A
Splendor
of Letters

ALSO BY NICHOLAS A. BASBANES

A Gentle Madness

Patience & Fortitude

Among the Gently Mad

HARPERCOLLINS*PUBLISHERS*

A
Splendor
of Letters

The
Permanence of Books
in an Impermanent World

NICHOLAS A. BASBANES

HarperCollins books may be purchased for educational, business, or sales promotional use. For information, please write: Special Markets Department, HarperCollins Publishers Inc., 10 East 53rd Street, New York, NY 10022.

FIRST EDITION

Designed by Claire Vaccaro

Printed on acid-free paper

Library of Congress Cataloging-in-Publication Data
Basbanes, Nicholas A.
A splendor of letters : the permanence of books in an impermanent world / Nicholas A. Basbanes.—1st ed.
p.   cm.
Includes bibliographical references and index.
ISBN 0-06-008287-9 (acid-free paper)
1. Books—History.   2. Written communication—History.   3. Cultural property—Protection.   4. Library materials—Conservation and restoration.   5. Library materials—Reproduction.   6. Archival materials—Conservation and restoration.   7. Archival materials—Reproduction.   8. Digital preservation.   9. Censorship.   I. Title.

Z4.B397 2003

302.2'244'09—dc21   2003047821

03   04   05   06   07   NMSG/RRD   10 9 8 7 6 5 4 3 2 1

For my wife, our daughters, and our parents,
and to the unending wonder of the continuum

Contents

All just criticism will not only behold in literature the action of necessary laws, but must also oversee literature itself. The erect mind disparages all books. What are books? it saith: they can have no permanent value. How obviously initial they are to their authors. The books of the nations, the universal books, are long ago forgotten by those who wrote them, and one day we shall forget this primer learning. Literature is made up of a few ideas and a few fables. It is a heap of nouns and verbs enclosing an intuition or two. We must learn to judge books by absolute standards. When we are aroused to a life in ourselves, these traditional splendors of letters grow very pale and cold. Men seem to forget that all literature is ephemeral, and unwillingly entertain the supposition of its utter disappearance. They deem not only letters in general, but the best books in particular, parts of a preëstablished harmony, fatal, unalterable, and do not go behind Virgil and Dante, much less behind Moses, Ezekiel, and St. John. But no man can be a good critic of any book, who does not read it in a wisdom which transcends the instructions of any book, and treats the whole extant product of the human intellect as only one age revisable and reversible by him.

RALPH WALDO EMERSON,
"THOUGHTS ON MODERN LITERATURE"

Preface

T here is a wonderful flashback scene in the 1977 Woody Allen film *Annie Hall* in which nine-year-old Alvy Singer is brought by his concerned mother to the family physician to articulate his depression, the stated reason being that the big bang theory of celestial expansion and retraction—something the boy has just read about in a school book—assures ultimate annihilation for everyone and everything, thus rendering every mortal endeavor irrelevant and without purpose. When Alvy is asked by the kindly Dr. Flicker the reason why he refuses to do his homework, the disconsolate lad replies with a simple question of his own: "What's the point?" As the Singer character grows older and more neurotic, his cosmic concern goes well beyond the ultimate fate of the planet to embrace the mystery of existence itself. "I'm obsessed with death," Alvy confesses at one point, and the two gifts he gives to the upbeat Annie after they become lovers are weighty books on the subject, Ernest Becker's *The Denial of Death* and Jacques Choron's *Death and Western Thought,* which is another side of his droll personality entirely. But that resonant line from his youth contains a certain verity to it, one that is not so easily dismissed when the subject is human achievement, and why the innate desire we all have to pass on a record of what we have accomplished to the next posterity should matter so much.

Over time, communication across the generations has typically come by way of the written word, carried out in a striking variety of ways and recorded on an astonishingly rich medley of surfaces, the impulse always being to make contact and to give an account of ourselves—which, it turns out, *is* the point of the exercise. In a famous passage in his

Areopagitica (1644), John Milton argued passionately that books—and the implicit understanding in that usage was writing in *every* form and on *every* conceivable kind of surface—are the "precious lifeblood of a master spirit, embalmed and treasured up on purpose to a life beyond life." That conviction forms the central premise of this book.

As an activity to enjoy in her later years, the British novelist Rose Macaulay (1881–1958) traveled the world in search of abandoned ruins, not to study old buildings with the trained eye of an archaeologist or the analytical temperament of an architect, but as an admitted "pleasurist" intent on reveling in what she called "the stupendous past," and to ponder freely on the "growth and development of this strange human reaction to decay." She claimed as kindred spirits the eighteenth-century writer Thomas Whately, who believed that a "monument of antiquity is never seen with indifference," and the American novelist Henry James, who called his own taste for "ruin-questing" the one recreational activity above all others that involved "a note of perversity." Writing her *Pleasure of Ruins* in the years immediately following the unprecedented devastation of World War II, Dame Macaulay was ever mindful of an "extremely ruinous world" in which "there are, above and under the earth, far more ruined than unruined buildings." Regardless of whether her journeys brought her to the stark plains of Troy, the toppled monuments of Corinth, the column-strewn terraces of Persepolis, or the lost cities of Babylon, the motivation inevitably involved "orgiastic conjuring" in her mind's eye of places "as they stood two thousand odd years ago," all the while realizing that "this broken beauty is all we have of that ancient magnificence; we cherish it like the extant fragments of some lost and noble poem."

For a good number of people around the world, "ruin-questing" provides an enthralling intellectual exercise of "once upon a time" and "what if," but for all the majesty and wonder of scattered artifacts, what remains behind is still the result of happenstance, and any meaningful message that is passed on from ancient relics must be divined by the beholder through intuition or perception—unless, of course, there is the added availability of a text. A visit to the frozen-in-time ruins of Pompeii reveals a city preserved by volcanic ash and rock, with villas, gardens, bakeries, temples, brothels, and bathhouses lying almost untouched through the centuries, with frescoes and mosaics as vivid as the day they were created, all "speaking" in a synergistic way that is without parallel in the history of archaeology. But what does not have to be surmised are the letters that endure there in profusion. "Scrawled on street corners, carved in stone or plastered on walls, the written word is everywhere in Pompeii," Colin Amery and Brian Curran Jr. marvel in an engaging monograph prepared for the J. Paul Getty Museum and the World Monuments Fund. Sometimes terse, sometimes vulgar, these inscriptions are essential all the same, offering a "unique glimpse into the vanished world" of the doomed city.

The announcement in 2000 by the French maritime archaeologist Franck Goddio that he had located a pair of legendary cities from antiquity four miles off the coast of Egypt buried beneath thirty feet of water was greeted with genuine enthusiasm everywhere. Like Pompeii, Herakleion and Canopus were stopped cold in their tracks by the forces of natural catastrophe, in the case of Herakleion, probably an earthquake at the beginning of the Christian era, in the instance of nearby Canopus, possibly a giant flood along the Nile River delta in the eighth century that caused the muddy sediment of its foundation to liquefy and collapse. Inspired by the writings of the classical authorities Herodotus and Strabo, both of whom wrote colorful anecdotal accounts of Herakleion, Goddio used nuclear resonance magnetometers, side-scan sonar devices, and echo sounders to comb Aboukir Bay for proof of its existence. After three years of probing through the silt, he and his crew were rewarded with a vast debris field of urban artifacts.

Yet for all the dazzling statuary, pottery, jewelry, gold, and coins that have been brought to the surface thus far—and an entire marine archaeology museum will be built in Alexandria to house them all—the definitive identification came with the discovery in 2001 of an immense granite slab installed at the customs port in 380 B.C. by King Nektanebos I. The inscription incised on its face established a 10 percent duty on all Greek cargoes, and included a text that is identical to one found in the ruins of another city along the dried-up bed of the Canopic mouth to the Nile in 1890. The only difference between the two stelae were the names of the cities, in this instance Thonis, the Egyptian name for Herakleion, which the Greeks who colonized the outpost in Hellenistic times had named for the god Hercules. "We were the first to receive this message from the past," Goddio said in an interview. "Suddenly, we felt that we had made direct contact with the ancient world."

About the same time that these discoveries were being heralded around the world, a reporter for the *Cape Cod Times* was interviewing a retired scientist for the Woods Hole Oceanographic Institution in Falmouth, Massachusetts, about a remarkable telephone call he had received from a stranger in the Bahamas, an Englishman named Sir Nicholas Nuttall, who had recently left a message on his answering machine with the cryptic news that he had "found the bottle" on Old Fort Beach near Nassau. John Porteous told the journalist that he had forgotten entirely about the curiosity he had tossed over the side of a research ship into the North Atlantic thirty-one years earlier, but his memory was jogged in the course of several conversations he subsequently had with the man, a person like himself, it turned out, who also was an oceanographer—an ideal recipient, in other words, for a letter scrawled out on corrugated paper giving the coordinates of his precise location at sea, along with his name, address, and the date, August 27, 1969. "To reach Nassau from up North, I guess your bottle must have gone past the Azores and then south and west like Christopher Columbus," Nuttall wrote in a follow-up letter to Porteous. "What a voyage!"

The image of an uncertain voyage of the written word through the seas of time is central to *A Splendor of Letters*, which is why I was so taken by the chance discovery of this newspaper article in the summer of 2001 while enjoying a few days of relaxation on Cape Cod with my family. The disclosure contained in the bottle was of no great significance, to be sure; it was the extraordinary journey itself—a fragile carrier of information making its way across a vast ocean—that mattered most to me, especially in these times of great technological change, when the idea of the book itself is being discussed with unceasing regularity, when issues of preservation and relevance are at the heart of the discourse, when destruction of culture so often involves the destruction of books. It is a sad fact of history that so many efforts to record the milestones of human endeavor have failed over the centuries, but the enduring wonder is that so much has survived the long haul. Thus it is that the story of "a little glass bottle that could" is an inspiration for me, one that is especially pertinent for a writer who is obsessed with books in every imaginable sense and nuance of the word. I am fascinated by their history and composition, by the many shapes and forms they have assumed over time. I want to know everything I can about the people who write them, make them, preserve them, sell them, covet them, collect them, fear them, ban them, destroy them, and, most of all, about those who are moved, entertained, instructed, awed, and inspired by them—those, in short, like the medieval bibliophile (indeed, he invented the word) Richard de Bury, who regarded them as the "heavenly food of the mind."

A Splendor of Letters completes a trilogy of bibliophilic efforts that began in 1995 with *A Gentle Madness: Bibliophiles, Bibliomanes, and the Eternal Passion for Books* and continued in 2001 with *Patience & Fortitude: A Roving Chronicle of Book People, Book Places, and Book Culture.* My respect and appreciation go out to all the people who have helped me through what has truly been a life-affirming exercise—there are dozens of them, and they are recognized in the heartfelt acknowledgments of those earlier books—with particular thanks in order here to Terry Belanger, founder in 1972 of the Book Arts Press at Columbia University, and since 1992 happily located at the University of Virginia at Charlottesville, where he also is university professor and director of the Rare Book School, for reading and commenting on this book in manuscript, and to Hugh Van Dusen, my trusted and valued editor at HarperCollins who saw merit in separating and expanding what in its first incarnation was a discrete section of one book into the richer examination it has become here. For Connie—my wife and partner in all things good and worthwhile—words, as always, are never enough to express my love and gratitude. May the voyage continue, with godspeed, fair winds, and following seas.

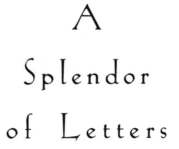

A
Splendor
of Letters

I.

Marbles and Names

At the core of a high-stakes political speech that has survived the passage of twenty-four centuries is a caustic aside on the merits of safeguarding written testimony and the need to archive documentary material. Cleverly framed as part of a devastating attack on a detested opponent, the biting comment was delivered in 330 B.C. by Aeschines, a renowned orator active in the daily affairs of Athens, and the sworn enemy of Demosthenes, the greatest public speaker of antiquity. The two men had become bitter rivals during a protracted effort to prevent Philip II of Macedon from consolidating control over all of Greece, with each championing different strategies for containment; both approaches had failed resoundingly, and now a legal proceeding had been convened to assess the blame. At issue was whether a proclamation awarding a gold crown of glory to Demosthenes six years earlier should be rescinded on the grounds of incompetence, or allowed to stand. Aeschines knew that if he had any hopes of humbling his charismatic rival, he had to reinforce his views with facts, not heated speculation. Addressing a legal assembly of citizens known as a *graphē paranomōn*, he built his attack around this tart observation: "A fine thing, my fellow Athenians, a fine thing is the preservation of public records. Records do not change, and they do not shift sides with traitors, but they grant to you, the people, the opportunity to know, whenever you want, which men, once bad, through some transformation now claim to be good."

To support his allegations, Aeschines asked that several documents housed in an official repository known as the Metroon—the sanctuary of the Mother of the Gods—be brought forth and read before the court of five hundred citizens that had gathered in a common meeting place at the base of the acropolis called the agora. In *On the Crown*, a brilliant rejoinder considered by classical historians to be his masterpiece, Demosthenes defended his comportment by artfully avoiding any substantive discussion of recent events, and the decree honoring his character was overwhelmingly sustained. Humiliated by this embarrassing rejection, Aeschines left Athens in disgrace and spent the remainder of his days teaching rhetoric in Rhodes, but his pithy rationale in defense of systematic record-keeping endures, and it suggests how highly documents were regarded in ancient Greece, particularly in a *graphē paranomōn*, where a preponderance of evidence, not prevailing public sentiment, was supposed to carry the day. It is worth noting that the *graphē paranomōn* proceeding, or a public action against an unconstitutional proposal, was introduced by Solon, the sixth-century lawmaker whose moderate precepts replaced the unforgiving code of Draco, the creator of laws so harsh they were said by Plutarch to have been written in the seventh century "not with ink, but blood." Regardless of the medium Draco used to document his pronouncements, the laws that bear his name marked the first time that Greek legislation was formalized in writing.

From a preservationist's point of view, the enduring lesson of the Aeschines-Demosthenes confrontation is that while the plaintiff's argument in praise of archiving has been passed on to our time through the miracle of textual transmission, the actual documents extolled in his speech—words written in their time on papyrus scrolls—have long since disintegrated. Paradoxically, all that has been unearthed from a first-century A.D. reading room located near the agora where Aeschines argued his point so heatedly is a rule inscribed on a marble tablet that governed access to its holdings: "No book is to be taken out because we have sworn an oath. The library is to be open from the first hour to the sixth." Like most other classical writings that survive in their original physical form, this edict endures because it was carved onto stone for display in a public place. But even then there were never any guarantees of permanence, as the Roman statesman, teacher, and occasional poet Decimus Magnus Ausonius (c. 309–392) suggested seven hundred years after the two Greeks had settled their scores in the shadow of the Parthenon. Remembered today largely for his lively correspondence and witty dedications in verse, Ausonius enjoyed poking through the shards of past cultures. In *On the Name of a Certain Lucius Engraved in Marble*, he considered a worn inscription marking the grave of some long-forgotten dignitary. He noted in this rumination that the deceased's forename began with the "single sign" of an L, and that it had been chiseled in front of what he believed to be an M, but which was incomplete, "for the broken top is flaked away where the stone is cracked, and the whole letter cannot be seen." So what, he wondered, was the name of this once prominent man whose identity had been buried in the dunes of time?

> No one can know for certain whether a Marius, or Marcius, or Metellus lies here. With their forms mutilated, all the letters are confused, and when the characters are jumbled all their meaning is lost. Are we to wonder that man perishes? His monuments decay, and death comes even to his marbles and his names.

Further evidence of that gloomy certainty comes in *The Antiquities of the Jews,* a sweeping history of the world from the time of the Old Testament to the reign of the emperor Nero written by the Romanized Jewish priest, scholar, and historian Flavius Josephus (A.D. 37–100). In chapter 1 of the work, Josephus told how Seth, the third son of Adam and Eve after Cain and Abel, became patriarch of an industrious clan of savants who were the "inventors of that peculiar sort of wisdom which is concerned with the heavenly bodies, and their order." Aware of Adam's prophecy that the earth was to be "destroyed at one time by the force of fire, and at another time by the violence and quantity of water"—but not sure which cataclysm would come first—these early astronomers were said to have undertaken what could be argued was the first documented attempt to make backup files of important data as a hedge against disaster, and as further insurance, they did it with two different recording surfaces. Josephus wrote how the descendants of Seth constructed two pillars, "one of brick, the other of stone," and "inscribed their discoveries on them both, that in case the pillar of brick should be destroyed by the flood, the pillar of stone might remain." For added protection, the duplicate was erected at a distant location "in the land of Siriad," where, Josephus asserted, it had remained "to this day," which may well have been the case two thousand years ago, when his history was written, though no trace of such a spire has come down to modern times. Indeed, most scholars today regard the tale as apocryphal, though illuminating all the same, given the clear suggestion it provides that even the earliest of chroniclers saw merit in seeking out alternate writing materials for their most important inscriptions, and for further protection, to retaining copies in multiple locations.

There is wisdom to be gleaned from this example, since now, as then, the setting down of what Ralph Waldo Emerson in a trenchant essay on the eternal power of writing called the "splendor of letters" remains only half the task at hand; ensuring that what has been recorded is passed on properly to the next generation—"migration of data" is the expression now in vogue—makes up the rest. As understood today, the word *preservation* is fraught with multiple meanings and connotations, particularly as it applies to the written record. For some curators, archivists, and librarians, preservation involves the attempt to save artifacts from physical deterioration and is synonymous with the goals of conservation. For custodians with a contrary view, the overriding obligation is to save "intellectual content" through the use of "surrogates," rendering the original carriers of information superfluous, and thus disposable. On yet another level, preservation considers whether limited storage space should be allotted indefinitely to materials that are rarely consulted, or if certain items are so peripheral to current interests that they should be discarded altogether. The concern in these cases is not crumbling paper or fragile bindings, but texts that prevailing fashion has judged to be no longer pertinent, instructive, or amusing, and therefore much too burdensome to store forever. At a time when many libraries are quietly ridding themselves of the same obscure materials, there is growing uneasiness over the possibility that a discard might be the last copy of a particular title still being held in any institutional collection, and that with its banishment from the stacks, that work—regardless of its literary or historical merit—is lost, not only to formal scholarship but to casual discovery, which some people contend is just as egregious a cultural offense.

In 1952, three documents known collectively as the Charters of Freedom—the Declaration of Independence, the Constitution of the United States, and the Bill of Rights—were placed in bronze and glass cases at the National Archives in Washington, D.C., hermetically sealed from all outside elements, and for half a century the centerpiece attractions for visitors taking part in a solemn ritual that could be argued is the American secular equivalent of a trip to the Sistine Chapel in Vatican City for Roman Catholics, or a pilgrimage to Mecca for Muslims. To make sure the charters remained beyond harm's reach, the designers made elaborate provisions for lowering them each night twenty-two feet into the reinforced entrails of the central rotunda where they were displayed, deep enough and secure enough, it was hoped, to survive a nuclear attack. What these formidable measures have never been able to prevent, however, is the inexorable passage of time and the effect aging has on all organic materials. It was in tacit recognition of this unforgiving reality that a $4.8 million project to construct seven new titanium and aluminum encasements for the documents was undertaken in 1999. Using space-age techniques developed by the National Aeronautics and Space Administration, the delicate operation was expected to be finished in September 2003. Protective measures taken included substituting the mixture of helium and water vapor—pumped in as a preservative five decades earlier—with argon gas, and replacing the deteriorating bulletproof glass plates that were believed to have been causing surface damage to the documents with new laminated plates that can be removed as necessary in the future. This is not mummification of iconic objects, to be sure, but it comes as close to achieving the Egyptian ideal of eternal life for fragile documents as current technology allows.

Beyond the parchments themselves is context, and *why* such heroic attempts at artifactual immortality are justified in this day and age, especially when the words in question, and the sentiments they express, are in no danger of disappearing from the face of the earth. The idea that the sanctity of a nation's founding principles is legitimized by the existence of six sheets of fading documents is by no means unique to the United States of America, of course, or even to politics for that matter, as the veneration of "sacred texts" among the world's great religions makes abundantly apparent. During World War II a manuscript copy of the Magna Carta was stored in Fort Knox, Kentucky, to protect it from the Luftwaffe's bombs, while three other original copies of the thirteenth-century compact remained in England. A question thus arises: If through some catastrophe each of those copies, along with the generative covenants of the American Republic, had been destroyed in enemy attacks, would the words they contain be any less valid in facsimile, or would the last, or oldest copy of the texts, as Umberto Eco playfully pondered in his provocative novel *Foucault's Pendulum,* then become the "original" document? Eco, it happens, is a medievalist who believes that the most compelling evidence is primary evidence, and it was no coincidence that a purported copy of an Aristotle text now forever lost played a central role in his best-known fictional work, *The Name of the Rose.* Like the late Stephen Jay Gould, the American paleontologist and author of numerous best-selling books on science, who told me during a tour of his private library in lower Manhattan in 1998 that he got a "special feeling" whenever he worked with primary materials, Eco is inspired to produce his most insightful commentary when he is able to handle authentic documents, not surrogate copies in facsimile or on microfilm.

"But what do I do if I want to examine the Book of Kells?" Eco asked during a wide-ranging interview in his sprawling Milan apartment. That extraordinary manuscript, he reminded me, was written on vellum by British or Irish scribes around the year 800, and has been kept under tight security for more than three hundred years at Trinity College in Dublin, where more than 250,000 people queue up in the Long Room of the main library each year to catch a glimpse of this European treasure, a viewing that lasts no more than a few seconds for each pilgrim. Since 1953 the book has been bound in four volumes, with two of them opened at any one time, one to display a major decorated page, another to show two pages of script. "There are 680 pages in the book," Eco said. "You can do the math for yourself: but at that rate I would need close to a year in Ireland to see the entire text just once."

Eco offered this wry comment as he was showing me a section of his home library devoted to the shelving of various books in facsimile, including an impressive reproduction of *Les Très Riches Heures* (The Very Rich Hours), a gloriously illuminated fifteenth-century Book of Hours that French officials do not allow to be viewed at all, not even by accredited scholars. Commissioned in 1410 by Jean, duc de Berry (1340–1416), the brother of King Charles V of France and a patron of French manuscript painting, the exquisite original was crafted over seventy-five years by a succession of book artists known as illuminators, first by the Flemish brothers and miniaturists Pol, Hermann, and Jehanequin Limburg, later by Jean Colombe, who was hired by the duke of Savoy to complete the job. Arguably the finest example of the illuminator's art in existence, the manuscript is kept in a vault a few miles north of Paris at Chantilly in the Musée Condé, a moated château that was once the elegant home of the duke of Aumale and his successors. "My overriding duty is to preserve the manuscript," the curator responsible for its safekeeping said in 1987 of the decision to keep the document forever sequestered. "No one will be allowed to see it again," he said, and the edict remains in force to this day. Now, the quarter million or so people who visit that museum each year see an elegant facsimile, not the original. "These facsimiles can be very expensive items in their own right," Eco said, noting with relief that all of the examples in his collection came to him as complimentary copies from publishers hoping to solicit a favorable comment or two for their promotions from the world-famous semiotician and medievalist.

When it was issued in 1980 by Faksimile Verlag Luzern of Lucerne, Switzerland, the fine-art facsimile edition of *Les Très Riches Heures*, limited to just 980 copies, was priced at $7,000 each, and sold out quickly. A

1990 reproduction of the Book of Kells, printed in an edition of fifteen hundred copies by the same company, went for $15,000 a set. In both instances, extraordinary measures were taken to make every printed page resemble the original leaves of the unique manuscript copies. The reproduction process used ten-color separations enhanced by lasers and handmade lithographic plates, with modern inks printed on paper that closely matched the texture of quill on animal skin. Each leaf, moreover, was cut to the irregular sizes of the originals, and holes bored through the parchment over the centuries by insects were replicated as faithfully as possible on the new papers. "It is a marvelous thing," enthused Philippe de Montebello, director of the Metropolitan Museum of Art in New York, when presented with proofs of the first prints, but what he was holding was a surrogate all the same.

"The driving historical question is this," the social historian Hillel Schwartz wrote in *The Culture of the Copy*, a provocative examination of "striking likenesses" and "unreasonable facsimiles" in contemporary life: "How has it come to be that the most perplexing moral dilemmas of this era are dilemmas posed by our skill at the creation of likenesses of ourselves, our world, our times? The more adroit we are at carbon copies, the more confused we are about the unique, the original, the Real McCoy." The central dilemma posed by Schwartz in his 1996 book took on an almost surreal note two years later at an exhibition mounted by the Royal British Columbia Museum in Victoria that purported to feature the "notebooks" of Leonardo da Vinci (1459–1519), a legacy comprising fifteen thousand pages of drawings, verbal asides, ingenious plans, penetrating thoughts, and creative scribblings. But instead of showcasing the authentic handiwork of Leonardo, the museum hung 150 photographic reproductions produced in a Florence workshop, each carefully framed as though it were the "real thing."

The actual notebooks from the maestro's oeuvre, meanwhile, remained securely stored in the scattered collections of their current owners, Queen

Elizabeth II of England, the Biblioteca Ambrosiana in Milan, and Microsoft billionaire Bill Gates, who acquired a seventy-two-page Leonardo journal at a Christie's auction in 1994 for $30 million. As far as the art critic for the *Vancouver Sun* was concerned, the entire premise of the exhibition was disturbing. "Is it the ideas sketched here that we are meant to admire?" Michael Scott asked. "If so, why are we looking at the reproduction of centuries of fingerprints and mildew and foxing paper? It would make so much more sense to show us photographically enhanced material, to translate Leonardo's odd mirrored handwriting and to animate or otherwise clarify his sketches." Or was it instead, Scott wondered, "the mark of the master we're meant to learn from? But then how can a photograph, however skillfully made, stand in for graphite on paper, for the smudge of the artist's fingers, for the precise size and orientation of the image on the original paper? None of this can be judged from a photo."

Central to the complaint voiced by the Canadian critic is the presumed value of the artifact as a cultural talisman. Put another way, does the first "container" have relevance in and of itself, or is it the information it conveys—and the information alone—that must be safeguarded above all else? This very concern is being debated with increasing frequency at academic and professional conferences around the world, and it was the focus of a major study commissioned in 1999 by the Council on Library and Information Resources, based in Washington, D.C. Worthwhile opinions and recommendations emerging from these inquiries were articulated in a report issued by the task force in 2001, but few pronouncements will have more immediacy than those expressed in a criminal court proceeding convened in New York City in the waning months of the twentieth century to pass sentence on a book thief who had pled guilty to stealing hundreds of rarities from Columbia University. At issue before the court was a hotly contested debate that considered the difference between the "monetary value" and the "cultural value" of the stolen articles, and whether or not one element is a reliable barometer of the other. On April 24, 1998, a U.S.

District Court judge ordered Daniel A. Spiegelman of Yonkers, New York, to serve five years in prison, flatly rejecting a recommendation from *both* the prosecution and the defense that he impose a term of about half that length. Judge Lewis A. Kaplan also ordered that Spiegelman pay Columbia $314,000 for costs associated with conservation and reparation. In pronouncing sentence, Kaplan declared that the monetary value of the rare maps, books, letters, and manuscripts, appraised by experts at $1.3 million, was not equal to the gravity of the crime. "Mr. Spiegelman," the judge said, "you have deprived a generation of scholars and students of the irreplaceable raw materials by which they seek to discern the lessons of the past and help us to avoid repeating it. That's what differentiates your offense from a simple theft of money or other easily replaceable property."

In pushing for a maximum of three years' imprisonment—which would have amounted to time served while awaiting trial and sentencing— Spiegelman's lawyers had argued that some of the items had never been consulted by researchers while they were kept at Columbia, suggesting that their intellectual merits had been overstated by the prosecution. The defense argued further that some early presidential papers taken by Spiegelman had "limited scholarly value" because they involved political "appointments to minor positions," and "little use had been made of them, even though they have existed for some two hundred years." Another archive he stole contained 133 letters and documents relating to Thomas Edison's development of the telegraph; these could not have been very valuable either, the defense maintained, since university curators had never bothered to catalog them individually.

To counter this claim, nine prominent scholars wrote letters to the court, a few to refute the suggestion that photocopies previously made of some of the materials had minimized the impact of their loss. "Such an act has graver implications," the eminent art and social historian Simon Schama declared. "For in rare book and manuscript libraries lie the artifacts of our common memory; the documents by which we can reconstruct the life and culture of our ancestors, and by so doing understand our kinship to them. To steal or mutilate such works is not only a violation of that kinship, a form of tomb robbery, it also inflicts a brutal wound on our remembrance." H. Elliot Wales, Spiegelman's lead lawyer, countered that the stolen material represented a minute fraction of the university's collection of half a million rare books and 28 million pages of manuscript. "Multiply that huge number by the considerable number of great depositories of rare books and manuscripts in the Western world, and we now realize that we are dealing with astronomical numbers of books and manuscripts which have been characterized as 'rare' by our scholars and librarians." Within that context, the lawyer argued, "Spiegelman's theft appears like but a single star in the vast terrain of the Milky Way, discernible only to an MIT astronomer, with a Hubble telescope."

When it came time to render a sentence, Kaplan rejected the defense arguments summarily and agreed with the librarians and scholars that primary documents "have significant scholarly value" apart from their content. In his written opinion, the judge addressed the difficult issue of placing a dollar value on "priceless" material by quoting from the testimony given by Jean W. Ashton, director of the university's Rare Books and Manuscript Library: "A document worth $10 on the market may well be the key to an argument that is made by a scholar which influences thousands of people," she had told the court. Kaplan also took note of Ashton's testimony regarding a late-fourteenth-century French manuscript of the *Roman de la Rose* by Guillaume de Lorris and Jean de Meung, stressing that even though a photocopy of the document existed, the facsimiles do not "show in any detail the depth, the gilt work, the hand painting," nor do they "show the line markings where the scribe lined it, lined up his text, the pin markings where the piece of parchment or leather was pinned to the board. They don't show the texture of the parchment at all and they give a totally inadequate sense of the look and feel of the manuscript and are very hard to read, actually, as well."

In a 1998 interview with me, the Reverend Leonard E. Boyle, a world-renowned paleographer and medievalist who served as librarian of the Vatican Library from 1984 to 1997, recalled several instances from his own experience where scholarly investigations that had been limited to the study of microfilm resulted in the drawing of erroneous conclusions. In one instance, a medieval commentary on the twelfth-century Italian theologian Peter Lombard believed to have been written by Thomas Aquinas was rejected for inclusion in a critical edition of the saint's writings on the basis of a faulty reading by an eminent French scholar who had not seen the original text. Father Boyle later determined that the scholar had failed to take note of an important notation written in a margin of the manuscript that would have resolved the issue. "I discovered the omission myself one summer when I was attending a conference in Oxford. Something had disturbed me about all of this, so I nipped away from the conference and went over to the Bodleian Library where the original manuscript is kept. I looked at it, and I found a note in the margin that clarified the entire situation, one that the man who had written the article had never considered, and which would have made all the difference in the world in his interpretation. I said to myself, 'Well, go to hell, he never saw the manuscript!' He was working from a microfilm, and the microfilm had not picked up what was in the gutters! It came to me as a revelation, and this was borne out later by an examination of the microfilm. What you must remember is that the person who is making the microfilm is a technician, a photographer. He doesn't know what you want. He thinks all you need is the text, not the whole opening, as we call it. So none of the marginal notes were included in this particular manuscript, only the text, and I would not be at all surprised to learn that this sort of thing has happened in many other instances as well."

Coming as it did seven years after the book thefts of Stephen C. Blumberg had made headlines around the world, the Daniel Spiegelman affair did not generate much attention outside the library community, especially since the defendant had been driven not by passion for the items he stole, but simply by greed. Blumberg's lawyers had claimed that their client was insane when he stole more than twenty-five thousand books conservatively valued at $7 million from several hundred North American libraries, and they pointed to the fact that he kept them all lovingly shelved in an old Victorian house in Ottumwa, Iowa, not as objects for sale in the antiquarian market.

Spiegelman had been arrested by Dutch police on June 8, 1995, after Jean Ashton received a tip that material discovered missing from Butler Library a year earlier was being offered for sale to dealers in Germany, Switzerland, and the Netherlands by a man calling himself William Taylor; she immediately alerted the Federal Bureau of Investigation. When taken into custody, Spiegelman was carrying two fake U.S. passports and licenses to drive automobiles from Saint Kitts, Nevis, the Cayman Islands, and the Bahamas. He also had a forged Columbia University identification card in his possession, exactly the kind of document that would have allowed him admittance to the library, although how he managed to secure access to the rare materials themselves remains a mystery. It was later disclosed that Spiegelman had been convicted in 1984 on charges of forging government documents. He was returned to the United States in 1996 after admitting that he had stolen the materials.

Among the other items he removed from Columbia were a thirteenth-century textbook on Euclidian geometry; two papal bulls from 1160 and 1202; three fifteenth-century printed books known as incunabula ("from the cradle"), including a 1493 edition of the Nuremberg Chronicle; twenty-six medieval, Renaissance, and early modern documents; 284 historical maps dating from 1628 to 1891; twenty-six presidential letters and documents, including six pieces of correspondence from George Washington, four of them sent to John Jay—one on the occasion of the first session of the United States Supreme Court; and eight letters from John Adams to William Tudor, the nation's first judge advocate general. Permanently lost, and presumed to have been sold, were a number of medieval and Renaissance manuscripts, including an illuminated Book of Hours from the fifteenth century, some 250 maps sliced out of a seventeenth-century Dutch atlas, and several documents signed by Abraham Lincoln and Thomas Jefferson. In departing from the prosecution's recommendation for leniency, Judge Kaplan offered this explanation for imposing a stiffer term:

> In callously stealing, mutilating, and destroying rare and unique elements of our common intellectual heritage, Spiegelman did not simply aim to divest Columbia of $1.3 million worth of physical property. He risked stunting, and probably stunted, the growth of human knowledge to the detriment of us all. By the very nature of the crime, it is impossible to know exactly what damage he has done. But this much is clear: this crime was quite different from the theft of cash equal to the appraised value of the materials stolen, because it deprived not only Columbia, but the world, of irreplaceable pieces of the past and the benefits of future scholarship.

Barely eighteen months after Judge Kaplan read his condemnation in open court, the Associated Press dispatched a five-hundred-word story reporting that Spiegelman had been arrested again after trying to sell another trove of stolen autograph material, this time to a Greenwich, Connecticut, bookseller who became suspicious of the material being offered to him, and alerted police. Documents later recovered included papers and letters signed by Presidents Thomas Jefferson, James Monroe, John Quincy Adams, Andrew Jackson, and James K. Polk, and a manuscript signed in 1504 by King Henry VII of England. Spiegelman, it turned out, had not been serving out his five-year term behind bars after all, but in a Manhattan halfway house. His movements supposedly were supervised, but they obviously were not so restricted that he was unable to resume his illicit activities. Brought to trial once again, this time on charges of carrying stolen property across state lines, Spiegelman pled guilty in February 2000 and was sentenced by U.S. District Court Judge Loretta A. Preska to serve another two years in prison, with an additional three years of supervised parole. At his release in 2002, according to Jean Ashton, fully a quarter of the items he stole from Columbia remained missing and unaccounted for.

Outside of the Spiegelman case, "cultural worth" is a phrase that appears repeatedly in the continuing debate over conservation policies, particularly in instances where they involve the use of microfilm and digital imagery as modes of textual preservation. This concern is made more acute by nature of the duplication process itself. Whenever brittle books, journals, and pamphlets with little monetary value are microfilmed or digitally scanned—and if the making of undistorted images is a priority—the deteriorating volumes are routinely cut apart at the spine ("guillotined" is the more colorful phrase used by professionals) and the unsecured leaves are then laid on a flat surface for copying. While this process succeeds in eliminating curvature in the new images, it usually represents a final act of service for the objects being copied, and is typically followed by a trip to the local incinerator, landfill, or pulping plant, although in some instances the originals are turned over to secondhand booksellers at a price that rarely exceeds the cost of scrap paper.

When archivists and conservators reproduce unique objects, their primary motivation is to create a "doomsday copy" in the event of a catastrophe, to ensure that the content, at least, is safe from obliteration. With the specter of nuclear conflict a horrifying possibility during the years of the Cold War, an ambitious project proposed by Pope Pius XII was begun in 1965 to make backup copies of medieval manuscripts held in monastic libraries and archives throughout the world, materials that exist, for the most part, in single copies. Working with a bequest from the James J. Hill Foundation, a midwestern philanthropic group named for the Gilded Age railroad baron whose estate provided funds for the project, a Benedictine order of monks based at St. John's University in Collegeville, Minnesota, established the Hill Monastic Manuscript Library. During its first thirty-five years of operations, the abbey sent photographers to monasteries in Europe, the Middle East, and North Africa, and reported copying 25 million pages of manuscript contained in ninety thousand volumes. Many of these documents include hand-painted illuminations and decorations and are resplendent in a number of vivid colors, but since the vast majority of microfilm images exist only in black and white, it is the content that is being copied, not the physical appearance of the artifact itself, which some observers consider a significant shortcoming. The reason usually given for this strategy is that archival images made in color are more expensive to produce, and the dyes tend to fade quickly. The color process, in short, is not considered reliable over the long term.

Despite this drawback, black-and-white microfilm has proven remarkably durable since its introduction in the 1930s, and as an information tool, it gives libraries access to material that would otherwise be unavailable to them. By drastically reducing the need for storage space, microfilm has become the option of choice for maintaining file copies of daily newspapers, which are printed on highly acidic newsprint and pose numerous obstacles to preservation. From 1927 to 1953—a period of twenty-six years and comprising about ninety-five hundred issues of "all the news that's fit to print"—America's premier journal of record, the *New York Times*, printed a limited run of each day's final edition on archival-quality rag paper, selling the copies in large bound volumes on the assumption that newspapers printed on nonacidic stock would serve as invaluable research tools for generations of scholars. A complete set of these broadsheet copies is on deposit in the New-York Historical Society, their pages a bit heavy to the touch, perhaps, but otherwise crisp, creamy, and showing no sign of the sickly jaundiced texture so common to aging newsprint. The service was terminated when it became apparent that microfilmed copies could be produced more efficiently and take up a lot less storage space than the awkward volumes. Even the *New York Times* does not have a complete set of its own rag-paper edition; in fact, the *Times* does not keep a hard-copy collection of the newspapers it publishes in any format, only samples that reflect changes in design and composition, and selected copies that include coverage of historic events.

"The microfilm copy is our preservation copy," Charles G. St. Vil, the retired archivist of the newspaper, told me in a 1999 interview, pointing out that the same policy for keeping archival copies of newspapers applies at most major repositories in the United States, including the Library of Congress, and that it extends to editions that contain color photographs, a feature the *Times* began phasing into its sections in 1997, but which are reproduced on microfilm only in black and white. "What we keep is the information, not the paper," he explained. When the newspaper needs a hard copy of a back issue of its own publication, the solution is simple: "We go out and buy one from people who deal in old newspapers." Visitors to the *New York Times* website on the Internet, meanwhile, are offered the opportunity to view authentic front pages from the past and to see firsthand how important events were reported as they broke "On This Day" in history. Alert readers who click onto this option will notice in a credit line at the bottom of the screen that the "pages" on display are actually microfilmed images furnished by UMI, the acronym for University Microfilms Inc. of Ann Arbor, Michigan, a division of Bell and Howell, and the world's largest producer of microfilmed copies. Fully 98 percent of all university dissertations accepted by American institutions are filmed by UMI, with fifty thousand or so added each year. At century's end, the company's inventory included 1.7 million doctoral and master's theses, comprising more than 210 million pages.

Founded in 1938, University Microfilms was the brainchild of Eugene B. Power (1905–1993), a Michigan inventor and entrepreneur whose first big contract came in 1942 when he was hired by the British Museum Library to make backup copies of every book in its collection printed in England prior to 1640. What gave the program particular urgency was World War II, and the well-founded fear that a sustained bombardment of London had the potential to destroy a considerable segment of the nation's literary heritage. In his autobiography, cleverly titled *Edition of One,* Power wrote that his motivation to develop a system that would produce microscopically compressed photographs on long strips of black-and-white film was driven by the idea of introducing an "economical method of producing a single copy" of any book—a doctoral dissertation, for instance, that could be issued individually and on demand. "Each copy made would be to fill a specific order. I could keep a vault full of negatives; therefore, no title need ever go out of print." Beyond the convenience of being able to "publish" a book on a strip of film was the promise the development held out to create "preservation copies" of information written or printed on other surfaces.

During the war, Power's skills were put to good use by American and British intelligence services. He was assigned to work in London for General William Donovan, head of the Office of Strategic Services. "British agents were gathering printed materials of all kinds in continental Europe and sending them back to the Foreign Office by various means," he recalled, items that included books, periodicals, newspapers, commercial catalogs, and underground newspapers. "I was granted twenty-four hours to photograph them for our use and for the British library organization, Aslib, which wanted German scientific periodicals." Power said the copies he made served many purposes, including source material for the preparation of propaganda broadcasts. "We were able to provide them with the news only six days after it was published in Germany and by the French Underground. The catalogs were used by our intelligence analysts as a guide to enemy supplies of various goods. For example, they determined that the Germans were running short of ball bearings, because a series of technical catalogs listed substitutes for ball bearings in their specifications. That information was the catalyst for the daring daylight bombing raid of October 14, 1943, in which our B-17s attacked the ball-bearing factories at Schweinfurt."

After the war, Power began looking for new ways to expand his business, and in 1947 he "came up with an idea" that he thought "would be a genuine breakthrough," a revolutionary new service "that would allow libraries to keep periodicals on microfilm instead of storing the original copies in bound volumes." The idea caught on, and that success was followed in 1948 by an invitation from the *New York Times* to film all current and back files of its newspapers. "There were howls of outrage from one end of the country to the other, because I actually advocated throwing away printed materials," he freely admitted. "Over time, however, the value of our service began to sink in and the logic of disposing of paper copies in favor of microfilm files became obvious. To my surprise, the first users of the service were mostly smaller libraries. The big ones took longer to come around."

In the decades that have passed since its introduction, microfilm has proven to be a reliable medium, although there is a decided drawback to its use, one that Power described in passing as an engineering problem that had to be solved. For the first time in the history of human communication, access to huge reserves of stored information required the use of a mechanical interface, not just knowledge of the language being used or the ability of people to understand it. Anyone who wants to see microfilmed data, in other words, has to employ the services of a device euphemistically known as a reader. Because very few individuals have these machines in their homes, the use of microfilm is confined for the most part to the audiovisual rooms of libraries and research centers. Not only does the mechanical "reader" have to be in good working order—never a certainty, as veteran researchers will readily attest—but it requires electricity to power the projection lamp, a crank or an electric motor to advance the film, and, if hard copies are to be made of desired material, a liberal supply of quarters and dimes or an active credit card to activate the camera.

Still, for all these logistical details, few people would dispute that microfilm performs a valuable cultural service. Where opinions divide heatedly—and it is the salient issue at the center of Nicholson Baker's 2001 book *Double Fold*—is the policy maintained by most major institutional libraries of discarding the bulky originals once the copies are made. One of the most consequential applications of the medium performed to date was accomplished two years before Eugene Power died, and the repercussions are still being felt today. On September 22, 1991, William A. Moffett Jr., at that time the librarian of the Huntington Library in San Marino, California, made front-page news around the world by taking what amounted to a Gordian knot approach to resolving a pitched battle then being waged several thousand miles away in the Middle East over access to the archive of ancient biblical documents known as the Dead Sea Scrolls. Renowned for its collection of English literary books and manuscripts and Americana, the Huntington Library became a major player in this controversy in the unlikeliest of ways. In 1978, a philanthropist who had underwritten a duplication project of the ancient Hebrew and Aramaic manuscript fragments discovered thirty-one years earlier in the Qumran caves near the Dead Sea gave the library two spools of film containing complete copies of the texts, the vast majority of which had never been published before. The reels were locked in a basement vault at the library, and largely forgotten. Unlike other institutions that had been given microfilm copies of the scrolls, the Huntington was never required to sign an agreement limiting their use, allowing Moffett to authorize access as he saw fit. By freeing up all of the information maintained in the library, his action had the residual effect of clearing the contentious logjam in Jerusalem, where a cartel of biblical scholars had imposed strict control over who could see the original documents and who could not.

Two years earlier Moffett had been the keynote speaker at a conference of the Association of College and Research Libraries (ACRL) meeting in Atlantic City, New Jersey, and used the site of the gathering—the convention hall of a busy casino-hotel—as a point of entry into an address he titled "The Librarian as Gambler." In his remarks, Moffett reminded his colleagues that their greatest responsibility as librarians was to defend the integrity of their collections, and that "there are things worth taking chances for." Not long after returning to California from the conference, Moffett found himself in the unenviable position of having to practice exactly what he had just preached when the spools of microfilm turned up in a Huntington Library safe during a routine inventory of its contents. "For years I have been telling people that a library is nothing more than the custodian of information embedded in various images, and that it is unethical to restrict access to them," he told me during one of the many conversations we had in the years I was researching *A Gentle Madness*. "It was a situation of my having to put up or shut up." For the decisive action he took, Moffett was proclaimed the "liberator of the Dead Sea Scrolls," and when a new translation of the parchments appeared in 1996, the translators put his contribution into sharper perspective: "This victory over scholarly secrecy and possessiveness made the book you hold in your hands possible."

But what has to qualify as the most far-reaching intellectual achievement secured through the study of "surrogates" is not the liberation of the Dead Sea Scrolls by microfilm, but the ability of the French linguist Jean-François Champollion (1790–1832) to make sense out of Egyptian hieroglyphics by relying almost entirely on imperfect copies of the ancient marker known as the Rosetta Stone. Named for an ancient town in the Nile River Delta where it was discovered in 1799 by a French army engineer during Napoleon Bonaparte's three-year occupation of Egypt, the stone had been incised with the text of a royal decree in three different scripts: Egyptian hieroglyphic, demotic, and, most important, Greek, which was a known and understood language. For scholars of ancient stone inscriptions known as epigraphers—the word *epigraphy* is derived from the Greek *epi graphein*, meaning "to write on"—the challenge was to use the known language as an instrument to decipher the hieroglyphics, which had been in use for more than three thousand years, but up to that time had been impenetrable for fourteen centuries. The second version of the Rosetta text, known as demotic, was a documentary script embodying a form of the Egyptian language as it was used during the reign of Ptolemy V, whose coronation in 197 B.C. was celebrated by the formal proclamation. The ramifications of what was at hand was apparent to everyone, and there was no shortage of talented people eager to take a stab at achieving scholarly immortality. But direct access to the original text—in this case a triangular slab of rock—was complicated by the vicissitudes of international politics.

In 1801, the stone was ceded with greatest reluctance by France to England under Article 16 of the Capitulation of Alexandria. Before the prize was carted off to London, however, French savants were able to make a number of impressions in a variety of formats. The orientalist Silvestre de Sacy, a teacher and mentor of Champollion, had several rubbings to work with in his unsuccessful attempt at decipherment. One of these was made on January 24, 1800, by using the stone as a printing block, producing a reverse image with the figures appearing in white on a black background. The savant Nicolas-Jacques Conté treated the slab as if it were an engraved plate, pulling prints of the text in black on a white sheet. Once the stone was in England, several plaster casts were made, with copies sent to Oxford, Cambridge, Edinburgh, and Dublin Universities. Of these, only the one in the Ashmolean Museum at Oxford is known to survive. Printed facsimiles of the three texts were subsequently distributed among the scholarly community. A reminder of just how extensively the stone had been used as an engraving block came in 1998 when a cleaning at the British Museum revealed traces of black printer's ink in the crevices of the inscriptions.

In 1814, Champollion began a correspondence with Thomas Young (1773–1829), an English scholar known for his work on optics and the theory of light, and the leading contender to be the first to decipher hieroglyphics. Champollion informed Young that his examinations were being impeded by the quality of the copies he had to work with, one of them an engraving made by the English Royal Society of Antiquaries, the other a French copy that differed in several key respects. Seeking clarification on several substantive points, the precocious son of a provincial bookseller expressed confidence that he would be able to expedite a decipherment if only he could acquire a fresh cast of the inscriptions. Young—who was then foreign secretary of the Royal Society and custodian of the stone— checked the specific passages Champollion had cited and passed his findings along to the young man, but opted against sending him a new copy, although he did offer a teasing tidbit of commentary to his enthusiastic French rival, who was just twenty-two years old at the time: "In most of the places that you have cited there is some obscurity in the original features which are a little confused or worn, and it is only by comparing the various parts of the stone that one can be assured of the true reading." Defenders of Young would later assert that it was he, and not Champollion, who had been first to crack the ancient puzzle, but that claim has been soundly rejected.

The final breakthrough was made possible by the sudden availability of yet another series of bilingual inscriptions copied from an obelisk removed from the temple of Philae in Aswan and taken to England in 1821 by William John Bankes, an antiquarian and close friend of Lord Byron. Young had access to this text well before a lithographic print was sent to the French Institute in Paris, but ignored it altogether. Champollion had already tentatively identified the names of Cleopatra and Ptolemy; this new material supported his theory that what he was looking at were alphabetic signs, giving him exactly what he needed—corroboration—to crack the ancient code. On September 27, 1822, he announced his preliminary findings in a fifty-page letter read before the Académie des Inscriptions et Belles Lettres in Paris.

His legacy secure, Champollion traveled to England with his older brother and lifelong champion, Jacques-Joseph, in 1824, and finally saw for the first time the stone he had deciphered from imperfect copies, pausing, one can only assume, to reverently touch the artifact that would forever be associated with his name. There is no reliable account of what transpired during the viewing, but it had to have been a profoundly moving moment. Later that year, Champollion traveled to Turin to examine the extraordinary collection of Egyptian artifacts assembled by Bernardino Drovetti, an Italian diplomat and antiquarian who had served Napoleon as counsel general in Alexandria. He wrote his brother an update of his activities, stressing how important it is to work with original inscriptions: "I will continue my research and chase after the original monuments, the ONLY GUIDES that we can follow without the risk of being held back, as I have been *for ten years,* by the inexact inscriptions engraved in the great work of the *Commission of Egypt.*"

Four years before his untimely death from a complex of untreatable physical ailments, Champollion fulfilled a lifelong dream to visit Egypt, and became the first person in modern times to read hieroglyphics in their original settings. In one in situ examination, he determined that the magnificent temple at Dendera was dedicated to Hathor, the goddess of love and mirth, not Isis, as previously believed, and he was able to pinpoint the precise period of construction. He did not let the setting of the sun stop him from reading inscriptions on the outside walls, continuing at the task well into the night by moonlight. "I will not try to describe the impression which the great propylon and especially the portico of the great temple made on us," he confided to Jacques-Joseph. "It is grace and majesty brought together in the highest degree."

On the occasion of the two hundredth anniversary of the discovery of the Rosetta Stone, the British Museum mounted a special exhibition of stone inscriptions featuring pertinent examples from its vast holdings. "Museums are full of ancient voices," Richard Parkinson wrote in the catalog, pointing out that of the 110,000 objects in the institution's collection of Egyptian antiquities, "around a third are inscribed with a text of some manner." What every one of these writings offers as a consequence, he continued, is a chance "to access the past on its own terms," and it may well be for this reason that far and away the most visited exhibit at the British Museum is not the exquisite Parthenon friezes or the regal sculptures from the Mausoleum at Halicarnassus or any of the other dazzling artifacts from antiquity that grace the galleries of the venerable institution, but the irregularly shaped black stone notable simply for the matrix of ancient words carved in three languages on its smooth surface more than two thousand years ago. "While it is impossible to travel to the past, a measure of dialogue with the dead is possible. Reading texts over the shoulders of the dead, as it were, is among the most immediate ways of entering such a dialogue."

2.

Editio Princeps

※ ※

By the production of a cheap writing material, and its supply to markets both east and west, the Arabs made learning accessible to all. It ceased to be the privilege of only one class, initiating that blossoming of mental activity that burst the chains of fanaticism, superstition and despotism. So started a new era of civilization. The one we live in now.

ALFRED VON KREMER (1828–1889), *KULTURGESCHICHTE DES ORIENTS*

※ ※

S o long as the papyrus plant grew abundantly in the Nile River delta of Egypt, the use of tanned animal skins for writing was confined largely to the cattle and sheep regions of Asia Minor. Even the prolific copyists at Pergamum, the kingdom that gave its name to the word *parchment,* preferred papyrus for their texts; it was only when their rivals three hundred miles to the southwest in Alexandria placed an embargo on its export that they turned to the alternative source. In Book 13 of his *Natural History,* Pliny the Elder wrote an exhaustive discussion of these invaluable "marsh-plants" that proliferated in the "swamps" and "sluggish waters of the Nile." Because the manufacturing process of papyrus had been jealously guarded for centuries—Strabo wrote that all harvesting and production was rigorously controlled in Egypt by a government monopoly—Pliny scored something of a coup in A.D. 77 when he disclosed precisely how the strips were fabricated, pointing out that "our civilization or at all events our records depend very largely on the employment" of the material. Dard Hunter, the great twentieth-century historian of papermaking, considered Pliny's lengthy description of the process so significant that he reproduced it entirely in his seminal study, *Papermaking: The History and Technique of an Ancient Craft.*

Pliny noted that before the Egyptians figured out how to make writing surfaces from the ubiquitous marsh plant, they experimented variously with "palm-leaves and then on the bark of certain trees, and afterwards folding sheets of lead began to be employed for official muniments, and then also sheets of linen or tablets of wax for private documents." In his formula, Pliny gave instructions for trimming, stripping, and moistening the plants with water from the Nile, an unusually "muddy liquid" that he said had the "effect of glue." The sheets were then supposed to be dried in the sun and joined together, never more than twenty to a roll; like the various papers produced today, there were numerous grades of papyrus to choose from, with the best quality reserved for official reports. Other factors taken into account were "fineness, stoutness, whiteness and smoothness." The paste for joining strips together was made with high-quality flour mixed with boiling water and a sprinkle of vinegar. When the sheets were dry, they were beaten thin with a mallet and run over with a layer of paste; creases were removed by applying pressure.

On the matter of durability, Pliny reported that he had seen papyrus documents "in the hand of Tiberius and Gaius Gracchus written nearly two hundred years" earlier, and "autographs of Cicero, of his late Majesty Augustus, and of Virgil" from roughly the same period. For these writings to survive for any length of time it was essential that they always be kept dry. In an important survey of the Vatican Archives, the Reverend Leonard E. Boyle wrote that even though church fathers began conserving letters, acts of martyrs, and various other institutional records during apostolic times, very little material "that is original" from that period up to the eleventh century survives, "mainly because the Popes were very slow to change over from the traditional if uncertain papyrus to the more durable parchment."

The historian Suetonius wrote that Julius Caesar broke with convention by insisting that all of his dispatches to the Senate be written on animal skins. The first known mention of literature being published on parchment is found in the first-century epigrams of Martial (c. A.D. 40– c. 104), who praised the new codices for their compactness and portability. (Deriving from *caudex*, a Latin word for "wooden tablet" and "tree trunk," *codex* is used to identify sheets of manuscripts gathered in a volume that resembles the modern bound book.) Martial even named a shop in Rome where they could be purchased. "You who want my little books to keep you company wherever you may be and desire their companionship on a long journey, buy these, that parchment compresses in little pages." Significantly, the humorous statements known as epigrams that are synonymous with Martial—particularly those containing a witty word or phrase at the end often described as a "sting in the tail"—originated as stone inscriptions, mostly sepulchral or votive in content, and took literary form during Hellenistic times; the word *epigram* itself means anything written on an object. Despite Martial's cheery endorsement of parchment codices, another 150 years or so would pass from his time before they were used to record Christian texts, and it was not until the fourth century that they began to displace the traditional papyrus scroll. The very shape of the new codex required a stronger material that could be folded and bound, and for that parchment was ideally suited.

Paper, the next major development, is believed to have been introduced in China about A.D. 105 by the eunuch Ts'ai Lun, director of the imperial workshops, and was made from a macerated mixture of mulberry and bamboo bark, fish nets, hemp, and rags. Prior to that breakthrough, writing in China was generally done on thin bamboo strips known as slips, and silk, which was expensive. Successfully guarded as a valuable state secret for centuries, the formula was introduced to the Islamic world by Chinese artisans taken prisoner at a battle fought in Turkestan in A.D. 751. Facilitated by a rich supply of flax and hemp and a sophisticated network of irrigation canals, the process flourished in Samarkand, and quickly spread to Egypt and Morocco, but it took another four hundred years to reach Europe, where the first paper mills went into production in the twelfth century. For all its obvious attributes, paper did not become the preferred medium of written communication right away, and in some instances was scorned outright for what was perceived to be its fragile composition. When Frederick II of Germany (1194–1250)—the Holy Roman Emperor and one of the most learned men of his age—organized the Kingdom of Sicily in 1231, he quite explicitly decreed in a constitution known as the *Liber Augustalis* that all official documents be written on parchment, the only appropriate medium, in his immodest view, to preserve forever the legacy of *stupor mundi*, himself, "the wonder of the world."

Because the climate in northwestern Europe was not hospitable to papyrus, the preservation of Greek and Roman texts depended on the continuous making of new copies, a method of replication that today, in electronic terms, is called "migration." The practice was carried to hopeful extremes in the third century by the Roman emperor Marcus Claudius Tacitus, who believed himself a linear descendant of the famous historian Cornelius Tacitus (A.D. c. 56–c. 120) by virtue of sharing the same last name. As an act of homage to his presumed forebear, the emperor directed that imperial scribes make ten new copies of the master's works every year and deliver them to various libraries throughout the empire, a sure way, he was convinced, to ensure their long-term survival. This ambitious scheme did nothing to forestall the inevitable, as only a fraction of Tacitus's works passed on to the age of printing, each of them through circumstances bordering on the miraculous. Books 1 through 6 of the *Annals* have as their source a single manuscript on vellum now in the Biblioteca Medicea Laurenziana in Florence; *Annals* 11–16 and *Histories* 1–5 depend on another from the eleventh century.

Other thinkers of consequence were not nearly as fortunate. The works of the first-century historians Seneca the Rhetorician, Servilius Nonianus, Cluvius Rufus, Fabius Rusticus, Aufidius Bassus, and Velleius Paterculus disappeared largely through neglect or indifference. The writings of Heracleitus (c. 540–c. 480 B.C.), one of the most trenchant thinkers of classical Greece, are known to have been in circulation until the second or third centuries of the Christian era. All that survives of his works are about eighty quotations repeated by authors whose personal copies of his books have since vanished as well. A hint of just how many great works from antiquity have been lost is available in the most teasing of ways to anyone who takes the time to engage the eclectic ruminations of Aulus Gellius, a Roman writer from the second century A.D. who filled twenty volumes with his observations and commentary on a formidable variety of subjects, which in many cases included verbatim excerpts from many of the important writings of his time, along with snippets of his own commentary. Of the 275 authors he mentioned in *The Attic Nights,* a rumination he named in honor of the weeks he spent at a country house in Greece "assembling these notes during the long winter nights," fully half produced works that are either lost entirely or known only through fragments. In one telling sequence of *Attic Nights,* Aulus explained why it was that his musings were arranged in "the same haphazard order" that he "followed in collecting" the material, a casual method that might have him holding forth at one moment on the writings of the peripatetic philosopher Theophrastus or the histories of Hellanicus, followed perhaps by the comedies of Epicharmus, the epic poetry of Ennius, the annals of Quadrigarius, or the chronicles of Quintus Fabius Pictor—all of them writers whose works are now lost:

> Whenever I had taken in hand any Greek or Latin book, or had heard anything worth remembering, I used to jot down whatever took my fancy, of any and every kind, without any definite plan or

order; and such notes I would lay away as an aid to my memory, like a kind of literary storehouse, so that when the need arose of a word or a subject which I had chanced for the moment to have forgotten, and the books from which I had taken it were not at hand, I could readily find and produce it.

A similar phenomenon manifested itself in the writing of Photius (c. 810–c. 893), a ninth-century Byzantine theologian who twice served as patriarch of Constantinople. As a religious figure, Photius was active in the doctrinal upheaval that led ultimately to the rupture of the Greek and Roman wings of the Christian church known as the Great Schism, but it was his work as a literary diarist that makes him of compelling interest to scholars today, especially with regard to the detailed descriptions he wrote of 280 ancient books, half of which no longer survive in any form except in the succinct condensations he prepared for the private amusement of his immediate circle.

Beyond citing works that are now lost—a contribution that by itself would be significant enough in its own right—Photius's summaries achieve unprecedented depth by virtue of their erudite composition. In an opening dedication, Photius explained that he was preparing the descriptions for the edification of his brother, Tarasios, another theologian who was about to leave on a diplomatic mission to Arabia, and had requested, in his sibling's words, a "written account of the contents of such books as were read in your absence, in order to have some consolation for the separation which you sorely regret, and at the same time to obtain at least a summary and general knowledge of works you have not yet read in our company." Partly because the *Bibliotheca* was not meant for wide distribution—the title was assigned years later by others—it remained largely unknown for more than seven hundred years. Indeed, given the uneasy political and religious climate of the times in Asia Minor, the survival of the lengthy text itself borders on the improbable. Somehow, a copy made its way into the possession of Cardinal Vasilios Bessarion (1403–1472), the expatriate bibliophile from Constantinople whose matchless collection of Greek manuscripts became the core holding of the Biblioteca Marciana in Venice, though once deposited there, it did not attract serious scrutiny until the seventeenth century. "It is one of the enigmas of literary history that a work of such importance did not arouse more interest among the scholars of the Renaissance," N. G. Wilson observed in a truncated translation of the *Bibliotheca*, and even today the work is not nearly as well known as it might otherwise be.

Because the compilation was not intended for general circulation, Photius did not restrict himself to religious writings, and included secular works in a wide variety of areas, a few of which may well have been regarded by some of his contemporaries as scandalous, perhaps even heretical. In preparing the lengthy commentaries—a Greek printed edition of the complete text runs to 1,600 pages—Photius noted that he had arranged his choices "in the order in which our memory recalled each of them." Because he included a number of writings that have survived to our times—the works of Demosthenes, Galen, John Chrysostom, Lucian, Ctesias of Snidos, and Isocrates, for instance—it is possible to measure the quality of his observations against the existing texts. In his selective translation of the *Bibliotheca*, N. G. Wilson wisely concentrated his greater effort on descriptions of texts that have been lost. Thus it is that the modern reader can sense the narrative power of tales crafted by the storyteller Antonius Diogenes, or appreciate the observations of the historian Pamphila, a woman who was "born in Egypt and lived at the time when Nero was emperor of the Romans." Those with a penchant for poetry may be amused by the tropes of Olympiodorus, while those interested in the history of science can sample the writings of the physician Dioscurides. The names of other thinkers, scientists, philosophers, historians, and poets—

Eudocia, Conon, Sotion, Diodoros of Tarsus, Eunomius, Phrynichus, Epiphanius, Irenaeus, the litany of lost voices goes on and on—come at us like desperate calls from a shrouded sea.

When it came time to offer critical opinions, Photius did not pull his punches. The controversial assertions of the essayist Agapios, for example, were deemed "odious and impious," but obviously worth a cursory read all the same. He had the following to say about the handiwork of Sergius the Confessor, a historian whose works are otherwise unknown: "In style he has the distinction, more than others, of being clear and unaffected, through the simplicity of his vocabulary and the general structure and composition of his prose, so that he even gives the impression of extemporisation. His prose blooms with a natural grace and does not bear the imprint of elaboration. It is therefore a style most appropriate to ecclesiastical history, as he intended." Elsewhere, Photius enthusiastically recommended the work of a popular writer: "Read a novel by Iamblichus, a love story. There is less parading of indecency than in Achilles Tatius, but more display of immodesty than in the Phoenician Heliodorus. These three authors set out with virtually identical aim in writing a novel with a love interest, but Heliodorus is more serious and restrained, Iamblichus less so, and Achilles Tatius is indecent and shameless." It was learned observations such as these that prompted the English critic, biographer, and literary historian George Saintsbury (1845–1933) to anoint Photius the "patriarch" of book reviewers, basing his claim on the assertion that the Byzantine was the first person to have "dealt practically with literature from the reviewer's point of view." Of particular moment, of course, is the ironic fact that so many of the works Photius analyzed with such critical acumen are known today only by virtue of his reviews. For N. G. Wilson, the most pressing issue raised by the *Bibliotheca* involves the actual texts consulted by Photius: "Was he the proud owner of all the texts he had read, and if not, where was the library that supplied his needs? Unfortunately no clear answer can be given. Photius himself says nothing on this subject." It may well be that in some instances, Wilson concluded, "Photius presumably handled the last surviving copy."

Many other writings from antiquity, of course, have been deliberately destroyed over the centuries as a matter of political expedience, as I discuss presently in chapters 4 and 5, and religious zealots of every persuasion have had their moments as well. Almost all the works of Porphyry, a third-century philosopher pointedly hostile to Christianity, were sought out and burned in the fifth century, an approach that was rigorously followed for hundreds of years with the writings of anyone deemed heretical. Certainly one of the most egregious instances involved the Spanish physician Michael Servetus (1511–1553), a brilliant thinker who made the grave mistake of locking theological horns with John Calvin, the French-born lawyer-turned–Protestant reformer whose strict interpretation of Christian doctrine allowed little patience for the contrary views of an intellectual regarded today as a spiritual forebear of the Unitarian church. In 1533, Servetus's writing of the book *Christianismi Restitutio* (The Restoration of Christianity) resulted in this no-nonsense response from a group of politicians in Geneva who had been cowed by Calvin into putting him on trial for his life: "We condemn you, Michael Servetus, to be bound and taken to Champel and there attached to a stake and burned with your book to ashes." Of the one thousand copies of the *Restitutio* printed anonymously by Servetus, just three managed to survive the hateful dragnet to our time; in an extraordinary twist of circumstance, one of these turned out to be John Calvin's own annotated copy.

The practice of incinerating despised writings alongside the people who composed them was not entirely uncommon, as the prolific British writer P. H. Ditchfield made clear in *Books Fatal to Their Authors*, a sobering discourse assembled, in the nineteenth-century author's words, to enumerate instances of what he called *de libris fatalibus*. It is curious indeed, he mused, to consider just how many writers there have been who might otherwise "have lived happy, contented, and useful lives were it not for their insane *cacoethes scribendi*," a Latin phrase popularized by the Roman satirist Juvenal meaning an "incurable itch" for writing. "If only they had been content to write plain and ordinary commonplaces which every one believed, and which caused every honest fellow who had a grain of sense in his head to exclaim, 'How true that is!' all would have been well," Ditchfield lamented. One of the most diverting biblio-mysteries of recent years, Arturo Pérez-Reverte's 1993 novel *The Club Dumas*, poses just such a premise; the printer of a seventeenth-century instruction manual for summoning the devil is burned at the stake, prompting a twentieth-century rare-books dealer and dabbler in the occult to recover the few fragments that managed to survive, with surprising consequences.

For classical authors who set their thoughts down on papyrus, however, the worst enemy of the muses was not writer's block or outraged readers bent on getting even, but a ravenous adversary that caused incalculable damage well into the age of paper. "In old wax, as in wood, there is found an animal which seems to be the smallest of all creatures, called the acarus," Aristotle wrote in his *History of Animals*. "And in *books* there are others like those found in cloth, and they are like scorpions without a tail, the smallest of all." In *The Enemies of Books*, William Blades (1824–1890), a respected London printer and astute historian of his craft, placed insects and "other vermin" near the top of his list of perennial library despoilers, ranking them with fire, water, mold, dust, household servants, collectors, children, and atrocities arising out of neglect, ignorance, and bigotry. Blades commended the seventeenth-century physicist Robert Hooke for providing the first analytical account of bookworms in *Micrographica*, a pioneering report of scientific experiments performed with the aid of a microscope, and he was pleased to give credit where it was due. But Blades was nonetheless distressed by a number of "absurdly blundering" errors he found in Hooke's description of the grotesque "little creature" identified as the *Anobium*, and offered the results of his own investigations into the behavior patterns of the book-eating pest. Blades was a dogged researcher, as this excerpt demonstrates:

In December, 1879, Mr. Birdsall, a well-known book-binder of Northampton, kindly sent me by post a fat little worm, which had been found by one of his workmen in an old book while being bound. He bore his journey extremely well, being very live when turned out. I placed him in a box in warmth and quiet, with some small fragments of paper from a Boethius, printed by Caxton, and a leaf of a seventeenth century book. He ate a small piece of the leaf, but either from too much fresh air, from unaccustomed liberty, or from change of food, he gradually weakened, and died in about three weeks. I was sorry to lose him, as I wished to verify his name in his perfect state.

In an authoritative work on the transmission of Greek and Latin literature from classical times to the age of print, the British scholars L. D. Reynolds and N. G. Wilson cite a crucial time in the fourth century when the favored form of writing surface was moving from papyrus scrolls to parchment sheets bound in the shape of what are still regarded as conventional books, placing a wealth of classical literature at great risk of being lost. "There was the danger that little-read works would not be transferred to codex form, and in time their rolls would perish," they wrote. "A voluminous author, if some of his rolls were not available at a critical moment, might never recover his missing books."

Another key juncture in the history of textual transmission came in the ninth century, when the scarcity of parchment and the need for greater writing speed gave rise to a compact script known as minuscule. This development led to abandonment of the larger character, known as uncial, which took up far more space and could be written less quickly; by the end of the tenth century uncial was used only for specialized liturgical books. A general assumption frequently made, though not proven, is that whenever a copy was made, the original was discarded, and the new version became the source for all future copies, along with whatever errors were made by the copyist. Classical texts not selected for renewal were lost, "not because pagan authors were under attack, but because no one was interested in reading them, and parchment was too precious to carry an obsolete text." Parchment, it is worth emphasizing, has always been an expensive commodity, and when certain texts fell out of favor, it was customary to recycle the old sheets and use them for writings that were in greater demand. This was accomplished by removing the original writing from the surface of the animal skins and creating what is known as a palimpsest. First used in the seventeenth century, the word derives from a Greek expression meaning "scraped again" or "rubbed smooth," and identifies cultural riches found by scholars digging for material "buried under nothing deeper than the dust of ages."

The best-known palimpsest of recent times made headlines around the world in the fall of 1998, when it was sold in New York for $2.2 million after a claim of ownership by the Greek government was rejected in a U.S. district court. Appearing on the surface of the document are the words of a Greek Orthodox ritual from the thirteenth century, an interesting but by no means irreplaceable piece of writing, and hardly the kind of artifact to ignite an international incident. Barely visible in light detail beneath these writings, though, appear copies of six texts of the mathematician and inventor Archimedes (c. 287–212 B.C.), two of which are not known to survive anywhere else. Of these, the mathematical proof known as "On Floating Bodies"—the source of the apocryphal "Eureka" story—was unknown in Greek until discovered in this tenth-century palimpsest by Johan Ludvig Heiberg, a Danish classicist who was inspired to scrutinize the crudely bound swatches of parchment with a magnifying glass in 1906. In the other text, "Method of Mechanical Theorems," Archimedes showed how two-dimensional areas can be calculated by adding the lines on the surface, and how the volume of a solid can be determined by summing up the planes that intersect it. Unknown until extracted from this palimpsest, the treatise is now regarded as an antecedent of the calculus developed by Isaac Newton and Gottfried Wilhelm Leibniz nineteen hundred years later. To the great good fortune of posterity, the lower, tenth-century text had been recorded with ink concocted from deformities that grow on oak trees known as galls; when crushed and mixed with iron salts and water, the resulting dye, known as "iron gall," is high in tannic acid and bonds permanently with parchment. The thirteenth-century Greek monk who used the Archimedes sheets for his prayer book was able to scrape off the three-hundred-year-old original writing, but he could not make it disappear altogether. When the codex was acquired by an anonymous buyer at Christie's, Nicolas Barker suggested that the seven-figure price paid was undoubtedly a record for writing that is almost "invisible to the naked eye."

Palimpsests are also credited with preserving important works by Terence, Pliny the Elder, Pliny the Younger, Sallust, Seneca, Virgil, Ovid, Lucan, Juvenal, Persius, and Fronto. A fragment of the third-century B.C. Euripides play *Phaethon* appears on two parchment leaves that had been written over in the sixth century to produce a codex of the Pauline Epistles. The *Institutes* of Gaius was found under a treatise of Saint Jerome in 1816 by the German historian Barthold Niebuhr at Verona. The *De republica* of Cicero, written out in uncials on parchment in the fourth or fifth century, was discovered in 1822 by a cardinal doing research at the Vatican Library; sometime in the seventh century, a monk at Bobbio had layered a commentary of Augustine on the Psalms over the original Cicero text. In the late sixth or early seventh century, Seneca's *De amicitia* and *De vita patris* were covered over with sections of the Old Testament. To prepare a Syriac treatise by Severus of Antioch, a ninth-century scribe used a selection of leaves, some from sixth-century copies of Saint Luke and Homer, others from a

Euclid of the seventh or eighth century; this triple palimpsest is now in the British Library. In 1950, a team of scholars entrusted with microfilming the great accumulation of manuscripts maintained at the Monastery of Saint Catherine on Mount Sinai in Egypt discovered "a unique tri-lingual quintuple palimpsest," and promptly christened it the Codex Arabicus. Remarkably, it contains five layers of writing—two in Syriac, one in Greek, and two in Arabic—making it "unmatched in palimpsest history," according to a scholar who has studied it. Other notable examples of the phenomenon include a text of Plautus now at the Biblioteca Ambrosiana in Milan and a copy of Livy at Verona, both from the fifth century.

"One cannot consider these facts without marveling at the slenderness of the thread on which the fate of the Latin classics hung," Reynolds and Wilson marveled. "In the case of many texts, a single copy survived into the Carolingian period, and often a battered one at that." A fifth-century manuscript of Livy survived until the sixteenth century without ever being duplicated in another copy. "A mere mishap, and five more books of Livy would have disappeared without a trace." With the invention of movable metal type in the fifteenth century came the multiplication of copies, and the likelihood that fewer texts would disappear. But primary material continued to perish nonetheless, and many important writings survive today only in their printed versions, not the earlier manuscripts critics so often regard as essential in assessing the flow of the creative process.

The earliest editors of the plays of William Shakespeare, John Heminge and Henry Condell, tantalizingly noted in the preface to what has become known as the 1623 First Folio of the playwright's dramatic works that their monumental contribution to Western civilization—along with the King James Bible one of the two most important books ever printed in the English language—was "published according to the true original copies." Whether or not Heminge and Condell were referring to holographic drafts in Shakespeare's hand or to official prompt copies owned by the King's Men, his company of players, is a matter of continued debate. Either way, none of these "true original copies" survives in any form, only the edited version Shakespeare's colleagues prepared from material left in their possession after his death in 1616, and ushered through Isaac Jaggard's press seven years later. There are no known manuscripts for the poetry of Edmund Spenser (1552–1599), Michael Drayton (1563–1631), Andrew Marvell (1621–1678), or Henry Vaughan (1622–1695) either, nor is there any known manuscript of Jean-Baptiste Poquelin, the French national playwright known as Molière (1622–1673), just the printed editions of their works. The only poem in the hand of Sir Philip Sidney (1554–1586) to survive does so because it was written in the margin of a book that was considered valuable enough in its own right for someone to save.

We can be thankful, at least, that in each of these instances copies were made of the originals, and that a determined attempt was made to preserve their intellectual content. The unremitting fear among curators, archivists, and historians is that steps will not be taken to safeguard irreplaceable records of human achievement at key moments of technological transition, and that many writings will disappear through the combination of apathy and neglect. The word *incunabula*, literally meaning "from the cradle," is used to describe printed books from the time of Gutenberg in the 1450s through 1500. Since the first press to operate in North America did not begin operation until 1639, seventeenth-century books printed in the New World are sometimes called "American incunabula," and many books published during that period, and the century that followed, have been lost as well.

Every generation makes choices about itself, choices about what it regards as worth preserving and passing on, choices about what it decides to discard and let go. The Greeks wrote ephemeral material on wax tablets that were smoothed over and used again and again, a clear indication that not every syllable was intended for historical scrutiny, and the word *palimpsest* itself identifies a carrier of information that has been "scraped clean" for repeated employment. People have been inscribing important information on stones for centuries with the intention of making it immortal, but there also are the decidedly casual writings—scrawlings on a beach at low tide, for instance, or graffiti sprayed on the side of a building—that measure their existence by the hour or the day, the week or the month, the movement of the seas. Somewhat less perishable, but doomed to decay and decomposition all the same, are the tattoos that human beings throughout history have had incised on their skin with the clear understanding that what has been "written on the body" is not likely to outlast the carrier of the message. In the Sierra Nevadas of the southwestern United States, detailed drawings and concise biographical markings carved on the smooth bark of slender aspen trees by an expatriate community of Basque sheepherders in the early years of the twentieth century were meant to endure so long as the trees themselves remained firmly rooted in the ground. Some fifteen thousand of these aging dendroglyphs and arborglyphs have been documented in the high country by the U.S. Forest Service, but thousands of others have been lost to the vagaries of nature.

At the other extreme are the petroglyphs that were carved on stone many generations before sophisticated writing systems were devised, and endure in abundance all over the world, in North America most dramatically just outside Albuquerque, New Mexico, in a 7,236-acre preserve known as Petroglyph National Monument, home to hundreds of archaeological sites and an estimated twenty-five thousand images carved by native peoples and early Spanish settlers. Many are recognizable as animals, people, brands, and crosses; others are more complex, their meaning understood only by the carvers.

And then there are the materials of expedience, the writing surface of the moment—a cocktail napkin, a matchbook cover, the back of an envelope, a torn scrap of newsprint—and writing instruments that are just as improvisational—a stick of lipstick, a charcoal briquette, a can of spray paint, and, most fleeting of all, a finger run across a fogged glass window—creating in the vast majority of instances an idle missive of little substance that is not intended for unborn eyes. But there are cases in which materials meant to be disposable become carriers of consequence that do endure; I was reminded of this possibility when I was shown the manuscript copy for the third edition of *Leaves of Grass* in the Alderman Library at the University of Virginia, each page now tucked into a nonacidic sheathe and arranged in a loose-leaf notebook. As an employee in the tax office for the state of New Jersey when much of the work was under composition, Walt Whitman found it convenient to use scraps of paper of various shapes, sizes, and colors he had picked up at the office for his poetry, penning lines of verse on the back side of invoice sheets printed with the letterhead of the department on the front, little realizing that these fragments would become as much a part of his literary legacy as the printed versions that emerged from them.

One of the more popular artifacts on public view at the John Fitzgerald Kennedy Library and Museum in Boston is the husk of a coconut shell glazed and mounted in a wooden display case. Etched on the surface are these words: NAURO ISL COMMANDER. NATIVE KNOWS POS'IT. HE CAN PILOT. 11 ALIVE. NEED SMALL BOAT. KENNEDY. In July 1943, Navy Lieutenant Junior Grade Kennedy and ten members of his crew from *PT-109* had been stranded in a South Pacific atoll after being rammed by a Japanese destroyer; twenty-three years old at the time, the man who one day would be known to the world as JFK used his pocket knife to whittle the message on the only writing surface he could find, and asked one of the islanders he had befriended to pass it on to his superiors. Hailed in civilian life as a war hero, Kennedy kept the coconut that saved his life in the Oval Office of the White House throughout his presidency.

For Allied air crews flying bombing missions over Europe during World War II, a British company best known for the printing of such board games as Monopoly, Waddington PLC, came up with a plan to produce thousands of detailed maps on silk, rayon, and mulberry leaf paper that could be consulted in the event they were shot down behind enemy lines. The idea was to have a map that could be folded and concealed in the hollow heel of a boot or a cigarette package, one that would not rustle in the event of a body search and was resistant to water. As a further aid to navigation, tiny compasses were concealed in buttons and fountain pens. The silk maps were so popular among combat pilots that an effort was mounted to smuggle copies into prisoner-of-war camps to assist captured soldiers who were contemplating escape and needed guidance to make their way through a hostile countryside.

Just as improvisational was the use in several Confederate states during the Civil War of wallpaper for newsprint, the best-known example being the editions for June 16, 18, 20, 27, and 30, and July 2, 1863, of the Vicksburg, Mississippi, *Daily Citizen*, produced during the siege of Vicksburg, Mississippi, by the secessionist editor James M. Swords. Each was a single sheet, four columns wide, and printed on the back of paper intended to decorate the walls of elegant southern homes, requisitioned for alternate service in the face of severe paper shortages. A galley of type prepared for publication on July 4, 1863, was abandoned by the printers as the city fell to forces under the command of General Ulysses S. Grant. Two thirds of the last column was modified by the Union soldiers, and concluded with these words: "This is the last wall-paper edition and is, excepting this note, from the types as we found them. It will be valuable hereafter as a curiosity."

Among numerous ancient cultures, pieces of clay or pottery known as ostraca were used as a form of notepad for school lessons and for the composition of short letters, receipts, and administrative documents. Most were written with ink, but some were incised with a sharp instrument, and none was intended to last the long haul. The word *ostraca* is Greek for "shell" or "potsherd" and is frequently associated with ballots that were cast by Athenians in trials that often resulted in a punishment of exile known as ostracism, hence the name, but important examples from biblical times have been recovered in digs throughout the Near East. At Tell ed-Duweir in southern Israel, thirty miles southeast of Jerusalem and fifteen miles west of Hebron at the site of the ancient city of Lachish, twenty-one letters written on shards of pottery were found in 1938 and 1964 in what was once the guardroom of a huge gate between the outer and inner city walls. Later determined to have been communications exchanged between military commanders during the reign of Zedekiah, the last king of Judah, about 590 B.C., they had rested for about twenty-five hundred years until their recovery, and they are thought to have been written prior to the taking of Judah by the Babylonians. Their content suggests that the city of Azekah had recently fallen, a key piece of information for historians, since Lachish itself was overrun just after the last of the letters was written, in 588 B.C. The only city that had not been taken at that point was Jerusalem, which was sacked shortly thereafter, and the Temple of Solomon burned. These letters, as a consequence, are immensely important because they confirm, in a remarkably immediate way, the order of destruction of the last cities of the Judean kingdom. They also establish modern-day Tell ed-Duweir as the ancient Judean city of Lachish, a positive identification that had eluded archaeologists for decades.

The widespread use of an entirely different kind of ephemeral writing device during the sixteenth and seventeenth centuries was established recently by a University of Pennsylvania educator who had been trying to explain the meaning of an obscure metaphor that is at the center of a defining scene in *Hamlet* toward the end of act 1, shortly after the troubled Prince of Denmark confronts the ghost of his murdered father. In a searing speech in which he vows vengeance on his uncle Claudius, Hamlet makes the following declaration:

Yea, from the table of my memory
I'll wipe away all trivial fond records,
All saws of books, all form, all pressures past,
That youth and observation copied there,
Within the book and volume of my brain,
Unmix'd with baser matter.

Although the sentiment being expressed is clear enough, exactly what kind of object Shakespeare was using as an image when he had Hamlet pledge his intention to "wipe away all trivial fond records" from the "table" of his memory had perplexed scholars for years. In February 2002, Peter Stallybrass, a professor of English at the University of Pennsylvania who conducts a seminar on the history of "material texts," announced that he had located a palm-sized writing notebook known as a "table" at the Folger Shakespeare Library in Washington, D.C., that was made in England in 1604. His research determined that groupings of blank leaves bound in the volume had been covered by a kind of plaster that could be written upon with a stylus and wiped clean with a rag or sponge. Stallybrass estimated that thousands of these curiosities were in use in England during Elizabethan and Jacobean times, all presumably acquired with the idea that nothing recorded in them was meant for posterity. The coated pages were sold blank and often bound with pages of preprinted texts bearing practical information such as the dates of fairs, pictures of coins in circulation, and the multiplication table. The example Stallybrass examined at the Folger bears the fairly conclusive title of *Writing Tables with a Kalender for xxiiii. yeeres.*

For those among us today who grouse about why well-meaning people from the past would dispose of information that we regard as essential to understanding their culture, it is sobering to be reminded that the rubber eraser is a fairly recent innovation, hailed by one eighteenth-century historian of practical discoveries as a "very convenient method of wiping out writing made with a black-lead pencil." That innovation was carried a step further in 1858 when an American inventor received a patent for making a wooden writing stylus outfitted with a "piece of prepared rubber" glued on at one end. In his painstaking history of the "design and circumstance" of the pencil, the civil engineer Henry Petroski told how this practical method of eliminating unwanted writing was greeted with opposition by educators in many schools throughout the United States, the central argument being that "the easier errors may be corrected, the more errors will be made."

While writing with a pencil produces writing that *might* be erased, writing with a stick of chalk on a slab of black slate or green composition board is writing that is virtually *certain* to be wiped away, usually with one swipe of the hand and in a puff of white powder, as many millions of schoolchildren past and present can readily affirm. But what happens when it is evident that two chalkboards marked in haste with the duty roster for the 9 A.M. to 5 P.M. shift at the 159 East Eighty-fifth Street station house in New York on September 11, 2001, all of a sudden have become historic artifacts? Of the thirteen firefighters from Engine Company 22 and Ladder Company 13 who rushed off to the World Trade Center in lower Manhattan shortly after arriving for work that fateful morning, only four came back alive. "The very idea that there had been preserved—in the fugitive material of chalk on slate—the names written by men who went to their death is just so poignant," Philippe de Montebello, director of the Metropolitan Museum of Art, said eight months after the terrorist attack on the Twin Towers, explaining why a team of experts from his conservation unit had spent several weeks trying to come up with a way to safeguard forever jottings that were meant to last no more than a day. The most daunting challenge to be overcome was explained by Tony Frantz, head of the museum's conservation laboratory: "On slate, the only bond is mechanical, as microscopic pieces of chalk bond onto the roughness of the slate. Chalk is very likely to detach from the slate surface—and was designed to do so. Thus, the eraser." The solution? A pair of two-hundred-pound oak frames punctuated by brass aerators inset with copper screening, each fitted with panes of double-laminated automobile safety glass to sheathe the chalkboards. "They have now become iconized," Frantz said. "They have taken on an almost religious significance."

The discoveries of the English archaeological explorer M. Aurel Stein (1862–1943) on the ancient Silk Road caravan routes of central Asia—most spectacularly some seven thousand complete scrolls and an equal number of fragments from a sealed chamber in the Caves of the Thousand Buddhas near Dunhuang—comprise some of the greatest textual finds in history. Mortared behind a brick wall and forgotten for a thousand years were 1,130 bundles sewed in cloth, each containing a dozen or more rolls of paper, the vast majority of them manuscripts. Included among them was a sixteen-foot-long document containing the words of a famous Buddhist text known as the Diamond Sutra. Now a prize possession of the British Library, the roll, made up of seven sheets pasted together, was produced in A.D. 868 by the Chinese printer Wang Chieh, who devised a process of rubbing soft paper on inked blocks of engraved wood to produce identical copies.

Although Dunhuang remains Stein's most spectacular triumph, he had other adventures that were equally satisfying. In *Sand-Buried Ruins of Khotan,* he wrote about his probings at an abandoned settlement in India located "beyond the point where the Niya River now loses itself in the desert." Digging in that wilderness, he found a variety of ancient documents written in Kharosthi script from the third century A.D., some on wood, others on leather. "It was not sand from which I extracted tablet after tablet, but a consolidated mass of refuse," he was pleased to admit. "All the documents on wood, of which I recovered in the end more than two hundred, were found scattered among layers of broken pottery, straw, rags of felt and various woven fabrics, pieces of leather, and other rubbish." These documents were of great significance, he believed, since they represented "the first specimens as yet discovered of leather used for writing purposes among a population of Indian language and culture."

Stein called one chapter in *Ruins of Desert Cathay,* a two-volume account of his explorations in China, "Records from an Ancient Rubbish Heap," and told of a dig at Lop Nor where he uncovered evidence of another highly organized civilization, also from the third century A.D. "On the south to a height of four to five feet, gradually diminishing northwards, lay a mass of consolidated rubbish consisting of straw and stable refuse. But we had scarcely commenced digging up this unsavory quarry when Chinese records on wood and paper cropped up in great number, especially from layers two to three feet above the ground level." The "odours were still pungent," he continued, but his labors were "to the end amply rewarded by finds," some of them documents that he was delighted to report were "perfectly preserved."

Textual discoveries in the "rubbish heap" of numerous other past cultures are not at all uncommon and, as these examples indicate, they involve many forms of writing surfaces. What remains by far the greatest concentration of papyrus documents retrieved anywhere to date was found layered beneath a range of enormous trash piles that had accumulated over a period of centuries outside an abandoned city near a branch of the Nile River that once flourished as a provincial capital. Known to its Hellenistic and Roman residents as Oxyrhynchus, the desert settlement was named after a sharp-nosed fish sacred to the Egyptians. Surrounded in antiquity by a wall three miles in circumference, Oxyrhynchus once had colonnaded streets that crossed in a central square and a theater that could seat eleven thousand people. Quays lined its eastern flank, and off to the west was a trail that linked up with the camel routes to Libya.

Bereft of any outstanding temples, monuments, or palaces that would keep its memory alive after the Arab conquest of Egypt in the seventh century, Oxyrhynchus had retreated into obscurity and remained that way until 1896, when it became the focus of renewed attention. Farmers in the region had discovered that soil covering an arc of ancient mounds just outside the ruined city made for excellent fertilizer, and as they dug deeper and deeper into the ground, they came across fragments of papyri. Alerted by reports that curious materials from Oxyrhynchus were showing up in the street bazaars of Cairo, Bernard Pyne Grenfell and Arthur Surridge Hunt, a pair of Oxford University scholars adept in excavation and decipherment, began searching the desert site. Over the next twenty years they removed fifty thousand papyrus fragments from the sandy pits, many of them lying thirty feet below the surface. Most of the documents related to government administration, taxation, and private affairs, and offered extraordinary insight into domestic life of the Greco-Roman period in Egypt, but there were some exceptional literary finds as well.

Virtually every known verse written in the seventh century B.C. by the lyric poet Sappho, to cite the most prominent example, derives from fragments of her work recovered at Oxyrhynchus; according to one Oxford papyrologist working on the trove today—only 5 percent of the fragments have been translated over the past century—the woman's erotic verses were considered too scandalous by medieval monks to copy, and would have been lost entirely if not for the scrap heap of Oxyrhynchus. In 1963 the Oxford scholar Godfrey Bond, a Bletchley Park code-breaker during World War II, pieced together the scattered parts of *Hypsipyle,* a lost play of Euripides about the wife of Jason the Argonaut that had been found at the site, and arranged it in proper order. In 1990 the British playwright Tony Harrison adapted four hundred lines of *Ichneutae* (Trackers), a recovered farce by Sophocles and one of only two satyr plays now extant from classical times, into a production he called *The Trackers of Oxyrhynchus;* it had a short run at the National Theatre in London.

Another dig uncovered a complete comedy by Menander, a third-century B.C. Greek dramatist whose entire oeuvre was considered lost until several of his works turned up in the desert dump. During their two decades of collaboration, Grenfell and Hunt edited sixteen large volumes of material from the ancient discards they reclaimed from the sand. Four volumes of "select papyri"—two of them dealing with nonliterary subjects, two of them literary—are available in compact editions from Harvard University Press in the indispensable Loeb Classical Library series of Greek and Latin translations. Oxyrhynchus itself has since become known in archaeological circles as "waste paper city."

About the same time that Grenfell and Hunt started their search for tattered treasures in the Egyptian desert, an interesting twist to the Oxyrhynchus scenario began playing itself out 120 miles to the northeast in a neighborhood of Old Cairo known as Fostat. There, in the winter of 1896, the most important concentration of ancient Hebrew documents ever to be recovered apart from the Dead Sea Scrolls bonanza of half a century later was exposed to the light of day by Dr. Solomon Schechter, a Cambridge University scholar acting on a tip passed on to him by two tourists just returning home to England from Egypt.

Throughout their history, Jews have treated written words, especially those invoking the name of God, with the utmost respect. In keeping with this tradition, Jewish custom has always stipulated that when their days of usefulness have come to an end, worn-out books be "laid to rest" in a rite that has all the gravity and ceremony of a formal funeral. But until one of these burials can be arranged—and they are performed at irregular intervals—spent books are kept in a secure annex of most synagogues known as the *genizah,* a generic Hebrew word variously translated to mean "storage," "treasury," "archives," and "burial." Dr. Schechter himself explained the custom in an article for the *Times* of London: "When the spirit is gone, we put a corpse out of sight to protect it from abuse. In like manner, when a writing is worn out or disused, we hide the book to preserve it from profanation. The contents of the book go up to heaven like the soul."

In the curious instance of what would become internationally known as the Cairo Genizah, an enormous accretion of papers and parchments that had been stockpiled over a thousand years never made it to the cemetery at all, and lay in a windowless attic at the back of the Ben Ezra Synagogue. Built in the ninth century, the holy place was described by the Spanish Jewish traveler Benjamin of Tudela in the 1200s as already being "very ancient." The synagogue was rebuilt in 1890, but the *genizah* itself remained untouched, and through a stroke of good fortune—the reasons remain vague to this day—a quarter of a million pieces of paper and parchment had never left the loft. They were spared further deterioration by dint of the dry Egyptian climate, the same conditions that allowed so many papyri to survive at Oxyrhynchus. An even greater mystery was that the documents were not limited to religious texts and commentaries, usually the case in a *genizah*, but included correspondence, court records, business agreements, marriage contracts, musical scores, medical prescriptions, and a host of materials dealing with such decidedly lay subjects as magic and mysticism. In addition to Hebrew, other languages represented were Aramaic, Arabic, Coptic, Persian, Judeo-Arabic, Spanish, even some early examples of Yiddish.

Schechter had traveled to Egypt with the idea of gathering what he could for Cambridge University, where he was a world-renowned reader in Talmudic studies. "I am just back from the Genizah, and brought two big sacks with fragments," he wrote his wife, Mathilde, after an arduous day spent in the stifling attic. "I must have a bath at once. You have no idea of the dirt." In a letter to Mayer Sulzberger, an acquaintance in Philadelphia who would be instrumental in bringing him to the United States, Schechter wrote that he was finding "valuable treasures" on a daily basis. "A whole unknown Jewish world reveals itself to us."

Some of the documents he found date back thirteen hundred years and include the oldest text of the Talmud ever found, discovered on a scroll that was prepared in the eighth century. Some sixty fragments in the hand of Moses Maimonides (1135–1204), the foremost intellectual of medieval Judaism and the physician to Saladin, sultan of Egypt, were recovered. Maimonides wrote extensively on philosophy, logic, mathematics, medicine, law, and theology, and worshiped at Ben Ezra. Among numerous "lost" books found lying in the attic was a tenth-century Hebrew version of the *Wisdom of Ben Sira,* a collection of proverbs and common sense known as Ecclesiasticus dating from the second century B.C. Until its discovery by Schechter, the text was available only in Greek and Syriac translations used by the Christian Church.

More than a century after Schechter's forays into the attic were announced to the world, scholars were still poring over the materials. Five years after turning over 140,000 fragments to Cambridge University—a little more than half of what was found—Schechter moved to the United States to transform the Jewish Theological Seminary in New York into a scholarly institution, and arranged for some of the Cairo holdings to go there. Smaller collections are maintained at a number of other institutions in Britain and France. In November 1999, New York University announced that it had received a "substantial" grant—$5 million according to one press account—from a Canadian philanthropist and collector of Judaica, Albert D. Friedberg, to undertake a seven-year program committed to cataloging, transcribing, and publishing the thousands of Cairo Genizah materials that remain unexamined.

In stark contrast to the almost unfathomable mass of the Cairo Genizah are the contents of a single clay pot found in the early 1990s in the ancient Buddhist kingdom of Gandhara, an area located in what today comprises parts of eastern Afghanistan and a section of northwest Pakistan. Inside the jar were twenty-nine scrolls made from the bark of birch trees, each inscribed with texts written in the Kharosthi script once peculiar to the region. Acquired in 1996 by an "anonymous donor" for a sum said to be in the "high five figures," the fragments were transferred to the British Library through an "anonymous dealer" as a gift. "These birch bark scrolls are believed to be the oldest surviving Buddhist texts ever discovered," the Dalai Lama wrote in a foreword to a detailed account of the fragments, published jointly by the British Library and the University of Washington and an event the religious leader hailed for giving the writings a wide audience. "Despite the great respect that Buddhists universally have for their scriptures, there is sometimes a risk of books being venerated from a distance rather than read. This is all the more likely when the manuscripts concerned, like these, are extremely rare and fragile."

Richard Salomon, a professor of Asian languages and literature at the University of Washington, was brought in by the British Library to head the team working on the scrolls, which were carefully sectioned off and tweezed into delicate fragments for analysis. In *Ancient Buddhist Scrolls from Gandhāra,* the first of what will be several scholarly reports on the texts, Salomon wrote that no "reliable information is available as to the circumstances, location, and date of the discovery of the manuscripts and associated material," an especially regrettable circumstance, he acknowledged, since "the loss of a proper archaeological context seriously diminishes their scholarly value." In a telephone interview, Salomon told me the precise location of the discovery site remains sketchy at best, but he added his belief that the fragile scrolls—"looking for all the world like a box of stale cigars" when they arrived at the British Library—had been placed in a form of "Buddhist Genizah" about two thousand years ago, probably a hemispherical mound containing religious relics known as a *stupa.* "The scrolls were damaged somewhat by the people who discovered them," he said, "but there is little doubt from what we have been able to determine that they had already deteriorated considerably before they were placed in the clay pot, and there is even some internal evidence in the scrolls that suggests a form of deaccession." Salomon's theory, advanced at length in his published account, is that "the fragments were probably pieces of worn-out texts that had been discarded and were accorded ritual burial in a pot that was interred within the precincts of a Buddhist monastery."

Written in black ink with a split-reed pen on sections of bark that had been glued together to form long strips, the fragments, sixty altogether, represent about twenty-five texts, including some sermons of Siddhārtha Gautama, the religious philosopher and sage known as the Buddha, who died about 483 B.C. The texts are thought to have belonged to a long-lost sect that dominated the region of Gandhara two thousand years ago, and helped to bring the religion derived from Buddha's teachings into central and east Asia from India, where it has since disappeared. Pushing back the calendar as far as possible is of particular significance, since so much of Buddha's instructions were memorized by his disciples and passed on orally for close to five hundred years before being written down in the first century B.C. "There was a gradual transition to written tradition," Graham Shaw, a deputy director at the British Library involved in the project, said. "As we get closer to Buddha's own time, we are closer to the transition and closer to the oral tradition. The early texts may also tell us something about the nature of the transition of Buddhism to Central Asia and then to China."

Once again, the circumstance of climate and geography played a vital role in extending the life of discarded writings, with the cold, dry, high terrain of the mountains acting as a preservative agent. Unlike the formula for making papyrus sheets, which as we have seen was passed on to us by Pliny the Elder, the process used for preparing birch-bark strips to receive ink has been lost. "Unfortunately," Salomon wrote, "the delicate condition of the British Library manuscripts, which are now permanently encased in glass, does not allow for technical studies of their material and preparation."

. . .

Sifting through a swale of rubbish clogged beneath a cushion of mud outside Hadrian's Wall in the northern region of Northumberland, a British archaeologist had the shock of his life when he began to examine a sodden object about the size of a postcard. "They were two tiny sheets pressed together," Robin Birley remarked later about his 1973 discovery, made just outside the ruins of an old Roman fort called Vindolanda by occupants of the garrison stationed there two thousand years ago. When Birley pried the pieces apart, he caught a quick glimpse of some notations that quickly vanished in the atmosphere, then turned to black. Conservators at nearby Durham University used infrared beams to determine that Birley had found a letter written sometime around A.D. 80 by a soldier stationed at the post, making it the oldest example of Roman writing ever found in Europe, and the oldest piece of correspondence sent from one ordinary citizen in the sprawling empire to another. Over the next three decades of continuing excavation, Birley and his colleagues found fifteen hundred specimens in the Vindolanda pits, many of them personal letters, others official documents, including one that reported troop strength at 750 men, with more than half of the contingent off on leave. Another memorandum dismissed thoughts of any threat from the overmatched natives in the region, calling them *Brittunculi*—a word found nowhere else, and translated to mean "wretched Britons."

The trench had been used as a general disposal area by the garrison foot soldiers, and was dug just outside the general commissary. Most of the letters were casual correspondence and routine administrative documents jotted down on inexpensive materials, including a personal letter to Sulpicia Lepidina, the wife of the base commander, inviting her to a birthday party. Most of these "leaf tablets," as they have come to be called, had been written on thin sheets of birch or alder wood in carbon ink with "dip-and-scratch" stylus pens, several hundred of which were also found in the debris. The slices of wood—none of the letters found were cut from bark—were hinged, folded, and tied together through perforations. Some of the tablets show evidence of having been partially burned, in all likelihood set on fire along with the other rubbish, but were saved, it has been theorized, by a rainfall that doused the flames. It was the further intervention of nature—sealing blankets of mud and turf—that enabled these documents to carry their messages forward to modern times. The official files of the detachment—recorded, presumably, on papyrus or parchment and kept in the *principia,* or administrative headquarters— traveled with the unit when it was reassigned to other duties on the continent in A.D. 105 and have all long since vanished. Rome ended its four-hundred-year occupation of Britain entirely early in the fifth century. A Centre for the Study of Ancient Documents established in 1995 at Oxford University is using high-resolution digital imagery—the same kind of technology used to diagnosis breast cancer and glaucoma—to make enlarged three-dimensional copies of these strange missives from the past and to enhance their interpretation. Alan K. Bowman, director of the center, has written several books on the leaf tablets, including *Life and Letters on the Roman Frontier,* a lively translation of some of the more interesting examples exhumed thus far.

The words Sir Aurel Stein used to characterize several of his major finds in India and China are appropriate to Vindolanda, as they are for the rich vein of papyrus fragments mined at Oxyrhynchus, and for many of the other extraordinary textual discoveries of recent history, be they writings on wood, bark, bamboo, leather, paper, parchment, slivers of pottery, or copper sheets. "It is mainly to the unsavory associations of the dustbin," Stein wrote in *Sand-Buried Ruins of Khotan,* "that we must ascribe the remarkable state of preservation shown by the great mass of these precious records."

3.

The Ozymandias Factor

※ ※

I met a traveller from an antique land
Who said: Two vast and trunkless legs of stone
Stand in the desert. Near them, on the sand,
Half sunk, a shattered visage lies, whose frown,
And wrinkled lip, and sneer of cold command,
Tell that its sculptor well those passions read
Which yet survive, stamped on these lifeless things,
The hand that mocked them, and the heart that fed:
And on the pedestal these words appear:
"My name is Ozymandias, king of kings:
Look on my works, ye Mighty, and despair!"
Nothing beside remains. Round the decay
Of that colossal wreck, boundless and bare
The lone and level sands stretch far away.
PERCY BYSSHE SHELLEY, "OZYMANDIAS"

※ ※

The French art historian Alain Schnapp has written that "from the moment of their emergence as a cultural and biological entity" many thousands of years ago, human beings "have in one way or another collected, preserved and hoarded items which have no other significance than as carriers of messages from a more or less remote past." That crisp certainty in and of itself, he continued, is why every archaeologist has a cardinal responsibility to look beyond the detritus of the past to the here and now: "We have to engage with the idea that other human beings, maybe tomorrow, maybe in a few hours' time, maybe a few centuries from now, will look upon our traces."

A bold attempt to transfer just such a greeting to the distant future was undertaken on August 20, 1977, and September 5, 1977, when two *Voyager* spacecraft were launched from Cape Canaveral, Florida, on photographic reconnaissance missions to the outer planets of the solar system. Hurled into the heavens by a pair of *Titan III-E Centaur* rockets, the robotic wanderers were rigged to transmit streams of data back to Earth for up to fifty years. After completing the first phases of their assignments, they headed off on a billion-year journey into the depths of the cosmos with another task on their agenda. Attached to the support panels of each spacecraft is a gold-coated copper phonograph record containing messages for any extraterrestrial trawler that might by chance pluck it from the heavens. Encoded digitally into the grooves of the twelve-inch disks are the images of 118 photographs depicting the people of Earth and aspects of its civilization, along with ninety minutes of music, greetings in sixty human languages, and a snippet of a whale song. As a helpful touch for the would-be discoverers, a sequence of operational instructions the astronomer Carl Sagan called "scientific hieroglyphics" was engraved on the slip-jackets. To track the 33 rpm records, a stylus was set in place alongside each unit; the aliens will be required to provide their own tone arm, amplifier, video monitor, and power source.

Sagan, who organized the deep-space message segment of the project for the National Aeronautics and Space Administration in the 1970s, likened the mission to casting a fragile glass bottle into a bottomless sea. By the time he died in 1996, the *Voyagers* had produced the most extensive collection of planetary data ever generated by any spacecraft, returning trillions of bits of information that scientists believe will keep them busy for decades, with more material still arriving. The resilient instruments will continue beaming signals to receivers on Earth for years to come, probably through 2020, perhaps even to 2030. But once the transmitters are silent, the 1.25-pound copper disks will continue on their journey, wandering calmly through the blackness of a frigid void where there is no erosion. As the *Voyager*s circle the center of the galaxy, their messages of greeting will remain unblemished by deterioration. "Billions of years from now, our sun, then a distended red giant star, will have reduced Earth to a charred cinder," Sagan predicted shortly after the launchings. "But the *Voyager* record will still be intact, in some other remote region of the Milky Way galaxy, pre-serving a murmur of an ancient civilization that once flourished—perhaps moving on to greater deeds and other worlds—on the distant planet Earth."

For those of us who will remain forever earthbound, a consideration of what might well be called the Ozymandias factor comes into play with a physical examination of *Murmurs of Earth,* the detailed account Sagan and his colleagues wrote in 1978 of the "interstellar record project" they had just coordinated for NASA. My copy of the book—which I received as a review copy in the year of publication, and is now out of print—has been handled no more than two or three times over the past two decades, and has never been exposed to sunlight. Despite this limited level of stress, the inside surface of the dust wrapper and the edges of the pages have started to yellow, obvious signs of decay, and clear evidence of a text that was printed on acidic paper, what in common parlance is known as a brittle book. It is still in good reading condition, and will remain so for years to come, but unless chemically reversed, the process of deteriora-tion is inexorable. If this particular copy is deemed worthy of long-term preservation, it will have to be treated at some point in the future; other-wise, it is doomed to disintegration.

John Milton's impassioned declaration in the *Areopagitica* that books are the means to achieving "life beyond life" assumes that a durable medium will be available to facilitate the transmission of knowledge. Historically, the preservation of information has involved various compromises, with the more durable materials typically being the most cumbersome to manufacture and store, while those most efficiently produced are more vulnerable to deterioration. The nineteenth-century British historian Thomas Babington Macaulay (1800–1859) took oblique note of these trade-offs in a biting essay putatively directed at the Royal Society of Literature, with whom he maintained a long-running feud. To make his point, he told the whimsical tale of an imaginary Babylonian monarch who ruled "about four hundred years after the Deluge," a beloved leader he called Gomer Chephoraod:

> He made good laws, won great battles, and whitewashed long streets. He was, in consequence, idolised by his people, and panegyrised by many poets and orators. A book was then a serious undertaking. Neither paper nor any similar material had been invented. Authors were therefore under the necessity of inscribing their compositions on massive bricks. Some of these Babylonian records are still preserved in European museums; but the language in which they are written has never been deciphered. Gomer Chephoraod was so popular that the clay of all the plains round the Euphrates could scarcely furnish brick-kilns enough for his eulogists. It is recorded in particular that Pharonezzar, the Assyrian Pindar, published a bridge and four walls in his praise.

Like all good satire, Lord Macaulay's entertaining premise is not entirely without foundation, as a huge panel of inscriptions carved on the side of a rising cliff twenty miles outside of Tehran in Iran might suggest. There, near a well-worn camel trail at a place known as the Great Rock of Behistun (or Bisutun), Darius the Great (550–486 B.C.) of Persia had ordered a celebration of his victory over the usurper Gaumata and nine rebel chieftains inscribed in bas-relief on the sheer face of a bloodred slope about three hundred feet above the ground. Royal scribes fashioned tributes to their monarch in the three principal languages of the empire:

Babylonian, Old Persian, and Elamite, an ancient tongue of southwest Iran. Each was a variation of cuneiform, the wedgelike script most commonly associated with clay tablets (*cuneus* is Latin for "wedge"), and the "lingua franca" of the eastern Mediterranean world at the time.

To protect the accolade from desecration, the surface surrounding the twelve-hundred-square-foot commendation was smoothed over, making it nearly impossible to reach without benefit of scaffolding, and, paradoxically, rendering it virtually impossible to read from the ground with the naked eye, let alone allow anyone to produce accurate copies many centuries later. Some twenty-two hundred years after the words had been carved into the cliff, a contemporary of Lord Macaulay—an adventurous British diplomat and former cavalry officer with a remarkable flair for exotic languages—began making rubbings of the words with the hope of facilitating a decipherment. Sir Henry Creswicke Rawlinson (1810–1895), a onetime champion polo player who prided himself in his athletic prowess, undertook the project in 1835 while serving as an officer with the East India Company, four years before the unveiling of the daguerreotype ushered in the age of photography (a coinage from the Greek that means "writing with light") and altered forever the way precise visual images could be captured. A delegation of French antiquarians had already declared the inscriptions impossible to copy, but Rawlinson was determined to make accurate impressions of every carving on the cliff, and to achieve that goal, he had to take some extraordinary steps. He began by lowering himself by rope from a ledge high above the carvings; as he became more familiar with the hill, other means of access were improvised. In a lecture delivered to the Society of Antiquaries of London in 1850, he described some of the creative methods he had employed:

> On reaching the recess which contains the Persian text of the record, ladders are indispensable in order to examine the upper portion of the tablet; and even with ladders there is considerable

risk, for the foot ledge is so narrow, about eighteen inches or at most two feet in breadth, that with a ladder long enough to reach the sculptures sufficient slope cannot be given to enable a person to ascend, and, if the ladder be shortened in order to increase the slope, the upper inscription can only be copied by standing on the topmost step of the ladder, with no other support than steadying the body against the rock with the left arm, while the left hand holds the notebook, and the right hand is employed with the pencil. In this position I copied all the upper inscriptions, and the interest of the occupation entirely did away with any sense of danger.

For all his bravado, Rawlinson still found copying the Babylonian inscriptions a treacherous enterprise, and while the intrepid adventurer acknowledged that a passable copy could have been sketched in longhand with the aid of a good telescope, he was set on making direct casts of every figure on the cliff. Told by local shepherds that this section of the slope was "unapproachable," Rawlinson thereupon retained the services of "a wild Kurdish boy" blessed with uncommon physical resilience and dexterity. He told of the youngster's assault on the "near-perpendicular" mountain while seated on a "swinging seat, like a painter's cradle," and how the lad made "the paper cast of the Babylonian translation of the records of Darius" by following his shouted directions from the ground below.

As for the casts themselves, Rawlinson called the method he applied to making them "exceedingly simple" to master. Sheets of paper were spread on the rock, moistened, then beat into the carved crevices with a "stout" brush, and allowed to dry in the sun. The result was "a perfect reversed impression of the writing." These extraordinary molds, made under the most forbidding of conditions, were "almost of equal value for the interpretation of the Assyrian inscriptions as was the Greek translation on the Rosetta Stone," Rawlinson told his colleagues with justifiable pride. "The inscription is probably the most important document of the entire Ancient Near East," Sheila S. Blair agreed in an important study of monumental inscriptions, "for it was the key to deciphering cuneiform writing and thus comparable to the Rosetta Stone for Egyptology." But there is a sadly ironic coda to the story. Unlike the Rosetta Stone, the Darius casts, or "squeezes," as they were called, were made of massed clusters of paper. Once their usefulness was exhausted, they were laid flat in a musty storeroom of the British Museum basement, forgotten for decades in a cavernous building that now contains more than 7 million objects, and eaten beyond recognition by generations of foraging mice.

Rawlinson's acrobatic feats at Behistun would not be the only time an energetic explorer risked his life to facilitate the study of an ancient text. When the Italian archaeologist Federico Halbherr traveled to Crete in 1884 in search of classical carvings, the danger came from hazards encountered well below ground, not from any cliff towering high above it. Halbherr began his investigations on the southern side of the island in a plain bordered by Mount Ida, the mythological birthplace of Zeus, at the site of an ancient city known as Gortyn. He had been enticed to the area by reports of some inscriptions encountered twenty-seven years earlier by a team of French archaeologists, with indications that much more remained yet to be uncovered. The immediate problem was not one of excavation, since digging, however problematic a process it may be to ensuring the integrity of an archaeological site, is not usually considered a life-threatening exercise, if carried out deliberately. But in the centuries that had passed since the destruction of Gortyn by Arab pirates in A.D. 824, a sluice from the nearby river Lethaeus had been diverted to power a water mill improvised above a Roman theater known as the Odeion, which had been built during the reign of the emperor Trajan in the first century A.D. That building had been erected after an earthquake destroyed a Hellenistic structure on the site, using a dozen marble stones bearing a Greek legal code as part of its foundations. In time, the slabs, twenty-seven feet long and five feet high, formed part of a retaining wall cobbled together by the local residents to channel the water. The idea of shutting down a perfectly functional mill did not sit well with its operators, who expressed their displeasure with Halbherr's incessant probings by raising the sluice gates one day while he was below examining the slabs, allowing a torrent of water to come rushing in, though not quickly enough to drown him. The harrowing experience persuaded the Italian that formal permission from the Greek government to continue with his work would be a prudent precaution to take. When finally exposed, the twelve tablets were determined to contain the foundation of an entire legal system, including rules of civil procedure, offering tremendous insight into the social system of the classical era. Dated to 450 B.C., the laws are inscribed in the script of a Doric Cretan dialect that reads from right to left on the first line, then left to right on the next, continuing in this fashion in a configuration known as boustrophedon—a usage from the Greek meaning "as the ox plows" to suggest the alternating directions it follows— accounting for six hundred lines all told. Today, the inscriptions remain in place on the original site, in the north round wall of the Odeion.

Squeezes of the code, meanwhile, are included among the 450 direct impressions on paper of ancient inscriptions maintained by the Museum of Classical Archaeology at Cambridge University in England, a repository that is notable for the fact that *nothing* in its vast inventory is original. Everything—including some 650 full-sized Greek and Roman sculptures made directly from authentic statuary—is a copy, a circumstance, in an oddly convoluted way, that has some advantages as teaching tools over the originals. The best-known reproduction in the museum is the Peplos Kore, a statue of a young woman wearing an intricate garment known as a peplos, and dating from 530 B.C. The plaster copy has been carefully painted to indicate what scholars believe was probably the appearance of the original statue, something that would never have been attempted with an authentic work of art, and would not have been considered for the reproduction either had the museum not acquired a second cast in 1975.

Even though it has been known for centuries that the Greeks painted their marble sculptures with vivid colors and decorated them with jewelry—Pliny the Elder wrote of the practice in the first century A.D.—some observers might still regard that kind of reconstruction as fanciful conjecture. Such is not the case with the museum's copy of a sculptured frieze known as the Lysikrates Monument, however. Molded in situ in the eighteenth century, the two-hundred-year-old cast preserves many figures, including an image of Dionysius seated with a panther, that have since been eroded on the original by the polluted air of Athens, one instance in which the facsimile of a creative work is more faithful to what once was than the original itself.

When the librarian of the Biblioteca Nazionale Marciana in Venice, Dr. Marino Zorzi, placed an ancient manuscript known to scholars as the Venetus A in my hands during a visit to his library, he was allowing me to hold the earliest known version of Homer in the world, a gift to the people of Venice in 1468 from Cardinal Vasilios Bessarion, a Greek refugee to Italy from Constantinople who was prominent in the failed effort to reunite the eastern and western branches of the Church in the aftermath of the Great Schism, and a bibliophile for the ages. This text is crucial not only because it transmits the earliest surviving version of the *Iliad,* but also for the commentaries that have been written in the margins, some making reference to learned works that have long since disappeared. As old as the manuscript is—and it had survived for thirteen centuries when I was permitted to touch the vellum leaves—it is still twelve centuries removed from the poem's estimated time of composition. Its survival as a text, in other words, relied on earlier copies that have long since vanished or been destroyed. "What you held in Venice is the oldest version we have," Stephen G. Nichols, the head of the task force established late in 1999 to develop a strategy for determining the "place of the artifact in future libraries," told me in an interview. "Granted, it's not a 500 B.C. Homer, but it's not a Penguin edition either; so for a scholar, yes, the earliest is the most important. The surrogate does, in a sense, become the original in an instance like this."

Several hundred years before Homer composed the *Iliad* and the *Odyssey*, a poem known today as the *Epic of Gilgamesh* was written in Akkadian, the main Semitic language of ancient Babylonia and Syria. Unlike the Greek epics, which have enjoyed an unbroken run of popularity, the Mesopotamian tale describing the exploits of Gilgamesh, king of the Sumerian city-state Uruk, disappeared along with the ancient culture that sustained it thousands of years ago. In 1845 Austen Henry Layard (1817–1894), a British adventurer driven by boyhood readings of *The Arabian Nights*, began digging into a series of covered mounds at Nimrud, the biblical region of Calah in Mesopotamia—Greek for "between the rivers" of the Fertile Crescent, the Tigris and the Euphrates—and was rewarded with the discovery of several Assyrian palaces. His impressive finds led him to undertake further excavations near the modern city of Mosel at Kuyunjik, where he uncovered Nineveh, at one time the largest city in the known world. Built in 701 B.C. by Sennacherib, king of Assyria from 704 to 681 B.C., the city fell to the Medes in 614 B.C. Deserted, sacked, and burned, the palace ruins were quickly covered over by the blowing desert sands. Traveling through the region just two hundred years later, the Greek historian Herodotus could find no trace of Nineveh, and for close to two and a half millennia after that, every chronicle written of the Assyrian empire was based on legend and guesswork. But that all began to change in 1847 with Layard's spectacular discovery.

The Englishman focused his immediate attention on the massive sculptures located throughout the palace, and worked assiduously to get the finest examples back to London as quickly as possible. Of secondary interest were the thousands of incised clay tablets he found lying about the royal archives of King Ashurbanipal (sometimes spelled as Assurbanipal), whose long reign (668–627 B.C.) was acclaimed for its commitment to literature and the arts. Layard's crew burrowed more than three kilometers of tunnels around the walls of the palace, clearing seventy-one rooms of their sculptures, and causing severe structural damage that today would be considered inexcusable. Additional difficulties arose from the fact that Layard, who was not a professional archaeologist, kept no systematic logbooks of where each clay tablet and cylinder was found. In some instances fragments were lying a foot deep on the floor of the chamber. Not wanting to waste more time than necessary, Layard had them loaded haphazardly by the thousands into wicker baskets and shipped to England without first documenting their original locations; as far as he was concerned, rigorous scholarship could come later in the British Museum. The future parliamentarian acknowledged as much in one of several best-selling accounts he wrote of his discoveries; the Ashurbanipal tablets, he proclaimed, "furnish us with materials for the complete decipherment of the cuneiform character, for restoring the language and history of Assyria, and for inquiring into the customs, sciences, and we may even add, literature of the people," adding almost parenthetically that many years "must elapse before the innumerable fragments can be put together and the inscriptions transcribed."

As events turned out, Layard's prediction was pretty much on target. On December 3, 1872, George Smith, a protégé of Henry Creswicke Rawlinson, informed a packed gathering of the Biblical Archaeological Society in London that he had arranged dozens of tiny clay pieces in patterns much like a jigsaw puzzle to reveal portions of a Great Deluge tale that celebrated the exploits of an ancient king called Gilgamesh who ruled in Mesopotamia about 2700 B.C. What electrified the London audience was Smith's disclosure that the poem told of a catastrophe in ways that were strikingly similar to the Great Flood of Genesis, but composed a thousand years *earlier* than the writings of the Old Testament. Hopeful of fleshing out further episodes of the tale—and underwritten by a grant from the *Daily Telegraph*—the British Museum dispatched Smith to Nineveh with a commission to locate additional specimens. Five days after arriving at the site, he found a fragment that contained seventeen lines of inscription "relating the command to build and fill the ark." Over the next few weeks, and during another probe undertaken a year and a half later, Smith located hundreds of additional pieces.

All told, about fifteen thousand words of the poem were derived from the Nineveh tablets. Since then, fourteen additional sets of fragments have been found in Turkey and Iraq, persuasive evidence of how influential the Gilgamesh tale was throughout Mesopotamia. About a third of the epic remains missing, though there is hope that the entire text will one day be recovered, some of it, perhaps, lying among the 120,000 tablets stored in London, many of them still unexamined and uncatalogued. That such an eventuality is not impossible was underscored in 1998 when an American researcher announced that he had located the words needed to complete the beginning lines of the poem. "It's the most important piece of evidence on the opening of the epic we've had for one hundred years," Theodore Kwasman said of his discovery, and he had found the tiny pieces lying in a glass-topped box on a wooden shelf in a back room of the British Museum. Unlike the texts of Homer, which undoubtedly experienced numerous modifications in the centuries leading up to the writing of the Venetus A manuscript that the Greek expatriate Cardinal Bessarion brought to Italy in the fifteenth century, the cuneiform tablets are "pure" in the sense that they have not been "contaminated" by the repeated intervention of editors and copyists over the past twenty-seven hundred years. But as old as these tablets are, they too are copies of a poem that had an oral tradition extending a thousand years further back in time, and undoubtedly were modified over the course of their textual migration as well.

In 1975 a cache of clay tablets older than the ones removed from Nineveh was discovered by Italian archaeologists searching regions of northwest Syria for traces of a civilization thought to have thrived in the region a thousand years before the time of Moses. For thirteen dusty digging seasons, team leader Paolo Matthiae had concentrated his efforts on a huge mound known to natives as Tell Mardikh before finding what he would later describe in his memoirs as "the centre of the most ancient great culture of Western Asia yet to enter historical record," a long-lost city-state known in its time as Ebla. Historians would determine that Eblaite civilization reached its height around 2250 B.C., and that it had developed a written language that was lost for more than four thousand years. With the discovery of the tablets—two thousand of them complete, six thousand others in large fragments—it was possible to penetrate the daily life of this lost culture. As an added bonus, the tablets were found exactly where they had fallen when the palace was set on fire by invading Akkadians sometime between 2150 and 2350 B.C., making a precise determination of their original placement in the official repository readily discernible. Sifting cautiously through the debris, archaeologists concluded that all records in the State Archives had been classified by subject and stacked in baskets on wooden shelves. When the shelves went up in flames, all tablets on the upper levels slid toward the middle of the room, arriving on the floor in separate heaps. Baked to the hardness of ceramics, the clay documents remained couched in a bed of soft ashes, undisturbed across the centuries.

The Ebla tablets document the activities of various administrative offices of the government through three complete dynasties and parts of two others; one archive alone contains twenty-eight letters and royal decrees issued just before the city's destruction. On the north wall of the chamber, mythological texts were placed next to a grouping of magical incantations and judicial documents. Records concerned with the administration of arable land and the breeding of livestock were kept on lower platforms along the same wall. In the east corner were kept documents recording palace revenue from textile production and precious metals. Tablets shelved on the western wall kept track of economic production and goods designated for export. While 80 percent of the documents are administrative, the remaining 20 percent includes many literary texts, some of them written in Sumerian, others in Eblaite, including one lexical list that is believed to be the world's oldest dictionary.

"These documents now permit us to write the history of northwestern Syria during the second half of the third millennium B.C. and help us to better understand the early history and classification of the Semitic languages," Alfonso Archi wrote in the catalog of a 1985 traveling exhibition of artifacts found at Ebla. Giovanni Pettinato, the chief philologist of the Italian archaeological mission, voiced similar sentiments in his published account of the project: "A new world is opening up to scholarship and to the modern public because the combined efforts of archaeologists and philologists have succeeded in bringing to light tablets of clay which let the kings and functionaries and scribes of Ebla speak to us."

This heretofore forgotten civilization "speaks" to us, obviously, because its writings survived in sufficient abundance so that people skilled in decipherment had the latitude they needed to "receive the message." By contrast to this success, an obscure Mediterranean civilization we understand something about from objects found in their tombs and temples and by the scattered accounts of their successors—the Etruscans in the region of central Italy between the Po and Tiber Rivers known in the years before the ascension of Rome as Etruria—has very little to "say" to us through the written word, not because their savants failed to chronicle their culture in any systematic way, or, for that matter, because so few examples of what they wrote about themselves managed the long passage to our time, since hundreds of Etruscan documents written on a variety of surfaces survive, with more being recovered all the time. Most are prayers and epithets incised on stone tablets, sarcophagi, ash holders, and metal plates, and written or painted on walls and earthenware vessels, although there are a few enticing segments preserved on other media. But if there is any one language from the past that ranks above all others on the wish lists of epigraphers to penetrate, it would be this most elusive of dead tongues, especially since knowing more about who the Etruscans were could very well tell us a good deal about ourselves.

Herodotus claimed in the fifth century B.C. that the people he knew as Tyrrhenians were led to Italy from Lydia in western Asia Minor by a prince named Tyrrhenos to escape a famine (the body of water bordering the region the Etruscans inhabited in Italy is still known as the Tyrrhenian Sea). Before he became the emperor of Rome in A.D. 41, Tiberius Claudius Drusus (10 B.C.–A.D. 54) lived the contented life of a probing intellectual, and included among his output of writings a twenty-volume history of the Etruscans called the *Tyrrhenica*. In a speech preserved on a bronze tablet found at Lyon in 1524, Claudius asserted that he based much of his work on authentic "Etruscan sources," and he is the last scholar we know of who was fluent in the language. He had so much respect for these early inhabitants of his native region that in A.D. 47 he formed a college of Etruscan soothsayers known as the *haruspices* into an official academy of sixty priests. The order's tradition of divining the future through the interpretation of signs had been passed down from father to son, but died out as Rome began to abandon its interest in pagan influences. The college was disbanded early in the fifth century, its documents probably destroyed. Claudius's history was lost as well, along with an eight-volume work he wrote about Carthage. That the Etruscan corpus would have included much more than religious pronouncements is clear by the reputation the Etruscans enjoyed in their own time as scholars; according to Livy, young Roman aristocrats were sent to Etruria routinely to complete their education in much the same way that they would later go off for advanced study in Athens.

Particularly dispiriting is the fact that not a single literary or historical document of Etruscan origin survives, not even in Greek or Roman translation, raising the suspicion that many writings may have been systematically destroyed, and the likelihood is that this happened well before the emperor Constantine formally embraced Christianity in A.D. 324. When

Arnobius, one of the first Christian apologists and the author of seven books directed "against the heathen," declared in about A.D. 300 that "Etruria is the originator and mother of all superstition," the prospects for survival of the language were bleak, and there was no compelling reason to archive the old writings in any case. With the ascendancy of Rome, the Etruscans had already begun to abandon their language, and by the time of Augustus in the first century B.C., they no longer existed as an indigenous people. "There was thus no reason to preserve their texts by copying them in other books or volumes," the noted Italian linguist Larissa Bonfante has written.

There is no doubt, however, that the Etruscans developed a sophisticated means of documenting their thoughts. Writing is believed to have developed in Etruria about 700 B.C., with borrowings almost certainly from the Greek. The main problem confronting scholars studying the Etruscan language today is the simple fact that it resembles no other language they have ever encountered. In contrast with Linear B, which was an unknown script used for a known language—Greek—Etruscan is an unknown language written in a known script—the alphabet—in which each sign represents a different sound. "For an unknown language," one scholar has noted in exasperation, "many Etruscan words look very familiar."

About thirteen thousand artifacts bearing the distinctive Etruscan script are known today, and some words, perhaps 250 of them, have been identified. Most are the names of people and deities, though a few nouns and verbs have been determined. "There is no *point d'appui*," the Etruscan scholar Massimo Pallottino explained of the conundrum, using a melodic French phrase that translates literally as "point of rest," meaning, in essence, that there is no fulcrum upon which a more productive whole can be balanced. Especially enticing all the same, however, are the handful of longer inscriptions that have survived by way of a number of strikingly different writing surfaces. Certainly among the most enticing are three sheets of gold foil found at Pyrgi, the port city of Cerveteri some twenty-five miles northwest of Rome, in 1964. These writings are of keen interest because they bear texts in two languages, Etruscan and Phoenician, making them the closest artifact recovered to date that could be regarded as a bilingual inscription. From the Phoenician, which they can read, scholars have determined the ornate document to be a joint decree dedicating a temple to the goddess Uni. Dating from about 500 B.C., the text includes a quotation from Thefarie Velianas, ruler of the nearby Etruscan city of Caere during this period. That such a decree appeared as part of a reciprocal consecration is consistent with an alliance reported by Aristotle to have been forged at this time between the Etruscans and the Phoenicians, thus making the gold sheets a legitimate historical document. The longest Etruscan text on either tablet appears on sixteen lines, comprising thirty-six words, and though it parallels the Phoenician text, it does not provide a word-for-word translation, leading Bonfante to conclude: "It is no Rosetta Stone."

A bronze model of a sheep's liver found in 1877 near Piacenza in northern Italy is incised with what is presumed to be detailed directions for reading the heavens, with all instructions neatly contained in sixteen demarcated regions, each indicating a precise section of the night sky. Other important Etruscan artifacts include a writing tablet fashioned from ivory and layered with letters in gold leaf, and several pieces of pottery decorated with what clearly are syllables. A terra-cotta tile from Capua preserves sixty-two lines of text, with close to three hundred legible words; a lead sheet excavated not far from Pyrgi is notable in that several of the eighty words bear striking similarities to those carved on an inscription unearthed at another site. Among the most elegant of Etruscan "documents" have been the scores of intricately crafted metal hand mirrors, three thousand all told, recovered from the burial sites of what undoubtedly were wealthy women. "The number of surviving mirrors, their beauty and the interest of their scenes, often labeled with inscriptions, testify to the literacy, culture and wealth of the Etruscan women for whom they were made," Bonfante determined. A carved gem from about 450 B.C. fitted to be worn as a pendant, now in the Bibliothèque Nationale in Paris, pictures a young man seated at a desk, studiously reading figures from a tablet in his lap, with the word *apcar*—Etruscan for *abacus*, or counting board—visible. Although no wax tablets have been recovered, many attractively decorated bronze styli used to incise memos, correspondence, and routine transactions on them have survived; a stone relief dating from 500 B.C. pictures a well-dressed official recording the names of prizewinners at an athletic competition on a hinged tablet that, presumably, could have been closed when not in use, suggesting its portability.

Most extraordinary of all and, given the fragile nature of the writing surface, the most improbable as well, is a lengthy manuscript written on woven cloth known by the Latin name *Liber Linteus,* or linen book, that had been cut into strips and used as funerary bands on an Egyptian mummy sometime during the first century A.D. Exactly how an Etruscan book got to Egypt where it was used to bind the corpse of a woman is a matter of continuing conjecture, but the best guess is that once the object outlived its usefulness as a carrier of information, it was recycled in a manner not unlike the way old manuscripts were used to strengthen bindings in the early days of printing. The mummy was acquired in Alexandria by a diplomatic officer with the Austro-Hungarian Royal Chancellery in 1848, probably on the black market, and brought home with him to Vienna as a curiosity to be displayed in his home. Following the man's death in 1859, it went to the national museum in Zagreb, where it was examined in 1877 by the famous English explorer Sir Richard Francis Burton, who wrote about the strange writings two years later for the Royal Society of Literature, believing them to be an unknown form of runic script. In 1891, the Austrian scholar Jacob Krall correctly determined the text to be Etruscan, making the *Liber Linteus* the longest preserved inscription in the language recovered to date. With infrared lighting, some words that had defied detection in the nineteenth century are now legible, yielding a total of 230 lines of text comprising thirteen hundred words. The manuscript—about a third of the original survived—is believed to have been a kind of religious calendar indicating where and when various ceremonies were to have taken place, citing which gods were to be invoked, and detailing the offerings that were to be made. Although the artifact is unique—no other linen book from antiquity survives—there is no doubt that texts written on cloth existed in abundance; Etruscan sculptures picture linen books folded in the shape of an accordion in much the manner of a conventional codex. The mummy that occasioned the preservation of this extraordinary volume is on public display in the Museum of Archaeology in Zagreb, Croatia, while the bands that wrapped it are kept locked in a vault.

I n China, two caches of manuscripts unearthed in the latter decades of the twentieth century—one of seminal writings painted on a long silk scroll, the other bearing characters brushed on slender bamboo strips—ignited intense scholarly debate about the origins of the Daoist and Confucian traditions. In each instance, the information preserved on these surprisingly durable writing surfaces placed the composition of the *Daodejing*, also known as the *Tao Te Ching* (The Book of the Way and the Power), traditionally ascribed to the Daoist philosopher Laozi (Lao-tzu), at a much earlier period in history than supported by any previously known documents. Laozi is said to have lived in the sixth century B.C., and may at one time have been a keeper of royal archives in the Zhou court— he was a librarian, in other words—a circumstance that could have brought him into contact with the philosopher Confucius (551–479 B.C.), considered by some historians to have been Laozi's pupil. A burning point of contention among historians questions whether or not the works traditionally ascribed to Laozi were set down by him alone, or whether they were the product of several hands, a debate that was quickened by the discoveries of these two texts.

The writings on silk were found in 1973 at Mawangtui in south-central China near Changsha among a cache of funerary goods buried alongside the son of a midlevel government official. An inventory slip found in the tomb pinpointed the date of interment precisely to the Western equivalent of April 4, 168 B.C. Notable among the documents recovered were previously unknown maps, charts, and diagrams offering commentary on early Chinese philosophy, history, literature, astrology, astronomy, political thought, and science, including some illustrated medical texts employing the theories of Yin and Yang and the Five Elements of metal, water, wood, fire, and earth. There also were treatises dealing with the conduits of the circulation system; others listed diagnostic prescriptions for the treatment of four dozen diseases and medical conditions, including childbirth. Most of the writings were "documents of which we had no prior knowledge, though in some instances we knew of the item by name," the Dartmouth College scholar Robert G. Henricks, an international authority on classic Asian literature, wrote in summary of the recovered materials. But it was the two versions of the *Daodejing* that stimulated the most interest, and encouraged Henricks to prepare a translation of the material, which was published in 1989.

Four years after that, the contents of an obscure tomb dating to the fourth century B.C. uncovered in Guodian in Hubei province would push the composition of the *Daodejing* even further back in time. Scattered on the floor of the cramped chamber, possibly the burial site of a tutor to one of the crown princes of the Warring States period (476–221 B.C.) in the kingdom of Chu, were eight hundred bamboo strips, each as wide as a pencil and up to twice as long. When examined by scholars, it was evident that a discovery of the first magnitude had been made. The strips—known as *slips*—were found to contain some ten thousand Chinese characters, a thousand or so bearing what has since been determined to be the oldest extant version of the *Daodejing*. The nine thousand other characters, comprising fifteen texts, are believed to have been written by disciples of Confucius, including the teacher's grandson Zisi, in the first generation after his death. Only one of these texts had ever been seen before.

The Guodian grave was excavated in 1993 after it was determined that robbers had penetrated the previously unexplored site through a narrow hole. Fortunately, the looters ignored the *Daodejing,* which had been written with a brush on bamboo and tied together in three bundles with the other texts. To restore the faded writing, the two-thousand-year-old slips were immersed in solvents, then treated with preservatives. "They became so brilliant, as if the characters were written yesterday," marveled one Chinese conservator. In 2000, Henricks published a new translation of what he unashamedly declared were these "startling new documents." For Sarah Allan, a professor of Chinese studies at Dartmouth, and with Henricks cosponsor of an international conference mounted at the college in 1998 to discuss the ramifications of the texts, the cache was nothing less than the "Chinese equivalent of the Dead Sea Scrolls. They are works that are already changing our outlook on the formation of the early Daoist and Confucian traditions."

As these examples demonstrate, cultures have always had a choice of materials to select from for their writing, with the costliest materials typically used for crucial documents, even though the most exotic surfaces have not always proven to be the most durable. When members of a Jewish sect calling themselves the Essenes prepared the biblical texts known today as the Dead Sea Scrolls between 250 B.C. and A.D. 68, they wrote most of their material on parchment and stored them in stone jars, although some were on papyrus. Reduced mostly to tiny fragments over the passage of two millennia, the task confronting scholars has been twofold: assemble the pieces as faithfully as possible, then translate the texts. The discovery of these documents in a complex of eleven caves on the western shore of the Dead Sea known as Qumran in 1947 and their stormy existence since then have been well chronicled over the past half century. Among the most curious artifacts recovered was an object found in 1952 in Cave 3 and known today as the Copper Scroll, so designated because it contains words incised on two thin sheets of the corroded metal, which has proven far less resistant to the elements than cured goatskins. Joined with rivets and rolled into two scrolls, the metal had become so badly oxidized over the centuries that it was too brittle to be unfolded, which seriously jeopardized the integrity of the message it contained. In 1956 an English scientist devised a process that enabled him to cut the metal into twenty-three longitudinal strips, each curved into a half-cylinder, revealing information that seemed to pinpoint the whereabouts of an ancient fortune purportedly buried at sixty-four hiding places in the surrounding region. The size of the hoard—which has been sought unsuccessfully by modern treasure hunters handicapped by references to architectural landmarks that have long since disappeared—is estimated to have totaled sixty-five tons of silver and twenty-six tons of gold. According to one theory, the cache was buried around the time of the destruction of the Temple in Jerusalem in 68 B.C. to protect it from the Romans, and may just possibly have represented the combined fortune of the imperiled Essene sect.

Two years before the discovery of the Dead Sea Scrolls in the Qumran caves, an Arab camel driver who claimed to be digging for fertilizer—but who was probably poking through an obscure grave site for targets of opportunity he could sell on the black market—came across a cache of papyrus texts buried centuries earlier at the foot of a mountain in the upper Egyptian desert, about ten miles from the remote hamlet of Nag Hammadi. Carefully bound in thirteen leather casings, the documents had been packed in an earthen jar and were in remarkably good condition, their long-term survival partly due to the desert climate. Although set down on papyrus, they were not rolled into scrolls, as was customary for this writing surface, and which had been the case with the parchment documents found at Qumran. Instead, they took the shape of the modern codex and were inserted in protective coverings that bear a strong resemblance to the modern binding. Like the Dead Sea Scrolls, the Nag Hammadi Library codices are presumed to have been hidden at a time of great danger by the people who valued them, in this case the followers of an obscure religious movement known as Gnosis. Prior to the discovery of these codices, just fifty pages of original material offering insight on the group had survived to the twentieth century.

Dubbed the *Gnostic Gospels* by the historian of religion Elaine Pagels in an enormously popular work published in 1978, the fifty-two papyrus texts date from the early years of Christianity, with the period of composition for some of the documents determined to be around the same time that the New Testament gospels themselves were being set down. Written in the script of Egyptian Christians known as Coptic, the codices were translated from the Greek—they are copies of other documents, in other words—and they demonstrate how divided the followers of Christ were in these early years of the movement. One text, for instance, *Gospel According to Thomas*, identifies itself as a *secret* text, and makes the astounding claim that Jesus had a twin brother. Other assertions question the virgin birth and the bodily resurrection of Christ. Because writings such as these were denounced as heresy and routinely destroyed in the fourth century, when it is believed the Nag Hammadi codices were buried, it is no mystery as to why they ended up in an underground depository. Regardless of how readers of today may respond to their remarkable content, what is not in dispute is that these documents were written in multiple hands over a period of many years, and represent a variety of views, some of them conflicting, and comprise a *library* in every sense of the word. "The focus that brought the collection together is an estrangement from the mass of humanity, an affinity to an ideal order that completely transcends life as we know it, and a life-style radically other than common practice," James M. Robinson wrote in the standard translation into English of the Nag Hammadi Library. "Those who collected this library were Christians, and many of the essays were originally composed by Christian authors. In a sense this should not be surprising, since primitive Christianity was itself a radical movement."

Minoans living on the Mediterranean island of Crete in the second millennium B.C. also used a variety of materials for their writing, recording their most important documents on expensive organic materials, while keeping track of routine transactions on tablets made from clay, not surprising, since clay was an abundant natural resource for them. The net result is that weighty pronouncements inscribed for posterity on animal skins by these resourceful people have long since disappeared, while the minutiae of everyday life has held up remarkably well. As for the content, it remained impenetrable to modern scholars until 1952 when the English architect Michael Ventris, an amateur linguist obsessed since childhood with deciphering an unknown language, unraveled the Aegean script written on clay tables known as Linear B, so called because it was incised along horizontal lines, and to distinguish it from an earlier Minoan script designated by the archaeologist Arthur Evans as Linear A. The unbaked clay documents that became the focus of Ventris's attention were found in the royal palace of Minos, and were determined to be the notebooks of daily bureaucracy, records that detailed routine business activities, a good deal of them itemizations of produce and livestock. Of far greater consequence than their content were the implications of the discovery itself, since by cracking the code of the ancient syllabic script, Ventris established that variations of the Greek language were used in the courts of Knossos, Mycenae, Tiryns, and Thebes a full five centuries before the time of Homer. Prior to that breakthrough, the prevailing view was that the script had represented another language altogether; Ventris himself at one point thought it may have derived from Etruscan.

A much deeper mystery shrouds the meaning of a circular clay tablet known as the Phaistos Disc that was discovered by archaeologists on Crete forty miles southeast of Knossos. Unearthed during an Italian expedition to the island in 1908, the terra-cotta artifact continues to baffle scholars who seek to make sense of its script, its purpose, and the puzzling circumstances of its production. With a diameter of 6.5 inches and a thickness of about 0.6 inches, the grayish-brown object is remarkably well preserved despite its age, calculated to be on the order of thirty-seven hundred years. An approximate composition date of 1700 B.C. is suggested by other objects excavated in the same stratum of earth at Phaistos, which at one time was the wealthiest and most powerful city on the island. If that is in fact the date of composition, then the disc would be contemporary with Linear A, the oldest Minoan script of them all, which also remains undeciphered.

Each side of the disc is decorated with forty-five different characters appearing a total of 242 times. One sign, called the "plumed head" because it pictures a man wearing a sort of feathered bonnet in profile, appears nineteen times. A sign called the "helmet" was used on eighteen occasions, the "shield" seventeen times, a pointed symbol called the "boomerang" a dozen times. Others—the "column," the "ram," the "flute"—show up just one time each. All figures on both sides are arranged in the form of parallel lines that spiral away from the center. None of the characters are similar to any other script known to have been produced in Crete—or anywhere else, for that matter—leading some scholars to believe that the object was brought in from somewhere else. Because there is no variation between the same symbols, it is likely that stamps were used to create them, a circumstance that raises the tantalizing question of whether or not this could be the first known bearer of writing to be incised by means of a printing device. That quite likely is the case, according to Louis Godart, professor of Mycenean philology at the University of Naples, and the world's leading authority on the Phaistos Disc.

"The disc is of high-quality, well-levigated, fine-grained clay," Godart wrote. "After the characters had been imprinted on it, it was fired, acquiring the smooth, lustrous surface of majolica ware, and a lovely yellowish color." Given the state of technology at the time, the stamping devices in all likelihood were made of gold. John Chadwick, a Cambridge University scholar who worked with Michael Ventris on the decipherment of Linear B, went so far as to proclaim the disc to be the world's "first typewritten document," and he explained his rationale: "It was made by taking a stamp or a punch bearing the sign to be written in a raised pattern, and impressing this on the wet clay. The maker therefore needed to have as many stamps as there were signs in the script. It has the advantage that even complicated signs can be quickly written, and every example of the same sign is identical and easy to read." The purpose of a printing device, of course, is duplication, which means that the maker of the disc "must have intended to produce a large number of documents," although no other examples of the script have been found. Numerous theories have been put forward to explain the disc's meaning, though none have been accepted as particularly convincing, and as Louis Godart noted in his monograph, the puzzle of its existence is sure to go on:

> Why was it found where it was? What is its date? Where is it from? What does it mean? Is the inscription in a known script? Is the script alphabetic, syallabic or ideographic? What solution does it conceal? What message did its anonymous scribe leave for posterity?

In stark contrast to this mystery script that exists in just *one* tantalizing example is the language of the ancient Egyptians, which had a documented life span of almost thirty-five hundred years, with a rich variety of writing surfaces being employed over that long period. "English—as we can read it without too much aid—has so far survived for only 500 years (that is, back to Chaucer) and spans at best a thousand years, if we go back to Anglo-Saxon, which must be studied as a foreign language," the Egyptologist John L. Foster has pointed out. Despite the abundance of papyrus in Egypt through much of that span, that material was never considered reliable enough to record important historical records, which Egyptian policy required be written on stone, "with a pen of iron, and with the point of a diamond." Inscriptions made by Rekhmara, the vizier, or prime minister, of the pharaoh Thothmes III, stipulated that the codified laws of Egypt be recorded on animal skins. The text of one of the oldest chapters of the Book of the Dead has attached to it a rubric stating that it was found in the reign of the pharaoh Menkaura engraved on a block of alabaster. By the time of the Fifth Dynasty (c. 2700 B.C.), the standard copies of teachings relevant to the underworld were carved on the walls of burial chambers, and are found nowhere else; for this reason they are called the Pyramid Texts. In the time of the Middle Kingdom some seven hundred years later, these teachings were no longer the exclusive property of the ruler; they began to appear on the wooden coffins of lesser officials written in ink, and thus are known as Coffin Texts. Diplomatic dispatches were exchanged by way of clay tablets incised with the cuneiform script of Babylonia during the reign of Amenophis IV, the maverick pharaoh more familiarly known as Akhenaten, who ruled Egypt from 1352 to 1336 B.C., and whose queen was Nefertiti.

The unearthing of 350 tablets known as the Tell el-'Amârna Letters in 1887 at the site of Akhenaten's long-forgotten palace about 190 miles south of Cairo raised an interesting series of issues on this very point. Discovered by a peasant woman digging for rich soil to fertilize her garden, the tablets were dismissed at first as fakes since they were written on a medium not common to Egypt, and because they were incised in a foreign script. Because of these misgivings about their authenticity, the tablets passed from dealer to dealer in the antiquities market, most of them ending up finally in the Berlin Museum and the British Museum. It was only when the legendary curator of the British Museum, Sir Ernest

Alfred Wallis Budge, correctly identified the language as Akkadian cuneiform that their true significance was realized. Once translated, it was apparent that the tablets were official letters exchanged between the pharaoh and other rulers in the region. From that determination, it followed logically that clay would have been a convenient medium to carry on communications between governments. And cuneiform script, as S. A. B. Mercer wrote in the introduction to a 1939 translation of the Amarna tablets, was a language that Akhenaten could have used to carry on an international correspondence, "not only with his peers on the thrones of Babylonia and Assyria, but also with his representatives in Syria and Palestine." When the city he founded as a shrine to the sun god Aten was abandoned soon after his death, it "fell into ruins and was forgotten, as also were the archives of the king," a circumstance, in an odd way, that assured their long-term survival.

But in instances where writing had to be done at great length, it still made eminent good sense to use papyrus. For literary works, mathematical calculations, astrological charts, medical formulations, religious pronouncements, and ruminations dealing with the afterlife, the medium of choice was the more manageable scrolls. Although the word *paper* is derived from *papyrus*, it bears stressing that the two materials are not the same. The nature of paper is the matting together of fibers—wood, flax, or other cellulose-rich substances—while papyrus, as Pliny the Elder explained in exacting detail, was fashioned from the inner bark of a marsh reed, with long sheets produced by attaching strips together to make scrolls. It is from that characteristic that the word *volume*, which descends from the Latin word *volvere*, meaning "to roll up," derives. Similarly, *bible* comes from the Greek word *byblas*, meaning the inner bark of papyrus.

Because religious literature in Egypt was regarded for centuries as the exclusive province of the pharaoh—the only Egyptian, in fact, with a claim to immortality—there was no need for multiple copies to be made. It has been speculated that no more than 1 percent of the population in ancient Egypt could read at all, which is one reason why working knowledge of hieroglyphic script died out with the elite corps of priests and scribes accorded the privilege of understanding them. The word *hieroglyph* itself is instructive; the Greeks coined the term, meaning "sacred carved letters," to identify the pictographic writing of the pharaohs. The subsequent development of an alphabet brought with it the democratization of literacy; by simplifying the elements of spoken language to twenty or thirty characters representing different sounds, written communication became fairly easy to learn and practice, and comprehensible to large numbers of people not trained as professional scribes, a shift comparable in scope and impact to the arrival of the printing press in Europe during the fifteenth century.

The overwhelming majority of Greek and Roman papyri that have made it to our time have been discovered in Egypt, where sandy soil and a dry climate provided ideal conditions for preservation. Only one scroll from antiquity has been found on the Greek peninsula, and in that instance survival came as the result of a ritual intended to incinerate it. The carbonized document was discovered in 1962 during excavations at a burial site in the village of Derveni just outside of Thessaloníki in northern Greece; the completely charred top part of the scroll, known as the Derveni Papyrus, was lying in a funerary pyre. Working with two hundred tiny fragments, archaeologists were able to reconstruct twenty-four columns of text. They restored about fifteen lines per column, amounting to about a third of the length of the charred roll.

Assigned to the fourth century B.C., the text contains a previously unknown Greek poem in hexameters that is believed to have been composed in the fifth century. It includes an account of various funeral rites and beliefs, and a literary verse ascribed to the mythical poet Orpheus. The Derveni Papyrus is by far the earliest scroll written in Greek to survive, and has been the subject of intense scholarly inquiry. A colloquium held at Princeton University in 1993 devoted to discussion of this single artifact resulted in publication of an important monograph. The pieces are now displayed in the Archaeological Museum of Thessaloníki, best known for its collection of funerary objects recovered from the royal tombs in Vergina, site of the burial chamber of Philip II of Macedonia, the father of Alexander the Great.

The discovery of yet another text bearing ancient Greek poetry in the most unlikely of places made front-page news around the world in the fall of 2002, this time at an academic colloquium convened at the University of Cincinnati to discuss a scroll containing 112 poems written in the third century B.C. by Posidippus of Pella, a prominent writer of epigrams whose work was well known in its time, but, until the recovery of this scroll, had survived in only a handful of instances. Called the Milan Papyrus for the Italian city where the artifact is now kept, the scroll may well qualify as the oldest surviving example of a Greek poetry collection. Once again, the burial customs of the ancients, along with the practice of recycling discarded materials, provided the means of textual transmission, only in this instance the precise details of discovery remain hazy at best. What is known is that sometime in the 1980s or 1990s, a group of looters unearthed a mummified corpse in a desert region of Egypt southwest of Cairo called the Fayum, attracted to the desiccated specimen by the brightly colored layers of compressed papyrus that ancient morticians had placed over the chest of the remains. Known as a cartonnage, this particular contrivance was painted in red, white, and blue, and had flourishes of winged griffins, making it particularly desirable on the antiquities market. Once smuggled out of Egypt, the cartonnage was examined by a Swiss dealer who suspected its importance and circulated photographs of the object throughout Europe. "I don't think anyone knows the details of what happened, or if they do, they're not talking," Dr. Dirk Obbink, a papyrologist at Oxford University, told John Noble Wilford of the *New York Times*. It is for this delicate reason that so much of what happened remains cloaked in mystery. But once the significance of the papyrus strips were suspected, the layers were separated by soaking in warm water, then pressed and dried, revealing the residue of a script in carbon-black ink that was still legible. When news of this turn of events began to spread, an Italian bank acting for the University of Milan outbid a German university consortium to buy the scroll for what was reported to be about $1 million.

It was later theorized that the discarded strips were recycled and used sometime in the second century B.C. by an Egyptian mortician to pack the chest cavity of a corpse being readied for burial. The papyrus scroll itself, estimated to have been copied in Greek about 250 B.C., or around the time of their composition, contains about six hundred lines of poetry divided into nine sections. Prior to its discovery, scholars had identified two epigrams as being written by Posidippus, a Macedonian who worked in the Aegean region from about 280 to 240 B.C., and was renowned in his time as a writer of the short verses familiarly identified with Martial, but took on a more didactic character in his case. The two epigrams that were previously known were among the 112 found in the Milan Papyrus, so not only did the Milan Papyrus enrich the appreciation of an important classical writer by adding dozens of new examples of his work to the classical canon, it also shed light on the creative process, according to Peter Bing, a teacher of classics at Emory University, since it "provides us with the earliest detailed evidence of how an editor—perhaps the poet himself— organized a poetry collection."

Hundreds of petrified scrolls of much later vintage were discovered in 1752 buried beneath one hundred feet of volcanic earth in the seaside resort of Herculaneum in Italy. Digging for gold they believed might have been entombed in the eruption of Mount Vesuvius on August 24, A.D. 79, the excavators struck riches of a different sort in the library of an elegant building they promptly christened Villa Suburbana dei Papiri—Villa of the Papyri. Unlike Pompeii, which was covered by molten lava, Herculaneum was buried beneath an avalanche of consolidated mud and descending clouds of volcanic ash, a rock-hard mixture known as pyroclastic matter that seals everything it covers, making for an excellent preservative. Measuring 812 feet by 455 feet, the seaside mansion, at the foot of Vesuvius on the Bay of Naples, is believed to have been built by Lucius Calpurnius Piso, the father-in-law of Julius Caesar, and later owned by an Epicurean poet and philosopher known as Philodemus. It was never completely exposed by the treasure hunters, who conducted their diggings by way of tunnels burrowed around the perimeter. A speculative sketch of the villa was prepared by Karl Weber, a Swiss engineer involved in the eighteenth-century dig, which the American oil billionaire J. Paul Getty later used as the model for an art museum he built on a bluff overlooking the Pacific Ocean in Malibu, California.

Now in the custody of the National Library of Naples, the 1,826 carbonized scrolls were found stored on shelves in neat rows; a few were piled on a reading table in the middle of the room. They were so hard and blackened that excavators at first thought they were lumps of charcoal briquettes. In 1969 Dr. Marcello Gigante, professor of classical philology at the University of Naples, founded the International Center for the Study of Papyri of Herculaneum, and led the effort to renew excavating the site, which had been closed off in 1765, when it began to vent poisonous volcanic gases. Driven by hopes of recovering additional scrolls, the new digs began in 1984. "Works of Latin would have been abundant in this library," Gigante told the novelist Shirley Hazzard when she accompanied him on a descent into the villa three years later. "The papyri so far retrieved are in Greek. Now I would like to see Roman authors—Ennius, Lucretius, Cicero. The lost works, of course; but also the contemporary texts of writings we know only from copies made in later centuries. One might hope, for instance, for a contemporary text of Horace. Above all, of Virgil who, having the luck to be celebrated in his lifetime, saw his works much reproduced—and whose residence at Naples gave him local as well as universal fame. Then there are the unknown works, the revelations."

Although the Herculaneum papyri were discovered in the 1750s, it was late-twentieth-century technology that enabled scholars finally to pierce their carbonized veneer and determine their contents. Papyrologists working under the supervision of Gigante determined that fully eight hundred of the scrolls contain the writings of Philodemus (c. 110–35 B.C.), a contemporary of Lucretius and Horace, and like them a poet and follower of the philosopher Epicurus. What makes the Philodemus connection especially exciting is the strong belief that he lived at Herculaneum between 75 and 50 B.C., quite possibly in this elegant villa, and that the scrolls in the library may well have belonged to him. "They are written in Greek so esoteric that they would be hard to restore and to translate even if they had come to us in perfect condition," Gigante wrote in a preliminary account of his findings. In addition to Epicurean works, a number of Stoic texts, most notably the *Logical Questions* and *On Providence* by Chrysippus, were recovered, along with a work by a Latin poet about whom nothing is known except that he lived after 31 B.C., and that he wrote about the Battle of Actium.

Because 80 percent of the site has not been excavated, Gigante suggested that his team might yet discover some "provisional drafts" of works in progress in new digs, perhaps even some unknown texts. "We are dealing with an 'author's manuscripts,' " he said when excavations were about to resume in 1997 after several years of limited funding had forced a hiatus. "But even if we find known texts, we will be finding their oldest versions because today we know them through medieval copies. We would have the texts closest to their authors and could check the 'corruptions' of the texts through the ages."

Sadly, explorations were suspended at the villa in 1998 because of more funding problems, and with the death of Dr. Gigante in November 2001, hope for an expeditious resumption lost further momentum. In the spring of 2002, eight distinguished British and American classicists wrote a letter to the London *Times* calling on the international community to continue the work, noting that flooding now posed a "grave danger" to the precious manuscripts they believe still remain in other unexplored rooms. A two-year feasibility study, meanwhile, was ordered by the Italian government to determine whether or not excavations should continue.

4.

Ex Libris Punicis

Truth once lost in the annals of mankind leaves a chasm never to be filled.
ISAAC DISRAELI, *CURIOSITIES OF LITERATURE*

I know I am condemned and awaiting my turn,
Although deep inside me burrows a hope for a miracle.
Drunk on the pen trembling in my hand,
I record everything for future generations;
A day will come when someone will find
The leaves of horror I write and record.
HERMAN KRUK (1897–1944),
LIBRARIAN AT VILNA GHETTO,
"FOR FUTURE GENERATIONS"

In the totalitarian world of *1984*, a morally corrupt government maintains absolute power by systematically depriving its subjects of their identities and by denying them any hope of a cultural legacy. Writing in the late 1940s with the horrific examples of Adolf Hitler and Joseph Stalin fresh in his mind, George Orwell envisioned a bleak society in which a people's touchstones with the past are pulverized as a matter of public policy. "All history was a palimpsest, scraped clean and reinscribed exactly as often as was necessary," he wrote of a Ministry of Truth where the official record of past events is constantly tailored to suit immediate political needs. Orwell's nightmarish scenario has been described variously as a dystopian novel and as a biting contemporary satire that uses exaggeration as an effective literary device, but his chilling premise has many factual precedents. A slogan trumpeted by the novel's ruling elite suggests why tyrants and dictators of all eras have been encouraged to pursue such seemingly surreal goals: "Who controls the past controls the future; who controls the present controls the past."

One of the most portentous images to emerge from Germany in the years leading up to World War II was of roaring bonfires being stoked in city squares with piles of condemned books. The world knows now, of course, that the targets singled out for destruction went well beyond ideas to include human beings. *The Diary of Anne Frank* is by far the best-known domestic journal to survive World War II intact, but the larger reality of the Holocaust was that any Jew caught keeping a record of life under the Nazis faced the prospect of immediate execution. That young Anne's diary was not destroyed proved once again how artifacts that seem most perishable are sometimes the ones that endure. Tossed aside by a German officer impatiently searching a briefcase for valuables, the girl's writings were scooped up by a Dutch woman who had helped the family while they hid in the Amsterdam annex, and were thus saved for posterity. Another Jewish diarist whose recollections were discovered after the war at the Auschwitz death camp in Poland had written this plea: "Dear finder, search everywhere, in every inch of soil. Tons of documents are buried under it, mine and those of other prisoners, which will throw light on everything that was happening here." Salmen Gradowski, the man who wrote that passage, was one of several members of a concentration camp confederation known as the *Sonderkommando* whose clandestine scribblings were discovered hidden beneath the ashes of cremated victims. "Entrusted to us by the dead, these diaries line up in a funeral procession that has no limit, no end," David Patterson wrote in an important study of fifty Holocaust diaries. "And where does the procession lead? Into the soul of the reader."

One Jewish diarist who survived the war, Victor Klemperer (1881–1960), kept a journal from 1933 to 1945, some five thousand pages of manuscript altogether, which was discovered in the 1980s and published in two volumes in 1998 and 2000 under the title *I Will Bear Witness*. Because Klemperer was married to a "pure Aryan" woman, his status as a *problematische personlichkeit*—a problematic personality—enabled him to avoid deportation to a concentration camp, but he still had to wear a yellow Jewish star on his jacket in public, and the constant fear of summary judgment runs through the pages of his day-to-day reports. At one time a professor of romance languages in Dresden, Klemperer was an intelligent and literate man who prepared a detailed study of what he called "the functions and effects of Nazi language" and committed himself to writing about the unending challenge of staying alive, regardless of the punishment he risked by putting his observations down on paper. He kept the diary pages hidden in a Greek dictionary, sending them off periodically for safekeeping to a trusted friend who was under far less scrutiny. On May 27, 1942, Klemperer reported the results of an unannounced rifling of his home conducted by the Gestapo. "After the house search I found several books, which had been taken off the shelf, lying on the desk. If one of them had been the Greek dictionary, if the manuscript pages had fallen out and had thus aroused suspicion, it would undoubtedly have meant my death. One is murdered for lesser misdemeanors." He was determined, however, to proceed. "I shall go on writing. That is *my* heroism. I will bear witness, precise witness."

Of more than thirty-five thousand artifacts gathered for public display at the United States Holocaust Memorial Museum in Washington, D.C., among the most consequential is a rusted metal milk can unearthed in

Warsaw, Poland, on December 1, 1950, one of several such containers found buried beneath the rubble of the city at the end of World War II. Stored neatly inside each of these vessels was a cache of materials documenting the experiences of close to half a million Jews who had been forced by the Germans to live inside a tightly confined sector known as the Warsaw Ghetto. Among the seventeen thousand carefully packed items recovered from the containers were diaries, monographs, autobiographical vignettes, underground publications, and official notices, all assembled between 1940 and 1944 by a group that called itself *Oneg Shabbos*—Joy of the Sabbath, "O.S." for short. This remarkable effort was organized by Emmanuel Ringelblum (1900–1944), a respected historian who was skilled in the nuances of scholarly research and, by dint of cruel circumstance, also a man of destiny. When it became evident to him what the Nazis had in mind for the Jews of Poland, he set about creating an unimpeachable record of the outrage and suffering he knew they all were about to endure.

A graduate of the University of Warsaw with a doctorate in history—he wrote his dissertation on the "history of Jews in Warsaw up to the expulsion of 1527," and by 1939 had published 126 scholarly articles—Ringelblum set high professional standards for the project, and he took pains to train the makeshift staff he had assembled in the subtleties of building a sophisticated archive. "I laid the cornerstone for O.S. in October 1939," he wrote in an overview of his operation. "Comprehensiveness was the principle of our work. Objectivity was the second principle. We aspired to present the whole truth, however painful it might be." Of paramount importance was that "not a single fact about Jewish life at this time and place will be kept from the world." Ringelblum and his team knew their prospects for survival were slight, but they were set on perpetuating their heritage by every means possible. "There are illegal traveling libraries that circulate from house to house," he wrote in 1941. "There is a Talmud Torah attended by 700 students; rabbis are the teachers." Dur-

ing one three-month period in 1942 when 300,000 Jews were rounded up
for transfer to the Treblinka camp a two-hour train ride away, Ringelblum
provided firsthand testimony of what became the largest single deportation of the war. "Only a handful of our friends kept pencil in hand and
continued to write about what was happening in Warsaw in those calami-
tous days," he wrote later. "But the work was too holy for us, it was too
deep in our hearts, the O.S. was too important for the community—we
could not stop."

In the spring of 1943 Ringelblum helped organize an armed resistance
that made headlines around the world for its valor in face of impossible
odds, making him a marked man when the action, known as the Warsaw
Uprising, was crushed by the Waffen SS. Managing to evade capture for
eight months outside the ghetto boundaries, Ringelblum was finally discovered hiding in an underground bunker with his wife, their thirteen-
year-old son, and thirty-five other fugitives. They were all shot to death
on March 7, 1944, and dumped into a collective grave, but none of the
condemned betrayed the *Oneg Shabbos* project. "The historiography of
the Holocaust was an act of intellectual heroism," Leon Wieseltier wrote
when the Holocaust Memorial Museum was inaugurated on the Washington Mall. The mud-encrusted milk can that preserved Ringelblum's
journal, a vessel meant to convey life's most vital nutrient, occupies a
place of honor in the permanent exhibition devoted to the Warsaw
Ghetto. "For its faithfulness," Wieseltier concluded, "its color of rust has
turned a color of gold."

In striking counterpoint to the profound humanity of the Ringelblum
archive is the feral terseness of the post-action report prepared by SS
Brigadenführer Jurgen Stroop, the commander of the elite Nazi detachment assigned to crush the Warsaw Uprising in 1943, and forwarded to his
superiors as a memento of the victory. Bound handsomely in a volume of
speckled black leather for presentation to SS chief Heinrich Himmler, the
album is known today as the Stroop Report. Translated from the German,

the actual title, inscribed in large Gothic letters on a single sheet of paper, is "The Jewish Quarter of Warsaw Is No More!" The text was typed on white deckle-edged paper and organized in three sections. In the first part, Stroop offered a dispassionate account of his monthlong operation "to destroy the Jews and bandits in the former Jewish quarter of Warsaw." He then reproduced complete transcripts of the thirty-two daily reports summarizing the progress of the action he had filed by teletype to head-quarters. A final section consisted of fifty-four mounted photographs, thirty-nine of them accompanied by captions. The album began with these words: *Für den Führer und für ihr Vaterland*—For Führer and Fatherland. Three sets of the keepsake, each one looking for all the world like an ele-gant family scrapbook, were assembled, the most lavish of them all intended for Himmler's personal delectation; the other two were kept as souvenirs by Stroop and his immediate superior. Himmler's leather-bound copy was found by soldiers of the U.S. Seventh Army, and entered into evidence at the military tribunal proceedings conducted in Nuremberg after the war. Stroop never once contested the authenticity of its contents, and was hanged for his crimes against humanity.

Whether or not the brigadenführer ever intended a general audience for the album is unknown, but even if he had, there is no way he could possibly have anticipated the emotional pull several of the photographs in the third section, called simply "Pictorial Report," would have on the conscience of the world. One of them depicts a group of civilians being marched down the center of a Warsaw street by an armed escort of German troops, and was included in Edward Steichen's monumental *Family of Man* exhibition at the Museum of Modern Art in 1955. Another snapshot—captioned "Dregs of Humanity"—shows two emaciated men stripped of their clothes and facing what is presumably an execution wall. Perhaps the most widely circulated photograph of them all is of a group of women and children leaving the refuge of a seized building, their hands held high in the air. At the front of the line, a terrified child in short

pants, kneesocks, and peaked cap stumbles forward under the contemptu-
ous gaze of a helmeted soldier, an automatic weapon coolly trained on his
back. Stroop captioned this photograph "Pulled from the Bunkers by
Force." In a learned introduction to a facsimile edition of the Stroop
Report published in 1979, the Polish writer Andrzej Wirth characterized
the album as the classic example of "an obsession with documentation,"
and described the callous detachment of its bureaucratic language as the
"lingua of the technological age, to be studied for its use in relation to
mass murder."

There is further evidence that with their tenacious zeal for documentation, the Germans committed some effort toward preserving a historical
record of the people they had targeted for annihilation. In a steel vault on
the fifth floor of the Deutsche Bücherei (German National Library) in
Leipzig are nine thousand volumes known today as *exil* books, each iden-
tifiable by a bright yellow sticker affixed to the spines; these are works that
were banned by Hitler's propaganda minister, Joseph Goebbels, and
ordered kept under lock and key as official file copies. All of the others
that could be found, of course, were either destroyed or sold for scrap
paper and pulped under the supervision of party officials—but an artifactual record of what had been written by such "decadent" writers as Albert
Einstein and Thomas Mann was still retained.

Elsewhere in the Third Reich, a unit known as *Einsatzstab des Reichsleiter Alfred Rosenberg* (Special Detail of Reich Administrator Alfred
Rosenberg) was assigned the task of gathering Judaica throughout
Europe and shipping it to Frankfurt to form a core collection for the *Insti-
tut zur Erforschung der Judenfrage* (Institute for the Study of the Jewish
Question). Reichsleiter Alfred Rosenberg—the only Nuremberg defendant to be executed for war crimes as an ideologue—was the rector. His
chief lieutenant, Dr. Johannes Pohl, had studied Judaica at the Hebrew
University in Jerusalem from 1934 to 1936 by direction of the Nazi party,
and was spokesman for an academic program called *Judenforschung ohne*

Juden (Jewish Studies Without Jews). By 1942, the Central Bureau for Dealing with the Jewish Question had been established in Prague, using as a base of operations the Jewish Museum, which had been founded in 1906 but was closed during the years of German occupation. The names of seventy-seven thousand Czechoslovakian Jews who died in the Holocaust are inscribed on the walls of the sixteenth-century Pinkus Synagogue located in the old quarter of Prague, while the artwork, books, and artifacts these doomed people worked so diligently to safeguard—and today makes up the world's richest collection of Judaica outside of Jerusalem, some 150,000 items altogether—survive intact. It was later disclosed that the Nazis had kept these materials out of harm's way to use as exhibits in a "Museum of an Extinct Race" they planned to open after the war, scornfully mindful, perhaps, that for centuries the Jews had been known as "the People of the Book," a designation derisively given them by the Prophet Muhammad for their reliance on scriptures, but one they proudly embraced. "Paradoxically, the Nazis, who confiscated these objects with an intention to build a pathological 'research' and propaganda institute in Prague, instead laid the groundwork for a museum collection that for all time will document the inhumanity of their genocidal program," S. Dillon Ripley wrote in the catalog of a 1983 exhibition sponsored by the Smithsonian Institution featuring selected pieces from the Czechoslovak collections, aptly called *The Precious Legacy*. "During the final years of the war it could be only a warehouse for material remnants of a doomed people," Linda A. Altshuler and Anna R. Cohn noted in their contribution to the catalog. "Virtually overnight, the museum had become the repository of an entire people's material culture. The all too few survivors who returned to Prague encountered in shock and disbelief this awesome evidence of the destruction of tens of thousands of Czech Jews."

In the Soviet Union during the Stalin years, official photographs were routinely airbrushed and cropped to corroborate changing perceptions of reality, as a 1997 book, *The Commissar Vanishes*, has persuasively demon-strated; appearing in striking counterpoint alongside the fabrications gathered in that collection are the undoctored originals. Further evidence of just how institutionalized the practice of document distortion became was made clear in an exhibition of various graphic artifacts at the New York Public Library in 1984. Falsification of the historical record was so rampant that Russian censors commonly used the phrases "covered with caviar" to describe the act of obscuring objectionable material with thick black ink, and "covered with sour cream" for whiting out discredited words with heavy dabs of correction fluid. When a person became an "un-person," Marianna Tax Choldin wrote in the catalog, "all traces of his existence disappeared from printed works." In one inglorious incident, owners of the *Bol'shaya sovetskaya entsiklopediya*—the Large Soviet Encyclopedia of 1949—were mailed instructions to razor out a full-page portrait and two pages of text extolling the life and accomplishments of Lavrenti Beria, the Communist Party secret police chief who was purged and executed in 1953, and to paste in their place two pages of text and a one-page spread of photographs devoted to a discussion of the Bering Sea. Copies of both these entries—the purged and the approved, each beginning with the same four letters of the alphabet—are in the perma-nent collections of the New York Public Library; owners of the book in the Soviet Union were required to return the excised pages.

Dimitri Simes, a Russian scholar who immigrated to the United States in 1970, once recalled his impressions of going to Young Communist League meetings to David Remnick, author of the Pulitzer Prize–winning history *Lenin's Tomb* and now editor in chief of the *New Yorker.* "You not only had to agree with the ideas and policies being expressed in that morning's *Pravda*, you also had to use the exact same phrases to express your unfailing agreement," Simes said. "Just as dangerous, you always had to pay attention to any changes in party line and language. If, on a Thursday, you were still mouthing the language of Tuesday's *Pravda* without bothering to check if the script had changed, you were running a tremendous risk."

That the penalties risked by wavering from the party line were indeed tremendous—and involved considerably more than being declared persona non grata—is at the heart of *Invisible Allies,* one of the most powerful works written by Aleksandr Solzhenitsyn, though probably the least well known among his corpus. Published in 1995 as a supplement to *The Oak and the Calf* (1980), a riveting account of the Nobel laureate's ten-year effort to break through Soviet censorship and publish his historical novels, *Invisible Allies* was written as a tribute to the dozens of volunteers who secretly compiled documentation for Solzhenitsyn's forbidden research and placed themselves in immense danger by agreeing to conceal what he wrote in a variety of ingenious hiding places, then risked further harm by editing, typing, proofreading, microfilming, and smuggling what he wrote out of the country to the West. "I see their eyes and listen intently to their voices—more intently than I ever could in the heat of battle," Solzhenitsyn wrote in tribute. "Unknown to the world, they risked everything without receiving in recompense the public admiration that can mitigate even death. And for many of them the publication of these pages will come too late."

Although dramatic technological advances have made tinkering with factual records a sophisticated exercise, the practice is by no means new, having been employed for centuries in a variety of effective ways. The Romans punished individuals deemed guilty of committing crimes against the state by imposing on them a penalty known by classical scholars today as *damnatio memoriae,* "obliteration of the record," or, more literally, the "damnation" or "condemnation" of all "memory" pertaining to their existence. The procedure was employed widely from the fifth century B.C. through the sixth century A.D. and involved "the eradication of visual representations of the person, a ban of the name, and a prohibition of the observance of the funeral and mourning," according to

Charles W. Hedrick Jr., who wrote a learned study detailing one dramatic instance of its use. The incident he focused on first came to light in 1849 when workmen constructing a drain in the Forum of Trajan in Rome uncovered the base of a statue erected in A.D. 431 that had lain buried for hundreds of years. On the pedestal was an inscription that represented the "rehabilitation" of a prominent Roman citizen whose memory had been "obliterated" forty years earlier for political reasons that can only be surmised today. The formal pronouncement was carved on a slab that bore evidence of having been scraped clean of a prior inscription, making it a palimpsest in stone.

Many other instances of the practice were far less obscure. After the assassination of Julius Caesar in 44 B.C., all statues and dedications praising the conspirator Brutus were ordered expunged, although several survived. Suetonius wrote that after the death of the detested emperor Domitian in A.D. 96, the Senate directed that his inscriptions be "erased everywhere as soon as possible, and all memory of him was to be destroyed." An unusually infamous instance of a *damnatio memoriae* decree came when the psychopathic emperor Caligula ordered his wife, Plautilla, executed, and the features of her marble bust rendered unrecognizable.

One of the more curious episodes of what could be regarded as an imposition of *damnatio memoriae* on an entire culture was occasioned by the Norman Conquest of England, and the transfer of power to a French-speaking nobility that considered all books written in Anglo-Saxon, or Old English, crudely archaic and disposable. Although not explicitly hostile to the dialect of the conquered natives, the Norman rulers considered their language vulgar and unworthy of preservation, and ordered it expunged from official repositories. Three centuries would pass from when King Harold died at the Battle of Hastings in 1066 to a time when another British ruler was fluent in the tongue of the English. During that long interval, French and Latin became the languages of record and daily discourse among the aristocracy, the courts, and the church hierarchy, and the switchover was brought about with a minimum of delay. In 1070 Lanfranc of Bec, a dominant figure in the theological, educational, and political life of eleventh-century Europe, left Normandy to become archbishop of Canterbury and to serve as regent of England during King William's prolonged absences. Despite the churchman's reluctance to accept such an ambitious assignment while in his late sixties, historians still regard him as one of England's great archbishops, even though the language of the Anglo-Saxons was never part of his worldview.

"After the Conquest the indifference and contempt with which the conquerors regarded everything Saxon must have been responsible for the destruction of nearly every manuscript written in the vernacular," Ernest A. Savage surmised in a respected survey of early libraries. Old English poems that did manage to survive are preserved for the most part in unique manuscripts, many of them as incomplete fragments, some found as scrap material used as reinforcement in the bindings of later volumes. Albert C. Baugh, a historian of English language and literature, believed that the abrupt cessation of creative writing in Britain at that time was brought on by "the rapid displacement of English bishops and English abbots in the monasteries, the eviction of the English language and English culture from the place they should have occupied in the national life, and the complete indifference of the new rulers to books in a language which they did not understand." By 1248, only four works written in Old English were reported to be still at the Glastonbury abbey, and they were described in a formal inventory as obscure and useless.

Spoken English, meanwhile, was passed on by the rank and file from generation to generation without benefit of a standardized grammar or a canon of recorded literature, and as events turned out, the same kind of dynastic contention that led to the shunning of the language in the first place contributed measurably to its triumphant resurgence. As the decades of occupation passed on, French nobles living in England lost control of their ancestral properties on the continent, and lines of inheritance and entitlement became increasingly blurred. In a summons delivered to Parliament in 1295 with the clear intention of stirring up chauvinistic sentiment among his subjects, King Edward I claimed that the "detestable purpose" of Philip IV, his counterpart in France, was "God forbid, to wipe out the English tongue." More than any other outside influence, it was the Hundred Years' War, fought intermittently between 1337 and 1453, that helped return English to prominence, particularly among an increasingly influential middle class.

In 1362, Parliament rescinded its decree of sixty years earlier and ordered that lawsuits once again be recorded in English; that same year, the lord chancellor broke with tradition and opened the chamber's proceedings with a ceremonial speech in the native language. While these developments were taking place, literary works known as Middle English romances composed in a distinctive alliterative verse began to appear with continuing frequency. Most of the compositions were French in origin, though some native traditions practiced before the Conquest had been transmitted orally. By far the best-known example of the genre, *Sir Gawain and the Green Knight,* was produced anonymously about 1375 by a chronicler known today as the Pearl Poet, and survives in a single manuscript copy through the efforts of Sir Robert Cotton, the seventeenth-century antiquarian who is also responsible for saving the tenth-century *Beowulf* codex, the Lindisfarne Gospels, and the unique manuscript copy of William Langland's *The Vision of Piers Plowman.*

The oeuvre of the poet John Gower (c. 1330–1408) offers another indication of how profoundly attitudes had begun to change, and how quickly they took place. A good friend of Geoffrey Chaucer (c. 1342–1400) and a prominent figure in the courts of Richard II and Henry IV, Gower earned an international reputation for his writing, and he achieved it by composing successive works in three different languages, all intended for the *same* audience. *Vox Clamantis,* an apocalyptic poem in 10,265 lines of elegiac couplets, was set down in Latin between 1379 and 1381, while *Mirour de l'Omme* and *Cinkante Balades* were verses written in a form of French peculiar to Britain called Anglo-Norman. But Gower's best known work, the *Confessio Amantis* (The Lover's Confession), was written about 1390 and, despite its Latin title, in English. In a prologue to the lengthy work, which consists largely of stories taken from Ovid's *Metamorphoses*, Gower took special pains to explain that he had turned to the vernacular tongue at the direction of King Richard II, who was eager to show solidarity with his English subjects. With the posthumous distribution of Chaucer's *Canterbury Tales* in 1400, the native language reemerged in full flower, greatly changed to reveal nuances of not only French but also the Italian that the poet mastered while serving abroad as a civil servant. Chaucer's impact was such that Thomas Hoccleve, his younger contemporary, anointed him "the first finder of our fair language."

F ew people would argue that the most effective method of crushing a people's hold on the past is to prevent a common heritage from being documented in the first place, which may help explain why teaching slaves to read was regarded as a criminal offense in much of the American South before the Emancipation Proclamation was issued in 1863. When I interviewed Charles Blockson for *A Gentle Madness*, the Philadelphia bibliophile said that the reason he became obsessed with creating what has become one of the world's great collections of African-American writing was to disprove a tactless remark made to him by an elementary-school teacher in Norristown, Pennsylvania, when he was in the fourth grade, that "negroes have no history," and that they "were born to serve white people."

One of the more dramatic cases of cultural management to be documented in what is now the United States involved the efforts of Phillis Wheatley (c. 1753–1784) to become the first African American to publish a book, and the first to achieve international acclaim as an author. From the time Wheatley had arrived in North America at the age of seven, she had been encouraged to learn Greek, Latin, and English in the household of the Boston family where she had lived as a domestic servant, and she quickly became celebrated in the local press for her incisive poems. But when Wheatley's master attempted to publish her work in 1771, problems arose. Before the young woman was allowed to proceed with the project, she was required to appear before a panel of prominent Massachusetts citizens. What, precisely, Governor Thomas Hutchinson, the Honorable John Hancock, the Reverend Charles Chauncey, and their fifteen colleagues asked Wheatley to demonstrate that day is uncertain. "Perhaps they asked her to identify and explain—for all to hear—exactly who were the Greek and Latin gods and poets alluded to so frequently in her work," Henry Louis Gates Jr. and Nellie Y. McKay speculated in *The Norton Anthology of African American Literature*. "Perhaps they asked her to conjugate a verb in Latin," or maybe they required her to recite from memory key passages from the texts of John Milton and Alexander Pope, "the two poets by whom the African seems to have been most influenced." Whatever the panel inquired of Wheatley that day, there is no doubt that she responded with satisfactory answers. Inserted as a preface to the collection of thirty-nine verses published later that year under the title *Poems on Various Subjects, Religious and Moral* was an "attestation" prepared by her examiners, and addressed directly "To the Publick." It stated in part:

> We whose Names are under-written, do assure the World, that the POEMS specified in the following Page, were (as we verily believe) written by PHILLIS, a young Negro Girl, who was but a few Years since, brought an uncultivated Barbarian from *Africa*, and has ever since been, and now is under the Disadvantage of serving as a Slave in a Family in this Town. She has been examined by some of the best Judges, and is thought qualified to write them.

Even with this ringing validation, no colonial publisher was willing to issue the work in print, so with the backing of her sponsors, Wheatley sailed to England and found a far more agreeable response to her work there. The first appearance of her slim volume in the fall of 1773 bears the imprint of a London bookseller, A. Bell, and was underwritten by the countess of Huntingdon. Today, the mahogany desk she used for her writing occupies a prime location on the second floor of the Massachusetts Historical Society in the Back Bay section of Boston, a material reminder of her accomplishment. Just how remarkable a personal triumph this was for a person in bondage to achieve becomes clearer when considered alongside the extraordinary steps an African-American slave in South Carolina—a man known today as Dave the Potter—took a century later to pass his words along to future generations. In Dave's case, the medium of transmission was not the printed page but glazed stoneware inscribed with a variety of signed messages, some of them clever plays on words, others short rhyming verses, all of them dated and signed "Dave."

That Dave learned to read and write at all, and that he had the courage to "publish" the fruits of his literacy on large pieces of earthenware meant for distribution to the general public, was no small achievement for a black man who came of age in South Carolina during the 1820s and 1830s. It was South Carolina, after all, that championed the extremist doctrine known as nullification, which claimed the right to declare null and void any federal law it deemed inimical to its interests; when that movement failed, the state was first in line to secede from the Union, first to open fire at Fort Sumter in 1861, and last—in the summer of 2000—to stop flying the Confederate flag over its capitol dome. Ironically, the oldest jar known to have been inscribed by Dave is dated 1834, the same year South Carolina passed legislation making it a crime to teach any Negro—slave or free—to read or write. That playful couplet was composed around the number of gallons the pot he made could hold:

Put every bit all between
surely this jar will hold 14

In addition to practical information like this, Dave's inscriptions include philosophical and religious meditations and witticisms. Jars referencing his personal feelings are especially prized by collectors.

I saw a leopard and a lions face
then I felt the need of grace

Occasionally, he considers his ancestry:

I wonder where is all my relations
friendship to all and every nation

Nobody knows for certain how Dave learned to read and write, although there is speculation that he became literate while working for Abner Landrum, an early master who also was the publisher of a small weekly newspaper, the *Edgefield Hive*. Landrum, it is thought, may have trained him to be a typesetter in the printing shop. If that was the case, Dave's days as a printer were short-lived. Edgefield, South Carolina, is pottery country—the clay deposits in the region are of such superior quality that the famed maker of fine English china, Josiah Wedgwood, once had three tons of the material shipped to his plant in Britain—and the stoneware industry is where skilled labor was best employed. Dave is known to have worked for no fewer than five manufacturers, and he produced thousands of clay jars in his lifetime, intended not as works of art but as objects of pure utility.

Although very little is known of Dave's life, he is assumed to have had great physical strength, given that some of the pots he turned by hand held up to forty gallons, among the largest produced in the nineteenth century. His earliest vessels were devoid of poetic inscriptions, possibly out of fear that he might be punished for his literacy. Six years after writing his first verse, Dave went silent for seventeen years, from 1840 to 1857, only signing and dating his work during that period. The last known jar attributed to his hand is dated March 31, 1864. "If Dave hadn't have left his mark on these jars, we wouldn't know anything about the contribution of African Americans to an important ceramic tradition," Jill Beute Koverman, an art historian responsible for piecing together the history of Dave's clay writings, told me when a traveling exhibition she curated was about to open at the Winterthur Museum in Delaware. Because Dave was regarded as "property" for most of his life, Koverman was able to track his movements by following a trail of old documents. His name first appears in an 1818 mortgage as a slave owned by Harvey Drake, a ceramics producer in the community of Pottersville, a mile north of Edgefield. Dave's constantly improving expertise as a master potter increased his value as a "commodity." In 1833 he was sold for $400; fourteen years later the price was $700. After the Civil War, Dave took on the surname Drake, a respectful nod, presumably, to his first master. Analysis of census data has led Koverman to believe that he was born in 1800 and died around 1870.

Koverman examined sixty vessels in museums that are known to have been made by Dave, and another seventy that are privately owned. "They are constantly turning up," she said. "Some come out of barns, one was found in a pantry." His pieces are included in the permanent collections of the Smithsonian Institution, the Philadelphia Museum, the High Museum in Atlanta, the Museum of Fine Arts in Boston, and the African-American Museum in Detroit. "Obviously, this man wanted to be known, otherwise, he would not have signed his name or dated more than one hundred and thirty jars that we know of, and probably many, many more. Unlike earlier potters who commonly stamped their initials or name near the base or along the upper walls of a vessel, he clearly and boldly wrote 'Dave'—often with a flourish."

To find a benchmark example in which a Final Solution was irreversibly implemented as the result of official policy, it is necessary to go back more than twenty-one hundred years to the systematic destruction of Carthage on the coast of North Africa by soldiers carrying out the explicit orders of the Roman Senate. Every vestige of a thriving metropolis was obliterated, and from that point forward the historical record was tailored in ways that suited the changing requirements of the victors, the most egregious example being the creation of a literary landmark that placed ultimate blame for the devastation on the dying curse of a jilted woman. That ingenuous interpretation came about in the most circuitous of ways. In 30 B.C., the emperor Augustus prevailed upon Publius Vergilius Maro, the poet known as Virgil, to commemorate his victory over Mark Antony and Cleopatra at the Battle of Actium the year before with an epic poem.

Because emotions still ran deep over the merits of the civil war just concluded, this was a risky assignment for any politically astute Roman to assume, and a number of literary figures, Horace and Propertius most prominent among them, had already found excuses to pass on the emperor's offer. Virgil accepted, but he wisely chose to celebrate Roman glory by reaching back to a time where he could combine mythology and legend with a smattering of history. Even then there was nothing especially glorious about the liquidation of an ancient enemy to extol, which may be one reason why Virgil tinkered with the *Aeneid* for eleven years, and why he left the work unfinished at his death in 19 B.C. with specific directions that it be destroyed. The poem was issued by his heirs anyway, and acclaimed a masterpiece throughout the empire almost immediately.

Virgil's way of dealing with what we might call the "Carthage problem," it turned out, was a clever application of poetic license in which the
obliteration of an ancient enemy was rationalized as a manifestation of
divine will, not a consequence of malicious intent. The poet maintained,
presumably with a straight face, that it was the Carthaginian queen Dido
who seven centuries earlier had set "the wheel of fate" in motion toward
destruction of her own country, a nation so advanced that it once had been
favored to be "the capital of all nations." As Virgil tells the story, Aeneas,
a lucky survivor of the ravages of Troy, is required by sacred mandate to
establish a new homeland in Italy. As he makes his getaway voyage out of
Asia Minor—he escaped the flaming ruins carrying his gravely wounded
father on his back—a pounding Mediterranean storm knocks his small
fleet off course, forcing him to seek refuge on the North African coast as
the pampered guest of the recently widowed Phoenician woman who tradition holds founded the colony of Carthage around 800 B.C. Before long
Dido is "smitten with a grievous love-pang" for the irresistible son of
Venus—the goddess Juno has worked her naughty wiles to perfection—
and she proposes a union with him in which they will rule Carthage "with
equal sovereignty." Aghast at the sudden turn of events, the god Jupiter
commands Aeneas to cast off for Italy at the first opportunity, and as he
sails away in the morning sun, a huge column of smoke rises from the distant shore, telltale evidence of Dido's smoldering funeral pyre. Just
before throwing herself on a sword, she had damned Aeneas and his
descendants for eternity: "Let no love or treaty unite the nations! Arise
from my ashes, unknown avenger, to harass the Trojan settlers with fire
and sword—today, hereafter, whenever strength be ours! May coast with
coast conflict, I pray, and sea with sea, arms with arms; war may they
have, themselves and their children's children."

In reality, of course, the destiny of Carthage would be ordained by
decree of the Roman Senate, not by the will of vengeful gods, and the reasons were economic and political, not unrequited love. The most thor-

ough writer from antiquity to discuss the three Punic Wars with any semblance of balance was Appian of Alexandria (A.D. c. 95–160), a lawyer of equestrian rank based in Rome and a devoted student of history whose writings, all in Greek, were drawn largely from earlier chronicles that are now mostly lost. Appian's voluminous work, according to Horace White, his best-known translator, "has been severely criticized for want of accuracy in details," and he is sometimes accused of having indulged in "historical novel writing" for his tendency to quote various principals without bothering to identify who is speaking. The Cambridge University classicist Michael Grant deemed him "all too ready to call in divine revenge as a cause of events" when a measure of "critical acumen" may have been more appropriate. Because Appian is the best source that we have on the Punic Wars, what he wrote is invaluable nonetheless. Of great value, too, are the writings of the Greek historian Polybius (c. 200–c. 118 B.C.), not for any element of objectivity, since as the friend and mentor of the conquering general Scipio Aemelianus, his unequivocally stated goal was to glorify the rise to dominance in the Mediterranean of the Roman Republic, but for the eyewitness testimony he was able to record of the destruction.

The prelude to the bloody denouement came in the First Punic War of 264 to 241 B.C., when Carthage ceded control of Sicily to its uneasy neighbor to the northeast. After two decades of relative peace, a dynamic new leader, Hannibal, engaged Rome in what would become sixteen years of combat, scoring a number of impressive victories along the way. In his most celebrated action, Hannibal marched an army of mercenaries from Spain across the Alps to the outskirts of Rome. His decision not to attack the city ensured ultimate defeat, and as a condition of peace, he agreed to the dismantling of his forces and to pay a heavy duty for fifty years. It was only through the magnanimous nature of the Roman people, according to Appian, that a far more severe punishment was not meted out. One Senate advocate of leniency—conveniently unidentified by Appian but quoted at considerable length—explained the Roman decision to grant mercy to its ancient rival, setting up a rationale for the extreme action that would come later on:

> Gentlemen, this is not so much a question of saving Carthage as of preserving our faith with the gods and our reputation among men—lest it be said that we, who charge the Carthaginians with cruelty, behave with greater cruelty than they, and while always exercising moderation in small matters neglect it in large ones, which, on account of their very magnitude, cannot even escape notice. The deed will be sounded through all the earth, now and hereafter, if we destroy this famous city, former mistress of the seas, ruler of so many islands, and of the whole expanse of water, and more than half of Africa, a city which in contests with ourselves has exhibited such wonderful success and power.

So the Romans, we are told, exercised some compassion this time around, only to have the Carthaginians show their gratitude by reasserting themselves as a force in the Mediterranean. Thus it came to pass that while on a diplomatic mission to Carthage in 153 B.C., Cato the Elder saw a thriving capital full of confidence at the revival of its strength, and he became alarmed at what he observed. The aging politician—known more descriptively by his contemporaries as Cato the Censor—returned to Rome with a new purpose in life, and from then on every speech he delivered in the Senate ended with three thundering words: *Delenda est Carthago*— "Carthage must be destroyed."

With the outbreak of the Third Punic War in 149 B.C., plans were set in motion to accomplish that strident goal. In the spring of 146 B.C., after three years of siege, Roman troops stormed the Carthaginian capital and advanced toward the elevated royal precinct known as the Byrsa. Appian tells a macabre tale of citizens being thrown from rooftops by the hundreds and clogging the narrow streets with blood and gore. Some 200,000 people were killed in the rampage, and another 50,000 were taken as slaves, but mass slaughter was just one part of the solution. The Senate had decreed that neither house nor crop should rise again in Carthage, and the reality is that neither did with any degree of permanence until the emperor Augustus allowed a colony of Roman settlers to occupy the territory a century later. The fire was said to have raged unchecked for days on end, and layers of carbonized stone unearthed in recent digs by UNESCO archaeologists offer grim evidence that the reports were not exaggerated. Whatever written records the Carthaginians had kept in their capital—and there is sufficient testimony to indicate that they had amassed great stores of knowledge over their seven hundred years of existence—were destroyed outright.

Qart Hadasht, the "New City" of Carthage, had been built by Phoenician colonists from Tyre on a ridge rising along the coast from La Goulette, the present-day seaport of Tunisia. By the seventh century Carthage had become the overlord of all Phoenician settlements in the region, ruling a trading empire that ranged from Tripoli and Libya in North Africa to the Atlantic coasts of Morocco and southern Spain, with a combined population of about 3 million people. "They became a match for the Greeks in power, and next to the Persians in wealth," Appian wrote. Appian offered a detailed description of the Carthaginian harbor, the waterfront, the elaborate fortifications they had erected, and their sophisticated urban architecture, mentioning specifically clusters of six-story buildings that stood on both sides of three main roadways. Recent excavations estimate that 120,000 cubic meters of earth were moved to build a rectangular outer harbor for merchant traffic, and another 115,000 for a circular anchorage reserved for warships.

The word *Punic*, which is synonymous with Carthaginian, is a derivation of "from Phoenicia," the eastern Mediterranean territory where the first alphabet was developed around 1000 B.C. Herodotus credited "these

Phoenicians"—they actually were itinerant Canaanites—with bringing "into Hellas the alphabet, which had hitherto been unknown, as I think, to the Greeks." An archaic stone inscription from Crete first translated in 1970—and predating Herodotus—uses the terms *poinikazen,* "to write," and *poinikastas,* "scribe." Both derive from *(grammata) phoinikeia,* "Phoenician letters." The Greeks, in turn, modified the alphabet and made it more useful by adding vowels.

For their own language, the Carthaginians evolved a distinctive derivation of the Phoenician alphabet, and like all Semitic writing, it read from right to left. To ensure textual uniformity throughout its colonies, schools known as *sopherim* imposed strict professional standards on scribal conduct, helping make Punic the official language of the Numidian and Moorish kingdoms. Punic words appeared routinely on coins of the realm throughout the region, and the language was spoken, if not written, well into the fifth century A.D. With the pulverization of Carthage, its territories became absorbed in the Roman province Africa Vetus, but many of the old traditions, the veneration of certain gods in particular, continued. A "Neopunic" religious inscription from the first century A.D., carved on a portico in honor of the Phoenician god El more than two hundred years after the destruction of the capital, was found at Lepcis, a "lost city" on the Mediterranean coast of modern-day Libya that flourished well into the third century A.D., and used both Punic and Latin to record formal pronouncements.

"Many of the Carthaginian institutions are excellent" and "justly celebrated," Aristotle wrote at a time when Carthage was at the height of its power in the fourth century B.C. "The superiority of their constitution is proved by the fact that the common people remain loyal; the Carthagini ans have never had any rebellion worth speaking of, and have never been under the rule of a tyrant." Aristotle described their form of government as "oligarchical," but quickly noted that "they successfully escape the evils of oligarchy by being wealthy, sending out one portion of their people after another to the cities. This is their panacea and the means by which they give stability to the state."

When Aristotle was writing his treatises in the fourth century B.C., the great library at Alexandria was still several decades away from being established by the successors of his protégé Alexander the Great. Like their Greek contemporaries, Carthaginian scholars, scientists, historians, explorers, and poets had already produced many books, and their architects had built spacious libraries to contain them. In carrying out the methodical destruction of the metropolis, Scipio Aemilianus is said to have spared one collection of particularly informative manuscripts and presented them as gifts to a cartel of African princes who had supported the Roman cause. Another twenty-eight highly regarded books on farming techniques compiled by the Carthaginian agronomist Mago were brought back to Rome and translated into Latin by the scholar D. Silanus. That text was later translated into Greek by Cassius Dionysius of Utica. Like all other Punic books, this seminal work is now lost, although Pliny cited "Dionysius's translation of Mago" as a principal "foreign authority" for the chapters in his *Natural History* on "Fruit Trees," "Fruit Bearing Trees," "The Nature of Cultivated Trees," "Crops, Their Nature," "Drugs Obtained from Forest Trees," and "The Nature of Self-Grown Plants." Pliny used the word *bibliothecae*—a library with many books— to describe what had been ransacked by the conquering legions, leading the French archaeologist Serge Lancel to surmise that the Carthaginian collections "could very well have imitated the example set in the seventh century by the Assyrian king Assurbanipal," and possibly even have been more sophisticated.

Another significant Roman reference to Punic books was made by Gaius Sallustius Crispus (c. 86–c. 34 B.C.), a contemporary of Caesar and Cicero known as Sallust who wrote authoritatively about a number of civilizations that had once thrived in Africa. For his source material, Sallust gratefully acknowledged the availability of books that had been translated into Latin especially for him during his tour as Rome's first governor of Numidia—the same books, perhaps, that Scipio was said to have presented to the African princes half a century earlier. "What men inhabited Africa originally, and who came later, or how the races mingled, I shall tell as briefly as possible," Sallust wrote in *The War with Jugurtha,* his best-known work, which deals with Rome's handling of an insurrection led by the Numidian prince Jugurtha in 112 B.C. What he had to say next about his technique is of particular interest here: "Although my account varies from the prevailing tradition, I give it as it was translated to me from the Punic books said to have been written by King Hiempsal, and in accordance with what the dwellers in that land believe. But the responsibility for its truth will rest with my authorities." Sadly, those books—Sallust pointedly called them *ex libris Punicis*—and the translations prepared for him by his African hosts have long since disappeared as well.

The nineteenth-century French novelist Gustave Flaubert discovered just how deplorable the lack of primary information on the subject was when he decided to set his novel *Salammbô* in ancient Carthage. To achieve verisimilitude, Flaubert spent a month in Tunisia getting a feel for the countryside and absorbing the ambience, although the narrative he conjured forth was not driven by any epiphanies he may have experienced in the field but by the long-held assumption that infant sacrifice was widely practiced by the Carthaginians. Without any solid documentation to hinder his imagination, Flaubert created a pagan society that routinely drops newborn babies from the outstretched arms of a bronze god into a pit of purifying fire. "I have undertaken something bold, my boy, something very bold, and there are plenty of hurdles to break my neck over before I reach the end," Flaubert wrote a friend about the novel that ultimately would take him three years to write. "Still, just think what I've let myself in for: trying to resuscitate an entire civilization about which we know nothing."

Thanks to modern archaeology, more details are known today than were available when Flaubert began work on *Salammbô* in 1858. A number of stone inscriptions, some of them quite compelling, have been located in various burial grounds, and hundreds of amphorae bearing the bones of children and animals have been found, lending some credence, in fact, to the old stories of infant sacrifice, although nothing conclusive has been demonstrated. Decorated ivory combs, coins, amulets, pieces of jewelry, scarabs, figurines, cups, and terra-cotta fragments of molds also have been retrieved from tombs, and other exciting work continues to this day. But for all the artifacts that have surfaced, only a few educated guesses can be made as to the complexity of the lost civilization. Unlike the libraries of Sumer and Ur and Nineveh and Ebla, where hundreds of clay tablets lay waiting in the ground for three thousand years to be discovered, the written records of Carthage were thoroughly erased by the conquerors. Sidi Mahrez, the fourteenth-century Muslim saint whose memory is enshrined in a grand mosque in Tunis—a city that came to prominence across the lagoon from Carthage in the years following the devastation—wrote a dirge for the routed culture, one he could mourn but never see:

> *Why this emptiness after joy?*
> *Why this ending after glory?*
> *Why this nothingness where once was a city?*
> *Who will answer? Only the wind*
> *Which steals the chantings of priests*
> *And scatters the souls once gathered.*

"It is remarkable that conquerors, in the moment of victory, or in the unsparing devastation of their rage, have not been satisfied with destroying *men*, but have ever carried their vengeance to *books*," Isaac Disraeli lamented in *Curiosities of Literature*, a splendidly eclectic series of essays published in the late eighteenth and early nineteenth centuries that offers modern readers many rich rewards. The first instance of such an atrocity taking place in the New World was carried out on the orders of Diego de Landa, a Franciscan friar obsessed with "cleansing" the native Maya of their pagan beliefs, and by cleansing what he meant was eradication of their recorded memory. On July 12, 1562, Landa ordered thousands of hieroglyphic codices that had been discovered in the ancient village of Maní to be burned in a huge conflagration that became known as the "burning of the books." Landa correctly determined that the Maya had once used the writings in the practice of their spiritual beliefs, and since converting the native population to Christianity was a top priority of the Spanish conquest, the logical course of action was clear. "We found a great number of these books," Landa wrote in a dispassionate account of his activities, "and because they contained nothing but superstition and the Devil's falsehoods we burned them all; and this they felt most bitterly and it caused them great grief."

Although nothing was done to restrain Landa from committing these atrocities, a few Europeans considered his action senseless. Writing twenty-four years after the fact, the Jesuit Joseph de Acoste concluded that the bonfire resulted from "a stupid zeal," and that "without knowing or even wishing to know the things of the Indies," Landa and his cohorts had determined that "everything is sorcery and that the peoples there are only a drunken lot and what can they know or understand. The ones who have wished earnestly to be informed of these have found many things worthy of consideration." Of the thousands of manuscripts produced by the Maya, just four codices are known to have been spared. They were sent back to Spain by the conquistadors as curiosities for the amusement of their superiors, and only one has since returned to the land of its origin. Three of the surviving codices are named for the European cities where they are preserved, Dresden, Madrid, and Paris; the book now kept in Mexico City, an eleven-page fragment dealing with funerary offerings, is called the Grolier Codex in honor of the Grolier Club in New York City, which sponsored an exhibition of Maya writing in 1971.

When the American explorer and diplomat John Lloyd Stephens arrived at the Maya ruins of Copán in 1839, he believed he had come across the remnants of a vanished society. "It lay before us like a shattered bark in the midst of the ocean, her masts gone, her name effaced, her crew perished, and none to tell whence she came, to whom she belonged, how long on her voyage, or what caused her destruction," he wrote in *Incidents of Travel in Central America,* a travelogue that appeared in 1841 with some fanciful illustrations executed by the English artist Frederick Catherwood. "All was mystery," he marveled, "dark, impenetrable mystery."

Recent archaeological evidence suggests that Classic Maya society began around A.D. 250 in the lowlands of the Yucatán, where inscribed and dated stone monuments were first erected, and ended at the beginning of the tenth century with a still unexplained phenomenon known as the "Maya Collapse." Like the Carthaginians before them, the Maya thrived as a civilization for about seven hundred years, and like the Carthaginians, their expertise in agriculture and commerce produced riches that made a great cultural flowering possible. Terraced temples, sacred pyramids, decorated monuments, and limestone palaces were built in city-states that stretched across the Yucatán Peninsula into what is now Honduras, Guatemala, and Belize. Craftsmen adorned these magnificent buildings with exquisite bas-relief carvings and paintings, and created sculptured and polychrome vases.

Along with their architectural accomplishments, the Maya had developed a writing system sophisticated enough to express any word that was in their language. Maya priests turned to their writings when they were performing rituals necessary for maintaining the harmony and balance of daily life. "The books were indispensable for knowing what god was to be venerated on what days and what were the exact ceremonial procedures that were necessary for carrying this out in the correct manner," Thomas A. Lee

Whiting pointed out in an important monograph. The fundamental purpose of the codices was not lost on Landa. "These people," he wrote, "used certain glyphs or letters in which they wrote down their ancient history and sciences in their books; and by means of these letters and figures and by certain marks contained in them, they could read about their affairs and taught others to read about them too." The four surviving codices deal entirely with astronomy, calendrics, divination, and ritualism. The Dresden Codex includes data on the cycles of the planet Venus and tables for predicting lunar eclipses; the Madrid Codex addresses ritualism and prophecy; and the Paris Codex describes ceremonies associated with the passage of the seasons. Radiocarbon analysis of the Grolier Codex produced a likely date of 1230, which suggests that the beliefs of the people and knowledge of the language were transmitted several centuries after the Maya state had collapsed, a phenomenon not unlike that associated with the Punic language.

When the Spaniards arrived in the 1500s, the Maya temples had been reclaimed by the jungle canopies, yet thousands of books remained securely preserved in what were the first libraries built in the Americas. Before reducing the volumes to ashes, Landa studied them as if they were an exotic kind of laboratory specimen. It is especially ironic, then, that the report he prepared in defense of his activities became the one essential tool that paved the way for decipherment of the lost language four hundred years later. For twentieth-century scholars, Landa's dispassionate manuscript "account of things in the Yucatán," *Relación de las cosas de Yucatán*, became the key to understanding the far more extensive inscriptions on stone that had not been destroyed. Landa wrote the *Relación* in 1566 after having been recalled to Spain by the Inquisition to defend his harsh policies in the New World; absolved of his actions, he returned in 1572 as the first bishop to the Yucatán, and the tract he wrote fell into obscurity. The chance discovery of a forgotten and uncataloged abridgement of the work in a Madrid library in 1862—an anonymous "copy of a copy" of the original manuscript that by then was lost—made possible the great breakthroughs that followed. "It is a fact of scientific life—at least, a fact of archaeological research—that the truly great discoverers have occasionally been extraordinarily sloppy," the noted anthropologist Michael D. Coe wrote in *Breaking the Maya Code*. How the copy of Landa's apologia arrived in the Royal Academy of History in Madrid nobody could say. "Nonetheless, it is not only a gold mine of informed speculation on all aspects of Maya life as it was in Yucatán on the eve of the Conquest, but also, in spite of the denial by generations of epigraphers, the true Rosetta Stone for the decipherment of Maya hieroglyphic writing."

In the tract, Landa told how the Maya prepared their paper from the bark of trees, applied a thin layer of lime plaster, then doubled the sheets to make a kind of folding screen. "They wrote on both sides of the sheet in columns, following the folds," he observed, noting how the finished product was then enclosed between elegantly decorated boards, sometimes binding them in the cured skin of jaguars. Landa's physical description of the codices corresponds with images that were painted on Maya vases. For modern-day scholars, of far greater significance was Landa's character-by-character description of the alphabet, which had been dictated to him by a native who had working knowledge of the language, along with drawings of their appearance. Landa was certain that he had discovered a unique tongue, as this entry in his journal demonstrates: "I will set down here an alphabet of these letters since their difficulty does not allow anything more. They used one character or glyph to represent all the aspirations of their letters and then they joined on to it part of another glyph and another for joining them together, and thus these could go on *ad infinitum*."

For years Landa's cursory description was scorned as worthless, but in the 1950s Yuri Knorosov, a Russian epigrapher, subjected it to a fresh examination and concluded that the signs in the Maya writing system, like Egyptian hieroglyphics and Sumerian cuneiform, represent syllables, not individual letters. To confirm his findings, the Russian translated the four books that had been spared from the flames in the 1500s. Because of Knorosov's efforts, scholars can now read the inscriptions on the stone monuments and stelae that survive in profusion. Some of the most spectacular examples are to be found at Palenque, Mexico, in a palace called the Temple of the Inscriptions, built by Makina Pacal, a Maya king known as "Great Sun Lord, Shield," who ruled from 615 to 683. In these courtyards, adorned originally with sculptures of plaster and stone, are panels of hieroglyphs that comprise the most extensive texts to be found at any Maya site, constituting a "critical mass of data" that has proven invaluable to modern scholars, with startling new discoveries being announced often.

Just three months after assuming control of Germany in a landslide election, the National Socialist Party began burning books in public squares throughout the Third Reich. "It is all being done to the accompaniment of torchlight parades, martial music and much patriotic speechifying," the foreign correspondent Frederick T. Birchall reported in a special wireless dispatch from Berlin that was carried on the front page of the *New York Times* on May 11, 1933. Birchall described a "funeral pyre of crossed logs, some twelve feet square and five feet high" that had lit up the drizzly night sky in the Operplatz, a "great square between the opera house and the university." The inferno was witnessed by what he conservatively estimated to be forty thousand people, with at least as many more lining the route to the square. Universities throughout Germany had orchestrated separate bonfires the same night, and sidebar items gave details of conflagrations carried out in Munich, Frankfurt, Breslau, and Kiel.

In Berlin, a procession of five thousand students formally dressed in colorful caps and gowns and singing Nazi songs had marched around the pyre, tossing their lighted torches into the pile. Once the flames were roaring, the doomed books and pamphlets were driven forward by the carload as offerings, and a student leader began reading a litany of condemnation into a microphone. "Sigmund Freud—for falsifying our history and degrading its great figures." The crowd cheered, and the books of Freud fueled the inferno. Erich Maria Remarque was denounced "for degrading the German language and the highest patriotic ideal," the signal to send his internationally acclaimed novel of World War I, *All Quiet on the Western Front,* up in smoke. "Emil Ludwig—burned for literary rascality and high treason against Germany!" the voice boomed out, and Ludwig's books were incinerated. The American authors Ernest Hemingway, John Dos Passos, Upton Sinclair, and Jack London were shown no mercy, and the writings of the Nobel laureate Thomas Mann went into the flames en bloc. When Helen Keller learned that her works had been earmarked for immolation, presumably because of her essays and lectures in support of socialism, world peace, and internationalism, she issued an open letter to the German students: "You can burn my books and the books of the best minds in Europe, but the ideas in them have seeped through a million channels and will continue to quicken other minds. I gave all the royalties of my books for all time to the German soldiers blinded in the World War with no thought in my heart but love and compassion for the German people." That detail notwithstanding, Keller's books still went up in flames. "The victims even included Count Coudenhove-Kalergi, the Japanese-Viennese author, who dreams of Pan-Europa," Birchall wrote. "He falls under the ban because it is not a Prussian Pan-Europa and, moreover, might be suspected of having a Socialist tinge." After the books of more than 160 "un-German" writers had lit up the night sky, Dr. Paul Joseph Goebbels, the minister of propaganda, ascended "a tiny swastika-draped rostrum" to declare that "Jewish intellectualism is dead" and that "National Socialism has hewn the way" for the future. "These flames do not only illuminate the final end of the old era, they also light up the new. Never before have the young men had so good a right to clean up the debris of the past."

When plans for the auto-da-fé were being finalized, Emil Ludwig (1881–1948), the biographer of Goethe, Napoleon, and Beethoven, felt it prudent to be out of the country, and expressed grim amusement when informed in Barcelona that he was considered worthy enough to be despised by the Nazis. "I shall experience one of the greatest satisfactions of my life tomorrow, for that is the day that has been set for burning all my works in Germany," he told a reporter the day before. "I will attempt to hear over the radio the crackling of the flames that are destroying all our literary labors."

In 1974, a German journalist asked Walter Mehring, a prolific writer associated with the dada movement in Berlin during the fast and loose years of the Weimar Republic, how he felt forty-one years earlier when he learned that he had been identified over a loudspeaker as a "Jewish subversionist," and that his books had been among those tossed in the flames. "They got my name wrong," he said dismissively, not bothering to note that his countrymen got it "right" two years later when they stripped him of his citizenship and ordered the Gestapo to arrest him on sight for purported crimes against the state. Mehring's offense was that he had been identified as a member of an avant-garde milieu of writers, musicians, and performers who had made Berlin one of the intellectual capitals of Europe during the 1920s, but were considered "decadent" and "subversive" by the new regime. Other artists who were part of what had been called the Cabaret Society movement were Bertolt Brecht, Kurt Weill, Walter Gropius, Fritz Lang, and Marlene Dietrich. The author of taunting poems, plays, and caustic song lyrics, Mehring became a man in transit, going from country to country, hiding place to hiding place. He finally was captured by German security police in 1940 and placed in an internment camp, but managed to escape and reach the United States through the assistance of a group established for the express purpose of helping imperiled artists. In America, Mehring wrote scripts in Hollywood, worked as a warehouse administrator on Long Island, and became a naturalized citizen. When Mehring died at the age of eighty-five in 1981, he had lived an eventful life, but what he had chosen to focus on in *The Lost Library*, a memoir written thirty years earlier, were the books assembled by his father in the years leading up to World War I and passed on to him as his sole inheritance. It was a gathering of wisdom that he came to appreciate fully only when forced to flee for his life, leaving it behind.

"I was driven out by highly cultivated barbarians, by technically trained primitives, by uniformed cannibals," he wrote angrily of the seven-year flight that took him back and forth across Europe, pausing at one point "in the gay and slowly parching oasis" of Vienna with the idea of being repatriated with his library. Through friends, and by "devious means" that he did not elaborate, Mehring arranged to have his "legacy of books" sent on to him in Austria. "In going to so much trouble I was flouting the basic rule of exile, which prohibits such pleasures as settling down where you like to be or reading whatever you enjoy." It was not any specific title that Mehring had wanted so desperately to read; there were plenty of books in Vienna he could get. "I was not so much interested in individual books as in the unique historical, aesthetic and philosophical configurations in my father's library," a gathering that together "formed his particular horoscope of the nineteenth century. And I wanted to examine that horoscope once more and to see its pattern, no matter how fantastic or catastrophic the prediction." When at long last the books did arrive, Mehring spent a week with them trying to "restore the original mosaic of the library" in his flat, occasionally resorting to his "visual memory" of where certain volumes had been located by their bindings and spine decorations. "Finally the job was done and the three walls of my furnished room in Vienna were covered. Returning late at night and switching on the floor lamp, I felt that the books formed a magical pentagram and other necromantic patterns, producing an atmosphere that was both homelike and eerie, and bringing the dead to life." At that point he began to "read madly," morning, noon, and night. "A man can become as addicted to reading as to any other intoxicant."

When Austria was annexed by Hitler on March 12, 1938, Mehring knew his days in Vienna were numbered. He called his landlord on the telephone, and was given a simple piece of advice. "You had better not come home again. You have had visitors and they have already taken your books with them." The realization was instantaneous:

> Never had I possessed my library so literally, so physically, as at that moment when I lost it. Never, not for decades, had I read it so thoroughly as I did right then, after the lightning had struck it. I ran through the books from A to Z. Never had I longed for it so intensely as then when I was leaving it in the lurch. Never had I felt that seductive power of its intellectual charms, its grace of form, as then when I was leaving it in an express train without turning back to look at it, or at this city of Sodom and Gomorrah where inno-cent readers like myself were being humiliated, butchered, dragged away from their desks, their libraries, their cafés and their beds into slavery.

Mehring left quickly, his eyes "fixed ahead" in front of him, "lest I be changed into a pillar of salt."

Up to the day of his death in 1929, Aby Warburg, the pioneering art historian and philanthropist the critic George Steiner would call "one of the seminal figures in modern culture," believed that the eighty-thousand-volume library he had assembled so assiduously over the previous forty years would outlast by generations the family banking fortune that had financed its formation. "Aby saw the coming threats to civilization and heard the jackboots marching," the historian Ron Chernow wrote in an exhaustive history of the Warburg family dynasty. "He believed his library could be an antidote to the menace."

Born in Hamburg in 1866, Warburg studied the history of art in Bonn, Florence, and Strasbourg, writing his doctoral thesis on Botticelli's mythologies. After completing his formal studies, he immersed himself in the archives of Florence, becoming a leading authority on fifteenth-century Italy. Throughout his life as a probing intellectual, Warburg was driven to understand how memory of the past affects the development of culture, focusing on the influence the classical tradition has had on European civilizations. To support this scholarly pursuit, he set about building a sophisticated open-access library, which in 1921 became the raison d'être for establishment of the Warburg Institute in Hamburg. Fritz Saxl, the institute's founding director, recalled what it was like to visit his colleague's house, where the material was gathered: "From floor to ceiling the walls were covered with books, the pantry became a stack-room, heavy shelves were hanging dangerously over doors, the billiard room had been changed into an office, in the hall, on the landings, in the drawing-room of the family—everywhere, books, books, books; and new books came in every day. Something had to be done."

In 1926 that "something" became the formal opening of the Warburg Institute's new home, built on a piece of land adjoining the family residence and equipped with such modern accoutrements as a pneumatic book-ordering system and sturdy steel shelving. As a motto, Warburg had the name of the Greek goddess of memory, Mnemosyne, inscribed above the entrance to the front door. It was a glorious beginning, but seven years later the Nazis declared the "Jewish Warburg Library" off-limits and closed to scholars. By then Aby had already died, and although his surviving brothers had never shared his passion for books, they were determined to protect the institute he had founded.

It was only through a legal loophole that the collections were not confiscated outright, a stroke of good fortune that gave the brothers a window of opportunity to engineer a massive exodus. Because 60 percent of the library had been inherited by Felix and Paul Warburg, who then were living in the United States, a statement was issued in Berlin declaring portions of it to be American property. Fortified with what everyone understood was nothing more than temporary immunity, plans were made for a daring flight to safe haven. Several options had been explored, including sending the library to New York University. The Dutch and the Italians had made offers of assistance as well, but in each instance an unconditional gift of the books was expected in return for providing asylum.

A far more agreeable solution came from London, where an ad hoc committee headed by Viscount Lee of Fareham proposed temporary lodgings in Thames House, with the understanding that the Warburgs would cover all expenses while the institute was there in exile. With this agreement in hand, the family moved quickly in December 1933; the entire library, including the fancy shelving and modern bookbinding equipment, was packed aboard two cargo ships, *Hermia* and *Jessica*, which were standing by at the Elbe River docks. The circumstance of Hamburg being a port city outside the immediate reach of Berlin may well have been the difference between evacuating the library safely and having it seized. Two weeks after the cargo had been unpacked in London, the Propaganda Ministry of Joseph Goebbels assumed jurisdiction of the matter, a turn of events that almost certainly would have prevented the books from leaving had time been lost in arranging for the departure.

When three years had elapsed—and with the Nazis still firmly in control of Germany—the decision was made to stay in England for good. The Warburg Institute moved to the Imperial Institute Buildings in 1937, and in 1944 it was incorporated into the University of London; fifty years after that it became a founding member of the university's School of Advanced Study. By 2000 the collection had grown to 350,000 highly specialized volumes, about 40 percent of which are not in the British Library. "The Anglo-Saxon culture that had struck Aby as such a lethal menace to mankind during World War I," Chernow wrote, "had ended up safeguarding his own legacy."

5.

From the Ashes

The stone which the builders refused is become the head stone of the corner.
—PSALM 118

In the early evening hours of August 25, 1992, Serbian nationalist soldiers nested in the craggy hills surrounding the besieged city of Sarajevo trained their artillery pieces on a graceful building that for four decades had functioned admirably as home to the National and University Library of Bosnia and Herzegovina. Shortly after 10 P.M., the gunmen opened fire with a barrage of incendiary shells from four elevated positions, using a proven targeting technique known as bracketing to measure the precise range for their volleys. Before long spotters were reporting direct hits on the structure's most prominent features, a stained-glass skylight and a rounded copper cupola, and within minutes the architectural landmark known to local residents as Vijecnica (Town Hall) was spewing flames high into the night sky. Attempts to save the irreplaceable contents were heroic, but in the end hopelessly futile. A makeshift crew that had ventured inside the doomed structure on the ground floor barely escaped serious injury when a band of narrow support columns in the old reading room began to explode from the intense heat, causing a section of the roof to come crashing down in a cascade of flaming rubble. Hampered by low pressure in the water mains, firefighters watched helplessly as the north wall collapsed and as the priceless patrimony of a beleaguered people went up in smoke.

Fueled by fifteen thousand meters of wooden shelving and a collection of books estimated to have numbered 1.5 million volumes, the fire smoldered for three days, filling the hot summer sky with clouds of searing fragments that one witness described as a blizzard of sooty black snow. Ignoring the threat of sniper fire coming in from the mountains, volunteers set up a web of human chains and removed 100,000 volumes from the stricken building. An official casualty list released by Bosnia's Ministry of Health disclosed that 14 people were killed and 126 wounded in Sarajevo on the day the library was attacked. Listed among the victims was Aida Buturovic, a thirty-two-year-old cataloger struck by shrapnel from a mortar shell while returning home after a frenzied night of saving books at the library; she died instantly from her wounds.

In addition to mass murder, the methodical obscenity used by the Serbs known as ethnic cleansing during the conflict included the destruction of cultural artifacts, and represented what horrified observers called a systematic "attack on memory" meant to eradicate every trace of a despised neighbor's existence. Killing the people, in other words, was viewed by the perpetrators as little more than a productive beginning to the larger task at hand. "What is more important in a library than anything else—than everything else—is the fact that it exists," the poet-librarian Archibald MacLeish proclaimed in 1971, an assertion that underscored how essential national repositories are to preserving a people's touchstones with their past. Losses at the Sarajevo library were especially crippling, since the holdings represented a common heritage that Muslims, Serbians, and Croatians had shared for more than four hundred years, gathered together after World War II under one roof when the new national library was organized, and the books and archives of the Bosnian Serb community known as Prosvjeta, and the Bosnian Muslim cultural society known as Napredak, became part of the combined collections. Among other materials incinerated were 155,000 rare books and manuscripts, substantial holdings of archival materials, musical scores, historical photographs, prints, and ephemera, along with complete sets of magazines, literary journals, and newspapers published in Bosnia-Herzegovina since the mid-nineteenth century. The entire periodicals collection was lost too, as were the library's card catalogs.

Built on the banks of the Miljacka River at the edge of the Ottoman quarter near the center of town, the building originally functioned as a municipal center for the city of Sarajevo, and was completed in 1896 when Bosnia and Herzegovina were part of the Austro-Hungarian Empire. Designed in a pseudo-Moorish style, Vijecnica (pronounced VYECH-neetsa) complemented the graceful mosques that distinguished the city's elegant skyline. On June 28, 1914, Archduke Ferdinand of Austria and his wife, Sophie, were assassinated by a Serbian terrorist after leaving a reception in the building, the event that set in motion the outbreak of World War I.

Established in 1945, the National Library was stocked with books from several collections that had survived the ravages of world war, and moved into the old town hall in 1951. Once the institution was designated official depository for works published in Bosnia and Herzegovina and the territory of Yugoslavia, its holdings began to grow rapidly. With formation of the University of Sarajevo in 1957, it became an academic research facility as well, and began an active exchange of materials with many of the world's major institutions. A number of important manuscript archives were acquired during this period, including those of the Croatian poet Silvije Stahimir Kranjcevic and the Serbian poet Aleksa Simic.

If the 1992 bombardment had been an isolated incident in the three-and-a-half-year war that claimed ten thousand lives in Sarajevo alone, Serbian denials of having deliberately earmarked books for destruction might not have met with such disbelief throughout the world. But three months earlier, the Oriental Institute in Sarajevo, repository for one of Europe's most extensive collections of Islamic and Jewish manuscripts, was also targeted by the Serbs. Lost in that assault were 5,263 bound manuscripts in Arabic, Persian, Turkish, Hebrew, and a local Serbo-Croat-Bosnian Arabic script known as *alhamijado* or *adʒamijski,* along with thousands of documents from the Ottoman era. Other attacks were carried out on the library of the Museum of Herzegovina, the Archives of Herzegovina, the library of the Roman Catholic Archbishopric in Mostar, and the Orthodox monastery in Zitomislic.

A year and a half after the National Library was destroyed, the American journalist Mark Danner asked Dr. Radovan Karadzic, the leader of the Bosnian Serbs, how a practicing psychiatrist, a published poet who once taught Shakespeare, could justify destroying such an irreplaceable cultural legacy. "It was a Christian building, you know, from the Austro-Hungarian period, and so the Muslims hated it," he replied, insisting that the Muslims had ignited the building themselves in an attempt "to gain the sympathy" of the world. "Only Christian books were burned," he claimed. "The others were removed." He was equally dismissive of matters relating to all the other charges as well, even any culpability for initiating mass killings. "The Serbs did not invent ethnic cleansing," he said. "The Croats did, in World War II."

Investigating what he described as "culturecide" during the war in Bosnia, British journalist Robert Fisk reported seeing widespread destruction of historic buildings and precious artifacts throughout the region formerly known as Yugoslavia. "It is sometimes a shock to find something that has survived," he wrote, noting his astonishment that the greatest treasure of the badly damaged sixteenth-century Karadjoz-Bey mosque, a fragile Koran handwritten and illuminated in gold in Baghdad during the 1300s, escaped incineration only because it had been placed for safekeeping beneath the floorboards of a grimy outhouse. "You have to understand that the cultural identity of a population represents its survival in the future," Jan Boeles, head of the Dutch delegation to the European Community Monitor Mission investigating possible war crimes, told Fisk. "When the Serbs blow up the mosque of a village and destroy its graveyards and the foundations of the graveyards and mosque and level them all off with a bulldozer, no one can ever, ever tell this was a Muslim village. This is the murder of a people's cultural identity."

Several thousand miles away from Sarajevo, in a ground-floor office of the Fine Arts Library at Harvard University in Cambridge, Massachusetts, an American librarian followed news of the destruction of the Oriental Institute in May 1992 with a growing sense of helplessness. András J. Riedlmayer, bibliographer in charge of the Documentation Center of the Aga Khan Program for Islamic Architecture at the university, first learned of the attack while browsing the Internet. A native of Budapest who moved to the United States as a child following the failed Hungarian uprising against the Soviet Union in 1956, Riedlmayer has a deep sense of displacement that is fueled by personal experience. "At first I thought the world would rise up in outrage," he told me in the first of several interviews I conducted with him for this book. "I assumed that professional groups everywhere would take some action, and that some international organization like UNESCO would issue a statement, at least, in support of our Bosnian colleagues. But there was nothing, not a murmur, nobody even took cognizance of the fact, let alone raised a voice in protest or tried to help. I was just absolutely flabbergasted." Riedlmayer vented his frustration by writing letters, making telephone calls, and posting appeals on various electronic forums, hoping to find others who shared his sense of outrage. "Nobody wanted to touch it with a ten-foot pole. The American Library Association, for one, said, 'We don't do politics. Burning books is a political act.' "

Then in August came word that the National and University Library had been destroyed, and once again the world press paid scant attention. Typical was the coverage accorded by the *New York Times,* which used an Associated Press dispatch on August 27, 1992, to report the bombing in four sentences; twenty months elapsed before the newspaper mentioned the bombing again. Determined to help the Bosnians reclaim at least part of their history, Riedlmayer focused his immediate attention on the most formidable challenge of all, how to deal with the loss of unique items such as manuscripts. When he learned that the losses at the Oriental Institute included thirty cabinets of microfilmed material, most of it obtained from foreign countries, a strategy began to take shape. Because libraries routinely build their international collections by exchanging microfilm with other institutions, it stood to reason that duplicate copies of Bosnian material existed in other parts of the world. Working with Amila Buturovic, a scholar now working in Toronto and the sister of Aida Buturovic, the cataloger killed in the attack on the national library, and Irvin Schick, a research engineer, Riedlmayer established the Bosnian Manuscript Ingathering Project on the World Wide Web, and launched an international appeal to help locate copies of lost originals, either in microfilm or photocopies of any manuscripts that visiting scholars might have made while conducting research in Sarajevo. "We are even interested in getting any handwritten notes that might have been made," Riedlmayer said. "We are also tracking down where lost original manuscripts were reproduced in publications. A lot of splendid manuscripts were used to illustrate coffee-table books, and if the resolution is good, sometimes you can read the text." That phase of the effort has succeeded in locating about a hundred pages of text.

The reclamation project is one of enormous hope, and when victories arrive, they arrive one by one. "The alternative is to do nothing, and by doing nothing you surrender," Riedlmayer said. In the first ten years of operations, the effort managed to locate about one thousand pages of photocopies that reproduce all or part of thirty different manuscripts, barely a dent in the 5,263 volumes of unique material and 200,000 documents that had been lost, but a hopeful start nonetheless. From Canada came the most exciting response so far. A retired scholar who had conducted research in Bosnia in 1981 sent full or partial copies of seventeen works, fourteen of them in Ottoman Turkish, two in Persian, and one in

Arabic, several of them copies of texts not recorded in other collections. The items included the full text of a collection of anecdotes written in Ottoman Turkish by an anonymous author in 1585; another was an excerpt from a sixteenth-century Ottoman work on the discovery of the New World, based on texts translated from Latin and Spanish.

Among more recently recovered items are photocopies reproducing thirteen Ottoman-era literary manuscripts made at the Oriental Institute by a retired Turkish scholar from Macedonia; Riedlmayer and his colleagues were able to trace the man to his home in Gostivar, west of Skopje, and persuaded him to make annotated copies of what he had for the ingathering project. Another group of recovered historical documents—a series of nineteenth-century court records from several Bosnian towns—had been copied in the 1980s by a German graduate student doing research for her thesis; the woman was tracked down in West Africa, where she had moved with her husband to work on a development project, and copies of her work ultimately were retrieved from storage. All of these materials have been digitally scanned and made accessible on the Internet.

Less problematic, but by no means simpler to organize, is the matter of rebuilding the library's collection of printed books. To this end, a parallel effort to the manuscript ingathering project, managed by Riedlmayer's colleague at the Fine Arts Library, Jeffrey B. Spurr, secured donations of monographs published by twenty-five university presses throughout North America. Some forty thousand books were gathered and sent to Sarajevo in five shipments between 1996 and 1999 by the Sabre Foundation, a nonprofit group that is committed to helping needy countries restock library collections destroyed by war or natural catastrophe, and to assist Third World countries in establishing new collections. "This program is a substantiation of what books are all about," Spurr said. "Books are mainly about the transmission of knowledge; that is why they are primary targets in wartime."

What was lost forever on the evening of August 25, 1992, can only be surmised, for the simple reason that along with thousands of books and manuscripts, the bibliographic record also went up in flames. But there are some clues in other libraries. An effort operated jointly by the University of Michigan and the Online Computer Library Center, Inc., of Columbus, Ohio (OCLC), searched the computerized records of collections maintained in its Online Union Catalog for mention of any materials relating to the history, literature, and culture of Bosnia, and assembled a list of titles in an effort to reconstruct a catalog. At the time of the first search in November 1996, the OCLC WorldCat database contained 36 million records; 103,983 matched one or more of the criteria that had been established, although a number were multiple hits. Of these, 78,766 records matched the language code for Serbo-Croatian, followed by 35,003 retrievals listing a Bosnian author as either the main entry or as an added entry. A detailed report of the findings can be viewed at the OCLC website, but clearly a meaningful first effort at some semblance of a reconstruction was made. In 1997 the University of Chicago's Regenstein Library announced it would reproduce a large set of reference materials it had located, including chronicles on the Ottoman Empire, almanacs published in Arabic in the late nineteenth and early twentieth centuries, political newspapers, and scholarly journals. The university also prepared a bibliography of twenty-seven hundred works contained in its libraries pertaining to Bosnia and Herzegovina, and presented that as well to library officials in Sarajevo.

"You can never re-create the library, but you certainly can reconstruct a library," Spurr said of these initial efforts. "You will never re-create what was. When the Oriental Institute burned, and its thousands of original manuscripts went up in smoke, there is no way that anything but a small fraction of those materials will be retrieved. But we have to do something." A decade after the firebombing, the old town hall remained an empty shell, its roof finally restored in 1997 with $825,000 committed by the Austrian government, but its future function still very much in question—a symbolic memorial of some kind has been proposed—though the likelihood of another library going inside remains a remote prospect. But hope, as the saying goes, springs eternal; on the occasion of the tenth anniversary of the attack in 2002, the European Union committed 1.5 million euros for use in repairing the building.

Toward the end of 1999 Riedlmayer and Amila Buturovic traveled to Sarajevo to attend a conference and used the occasion to turn over the material reclaimed by the ingathering project to that point. Riedlmayer would make similar trips in June 2001 and July 2002, but the significance of what he and his colleagues had achieved was felt most profoundly on that initial visit. It was a snowy November day, and as Riedlmayer and Buturovic walked across what used to be Sniper Alley to the combined headquarters of the National Library and the Oriental Institute in what was once the Marshal Tito Military Barracks, its exterior walls still riddled with the pockmarks of wartime, he sensed the full impact of what had been accomplished. "That first time is when everything we were trying to do felt real," he said. "We were carrying a large plastic shopping bag with seven hundred pages of manuscript on acid free paper, and a CD-ROM with image files for each page, all tied with library tape. We were bringing these shadows of burned manuscripts home." As Riedlmayer recalled the memory of the transfers for me, he was working on an ingathering program he had established that would do for the battered region of Kosovo and its lost library treasures what had been done for Bosnia. "People wonder why I worry about books when so many people have died and suffered," he said. "When I am asked that question, I point to Aida Buturovic. The two issues are really one. They are inseparable."

For those who wonder whether any significant form of large-scale reconstitution can ever take place in Sarajevo, there is a notable precedent to consider, one brought about by a deliberate book-burning that occurred seventy-eight years to the day before the National Library of Bosnia and Herzegovina went up in flames. Once again, it came as the result of failed politics run amok. When World War I broke out at the stroke of midnight on August 4, 1914, German troops stormed across the border with Belgium and raced across the countryside. Encountering weak opposition in the open fields, the kaiser's forces reported being constantly harassed by lone-wolf combatants known as *franc-tireurs,* or "free shooters," although doubt remains as to whether or not such a resistance was actually ever mounted, or cited merely as a pretext to justify the reprisals that were ordered. The German response was expressed most tellingly in the city of Louvain, home to a university founded in 1425 by Pope Martin V that had numbered among its faculty the cartographer Gerardus Mercator (1512–1594), the anatomist Andreas Vesalius (1514–1564), the humanist and philosopher Justus Lipsius (1547–1606), and the archetypal man-of-letters Desiderius Erasmus (c. 1466–1536), who pioneered the concept of a trilingual college—teaching in Greek, Latin, and Hebrew—at the institution.

Just three weeks after hostilities among the Western powers were declared, German soldiers occupied Louvain and began setting fire to eleven hundred buildings in the city, many of them masterpieces of Gothic and Renaissance architecture. In a rampage that went unchecked for six days, 248 civilians who had been taken as hostages were executed outright; others were used as human shields by the troops. Brand Whitlock, the American minister to Belgium during World War I and ambassador to the country afterward, wrote in a volume of wartime memoirs how hordes of "sinister figures in lurid grey" inflicted a "vast and appalling tragedy" on the medieval city. "The whole library, with all its riches, was deliberately and systematically burned," he wrote, describing an action that destroyed an irreplaceable collection that included one thousand incunabula and eight hundred illuminated manuscripts. In a private report conveyed to the Vatican in 1915, Monsignor Paulin Ladeuze, the university rector, lamented that "in nine or ten hours, all that remained of this enormous building and the 300,000 volumes it contained were four walls and ashes." When the university reopened in 1919, Ladeuze remained irate at what he had observed. "At Louvain," he declared, "Germany disqualified itself as a nation of thinkers."

The actual provocation for the atrocity remains unclear to this day— some accounts blame scattered sniper fire, others cite confusion and panic among inexperienced German troops—but historians agree that the action served no military purpose whatsoever. International reaction was so intense that ninety-three German professors, scholars who included Paul Ehrlich, Fritz Haber, Lujo Brentano, and Max Reinhardt, signed a declaration issued six weeks afterward on October 4, 1914, asserting that Germany had not "sinfully violated the neutrality of Belgium," and that the selective destruction of Louvain had been taken by German soldiers as a countermeasure "against frenzied inhabitants who had treacherously attacked them in their billets." The professors pointed out that most of the city had been left intact, although they failed to explain why the library had been singled out for immolation. Later examination of fifty diaries known as *Kriegstagebücher* kept by German soldiers corroborated accounts of widespread atrocities, however, including charges that they had used Belgian civilians as human shields and had engaged in widespread pillage. Hugh Gibson, another American diplomat who witnessed the atrocities, was told by a German commander that the city's fate had been determined at the highest levels: "We shall wipe it out, not one stone will stand upon another! Not one, I tell you. We will teach them to respect Germany. For generations people will come here to see what we have done."

On that point, at least, the German officer was correct. The eminent British military historian John Keegan ranked the destruction of Louvain— the "Oxford of Belgium," he called it—as among the "worst of all outrages" committed during World War I, and he credited this affront more than any other with mobilizing world opinion against Germany. "American as well as European universities denounced the atrocity and committees were formed in twenty-five countries to collect money and books for the restoration of the Louvain library." Within a month of the conflagration an international drive had been organized by President Lawrence Lowell of Harvard University. When the war ended four years later, Germany was required under terms of Article 247 of the Treaty of Versailles to make unprecedented reparations of "manuscripts, incunabula, printed books, maps and objects of collection corresponding in number and value to those destroyed in the burning by Germany of the Library of Louvain." In due course Germany turned over materials valued at 13 million marks to the Belgians. A new library designed by the New York architect Whitney Warren opened its doors on July 4, 1928; American Independence Day was chosen for the dedication as a gesture of thanks to the people of the United States for their help. By 1939 about 900,000 volumes were on the shelves, only to have history repeat itself a year later when Hitler's Wehrmacht occupied the city and exacted a comparable measure of spiteful retribution. Rebuilt and restocked anew, the library reopened once again in 1951.

Seventeen years after reopening for the second time in the twentieth century, the Louvain library took another unlikely turn, one that does not bear directly on the willful destruction of books but is instructive nonetheless. Until the end of the eighteenth century, Latin was the teaching language of Louvain. As it was replaced by French and Dutch—the languages spoken by the two competing segments of Belgian society—a polarity of interests developed among students and faculty that followed the language dispute that had been simmering throughout the country, with half the country populated by French-speaking Walloons, the other half steeped in the history and culture of Flanders and speaking a Dutch dialect known as Flemish. In 1968 the University of Louvain split into two "linguistic zones." Twenty miles to the south of Louvain, a parallel university, known as Louvain-la-Neuve, French for "the new Louvain," was opened on seven hundred acres of farmland, and a new city was built around it. Each of the two divisions—the French-speaking Université Catholique de Louvain and the Flemish-speaking Katholieke Universiteit Leuven—was given separate legal status. When it came to the library, it was agreed that books with even call numbers would remain in Louvain, those with odd numbers would go to Louvain-la-Neuve. The split extended to multivolume titles, right down the middle. Especially remarkable are reports that both sides are exceedingly comfortable with the results.

In the fall of 1996, Kemal Bakaršic had been traveling through much of the United States talking to people about the destruction of the National and University Library in Sarajevo and trying to mobilize international support for its reconstruction and replenishment. He had met with Hillary Clinton at the White House, addressed potential donors, and consulted with colleagues at institutions around the country. After a late-afternoon symposium at Boston College, he had agreed to join me at the Legal Sea Foods restaurant in the nearby Chestnut Hill Mall for a couple of beers and some fresh shellfish. "If my wife knew I was having oysters without her, there would be a divorce," he said in his heavily accented English, but there was no doubt he was willing to take his chances just the same. We were standing in the lounge of the crowded restaurant, drinking frosted mugs of Sam Adams lager at a counter and enjoying double platters of nicely chilled bluepoints garnished with freshly grated horseradish and plump lemon wedges. When the dishes had been cleared, I asked Bakaršic to describe for me the night four years earlier when Serbian gunners launched their attack on the National Library. Before the outbreak of hostilities in 1992, he had served as chief librarian of the National Museum of Bosnia and Herzegovina, a separate operation, and during the conflict as assistant minister in the Ministry of Culture, Education, Science and Sport charged with trying to rebuild the national library.

It was a busy weeknight, and the restaurant was mobbed with noisy people, so I held my tape recorder under Bakaršic's chin to pick up as much as I could.

"It was so hot," he said. "Summer in Sarajevo is most unpleasant, because we are surrounded by hills, and nothing moves. It was twenty-seven degrees Celsius scale, without water—*without water*—plus the smoke. And because there was no wind, the leaves of the books were floating very slowly. And really, you can capture a leaf in your hand, and you can *read* it before it disintegrates. The text is black, the background is gray, you can *feel* the heat, and the instant the heat goes into your palm, it all melts. But there is a moment where you have a final chance to make out a line or two, a word or two, and you realize you are the last person on earth who is able to do this. Then you see it crumble and disintegrate in your hands. This was the most horrible feeling. I tried to catch as many pages as I could, but what could I do except collect the ashes, because when you catch it, it just melts."

Bakaršic held his hands out, palms up, and gave a poignant pantomime of what it was like to reach helplessly for shards of a heritage that were about to dissolve into nothingness. He was just thirty-six years old the night of the attack, forty when we talked about it that evening in the Boston suburbs. By that time he had achieved a degree of international celebrity after it was reported that he was the person responsible for rescuing an ancient book known as the Sarajevo Haggadah, "the jewel of the National Museum," and for installing it in a safe deposit box in the Central Bank and keeping it safe from danger. Of particular moment was the ecumenical nature of this particular copy of a religious text produced in the Kingdom of Aragon around 1350 containing the readings for Passover, which is illustrated with sixty-nine hand-painted miniatures. It had been brought to Bosnia in the early 1600s by a community of Sephardic Jews expelled from Spain who sought refuge in Sarajevo, where Muslim, Jewish, and Christian craftsmen, merchants, scholars, clerics, and laborers had lived and worked in harmony, and where religious and cultural diversity was accepted as part of their daily lives.

Only a few manuscripts produced during this remarkably productive period of Hebrew book-making in Spain have survived, and none in the country of their origin. There were several convulsive disturbances over the next four hundred years, any one of which could easily have resulted in destruction of the book, but somehow it always managed to endure. In 1697 Habsburg soldiers under the command of Prince Eugene of Savoy ordered Sarajevo sacked and burned. "We let the city and the whole surrounding area go up in flames," he wrote in his diary, and he specifically recorded the destruction of 120 mosques. The city square was leveled and the synagogue razed, yet the Haggadah escaped. Huge quantities of books and artworks were seized and sent off to Berlin during the German occupation of World War II, and there were specific instructions to confiscate the Sarajevo Haggadah. Dervis Korkut, the director of the National Museum, is credited with smuggling the book out of the building and hiding it in a mountain village for the duration of the war— beneath the threshold of a peasant's front door by one account, in an apple orchard according to another.

The circumstances surrounding the book's survival half a century later suggested yet another irony. Unlike Vijecnica, which was built well within the interior of Sarajevo, the National Museum stood at the very edge of the city in the Grbavica district. When the barricades went up in March 1992, Bakaršic and his colleagues were determined to protect their collections. "I am the *kustos,* the custodian of the museum library," he said of his decision to hide the 200,000 volumes placed under his supervision. "I was absent from home for days at a time over the course of many weeks, and whenever I left the museum I kissed the walls and the doors, saying 'Please, God! Don't let the building get burned. Not yet!' "

Each night he would tell his wife, Marina, what he had accomplished during the day. "I would describe for her the books we had rescued, the titles and authors, the design, the front covers, all in great detail, as if making the confession of the last man who would ever see them." About two kilometers of books were removed over the next two months, and all of the museum exhibits, some of which had been there for 105 years, were preserved. Within a matter of days, the building was finally attacked and left in ruins. Bakaršic stessed in these discussions with me that he is a scholar with no political background or any agenda to promote. "I am a Muslim. I am an atheist. I am a computer man. I think I am a cosmopolitan kind of a guy. Marina's father is a Croat from Sarajevo. Her mother is a Serb from Banja Luka. We celebrate all the religious holidays, Muslim, Catholic, and Orthodox. Both my sisters are married to Croats. So we are mixed in every way. And with most people in Sarajevo, I believe you will find that the story is the same."

In a short essay he wrote of his experiences during the siege of the city, Bakaršic recalled the events of one night, April 22, 1992, with such clarity that he chose to set it down in the present tense. "At about 9:30 P.M., an 82mm mortar shell explodes in our garden, shattering the windows of the living room where we sit," he wrote. "Tiny particles of glass fill the air. We feel a warm blast, and smell the intense smell of explosives and melted glass. Are we still alive? For a moment, which seems to last about an hour, we do not know." The next morning—Shakespeare's birthday—Kemal and Marina noticed that a "very special" book in their household, the letters of 1926 between Boris Pasternak, Marina Tsvetsayeva, and Rainer Maria Rilke, had been knocked off the shelf by the concussion. "It is the first book I ever gave to my own Marina. Picking it up from the floor, we are terrified to find a large piece of shrapnel embedded in the cover. And yet, we are grateful, because a kind of miracle has occurred. From this morning on, we call this collection of poets' letters the Book that Saved Our Lives."

Bakaršic gave me a copy of this essay as I drove him back to Cambridge, where he was staying while in Massachusetts. I kept my tape recorder running during the ride from Chestnut Hill to Harvard Square, and for another half hour after I had parked the car. He spoke about his experiences the entire time. "I feel enormous guilt, because I lied to myself," he said at one point. "I always thought this madness would end soon. But I was wrong. Before the war, I was just a little baby. My life was books. I was sort of a homegrown dinosaur. My life was in the library. I spent endless hours there working on my Ph.D. thesis. I didn't read daily newspapers, I didn't pay attention to politics. I am just a librarian, and things happened the way they happened."

As to why the library was destroyed, there was never any doubt in Bakaršic's mind about the motives of the Serbs. "I was frightened to death," he said of his initial reaction. "Hearing the shells that were dropping one after the other, we all knew that the library was being fired upon deliberately, that it was the books they meant to destroy. The first attack lasted twelve minutes, and most of the shells hit the target." When the sun came up in the morning, he was greeted by the sight of pages falling from the sky.

"Even though our national library was burned to the ground, I don't think they were successful in military terms," he said. "I still think that if all the libraries are burned, there is still the possibility to reconstruct some portion of them. Why they choose to do this is outside my scope of understanding. They tried to do something evil, and they succeeded. The trouble is that I still do not believe that the library is gone. I still do not believe that the burning of the library happened. You know why that is? Because I do not have the right answer to why they did it."

To keep books alive during the darkest days of the siege, Bakaršic said that he and his wife drew on a library of the imagination they had established early on in their relationship. "It is very hard to destroy what you really love, and the books we cherish remain in our minds. Why do you read a book? You want to open your mind to a different experience. You are discovering words that do not have meaning by themselves. You can destroy the books, but you cannot destroy the vision."

During the long nights without electricity, Bakaršic said that he and Marina would recite favorite song lyrics to each other, then move on to verses of poetry and excerpts from beloved works of fiction. "We recite all the songs that we have ever heard. We sing to each other different kinds of tunes, and we sing them again and again. We summarize and repeat all the books that we have ever read. Then we reread the home library that we have, and then we do that again and again too, to keep ourselves busy, to provoke the fine feeling, the good vibrations. We stop this ritual, finally, by going to sleep. When I fall asleep, I start snoring, so I have developed a habit; if my wife goes to sleep first, I can easily fall asleep afterward, and then snore without bothering her, because she is a very sound sleeper. And only then do I stop this ritual of recollecting the memory of what we've read, what we've heard, what we've seen, because my wife at a certain point always says, 'Oh please, Kemal, shut up, you're repeating yourself.' Then I stop, and all these things end in dreams."

When a group of twenty Roman Catholic Armenian monks known as vartabeds arrived in Venice in 1715, their goal was nothing less than the preservation of an imperiled culture. Led by Abbot Mekhitar Petrosian of Sebastia (1676–1749), the exiles had been forced from their homeland in Asia Minor by the Ottoman Turks, their ancestral enemies. By picking Venice, the Catholic monks had chosen wisely, since offering sanctuary was a custom deeply rooted in local history. The first settlers of the scrubby islands in the marshy lagoon off the Adriatic coast of Italy during the sixth century had been refugees themselves, driven from their homes in what is now northern Italy by successive waves of Visigoths, Huns, Vandals, Ostrogoths, and Lombards. Their hope, largely realized, was that the barbarian hordes would bypass their odd settlements scattered about the shoals, preferring instead to plunder more accessible places. Acting in a spirit of solidarity—the welcoming hosts also considered the Ottomans an enemy, as Shakespeare makes clear in the play *Othello*, which is set in Venice—the Venetian Senate gave the Armenians title to a tiny island two miles north of the Lido that had been named for Lazarus, the diseased beggar the Bible tells us Jesus raised from the dead. Uninhabited at the time, San Lazzaro had been used in the twelfth century as an asylum for sick pilgrims, and after that as a leper colony. Custody of the island was granted to the congregation "in perpetuity," and the tiny outpost in the lagoon is still known as "the Armenian Island."

Historically, the region known as Armenia included areas in northeastern Turkey and Iranian Azerbaijan that form a continuation of the Anatolian plateau. According to tradition, the kingdom of Armenia was founded by Haik, a descendant of Noah, although modern scholars believe that the people known as Armenians came into Asia Minor from Europe in the eighth century B.C., and formed a distinct nation about two hundred years after that. Occupied successively by Persians, Macedonians, and Syrians, the Armenians declared their independence under a native dynasty in 189 B.C., only to be defeated later by Rome. Armenia claims the distinction of being the first Christian state, having formally embraced the new religion toward the end of the third century through the efforts of Gregory the Illuminator, a saint also known as the Apostle of Armenia. In the early fifth century A.D., the preacher and scholar Mesrop Mashtots (c. 350–440) constructed an alphabet consisting of thirty-six letters from a Greek model; two more letters were added later. What distinguishes the Armenian alphabet from its progenitors is that it provides a separate sign for each sound. The founder of several monasteries, Mesrop dispatched scholars to Constantinople, Alexandria, and Rome to collect literary manuscripts. Using them as primary sources, he personally translated the Bible into the Armenian language. By abandoning Greek and Persian, he had fashioned a distinctive medium by which the Armenians could record their literary, governmental, and religious texts, and it became the chief instrument through which they maintained a spirit of independence through centuries of oppression.

Arriving on San Lazzaro on September 8, 1717, Abbot Mekhitar found buildings "ruined and partly destroyed through long neglect and by the rain, at one time reserved for lepers and those suspected of being infected." The monks restored the existing structures, cultivated the small patch of open ground into a fertile garden, brought in fill to double the acreage, and set about the task of providing for the security of their heritage. An energetic program of gathering early books, manuscripts, paintings, tapestries, and native craft was initiated, with gifts and bequests actively solicited from Armenian expatriates living all over the world. One of Mekhitar's first orders of business was the establishment of a missionary school that encouraged research in Armenian history; then he undertook translating important literary works into Armenian, and Armenian works into more than thirty-five other languages.

In 1796, the abbot's successors established a printing operation on the island that continues to publish a wide variety of religious and secular works; about two thousand titles have been published during its first two centuries of operation. On August 17, 1810, Napoleon Bonaparte, who ruled Venice from 1797 to 1814, issued a decree ordering that the "Armenian Monks of the Island of San Lazzaro" be "kept in their present state," and that their school be known formally as the Academy of Science, a designation it retains to this day. The efforts of the Mekhitarist fathers to preserve their culture took on renewed importance in the twentieth century with numerous atrocities committed by the Turks against the Armenians. Indeed, when the legal scholar Raphael Lemkin coined the word *genocide* in 1944, he cited the wholesale massacre of Armenians in 1915 as the defining example of the phenomenon in the twentieth century. A Jewish native of Poland who lost forty-nine relatives to the Nazi Holocaust, Lemkin spent his life after the war working for passage of a United

Nations declaration condemning the practice of what Winston Churchill had called "the crime without a name."

George Gordon, Lord Byron (1788–1824), a resident of Venice between 1816 and 1817, made regular trips to San Lazzaro, and was enthusiastic about what he found on the tiny island. "I am studying daily at an Armenian monastery, the Armenian language," he wrote the poet Thomas Moore on December 5, 1816. "I found that my mind wanted something craggy to break upon; and this—as the most difficult thing I could discover here for an amusement—I have chosen, to torture me into attention." A day earlier, he proclaimed his enthusiasm at length in a letter to his good friend and publisher in London, John Murray:

> I had begun, and am proceeding in, a study of the Armenian language—which I acquire, as well as I can—at the Armenian convent, where I go every day to take lessons of a learned friar, and have gained some singular and not useless information with regard to the literature and customs of that Oriental people. They have an establishment here—a church and convent of ninety monks—very learned and accomplished men, some of them. They have also a press—and make great efforts for the enlightenment of their nation.

Byron had quickly mastered Italian during his stay in Venice, and found he wanted something more challenging to "twist my mind around" with "severer study." The monks on San Lazzaro were only too happy to indulge him. Rowed out daily by gondola, he was given a paneled room to work in, granted full access to the library's collection of illuminated manuscripts and printed books, and encouraged to enjoy moments of solitude in the garden, a state of quiet bliss he found especially relaxing during moments away from the "fathomless love" of his latest paramour, Marianna Segati, "a very pretty Venetian of two and twenty," and the wife of his landlord ("a very good kind of man who occupies himself else-where"). Studying under Father Paschal Aucher, Byron became fluent in the Armenian language, and as a gesture of compensation—the monks would not accept his money—he collaborated on the production of an English-Armenian grammar, and paid for its publication. He also asked Murray about the availability of Armenian typefaces at either Oxford or Cambridge, with the hope that some of the translations from San Lazzaro might be published in England. "I can assure you that they have some very curious books and MS., chiefly translations from Greek originals now lost." He was so engaged by the exercise on the island that he had "not done a stitch of poetry since I left Switzerland." In another letter to Murray, Byron inquired on the sale of books he had sent to England, and concluded with this admonition: "You must not neglect my Armenians."

A great champion of political liberty, Byron joined a band of Greek insurgents who had risen in 1823 against the Turks, and died of marsh fever the following year at Missolonghi. His memory is honored on San Lazzaro with a stone marker, and the second-floor room he used is preserved intact; a dashing portrait of the flamboyant Romantic poet hangs by his desk. Each day, eight public motor boats known as vaporetti depart the Lido for the twenty-minute ride out to San Lazzaro; visitors arriving at three o'clock in the afternoon are treated to a tour of the complex, including stops in a museum rich in porcelains, carvings, metal works, embroidered textiles, and coins, followed by the church and a modern circular building opened in 1970 known as the "house of the manuscripts." Some 150,000 books are kept in the monastic library, but this tastefully designed repository stands apart. It contains about five thousand Armenian manuscripts produced between the ninth and eighteenth centuries, many of them illuminated with marginal ornaments and exquisite miniatures. Three of the treasures—the Trebizond Gospel and the Gospel of Adrianople, both of the eleventh century, and a Book of Ordinations from the thirteenth century—were included in *The Glory of Byzantium* exhibition mounted at the Metropolitan Museum of Art in New York in 1997. In her catalog description, the medieval art historian Helen C. Evans noted how the Armenians had developed a "distinctive literary and artistic tradition nurtured by their religion, their language, their traditional social structure, and their literature," each of which has been protected for close to three centuries on San Lazzaro Island by the Mekhitarist congregation.

With the partition of Poland in 1795 among Russia, Prussia, and Austria—a territorial division by which the country ceased to exist as a state for one hundred and thirty years—a remarkable public collection of 200,000 books gathered by the brothers Andrzej Stanislaw Zaluski and Jozef Andrzej Zaluski was ordered removed from Warsaw to St. Petersburg in its entirety by Catherine the Great, creating in an instant a credible national library for her people, at the lamentable expense of the Poles. By that time the empress had already demonstrated an insatiable thirst for European treasures, buying up paintings, drawings, and books for the imperial collections. In 1765 she acquired the fabled private library of books amassed by Denis Diderot (1713–1784) in preparation for his monumental *Encyclopédie,* allowing the great French philosopher as part of the deal to take care of the materials in Paris for as long as he wanted, and paying him a handsome salary to serve as his own librarian. Diderot became quite enamored of Catherine—the 41,000 livres she gave him for his books and manuscripts was the equivalent of fifty years' salary—and he served as her unofficial agent in France, advising her on a number of key acquisitions. He once described the czarina as a woman with "the soul of Caesar and all the seductiveness of Cleopatra." Catherine added the seven-thousand-volume library of Voltaire—including fixtures and accoutrements as well as books—to the Hermitage collection in 1778. By the time of the October Revolution in 1917, Russian holdings would rank third largest in Europe behind the British Library and the Bibliothèque Nationale.

Back in Poland, the failure of a popular uprising against Russian domination led to further seizures from the Warsaw Lyceum in 1830, giving the Poles more reason than ever to fear for the survival of their collective memory, and prompting a group of patriots and intellectuals to form cultural retreats in other lands. In Paris, where a large community of émigré artists and intellectuals had set up residence, the Bibliothèque Polonaise was founded in 1838 to serve as a library in exile during the period of Polish partitions, which lasted for another seventy years. Preserving Poland's history, literature, religion, and culture became the main focus of the library's existence, although the collections were broadened into many other areas with gifts from immigrants who continued to carry precious materials with them to Paris. The library still operates at 6, quai d'Orleans on Ile Saint Louis on the Seine, the small island to the east of Ile de la Cité, in the shadow of Notre Dame Cathedral, and maintains a collection of 200,000 books, 2,600 manuscripts, 30,000 prints and photographs, and 800 maps and atlases. A room on the second floor is dedicated to the memory of Frédéric Chopin (1810–1849), the great composer and fervent Polish patriot who spent the final eighteen years of his life in Paris, and was one of the library's most enthusiastic members. Adam Mickiewicz (1798–1855), generally regarded as the greatest of Polish poets, was a founding spirit and frequent visitor to the Bibliothèque Polonaise as well. He taught Slavic languages at Collège de France during his long residence in Paris, and edited the radical newspaper *La Tribune des Peuples;* his desk, manuscripts, and family archives are preserved at the library.

"For the Polish people, the Bibliothèque Polonaise was the Polish national library at a time when there was no Polish state, and it was there years later during the dark days of the Cold War as an alternate voice to Communism," Vartan Gregorian, the former president of the New York Public Library and now the president of the Carnegie Corporation, told me in an interview. "I believe that libraries are sacred places, and the reason they are sacred is because they enable us all to extract what is important from the past and to preserve our collective memories. In this instance, the Bibliothèque Polonaise gave the Polish people a way to hold on to their noble heritage during many years of national trauma."

The rebuilding of a national library in Poland began when the country regained its independence in 1926, only to have its major holdings destroyed by the Germans during World War II as part of a systematic program to eradicate Polish culture, convert the native population into a servant class, and absorb their territory into German Lebensraum, or living space. Organized resistance to the Nazi occupation went beyond acts of sabotage to include formation of a clandestine library that circulated books to Polish scholars who were forbidden access to them by German regulations, but the losses were enormous all the same. Of 22 million volumes maintained in prewar collections of all Polish libraries, only 7 million are known to have survived. With the fall of the Soviet Union and the collapse of the Warsaw Pact in 1991, Poland was finally able to steer a truly independent course. Passage of a Library Law on June 27, 1997, codified the role of the national book repository within the country's library system, and defined its duty to preserve, disseminate, and celebrate Polish heritage.

During the five years that the Khmer Rouge imposed a reign of psychopathic terror on Cambodia in the mid-1970s, close to 2 million people died in an episode of mass murder so loathsome that the words *killing fields* were forged on the world's consciousness. Determined to break entirely with a "decadent" past, the insurgent leader, a former schoolteacher who called himself Pol Pot, renamed the small country of seventy thousand square miles the Republic of Democratic Kampuchea, and created a new calendar to begin with the "Year Zero."

Intent on creating a "pure" identity free of outside influence, and imposing his will through the unquestioning loyalty of his adolescent brigades, Pol Pot banned foreign languages, abolished money, seized private property, outlawed religious rituals, and ordered that children be taken from their parents and instructed in the ways of the new order. To expedite the dismantling of banks, universities, and religious pagodas, Phnom Penh was evacuated of all residents. Outside the capital city, the twelfth-century temple at Angkor Wat was left alone and abandoned to the elements, with all archaeological projects abruptly terminated.

An obvious target of the revolutionaries was the National Library of Cambodia, housed in a building built by the French in 1913 next to an ornamental garden located near the National Archives, and a visible symbol of the old order. Most of the books and all of the bibliographical records that documented a collection, estimated in the "tens of thousands," were tossed out into the streets and burned on the spot; the building itself was used as a pigsty during the years of Khmer Rouge occupation. The few volumes that survived were piled haphazardly in poorly ventilated storage areas and left to rot in the tropical atmosphere.

Even more menacing was the realization that it had become a crime to be literate, and highest on the list of "enemies of the people" were educated professionals. Terrified citizens who insisted they were not "tainted" or "infected" had the bridges of their noses examined for telltale signs of having worn glasses, presumptive evidence of being able to read, which meant a summary sentence of death. No attempt was made to conceal this policy of terror. "We must rid each Party member, each cadre of everything that is of the oppressor class, or private property, stance, view, sentiment, custom, culture, which exists in ourselves, no matter how much or how little," a writer for the official Khmer publication *Tung Padevat* declared in 1976.

According to one authoritative estimate, some 380,000 people who could be described as *intellectuals*—a group that included all scholars, artists, and writers—lived in Cambodia prior to the takeover. When the

Khmer Rouge were ousted in 1979, only 300 of these people were determined to be still alive. Of sixty librarians employed in Phnom Penh before the Khmer Rouge assumed power, three survived the massacre that followed. Out of six hundred skilled sculptors, five managed to stay alive. Just as devastated was the small corps of traditional court dancers whose graceful gestures are carved into the walls of the ancient temples at Angkor Wat. A master dancer named Chheng Phon avoided execution by pretending to be a peasant. Refusing to abandon the intricate movements that had been passed on to him by his mentors, he practiced his art under a mosquito net at night, and hid his songbooks inside the woven walls of a communal hut. All written records of the country's unique dances, however, are believed to have been destroyed. When Chheng Phon was able to teach once again, he tried to pass on what he knew to his young countrymen, but so much more had been irretrievably lost. "Since cultural knowledge rests within the bodies of the dancers, the fact that ninety percent died means much of the repertoire has been lost too," explained Toni Shapiro, an American anthropologist who has studied Cambodian customs.

With the return of some normalcy in the early 1980s, a modest international effort to help Cambodia reclaim its embattled past was initiated. One such program was undertaken by Cornell University in Ithaca, New York, which suddenly found itself in the odd position of maintaining the largest collection of Cambodian materials anywhere on Earth, about two thousand volumes all together, half in Khmer and the rest in French and English. In 1989 the university set up a preservation program in Phnom Penh that would try to save whatever materials remained, and to make microfilm copies for its own archival collections. Cornell's interest in this exotic outpost runs deep. Close to sixty courses specifically concerned with Southeast Asia are offered at the university in a broad range of departments, with another twenty or so dealing extensively with the region. Languages taught at the university include Burmese, Cebuano, Indonesian, Javanese, Tagalog, Thai, Vietnamese, and Khmer.

Arriving in Cambodia in 1989, the first order of business for John F. Dean, director of the Preservation and Conservation Department of the Cornell University Library, was fairly straightforward. "Before we could begin to make copies of anything, we had to instruct people in the basic principles of conservation," he told me in an interview in his Olin Library office. "We started with fundamental principles, things like placing the palm-leaf manuscripts in boxes lined with insect repellant." The university's readiness to help Cambodia came as the result of a number of converging circumstances, not least of which is the sophisticated preservation program it has in place, along with its pioneering projects in digital technology. Equally important is the university's preeminent position as a research center in Southeast Asian studies. "Cornell's Khmer language collections are the strongest in the world, stronger actually than those of the British Library and the Bibliothèque Nationale combined," Dean said. "The fact is that Cornell's collections are considerably stronger than a lot of national libraries in Southeast Asia, which means that any scholar who wants to deal with Southeast Asia in a serious way has to come here to Cornell."

Library and archival materials built to support the Southeast Asian program are concentrated in the John M. Echols Collection, and in extensive holdings maintained in the Department of Manuscripts and University Archives. The 320,000-volume Echols Collection includes 150,000 volumes and 110,000 micro-texts in vernacular languages, nine hundred titles, and 55,000 serial titles. Of 103 collections rated at level five among the university's library holdings—the most comprehensive research-depth ranking that can be assigned—38 are for materials in the Echols Collection. For 11 of those, the university has assumed what is known as Primary Collecting Responsibility, meaning that other institutions will usually defer to Cornell in cases where direct competition becomes an issue.

With the backing of the university and a modest grant from the Christopher Reynold Foundation, Dean and a graduate student attached to the Preservation and Conservation Department, Judith Ledgerwood, traveled to Phnom Penh in 1990 to assess the extent of the losses and to establish priorities. "I had just three weeks there during my first trip, and a good deal of that time was spent in training the staff in fumigation, cleaning, and repair," Dean said. Of immediate concern was the condition of manuscripts written on palm leaves, material that is particularly vulnerable to decay from mold and insect infestation. "Most of these palm-leaf manuscripts are not terribly old, perhaps a hundred years at the most, some more recent than that. Historically, the means of passing this material on has been for Buddhist monks to copy deteriorating manuscripts. They were the essential link to continued preservation. What we found when we arrived in Cambodia was that most of the monks had been killed by the Khmer Rouge. So for the immediate future the only hope is to preserve the surviving manuscripts as best we can, and to make preservation copies on microfilm as quickly as possible."

Palm-leaf manuscripts are made from mature leaves of a specific size. Sometimes the writing is applied directly to the surface, but usually the characters are incised with a sharp point and a mixture of lampblack and oil. To make a "volume," bundles of leaves are bound together by braided cords threaded through two holes, and secured at the front and back by wooden covers. The content, usually religious texts or folk tales written in a language once common in Southeast Asia called Pali, is generally very old. "These are very important collections, many of them unique," Dean said. "You have a tropical climate, tremendous war damage, and a government that is adamant about not letting any of the materials leave the country for treatment. So the obstacles you face are numerous." As part of a reciprocal arrangement, Cornell has been making copies of material from its own collections and presenting them to the Cambodian National Library. "What we are doing, in a way, is helping them reclaim the bibliographic record of their own literature," Dean said, noting that only 20 percent of the national collections survived the Khmer Rouge. Using the materials they have received from Cornell, the Cambodian Ministry of Education is preparing new textbooks to help rebuild the country's school system. In one instance, Judith Ledgerwood was able to present a Cambodian author who survived the carnage, Vandy Kaonn, with photocopies of the four books he had written on literature and society.

An unexpected archive of more recent vintage was discovered in a former Catholic high school that had been converted into an interrogation center known as S-21. "Something like fifteen thousand people were tortured and killed in there, men, women, and children," Dean said, figures that have been corroborated in *Voices from S-21*, a meticulous history by the Australian historian David Chandler that is based on his direct examination of the archival records. "S-21 was a total institution whose mission was to locate, question, and destroy the enemies of the Party Center," Chandler has written, noting that just seven inmates of the old school are known to have survived the nightmare. "Given its prisoner intake and the number of inmates who were executed by the facility, S-21 was probably the most efficient institution in the country," he added.

Both Dean and Chandler make note of the scrupulous nature of the record-keeping that was done in S-21. "The Khmer Rouge were fairly meticulous about their bloody work. They kept very large numbers of 'confessions' they had obtained under torture from these people, hundreds and hundreds of them," Dean said. Some four thousand "confessions" comprising about 400,000 pages survived; the rest were destroyed by the Khmer Rouge before their hasty evacuation. "The ones that were saved were stored in another building, sort of an overflow building, and that's why they made it through. It was just fortuitous, pure happenstance. Filming that material was probably as difficult as anything else we did, because we had a strong inkling all along that this material might disappear." The project to photograph the documents took four years to complete.

"We are the only institution that has a copy of these interrogations," Dean continued. "It required a tremendous amount of tenacity to film them. We had a camera in there, a generator in there, but we had considerable government opposition, and no written permission. When we first went in, the Khmer Rouge had been driven out, but it was the misfortune of the Cambodian people to be rescued by the Vietnamese, and neither the United States nor any other Western nation had any relationship with them. Consequently, it made Cambodia a sort of pariah nation. The only embassies there at the time were the East Germans and the Soviets. So it was not easy for us to do business, and very difficult to get things in or out. Every piece of equipment we wanted to bring in was regarded as strategic material by the United States government. What we ended up doing was to send all the equipment in through Singapore. When the film was shot, it was taken out in a diplomatic bag by the International Red Cross to Bangkok, and then airmailed to us here. We processed it immediately, inspected it, and if there was anything wrong, we would fax a message back to somebody in Bangkok, who would then give that message to the next person going into Cambodia."

In 1993 yet another archive was found in the old school, now known as the Tuol Sleng Museum of Genocide, by two freelance photographers from the United States, Christopher Riley and Douglas Niven, who wanted to locate whatever visual documentation they could find of these horrific crimes. "We came across an incredible historical archive which was clearly on the path to destruction," Riley explained to a wire-service reporter about their discovery. What they found pressed into a bank of dusty drawers were piles of photographic negatives, six thousand all together, gathering fungus and dirt. Given a grant, they began early in 1994 to clean and file the negatives, producing one set for Tuol Sleng, and another for Cornell. Simply stated, the black-and-white photographs show people who are about to be questioned, tortured, and killed. When the conservation project was finished, Riley and Niven gathered a selection of the photographs—mug shots, really—and published them in a book, *The Killing Fields.* A 1997 exhibition at the Museum of Modern Art in New York presented twenty-two of the haunting images.

"There definitely are parallels here with what you have been learning about Bosnia, only a lot bloodier, if that is possible," Dean told me. "You have a regime which set out to smash an entire culture. They killed almost all the librarians and archivists responsible for preserving most of the collections in Cambodia. Anybody who was a teacher, anybody who was educated, was singled out and murdered. They destroyed a great many of the materials in the National Archives and the National Library. So you have a society that was leveled. Under these kind of circumstances, how do you begin to rebuild? There is nothing in your national libraries. How do you start constructing textbooks in primary schools? You don't have any teachers. How do people learn about their history, when all of the materials have been destroyed? Sadly, systematic destruction like this is a very effective way to obliterate a culture."

Although Cornell is among the world's leading innovators of preservation technology, Dean does not believe access to electronic books will be the answer in Third World countries, at least not in the immediate future. "There are a limited number of computers for the library system in Cambodia right now, but they are basically used to produce catalog cards. And that is not so unusual. I am not at all hopeful that those libraries will be fully wired into the Web any time soon. You have to understand that getting typewriter ribbons is a major event for them. Technology is going to provide us with an opportunity to make the materials in our libraries more widely available, but a large part of the world is really going to be left out. Meanwhile, we've got to work with what we've got. Access to electronic communication in most Southeast Asian countries is always going to be difficult. Even if they are able to get some more computers, the ability to keep upgrading the equipment is going to be a great challenge for them. They just don't have the wherewithal to keep up."

A good deal of Cornell's efforts were in literature, and numerous microfilm copies were sent to Cambodia in a modest effort to "reseed" the country's national collections. "We filmed more than twenty-five thousand books in that area alone," Dean said, but as a practical matter, access to the microfilm requires the ready availability of microfilm readers. The university gave the National Library several viewing machines, but the process is cumbersome, and severely limited in the number of people it can reach. Dean put the mission in perspective: "One of the possible benefits of digital technology, and one of the advantages of digital imaging technology, is that, basically, you capture something, and having captured it, you have created a set of images that you can do a lot of things with. It's very flexible. Clearly, you can make those images available over the Web, but not, unfortunately, to countries that do not have access to the Web, or countries that are not up to speed with the prevailing technologies. More important, and I think this is where digital technology can have a real impact, you can replicate a printed volume very, very well, as we have demonstrated here at Cornell, at very high speed, and at low cost. The ability to reproduce books from those images, I think, is very powerful. Because it is digital technology, there is no generational problem. The millionth copy is every bit as good as the first copy, because it's either a zero or a one. So I think the real impact of digital technology on Third World countries may well be in the production of printed copies from digital images."

When I first met with E. Gene Smith in the summer of 1998 to talk about his bold mission to rescue thousands of Tibetan books from an uncertain fate, the onetime Far East field director for the Library of

Congress was playing host to a dozen savants who had been drawn to the cache of precious texts he had gathered over the previous thirty-five years, attracted not only by the plentitude of cultural treasure packed into the Greenwich Village brownstone he had just moved into a few weeks earlier, but for the knowledge and wisdom of the man who had brought it all together with such determined thoroughness. "We are the bees, and Gene is the honey," is the way one of the pilgrims, a Tibetan lama born in exile during the years that the Great Cultural Revolution was wreaking havoc in the land of his forebears, put it when I asked about his reason for coming to New York.

An inviting lunch had been prepared for this festive gathering, and as we sat around a long reading table on that warm July day, good feelings flowed in all directions. My tape recorder was lying in the center of everything, picking up what fragments it could of the conversation, making for a nightmare of transcription later on, but what came through loud and clear from every reach of the room was gratitude for what this most unlikely of bibliophilic Samaritans had accomplished almost single-handedly. When one particularly revered book was brought forth wrapped in a brightly colored silk sheath known as a *peruri*, every person to whom it was passed for examination pressed the volume to his forehead, then kissed it in an expression of high esteem.

"These people here today for the most part are teachers," Smith told me as we watched the ritual unfold. "This is one of the most famous texts in the Tibetan tradition; it is known as the Diamond Cutter Sutra, and what makes this copy so special is that it was never meant to be read outside of a certain circle. It is a text that was calligraphed by a great eighteenth-century lama for one of his students, and was passed on through the student's family. It became what is known as an itinerant, and was given to me as something of a relic. In the case of this work, the content is well known, it is a very traditional text, so the value is artifactual.

The lineage, unfortunately, is now ended, because the student who passed it on—his family—has died out."

At the heart of what Smith was trying to explain to me is a tradition of textual transmission known as the *lung*, which involves a process of reading aloud in the presence of a student. "What a good Tibetan teacher will say is, 'I am going to read this text in your presence just as my teacher has read it in my presence, and his teacher before him,' and so you sit there attentively while the lama reads it to you. Now this may sound strange, but this is the essence of the *lung*. And only after the teacher has given you the *lung*, will he give you a sense of each *word*, will he share an insight into the *meaning*. It is quite a different system of scholasticism, maybe to us it may not seem very efficient at all, but for the Tibetans I think it has proven quite efficient in a *total* context. Truth, after all, is only *true* within a *context*."

A year after that first meeting of ours in lower Manhattan, Smith moved his operation to Cambridge, Massachusetts, drawn there by an opportunity to help him establish the Tibetan Buddhist Resource Center, a nonprofit organization founded with the goal of putting digitally scanned copies of everything he had assembled on the Internet, where it could be widely distributed to everyone free of charge. Setting up shop in a converted duplex in a residential neighborhood, he worked closely with Leonard W. J. van der Kuijp of nearby Harvard University, chairman of the Department of Sanskrit and Indian Studies, and professor of Tibetan and Himalayan studies—a unit that would not exist, the scholar told me matter-of-factly, without the materials made available through Smith's efforts. "There is nobody in the world who knows as much about Tibet as Gene Smith," he said. "Gene is the dean of modern Tibetan studies. He doesn't like to hear this—he is a very modest man—but you will find any number of Tibetans who defer to him in many areas." For the program van der Kuijp directs at Harvard, there are two thousand books available in the university collections, "and if it hadn't been for Gene, there wouldn't be anything at all," he told me. "You will find this to be the case everywhere you look. In fact, without Gene, it is safe to say that this course of study would not be taught anywhere in North America. There simply would be no books—and by this, I mean, of course, *important* books, books that are totally necessary for scholarly inquiry."

I first learned about Smith at a time in the mid-1990s when I was beginning to document egregious instances of the willful destruction of books and the heroic efforts expended by a gallant few to preserve them. On more than one occasion it was suggested to me that an untold story of selfless determination was "out there" begging to be told, and that it involved nothing less than a one-man crusade to rescue a venerable tradition that had come perilously close to disappearing from the face of the earth. What made the story irresistible to me was the assertion that the person responsible for this extraordinary effort was a former Mormon from Utah who set out on this quixotic task in the 1960s at the urging of a mentor who had despaired at his own inability to pass on the insights of the ages without benefit of certain texts.

Smith's teacher, the Venerable Deshung Rinpoche Kunga Tenpai Nyima, tutor to the Sakya Phuntsok Phodrang, had moved to the United States in 1959 after the Chinese invasion of Tibet under the aegis of the Rockefeller Foundation, which had funded the establishment of nine centers for Tibetan studies in Europe and North America. One of these was established in Seattle at the University of Washington, where Smith— who had done undergraduate work at Adelphi and Hobart Colleges and the University of Utah—began graduate work in 1960. "What happened is that the Rockefeller Foundation decided to experiment and bring live Tibetans to a number of centers around the world and see what would happen," Smith told me. "The University of Washington was fortunate in that a very great bibliophile, a man with an encyclopedic mind and a passionate love for books—this person who became my teacher—went there, and not someplace else. My motivation at this point, quite frankly, was to stay out of the draft and not fight in Vietnam, but it wasn't long before I became deeply involved in this work." Focusing at first on anthropology and Inner Asian studies, Smith would spend the next five years with Deshung Rinpoche, asking questions, writing down in blue notebooks insights he received on "wisdom traditions" that took in "the entire range of traditional Buddhist culture, from Tibetan and Sanskrit grammar to Mādhyamika philosophy, from ritual to the arts."

One comment in particular from Deshung changed Smith's life entirely. "We had a handful of books at our disposal in Seattle, perhaps twelve or thirteen volumes, no more than that, and Deshung said to me at one point, 'If we are going to do our program, we need books. Why don't you go to Europe and make copies of what the people have there?' This was in 1962, I was twenty-six years old, and off I went that summer in search of copies at the other Rockefeller centers that had been set up. When I got back, I had a fairly sizable collection of material that had been copied for us, but Deshung said, 'Well, none of this refers to anything you want to study.' So I sort of sat every day at his feet from then until 1965 and continued to write down everything he said. I sat with him for an hour or two each day while he was doing his morning prayers and asked him questions. He finally said to me, 'Go out to India, study with the masters who are there. They will direct you to the things we need.' He told me what books to look for, and many of these were books that I would later arrange to have published through my work with the Library of Congress. Looking back, it was very fortunate that I happened to be in Seattle at the time that he was, because none of this would have ever happened without him."

Traveling under a fellowship from the Ford Foundation, Smith arrived in India in 1965, and for the next three years moved throughout the region among the exile community from Tibet, estimated to number as many as 100,000 refugees. In 1968 he was hired by the New Delhi Field Office of the Library of Congress and given supervision of a project that would shape the next three decades of his life, an undertaking that involved the gathering of written material brought out of Tibet after the Chinese takeover of the country, and the publication and distribution of selected materials to any institutional library in America that wanted them, free of charge.

One circumstance that made this effort achievable was the inspired interpretation of a federal program that had been established in 1954 with the ostensible purpose of providing surplus American wheat to "friendly" nations. A key element in the bill was the requirement that currency received in the transactions could be spent only in the countries that bought the food. Known as Public Law 480, or PL480, the rupees generated in India were made available through the Library of Congress to Smith, who began buying Tibetan texts, and arranged to have copies reprinted by local firms. It was through this program that superb collections were established at eighteen American libraries, the University of Washington, the University of Virginia, Indiana University, Yale, the University of Chicago, the University of Texas, the University of Pennsylvania, and the University of California at Berkeley among them. "I don't know if the far-sighted people in Congress who passed this particular bill had any idea that it would be used to save a threatened body of literature or not," Smith said, "but that's pretty much the way it turned out."

Remarkably, one institution that turned down the free books when they were being offered between 1965 and 1985 was Harvard University, an especially perplexing decision, given the fact that Harvard maintains the largest academic library collections in the world, and spends more money on books each year than any other university library. "I can't explain why Harvard declined an opportunity to receive free books, although one reason, I suspect, is because there was no curriculum in place they could support," Dr. van der Kuijp, who arrived at the university in 1995, told me. "But we have been playing catch-up ever since. Our collections here are nowhere near what they are at some of the other programs that got involved at the beginning. With Gene's help, however, we are getting there."

Of the materials Smith gathered specifically for the Library of Congress, fully five thousand are catalogued as "reprint" editions, meaning that once the materials were acquired, PL480 funds were used to produce new copies, and they represent "the entire corpus of Tibetan literature from the eighth century to the present," according to the official description of the collection. A good number of these are reproductions of a traditional form of Tibetan book known as xylographs, or impressions made directly from engraved wood blocks. Given the fragility of the originals, along with the very specific nature of the texts, these books—usually fastened together in the manner of a loose-leaf notebook—were never produced in abundance, and with the onset of the Cultural Revolution in 1966, their prospects for survival became grave, especially as swarms of Red Guards prowled the countryside with a mandate to eradicate all evidence of what were derisively known as the "Four Olds"—old ideas, old customs, old culture, and antiquated "habits of mind." Monasteries and temples such as Jokhang, Ramoche, and Norbulingka were looted during the rampage and shut down, in some cases damaged beyond repair. Drepung, a community of ten thousand monks, and Ganden, with three thousand, were leveled to the ground. Statuary and ritual objects were smashed and burned, religious and cultural activities, including the performance of traditional dances and music, were banned, and many monks were killed. Chou En-lai, the Chinese prime minister, directed that just fourteen temples in China and Tibet—one in each province, including the Potala Palace in Lhasa—be declared off-limits to the roving bands, but he imposed no similar restrictions on any of the others, which numbered in the thousands.

"He basically was following the Russian model that said you should keep a few sanctuaries around as living museums, you keep a few librarians, you keep some monks," Smith said. "Otherwise, it was the wholesale destruction of the old, across the board, and it prevailed throughout China and into Tibet. An incredible amount of literature was lost, but we also know now that a great deal was saved by many courageous individuals. There were instances were people buried books in the ground. And they stayed there for years. You must understand that books are magic to these people. To destroy a book means that you are losing something of yourself. So they had the fear of the Red Guards on the one side, and on the other there was this idea that these were objects that held some sort of magical power."

Dealing directly with émigrés who had found refuge in India, Nepal, and Bhutan, Smith began acquiring material, "everything under the sun," as Tashi Tsering, a scholar from Dharmsala, India, who traveled to Cambridge to work with the texts, said admiringly. "Buddhist philosophy. Some of the earliest examples of biography and autobiography in the world. Mathematics. Alchemy. Travelogues—Tibetans were great travelers and fond of writing about their experiences. A lot of great visionary writing." Equally important, Smith devised a method for cataloging and describing the works he had gathered, a systematic approach that would prove essential for the scholarly collections that would emerge from the material, and for many of the works that were reprinted in the PL480 program, he wrote knowledgeable prefaces that are considered so essential among Tibetologists that a number of them were published in 2002 in a scholarly edition titled *Among Tibetan Texts: History and Literature of the Himalayan Plain.* "Gene Smith opened more doors to Tibetan Buddhism than any scholar of the twentieth century," Donald S. Lopez Jr., professor of Buddhist and Tibetan Studies at the University Michigan, wrote in tribute. "These essays are the keys."

While Smith earnestly insists that he is not a bibliophile in the sense of being a conventional collector of rarities or curiosities, his activity over the past four decades as a gatherer of books suggests otherwise. This is due to the fact that at the same time that he was gathering books for the Library of Congress, he was acquiring even more materials for himself. "Yes, we have a lot of rare books here, although that was never my primary motivation," he said. "I am driven by preserving the cultural identity of a people. That has always been my driving principle. As for these books that I got for myself, I swear, I was doing it because I was *interested*. I was doing this because I thought, perhaps stupidly, that I could *read* all these books. But in the final analysis there were just too many." The immediate result is that Smith, by every credible account, is quite likely the owner of the finest private collection of Tibetan material to be found anywhere, a circumstance that he regards as an "awesome responsibility," one that he said occupies a good deal of his time and attention. A bachelor who has been only too happy to commit his resources to the acquisition of books, he now thinks long and hard about the future of the collection, and to ensuring that it will be readily available to scholars in the years to come. "That's where the Internet comes in," he told me. "My goal is to have everything scanned and available on the World Wide Web to anyone who wants access. That I must do before I die."

Though curators at many institutions in America would dearly love to have Smith's holdings enter their research collections, Smith said he wants to see them returned to the land of their origin, even to China, if there is a demonstrated commitment expressed by high officials there for their continued care. "I've always been afraid that something is going to happen to them, a fire, a catastrophe of some sort, whatever. So once we're able to scan everything, we will be able to distribute the content to everybody on the Internet. Then, the original artifacts—they can go back." He compared the spirit of this approach to a strategy put in place in 1971 in Bangkok by Peter Skilling, a Canadian scholar, with what is known as the Fragile Palm Leaves Project. In that effort, ancient Buddhist texts written on traditional surfaces, most of them plundered from nearby Cambodia, are being acquired as they appear in the marketplace, bought outright from vendors who are all too willing to break them up into single sheets and sell them off as antiques and curiosities to tourists and opportunists. Skilling has made clear his long-term goal of seeing the material he has rescued deposited in a national repository, but only after everything he has gathered is catalogued, copied, and given wide distribution, and when a stable government is in place in Cambodia to accept responsibility for it.

When I met Smith for the second time in June 2002, the fruit of four decades of collecting, some twelve thousand volumes, was everywhere apparent in his Cambridge duplex, piled neatly in every room except the kitchen, with some volumes stacked around the narrow bed in his cramped sleeping quarters. Once again he was getting ready to move, back again to New York, where new offices were to be provided at 115 Fifth Avenue, courtesy of the Shelley & Donald Rubin Foundation. "This, I hope, will be the final move," he said, with fingers firmly crossed for my benefit.

On April 15, 1971, the daily affairs of an island nation in the North Atlantic came to a standstill as two literary treasures of tremendous cultural significance returned to the land of their composition after spending close to two hundred years in a foreign land. In a rite of great pomp and ceremony, the *Codex Regius* (The King's Book), an anthology of ancient Norse myth that includes an epic known as the *Poetic Edda,* and *Flateyjarbók* (Flat Island Book), a unique collection of early Icelandic sagas dating from the thirteenth century, were transported to Iceland as precious cargo aboard a Royal Danish warship. The manuscripts had been taken from Iceland to Copenhagen in the early 1700s by a well-intentioned government antiquary and installed for safekeeping in the Danish Royal Library. Their return many decades later came in calm recognition of the former dependency's repeated attempts to reclaim the most cherished symbols of its heritage, manuscripts of its national narratives; by 1998, eighteen hundred other manuscripts were brought to Reykjavík for permanent installation in a modern research center that had been built specifically for them. One authoritative law journal hailed the repatriation as the most "outstanding example of a successful state-to-state restitution of cultural property" ever taken.

"We Icelandic people have very few visible memorials of our past," Vésteinn Olason, director of the Árni Magnússon Institute in Reykjavík and custodian of the manuscripts, told me in a telephone interview not long after the last sagas were turned over to his research center. "There are no ancient buildings here and very few medieval antiquities, so the sagas to Icelanders are what castles and royal palaces represent for the people of other nations. They are our principal links with the past." Notable for its glaciers, hot springs, geysers, volcanoes, snow-tipped mountains, sprawling desert plateaus, and surreal lava fields, the Icelandic countryside is undeniably breathtaking, but as Olason pointed out, not a landscape that is hospitable to the preservation of perishable artifacts. Just 20 percent of the land is considered habitable, and since the only trees that grow in any abundance are birch, buildings traditionally have been made of stone, sod, and logs that have drifted down from Siberia and Scandinavia. As a consequence, most of the nation's heritage comes in the form of medieval writings of explorations and derring-do known as sagas. Primarily a form of anecdotal prose that is both colloquial and concise, the sagas record, in distinctively intimate terms, the lives and experiences of the island's earliest inhabitants, and are the principal contribution of this tiny nation of 300,000 people to the canon of world literature. "Sagas can be religious, secular, truthful, or fictional," Olason said. "The one element they all have in common is narrative."

Settled during the ninth and tenth centuries by Norwegians, Iceland became Christian in 999, and remained independent for three hundred years before becoming a dependency of Norway, and then Denmark. Before colonizing Greenland, Erik the Red, the son of a Norwegian exile, lived in Iceland; his son, Leif Eriksson, is widely thought to have been the first European to explore the coast of North America, which he named Vinland the Good. In the twelfth century, Icelanders began using the Latin alphabet to record information in their own language. Their earliest literature was heavy on the saints and homilies, but a good deal of it was spun from tales of exploration. During the seventeenth century, Icelandic literature was regarded as an important source of Scandinavian history, and many manuscripts found in churches and farmhouses were among those sent to Denmark for safekeeping. The central figure in this removal was Árni Magnússon (1663–1730), a scholar and antiquarian who spent most of his adult life as secretary of the Royal Archives. In 1701 Magnússon was named chairman of a newly created Department of Danish Antiquities at the University of Copenhagen. As both public official and scholar, Magnússon took it upon himself to build a national collection of Scandinavian manuscripts, and he spent ten years off and on in Iceland searching for material. When Magnússon died in 1730, his collection of twenty-five hundred items was willed to the University of Copenhagen, at that time the only center for higher education in the Danish kingdom, which also included Norway. Money he left to publish textual editions of the manuscripts was used in 1760 to establish the Arnamagnæan Foundation.

When Iceland began a separatist movement in the early twentieth century, requests were made for return of the sagas. Seven hundred legal documents were turned over in 1927, but petitions for the more precious literary materials were continually rebuffed. It was only in 1944 when Iceland ended six hundred years of foreign rule to become an independent state that the claims began to be taken seriously. On May 16, 1965, the Danish Parliament enacted legislation permitting the return of all documents that could positively be determined to be "Icelandic cultural property," a qualification broadly defined to embrace any work written or translated by an Icelander, with content that is wholly or chiefly concerned with Iceland. To care for the national treasures, an Árni Magnússon Institute was established in Reykjavík as part of the University of Iceland. "The prose literature of medieval Iceland is a great world treasure—elaborate, various, strange, profound, and as eternally current as any of the other great literature treasures," Jane Smiley, the Pulitzer Prize–winning author of *The Greenlanders*, wrote in the preface to an English-language collection of the sagas, released in 2000. "Mysteries surround these stories—how were they composed and by whom? What were the motives of the authors? Why were they written in prose when the currency of medieval literature was poetry? How did their contemporaries understand them—did they ever read them, or did they hear them read aloud? But the questions fall away as we read the sagas and tales for ourselves."

At a time when museums and libraries around the world have been asked to return cultural materials to the places of their origin, the episode of the Icelandic sagas is pertinent. "The Danes were our masters for several hundred years, but I must say the repatriation of the manuscripts helped remove the resentments," Olason said. "It was a singular act of friendship on their part, since they were under no legal obligation to do this. They realized the significance these sagas had for Icelanders. They also understood that study of the manuscripts would be most effective in the country where the language is still spoken, since the underlying reality of the matter is that our language has changed very little over the centuries. If you can read modern Icelandic, you can read the sagas."

6.
Shelf Life

For certainly there is nothing which renders a Library more recommendable,
than when every man finds in it that which he is in search of, and nowhere else
encounter; this being a perfect maxim, that there is no book whatsoever, be it
never so bad or decried, but may in time be sought for by some person or other.
—GABRIEL NAUDÉ (1600–1653),
INSTRUCTIONS CONCERNING ERECTING OF A LIBRARY

I am a person whose home library includes numerous collections within collections, most of them discrete gatherings of works that reflect my personal interests and passions. Some are research tools that are useful in my work; others are quirky volumes that have piqued my curiosity from time to time, be they totally unknown nuggets that I run across at New England flea markets and yard sales, or obscure gems from my desiderata that turn up every so often gathering dust in the back rooms of secondhand bookstores, or in recent years been able to locate through use of the major Internet search engines. Because prior usage of old books is an appealing concept for me, I am not at all put off by intelligent annotations that have been written in the margins, especially when there are bookplates or ownership signatures to identify the readers whose wise perceptions have been passed on to me across the decades.

One area in my house is devoted entirely to a modest mélange of ex libris titles that have been discarded by various libraries from time to time either as "out of scope" and not pertinent to their collections, or merely because, in some opaque view, they have gone unused too long to justify occupying precious storage space any longer. My well-worn first-edition copy of *The House of the Seven Gables* (1851) was once the property of the Portsmouth Public Library in New Hampshire; I paid $8 for it at a country auction in Eliot, Maine, not so far from the town of Brunswick, where Nathaniel Hawthorne, the author of the novel, attended Bowdoin College. My lovely five-volume set of Plutarch's *Lives*, published by Little, Brown in 1885, bears the "discard" stamp of the Vineyard Haven Public Library. My copy of the 1876 edition of Thomas Frognall Dibdin's *Bibliomania*, beautifully illustrated with numerous wood engravings and in admirable condition, was once a reference in the Free Public Library in Concord, Massachusetts, and could easily have been handled by Ralph Waldo Emerson, a resident of the fabled literary community from 1834 until his death in 1882, whose own books now occupy an honored place in the special collections department of this historic institution. A few months after paying a secondhand bookseller $60 for that prize, my wife, Connie, and I were first in line at a spring tag sale mounted by the Worcester Art Museum in Worcester, Massachusetts. While I was poking through some tattered old Sotheby's, Christie's, and Parke-Bernet auction catalogs piled high on a folding table, Connie was examining the contents of a few cardboard crates lying nearby on the floor. In one box-lot marked $5 for the contents she found a bundle of old magazines tied together by twine, and promptly plucked from what very well might have been part of that evening's trash deposit a dozen issues of the *Dial*, an important nineteenth-century literary quarterly of considerable scarcity that boasts numerous first-appearance essays of Emerson, Henry David Thoreau, and Margaret Fuller, the founding editor. During a later examination of the October 1840 number, I came across an article by Emerson titled "Thoughts on Modern Literature," which includes several points that seem eerily pertinent to the general topic of durability, textual and otherwise, including one perceptive rumination on the matter of "universal books" that serves as the principal epigraph and provided the title for this book.

Because authoritative texts of Emerson's essays and lectures are available in a modern hardcover edition published by the Library of America—and can also be found in an on-line edition of his complete works, for that matter—the *content* of this provocative essay was by no means in jeopardy of being lost by the disposal of a few old magazines at a spring fund-raiser. But what had been rendered irrelevant in this instance was the "original carrier" of meaningful information in an important American journal, along with the physical context within which it was presented to its first readership. My wife and I were pleased to offer these orphaned *Dials* sanctuary in our home, and have declined several generous offers since then to part with them.

My acquisition in 2002 of a copy of Jesse H. Shera's *Foundations of the Public Library* (University of Chicago Press, 1949), a comprehensive work that traces the evolution of the public library movement in New England from the time of the Pilgrims to the establishment of the Boston Public Library in the 1850s, represented a bittersweet victory for me. Being able to add a book to my collection that I had coveted for some time was a welcome turn of events, since this was a title I knew something about, and had expended considerable energy to locate while doing research for my book *Patience & Fortitude,* which devotes several chapters to American library history. According to the Online Computer Library Center (OCLC) WorldCat database of forty-one thousand libraries in eighty-two countries, ten libraries in Massachusetts have the book, none in the central section of the state where I live. Unable, as a consequence, to obtain a copy locally, I had to make due with an interlibrary loan arranged by my friends at the College of the Holy Cross in Worcester. Though easily resolved, this was time-consuming just the same, so I have to say I was more than a bit miffed when I noticed that the secondhand copy I bought for $50 had a big "withdrawn" notice stamped on the front pastedown right above the bookplate of the Worcester Public Library, located just across Salem Street from Ben Franklin Book Store in downtown Worcester where I found it. Why such an important work of nonfiction, especially one pertinent to the evolution of the very institution that had owned it for more than fifty years, could have been deemed extraneous and discardable was beyond my comprehension, though "nonuse over a protracted period" was the reason cited when I inquired at the librarian's office.

I cite these few examples of institutional discards not because they are overly flagrant, but because they are drawn from my own modest experience. Indeed, they pale in comparison to those of other bibliophiles who routinely gloat over the "incredible" treasures they rescue from oblivion at library book sales. In an amusing essay titled "A Short Shelf Life," the English novelist Ian Watson boasted how from "piles of condemned texts" encountered at a succession of discard sales he had "rescued splendid volumes about the Crusades, the Jesuits, etymology, entomology and lots of other 'ologies.' " He wondered about the motivation to jettison these seemingly first-rate books by asking a simple question: "Are these titles all past their read-by date?"

The larger issue here is that the culling of books is an ongoing exercise that happens everywhere, on every conceivable level, and for a multitude of reasons, some of them perfectly defensible. Another case in point—one that illuminates in greater detail what one "library activist" in San Francisco cynically called the "workings of the de-selection chamber" during the operations that went on there in the late 1990s—presented itself to me one Sunday morning at the Cape Cod Book, Print and Paper Show, a popular event then held in a Barnstable, Massachusetts, community college gymnasium. While I was browsing through the crowded aisles, my eyes settled on a two-volume set of the 1908 London edition of *The North West Passage*, the Norwegian adventurer Roald Amundsen's

thrilling account of his first major voyage at sea, and one of the most difficult books on polar exploration to find on the open market, especially in
what booksellers call "collector's condition." Bound in dark green cloth
and illustrated with numerous photographs, each volume had a folded
map tucked inside at the back, as originally issued by the publisher; James
A. Visbeck, owner of Isaiah Thomas Books and Prints in nearby Cotuit,
had the set priced at $750, which later research would confirm was about
right for this title. Its only visible flaws were a few minor scratches on one
of the cloth covers, and what Visbeck called the "prior ownership" markings readily apparent on both volumes, specifically the bookplates of a
local public library affixed to the two front pastedowns, and the shelf
number 998 painted in indelible white ink on each of the spines.

Visbeck, a friend of mine of many years standing, told me he had
bought the books at a major discard sale held in October 1997 by the Sturgis Library, an institution established in 1867 as the first public library on
Cape Cod, and now one of seven branches operated by the town of Barnstable. Though by no means a big-city operation, the Sturgis Library is a
jewel of an institution nonetheless, one that enjoys a rich tradition of service to its community and the active support of a dedicated friends' group.
It was named for William Sturgis, a nineteenth-century shipping merchant
who made a fortune in the China trade and left the majestic old house he
had acquired to his hometown with the stipulation that it be used as a
library. Located on the Old King's Highway on the bay side of the Cape—
Route 6A on modern maps—the shingled structure was built in 1644 by
the Reverend John Lothrop, the founder of the village. A seventeenth-
century provenance—the house was built just twenty-four years after the
Pilgrims had settled in nearby Plymouth—supports the library's claim
that it is the oldest structure in the United States to function as part of a
public library, as well as the oldest building still standing in America where
religious services at one time were held regularly. Now attached as a wing
to a modern facility, the house is used to store an archive of genealogical

records and some fine special collections that deal with Cape Cod and maritime history.

One of the more interesting items kept on permanent display in the old dining room is a 1605 Bishop's Bible that Lothrop brought with him to the New World in 1634. This copy is unique by virtue of a mishap that is said to have occurred during the clergyman's arduous voyage across the Atlantic on the schooner *Griffin*. As the story has been passed down through the generations, a drop of hot tallow fell on the "good book" and burned a hole through several of the pages while the reverend was reading the scriptures one evening by candlelight. Before reaching America, the resourceful Puritan had mended the scorched sections with textiles scrounged up on the ship, and filled in the obliterated words in a calligraphic hand that closely matched the original type, recalling the damaged text entirely from memory. Now displayed under glass in a room that is notable for its beamed ceilings and wide-pine floors, the Bible is kept open to one of the repaired pages.

"I only got a few books at the Sturgis sale," Visbeck told me, and he suggested that if I really wanted to know more details about it, the person to speak with was Giles Hollingsworth, a bookseller from Georgia. "Giles got hundreds of wonderful things that day, and you are in luck because he has a booth at the fair right over there in the middle of the gym." Before making my way over to chat with Hollingsworth, I decided to examine some items brought in for the day by Cheryl Needle, a Chelmsford, Massachusetts, bookseller, who had set up her stock across from Visbeck. Among her offerings was *The Literary and Philosophical Repertory*, an early American periodical published in Middlebury, Vermont, and combined into two hardcover volumes issued in 1812 and 1817; the pair had been deaccessioned a few years earlier by the New England Historic Genealogical Society of Boston, and Needle had them priced at $175. She did not believe they were "last copies," and suggested that the American Antiquarian Society (AAS) in Worcester, the world's most complete collection of early American imprints, probably had the title listed. A later search of the OCLC database showed that the books are indeed there, but nowhere else among the thousands of member institutions who provide data on their holdings. Even Harvard University—the largest academic library in the world—does not have an original set, but does have two copies on microfilm. That tenuous duplication, apparently, was all the justification New England's most prominent genealogical society had needed to discard a reference work that has important connections to the region it serves.

After leaving Needle's booth, I introduced myself to Giles and Helen Hollingsworth, an affable couple who opened an antiquarian book business in the mid-1990s as an activity to enjoy in semiretirement. Both recalled the Sturgis Library sale with great relish. "It was one of those truly amazing experiences," Giles said, agreeing with his wife that it was nothing short of a "once-in-a-lifetime" opportunity; Helen Hollingsworth compared it to "digging for gold in the Sierra Nevadas." The Hollingsworths recalled that they had been driving through New England on an autumn vacation in 1997 and enjoying the spectacular fall foliage when they spotted an advertisement in the *Cape Cod Times* announcing a big book sale to be held the next day in Barnstable. "We decided to take it in, and from the moment we arrived, it was like going to book heaven," Giles said. "We were told later that they were raising money to put in a new elevator at the Sturgis Library." Because the Hollingsworths travel about the country in a van, they were able to buy aggressively, and wound up filling their vehicle "to the seams" with about a thousand books.

"We spent something like five thousand dollars at the sale," Giles said. "It was mostly nineteenth-century material; a lot of Civil War things, leather books for ten dollars a volume, all in pristine condition, absolutely breathtaking stuff. The thrill of a lifetime." Once the windfall had been brought to Atlanta and processed for resale, the books moved briskly. "We decided in this instance that the ex libris marking was a plus, not a minus, that it contained something that book people would appreciate for its historical significance alone. We described it as a 'prestige bookplate from the oldest library building in the United States.' " On their next New England vacation, the couple made it a point to visit the Sturgis Library once again. "We wanted to take a ride in 'our' elevator."

The following Saturday I paid a visit to the "oldest library building in the United States," and spoke with librarian Christopher Lindquist, who explained that the sale in question, representing at the time about 10 percent of the Sturgis collection, had been authorized by his board of trustees, and was held to help underwrite improvements mandated by the U.S. Americans with Disabilities Act, part of which included the installation of an elevator in the modern wing. "We had about seven thousand books that were gathering dust in the basement for at least fifteen years that nobody ever wanted to see, and which did not support our special collections in any way," Lindquist said. "Unfortunately we have, as you can readily see around you, only so much space here, and only so much money available for preservation. We went through everything very carefully, and we had everything professionally appraised, so I am confident that we got fair value for what we sold. I can also tell you that there were some 'last copies' in there, and that we held on to them. We also kept everything that supported our special collections."

Getting fair value for discards is relevant to the issue, since it is one way of ensuring that books are not headed for a landfill or a pulping plant, and that they are going to places where they will be welcome, although in many cases volumes containing valuable illustrations are bought by dealers who are interested only in stripping them of engravings, etchings, and lithographs that they can sell individually, and at great profit, on the antiquarian print market. In fact quite apart from the matter of dispersal policies at libraries is "book-breaking" itself, a practice that has run rampant for centuries. Virtually every leaf of illuminated manuscript in private and institutional collections has been removed at one time or other from a codex, just about every vintage map sold by cartography dealers has been cut out of an atlas, and every single example of what is called a "leaf-book" includes a leaf of text shorn from an important volume, and despite the great animus the practice engenders among most bibliophiles who preach the sanctity of the book, it is still very much in evidence today.

Most reasonable people would consider the wanton removal of illustrations from books that are in no immediate danger of deterioration, and are otherwise intact, a desecration of the first order. But anytime an original engraving from John J. Audubon's *Birds of America* is sold singly at auction or through private purchase, what is being sold is a hand-colored plate that has been removed from one of the original double elephant folios published in London between 1827 and 1838. Prices for these plates can vary anywhere from $3,000 for a good example of the autumnal warbler to $150,000 for the most coveted specimen of them all, the wild turkey, which Audubon gave pride of place in the first volume. It is not necessary to have a degree in calculus to figure out that exquisite engravings sold individually—and there were a total of 435 hand-colored etched plates inserted in each four-volume set—will generate more money when sold piecemeal, even though complete sets of Audubon do command hefty prices on those infrequent occasions when they appear on the market. On March 10, 2000, for example, Sheik Hamad bin Khalifa Al-Thani, ruler of the Persian Gulf nation of Qatar, spent $8.8 million at a Christie's auction for a set formerly owned by John, fourth marquess of Bute, more than double the price paid for a comparable copy at the H. Bradley Martin sale eleven years earlier, and twenty-five times more than what one brought in 1977. Beyond the arresting beauty of the *Birds of America,* part of this spiraling value derives from the fact that once a book of this stature has been stripped of its illustrations, a title that was *always* valuable becomes much dearer still. Only two hundred complete sets of the elephant folios were produced by W. H. Lizars of Edinburgh and Robert Havell and Robert Havell Jr. of London, and all were sold by subscription to people who knew in advance that they were getting an important book; according to the most recent census of copies, fewer than 125 sets have survived intact, with only 14 still in private hands, suggesting that at least 75 sets have been broken up over the past two hundred years, and sold piecemeal.

By far the most egregious book-breaking episode of recent times—indeed, a writer for the *Independent* in London called the incident in question an unprecedented act of "artistic vandalism"—was the decision in the 1970s of the late Arthur A. Houghton Jr. to dismember and sell in parts a unique manuscript copy of the Persian "epic of kings" known as the *Shahnameh*. Crafted over a twenty-year period in the early sixteenth century by some of the most gifted artists of the age, the majestic volume contained within its hard covers 258 folio-sized paintings, 759 illuminated pages of text, and an exquisite illuminated rosette, along with a 450-year-old binding that by itself was a dazzling creation. Composed about A.D. 1010 by a canonical poet known as Ferdowsī, the text of the *Shahnameh* celebrates, in sixty thousand metrical couplets, the lost imperial civilization of ancient Persia with stories, legends, myths, and folktales that were popular before the Islamic conquest of the seventh century. Because of the book's enduring cultural importance—it is regarded as the national epic of the Iranian people, the Persian equivalent of Homer's *Odyssey* and *Iliad*—having an exquisite personal copy was always regarded as de rigueur by every shah, with no example grander in scale and execution than the masterpiece crafted between 1520 and 1540 for Tahmāsp I. Given the paucity of surviving architecture, textiles, and other examples of decorative arts from the early Safavid dynasty, the Houghton *Shahnameh*—renamed for its final owner in much the same way that the friezes stripped from the Parthenon in the early 1800s were called the Elgin Marbles for the British peer who removed them from Athens to decorate his country mansion in Scotland—has been described as an art gallery unto itself.

A dedicated bibliophile best known for having built a remarkably rich collection of English poetry and prose of the Elizabethan, Jacobean, and Romantic eras, Arthur Houghton purchased the *Shahnameh* in 1959 from Baron Edmond de Rothschild, a French banker and collector of international renown who had taken special care to ensure that the miniatures were always protected from damage, rarely allowing them to be exposed to light. Believing that an institutional collection was the most appropriate home for a work of such unquestioned importance, Rothschild at first suggested selling the book to the Metropolitan Museum of Art in New York, where Houghton served on the board of trustees from 1952 to 1974, and as chairman from 1969 to 1972. A patron of the arts, Rothschild had already donated a number of important pieces to the Louvre Museum in Paris, and was one of the founders and principal benefactors of the Israel Museum in Jerusalem. On the recommendation of its trustees, however, the Met passed on the opportunity to get the *Shahnameh* and bring it to New York, at which point Houghton, the president of Steuben Glass Co. and vice president of Corning Glass Works, two lucrative family businesses, acquired it for himself, possibly with a mind toward giving the treasure to the museum at some point in the future, or perhaps even presenting it to Harvard University, where he placed the book on deposit shortly after acquiring it with the understanding that an elegant facsimile would be published by the university's academic press. Whether or not he intended eventually to give the book outright to his alma mater has never been disclosed publicly, though such a prospect certainly was regarded as a distinct possibility by curators there, since the university's prestigious Fogg Art Museum maintains a renowned collection of Islamic art, and since Houghton had already demonstrated his generosity to Harvard in other ways, most notably for having underwritten construction of the Houghton Rare Book and Manuscript Library at the university in the 1940s, and for having then presented the depository with an unparalleled collection of John Keats manuscript material.

"From what I could discern, time passed, and Arthur began to lose his patience with Harvard," Thomas Hoving, director of the Metropolitan Museum from 1967 to 1977, told me in the fall of 2002. "He wanted the facsimile published, and it wasn't going nearly as quickly as he wanted. So in frustration—perhaps it *was* pique, who knows—he pulled the book out of Harvard, brought it down to New York, and proceeded to do what he did with it there." In 1972, seventy-eight of the choicest paintings were removed from the book and presented to the Metropolitan Museum of Art, a turn of events that Hoving told me "was like getting a whole bunch of Michelangelo paintings from out of the blue." Because of the museum's nonprofit status, Houghton was able to claim a considerable tax deduction for his donation in return, though just how much he would actually be allowed to receive became a matter of some contention with the Internal Revenue Service. A prevailing assumption, one that Hoving did not dispute, is that had the IRS accepted as true value Houghton's estimate of the material he had already donated, the remaining plates may have been given at some point to the Metropolitan Museum as well. Had that scenario been the one that played out, all of the artwork from the *Shahnameh* would have remained together, if not between the covers of the book that had contained them for more than four hundred years, then at least within the walls of the same institution.

"I was flatly opposed to the breaking up of the book in any fashion," Hoving told me. "I confronted Arthur physically, personally, on the matter, but he was determined to do this, and he *was* the chairman of our board of trustees, after all; so at the end of the day we wound up with these fabulous plates, which our experts assured me were the very best of them all." Exactly how much Houghton asserted the plates were worth has never been disclosed, but it was enough to trigger an audit from the IRS. Hoving said the gift came to the museum at a time when the government was becoming increasingly suspicious of the deductions people were claiming for donated artwork, a concern precipitated by a flurry of embarrassing incidents in which paintings purported to have been painted by Pablo

Picasso and other luminaries were later determined to be frauds, and thus not worth a fraction of what had been claimed by their unwitting donors. "When the IRS disallowed Arthur's claim, he became petrified that the government was going to investigate *everything* that he was involved with, in particular that they would look into several of his charitable foundations, which we now know had acted as conduits for the Central Intelligence Agency during the Cold War. That, I firmly believe, was the concern that drove this highly intelligent man to do the impulsive thing he did with the rest of the *Shahnameh*. It was a totally stupid act on his part to break up this magnificent book and scatter the plates to the four winds, but he allowed his petty fears to take control of his common sense. You have to realize that this was a very arch, very patrician man who was unbelievably paranoid, kind of spooky to tell you the truth, and he had it in him to take offense at anything. What I believe he wanted to say to these people was, 'If you don't believe what I am telling you these plates are worth, then I will *show* you what they are worth.' " Corroboration of this impulsive side of Houghton's character is not difficult to find from other sources. In an otherwise laudatory obituary published in the *Independent* on April 4, 1990, the noted British bookman Nicolas Barker described Houghton as a "powerful" person "who made up his mind on anything and everything that came his way, and did not like to be thwarted."

As a first effort to demonstrate true market value, he offered what was left of the *Shahnameh* to the shah of Iran, whose third wife, Farah Diba, was in the process of building an enormous art collection for a new museum in Tehran. When Houghton's asking price, said to be $20 million, was rejected, he proceeded to consign seven folio pages from the book to Christie's in London. Choosing to offer just a few pieces for public sale at any one time, and making them available for purchase at infrequent intervals—not "flooding the market" is the phrase typically used in the art auction business to describe the strategy—would prove to be astute. On November 17, 1976, the seven pieces realized £785,000, with one lot alone going for £308,000, a record at auction for any Persian miniature. Houghton then authorized Agnew's in London, a Bond Street dealer, to sell another forty pages privately, with the remainder sent to Lloyds Bank in London. The next public sale was held at Christie's on October 11, 1988; this time, fourteen plates went under the hammer, bringing in a total of £976,800.

When Houghton died in 1990 at the age of eighty-three, there were still 120 plates remaining. To dispose of them once and for all, Houghton's estate worked out an ingenious barter with the Islamic government that had taken over Iran in 1979 and was discreetly trying to get rid of some "decadent" artwork bought by the deposed queen that by then were deemed to be unsuitable for public viewing. For the fragmentary remains of the *Shahnameh*, an arbitrary valuation of $20 million was agreed upon by the parties, with the same figure assigned to *Woman III*, a painting by the abstract expressionist Willem de Kooning that one Iranian critic had called a "savage, aggressive portrayal of a naked woman." The transfer took place on neutral ground at the Vienna airport in 1993. Returned to Iran in triumph, the miniatures—disbound, they were shipped in seven boxes—went on display in Tehran; the de Kooning painting, meanwhile, was sold privately for an undisclosed sum to the Hollywood film executive David Geffen. But the saga still had one more act left to play out, as four plates that had been removed from the book in the 1970s made their way back into the market a few years later. On April 23, 1996, they were sold at Sotheby's in London, with the first plate alone realizing £419,500. That figure, a new record, was eclipsed in a matter of minutes when the next lot brought in an astounding £793,500; the third plate was knocked down at £353,500, the fourth went for £397,500. "It was a great day for commerce," Souren Melikian wrote derisively in the *International Herald Tribune*, "but hardly for the preservation of cultural treasures."

Exactly how much money was realized altogether from this one book over the two decades it was being cut up and sold off in parts is not a matter of public record, though the prominent New York dealer John Fleming (1910–1987), who did a considerable amount of business with Houghton over several decades, is said to have quipped often that he was not the most successful bookseller of his generation as many of his colleagues had so frequently suggested, that "the ultimate honor belongs to Arthur Houghton and the great success he had single-handedly selling off that one book." All that exists today to suggest how magnificent an artifact that *one book* once was is a limited facsimile edition, *The Houghton Shahnameh*, exactingly produced by Harvard University Press, and released finally in 1981 with a list price of $2,500 per copy. In their learned introduction, the editors of the edition, Martin Bernard Dickson and Stuart Cary Welch, sidestepped entirely the delicate issue of how the original came to be broken up. In a lengthy essay published the following year in the *New York Review of Books*, however, the critic Michael Levy had this to say of the facsimile: "The present edition, reproducing every miniature, is not only a monument: it is a memorial to something that has been destroyed and can no longer be completely studied and appreciated in any other form."

As a cautionary tale, what the episode demonstrates more than anything else is how tempting it is to measure cultural treasures in terms of the hard currency they can generate as commodities, and not by artistic worth or merit. It was a similar realization, in fact, that motivated the trustees of the James Jerome Hill Reference Library in Saint Paul, Minnesota, to sell more than 100,000 books between 1980 and 1995, some of them uncommonly valuable and exceedingly scarce, including a complete set of the Audubon double elephant folio. The Hill Library case, in fact, offers an example of what can happen when a library created to serve the interests of scholarship discovers that its most valuable books are not instruments of learning they feel any obligation to maintain in the public trust, but "assets" that can generate capital on the open market. In this instance, a privately endowed institution established in 1921 with funds furnished by a Gilded Age railroad baron for the edification of the public sold a considerable research collection of printed books without any benefit of open debate, and one of the reasons later given was that it helped supply money for the purchase of computer equipment. Robert Rulon-Miller Jr., the local bookseller who handled most of the transactions for the institution's board of trustees, told me that the dispersal of the books, involving in many cases entire subject collections, went forward in an "extremely low-key" manner, with no probing news coverage to hinder its progress. It was only when some materials of unquestioned rarity were about to be sold, and when rumors began to circulate that the board itself remained bitterly divided over the mass dismantling of the collections, that outside interest was mildly aroused, but by that time it was a matter of too little attention coming along much too late.

Because the Hill Library was not built, stocked, or supported with municipal funds, and because James J. Hill, the man known as the Empire Builder, died intestate five years before work on the building was completed, its trustees have always been free to act as they wish without any formal "mission policy" passed down from the founder to restrict them. The direction they chose in the mid-1970s was away from what a thin majority of its board had felt was the need to keep materials that fewer and fewer people seemed interested in using, and which they were disinclined to continue maintaining. Since virtually anything the Hill family does makes news in Minnesota, the files of the Saint Paul and Minneapolis newspapers are filled with stories that report the comings and goings of its members, including periodic updates on a bitter feud that has raged over the course of three generations for control of an estate that once rivaled that of the New York financier J. P. Morgan. Though not nearly as well known today as Morgan, James J. Hill was very much a player in his rarefied league. Hill's entrepreneurial skills were legendary. His Great Northern Railway linked the northwestern United States from Saint Paul to Seattle, and provided a gateway to the markets of the Far East. By 1901, it was the nation's largest carrier, and is today part of the Burlington

Northern Railroad. Just as impressive were the timber, banking, and mining interests Hill had gathered under his control.

A native of Canada who received no formal education after the age of fourteen, Hill was a rugged individualist who firmly believed in giving people the tools they need to improve themselves. His gift of $750,000 for a library in Saint Paul was an enormous sum at the time, and it is clear from his correspondence that he wanted to establish an institution that would hold its own with the great repository that Pierpont Morgan had built adjacent to his house on Madison Avenue and East Thirty-sixth Street in Manhattan. Hill retained the New York architect Electus D. Litchfield to design the building, and appointed his speechwriter, biographer, and former *St. Paul Globe* editor, Joseph G. Pyle, to head the library. By all accounts, Pyle took the responsibility seriously and set about building a respectable collection.

Fifty-five years after the Hill Library opened its doors to the public, the trustees decided to downsize its services. G. Richard Slade, a grandson of James J. Hill who served as chairman of the board during the years of transition, told me in a telephone interview that when the library first opened in 1921, the intention of the original trustees was to be a general reference library in all areas except law and religion. "By the 1960s it became apparent that with our modest endowment we could never get the materials we needed to be a major force. So we finally voted to narrow the founder's vision and to concentrate on being a business information and reference library. And that has been the case since that time." The decision a few years later to "winnow out the holdings" that had been gathered by the original staff was the logical extension of that decision. "Our mission had changed," Slade emphasized, "and we were embarked on a new course."

In 1982 Robert Rulon-Miller Jr. of Saint Paul was invited to advise the trustees on how to exchange their books for hard currency. "My first direct dealing with the Hill Library was to take their fantastic collection of art books on consignment and bring them to New York for an auction," he told me in one of several conversations we had after his dealings with the institution had finally ended. "I really didn't know what the value of these particular books might be, so instead of making a direct offer, I decided to put them up for auction in New York. I loaded them on a truck and took them to Swann Galleries, where they were part of what became the most successful sale Swann put on in all of 1984. The Hill Library got something like $300,000 from that transaction, and you can pretty much say that the floodgates were opened up right there. It was then that they realized the true value of what they had, and it was at that point that they wanted to get rid of everything."

Over the next eleven years, Rulon-Miller was authorized to take about 100,000 books from the stacks, paying an average of $10 for every book he removed. "These were not rarities in any conventional sense of the word, but they were all terrific scholarly books. Name a subject, and they had it covered: architecture, travel, a naval section, an aviation section, it was all there. The only material they showed any interest in holding on to was anything relating to Minnesota or American Indians, because they figured that was local history, and anything that had something to do with business or industry."

Rulon-Miller said he had cultivated a ready customer for a major portion of the books in Bahrain, an oil-rich Middle Eastern kingdom of about 750,000 people. A College of Arts and Sciences at Bahrain University had opened in 1978, and its librarian, who had Minnesota ties, was eager to acquire books of proven scholarly merit. "Cost was not really an issue in this case, because the institution I was dealing with in Bahrain had more than adequate resources; what they wanted was the books, and I was pleased to supply them. I would estimate that I sent at least twenty-five thousand books from the Hill Library to Bahrain over a period of ten years, quite possibly a lot more than that. I can still see those great big wooden skids piled high with boxes that we used to take over to the

Minneapolis–Saint Paul airport. Each shipment was in the neighborhood of one hundred crates. This was a situation in which everybody made out well. The people in Bahrain got a very good deal, because a lot of these books were out-of-print titles that are pretty hard to find on the open market today. The Hill Library got a good deal because I paid them a fair price for every single item that I removed. The booksellers who dealt with me on everything I didn't send to Bahrain got a good deal too, because I fed a lot of terrific material directly into the trade."

Rulon-Miller calculated that he paid the Hill Library about $1 million for the materials he removed from the general collections. "There's no doubt in my mind that as this went on they realized they had assets on their shelves that they could use to generate capital, money they could use to repair the leaky roof or buy computers or strengthen the endowment." In 1987 the most valuable book of all, a complete set of John James Audubon's *Birds of America,* was consigned to Sotheby's for auction, with Rulon-Miller acting as the intermediary. Originally purchased by James J. Hill for $2,000 in 1891 for his personal library, the four volumes were expected to realize more than $1 million, but failed to meet their reserve when it was disclosed at the last minute that the engraved colored plates, although judged by the auction house to be in "very fine" condition, had been slightly trimmed around the edges, making them less desirable to collectors. The set was later sold privately to a Japanese university for $1 million. The Hill trustees justified the deaccession of the Audubons by arguing that two other sets of the folios—one in the rare books collection at the University of Minnesota, another at a library housed in the Minneapolis Public Library known as the Athenaeum—made the retention of a third set in the Twin Cities unnecessary.

After receiving another $1 million there, the trustees raised the stakes even further in 1993 by voting to sell more books from what had been James J. Hill's personal library, along with a run of fifty-six original watercolors painted in the mid-nineteenth century by the distinguished frontier artist

Seth Eastman, a career army officer who is remembered today for his remarkable skill as a pictorial historian of American Indian culture. During a seven-year posting at Fort Snelling in Minnesota in the 1840s, Eastman observed life among the Dakota and Ojibwa tribes with unmatched clarity and detail. The paintings in the Hill Library were prepared by Eastman for inclusion in Henry Rowe Schoolcraft's exhaustive six-volume work, *Information Regarding the History, Conditions, and Prospects of the Indian Tribes of the United States*, published between 1851 and 1858. James J. Hill bought them long before he expressed any plans for creating a research library. They were placed on deposit in the new building when the reference library opened in 1921, but were rarely put on public display. When news circulated that the Hill Reference Library intended to sell these materials, a local philanthropist and patron of the arts, W. Duncan MacMillan, a director of Cargill Inc., came forward with an offer intended to keep them in Minnesota. In a deal arranged by Rulon-Miller, MacMillan paid just under $1.8 million, and for that he acquired the Eastmans along with another six hundred rare books that also had been part of Hill's personal collection. MacMillan placed the paintings on long-term deposit in the Minnesota Historical Society, and sold the books privately to Rulon-Miller.

Among the high spots in this transaction was a copy of *The Viviparous Quadrupeds of North America* (1845–1848), with text by Prince Maximilian zu Wied-Neuwied and illustrations by Audubon. Rulon-Miller sold the book, known as Audubon's Quadrupeds, to a collector for $125,000. He turned a scarce book featuring hand-colored illustrations by Karl Bodmer, *Reise in das Innere Nord-America* (1839–1841), over to Donald A. Heald, a New York bookseller who specializes in color-plate books, for $225,000; Heald in turn sold it to a private collector for $500,000. The largest sum Rulon-Miller realized personally for any one title from the Hill collection was $375,000 for *The North American Indian* (1907–1930), a forty-volume set featuring the photographs of Edward S. Curtis, and usually referred to as the Curtis Indians.

Rulon-Miller said he stopped buying books from the Hill Library in 1995, and the reason for the termination then, he told me five years later, was that "everything of significance had been removed." He emphasized that his "conscience is completely clear" on the role he played in the massive dispersal. "I went to the trustees at one point very early on and advised them that if they wanted to keep the books where they were in Minnesota, they could probably put up $250,000 or so and do something really nice, perhaps negotiate an arrangement with the Saint Paul Public Library, which is right next door to the Hill Library, and which was eager to expand at the time. Who knows what they could have worked out? The Hills are a family that has a gazillion dollars at their disposal, they could do anything they have it in their mind to do. The point to be made is that I presented this to them as an alternative to deaccession, and they didn't want any part of it. So if someone was going to be their agent, I was elated that it was me they chose to represent them. The decision was theirs to make, and they made it. As long as they wanted to keep selling the books, I was only too happy to keep buying them. It was a unique opportunity for me, and I made sure all the books went to places where they are respected."

As to whether or not the people of Saint Paul—the people who James J. Hill designated as the ultimate beneficiaries of his largesse—got a "good deal" is another matter entirely, and one that Sheila ffolliott, a direct descendant of the benefactor and one of the dissenting trustees on the library board, raised in an essay she and her husband wrote for a lavish catalog issued by W. Duncan MacMillan to document the Eastman paintings he had just acquired. Sheila ffolliott is chair of the Department of Art History at George Mason University in Fairfax, Virginia, and a great-granddaughter of James J. Hill on her mother's side. The disagreement with other trustees remains a sensitive issue, and ffolliott has chosen to let what she wrote in the Seth Eastman catalog speak for itself. She did note in a telephone conversation with me, however, that her mother, Gertrude ffolliott, also a former trustee of the Hill Library, strongly opposed the mass deaccessioning of collections, and that in one rare public comment on the matter, told the *St. Paul Pioneer Press* that the sale reflected "a basic disregard for the most elementary morality which trustees of rare and important holdings ought to possess." In the same newspaper article Kathryn Gutzmann, a former assistant curator of the Hill Library, called what had gone on behind closed doors the "ongoing decimation of the library's treasures." Another Hill curator, W. Thomas White, said of the trustees, "If it's not bolted down, they'll sell it." But by the time that article appeared in print on July 2, 1995, everything of substance was gone.

"It seems incontrovertible that the Hill Library has turned its back on the materials so fundamentally related to the archival collections for which it assumed responsibility and therefore on those archival collections themselves," ffolliott and her husband, Shepard Krech III, an art professor at Brown University, wrote about the sale. "Instead it reconceptualized its rare holdings as 'portfolio assets,' and stripped itself of those assets. Unlike the library's earlier significant and equally quiet deaccession—an Audubon folio, for example—the sale of the Eastmans, as well as the books from Hill's personal library, involve the last vestiges of objects at the very core of the founder's life, as well as central to Minnesota history."

On the issue of deaccessioning in general, ffolliott and Krech had another observation: "The trust that libraries, museums, and other repositories hold with the public is fragile and is increasingly threatened. For institutions holding rare book and manuscript collections, the American Library Association has established standards for ethical conduct. While they do not prohibit de-accessioning, they stipulate that the process should be in accordance with a collections policy, deliberate, attentive to the donor's wishes and, above all, the public." The decision to strip the Hill Library of its collections, they concluded, was "tragic," and "cuts at the very soul" of James J. Hill's "vision for the library."

In his interview with me, Slade acknowledged that there had been "a lot of discussion" about the propriety of selling the rarities, but that a majority of members agreed to the deaccessions with the understanding that a portion of the funds would be committed to supporting James J. Hill's papers and archives, and strengthening the endowment. A part of the funds were used to purchase new computer equipment. "These were materials that were basically of an artistic quality, and were not part of the regular mission of the library," Slade said. "They weren't insured, and our legal counsel said that with that kind of an asset, if you can't take care of it, you ought to get rid of it."

I asked Slade if he thinks the library is functioning now in a manner that is consistent with the intentions of the founder. "It's doing just fine," he said. "But that's a qualified 'fine,' because the whole world is changing in ways that James J. Hill could have never imagined. The mystique of a library is disappearing. People simply don't want to go in them anymore from what I can see. What I do know is that James J. Hill was actively interested in books that went beyond the aesthetics. He valued them for the knowledge they contained. We at the library remain in an active self-examination mode right now, and we are looking at different ways to deliver services. Do I have any regrets about what we did? None. We made a decision to narrow the focus, and I'll stick by the direction we chose."

In stark contrast to the clean sweep brought off with a minimum of publicity in Saint Paul were the continuing woes of the New-York Historical Society at Central Park West and Seventy-seventh Street in Manhattan, which sold off significant pieces of a major art collection in 1995 during a financial crisis that had already forced it to close its doors to the public for two years. The fiscal problems of the prestigious nonprofit institution, with assets estimated to be worth between $1 billion and $2 billion on the open market, have been covered in detail by the *New York Times,* and were the subject of an exacting study written by Kevin M.

Guthrie that was funded by the Andrew W. Mellon Foundation, *The New-York Historical Society: Lessons from one Nonprofit's Long Struggle for Survival.*

What happened, briefly, is this: 191 years after it was established with a mandate to "rescue from the dust and obscurity of private repositories such important documents as are liable to be lost or destroyed by the indifference or neglect of those into whose hands they may have fallen," the New-York Historical Society found itself by the mid-1990s unable to care for the thousands of materials it had gathered so diligently. Faced with the prospect of imminent insolvency, the society decided to sell at auction selected items from its vast collections of artworks and curiosities, 183 valuable paintings most notable among them. A sale at Sotheby's raised $17.6 million, prompting the society to start delving through its holdings of 800,000 books and 3 million manuscripts, maps, photographs, prints, and architectural drawings, only a third of which had ever been cataloged, to find more "out of scope" items and duplicate titles that might generate additional cash. Once the depleted endowment had been raised to $22 million, the "fire sale" ended, and an affiliation with New York University was negotiated in 1997 to help catalog and preserve the library collections. The vast majority of the society's most important holdings—including, most spectacularly, 433 of the 435 original watercolors executed by John James Audubon for *Birds of America*—were declared safe from further deaccessioning, but the sale had struck a nerve, and there were no guarantees it might not happen again. "If you start cannibalizing your collections, for whatever worthy purpose," Richard Oldenberg, director of the Museum of Modern Art, said at the height of the crisis, "it's an abdication of responsibility by the people running the place."

Those very words would be echoed in August 2002 when word leaked out that the venerable Massachusetts Horticultural Society, custodian of what had been widely recognized as one of the strongest collections of botanical and horticultural literature in the world, was planning to offset years of fiscal indigestion by selling off its most precious holdings. Best known for the mammoth New England Spring Flower Show it mounts every year—begun in 1870, it is the longest-running extravaganza of its kind in the United States—the society had assembled a formidable repository of books in the years since its founding in 1829. Among the treasures stored in its vault were such botanical landmarks as Pierre Joseph Redouté's *Les Liliacées* (1814–1816), Giorgio Gallesio's *Pomona Italiana* (1817), Crispijn van de Passe the Younger's *Hortus Floridus* (1614), and Jean Louis Prévost's *Collection des fleurs et des fruits* (1804–1806), one of the earliest stipple-engraved and color-printed books to be produced.

The core of the collection was shaped by the taste, discrimination, and enthusiastic backing of numerous prominent nineteenth-century Bostonians. Among the more distinguished figures contributing to its formation was Dr. Jacob S. Bigelow (1786–1879), author of the groundbreaking text *American Medical Botany* (1817–1820), for which he drew many of the plates and devised the means of reproducing them through a color acqutint process. Equally influential were Thaddeus W. Harris (1795–1856), a librarian of Harvard College and author whose 1842 work, *A Treatise on Some of the Insects Injurious to Vegetation*, is still regarded as a standard reference, and Francis Parkman (1823–1893), the great historian of French America whose professional credits included a professorship in horticulture at Harvard University. According to Robert Fraker, a Massachusetts bookseller specializing in natural history who wrote a detailed survey of the collection in 1997—and who argued futilely against its wholesale breakup a few years later—the treasures represented a holding that was not likely to be replicated any time soon by any organization or individual. "When the first catalog of the Mass Hort collection was published in 1918, it called itself the finest horticultural library in the world," he told me. "The society received a number of major cash gifts not long after its founding, and its officers were empowered to form as good a botanical library as could be had. The twelve thousand dollars they got from Josiah Stickney in 1839 stipulated that the money be used strictly for library acquisitions, with the result that their agents bought from such people as Bernard Quaritch and John Wheldon in London, F. A. Brockhaus in Leipzig, Frederik Muller in Amsterdam, the very top people in the world at the time."

For years, the collection was made available to scholars, but as financial problems reached endemic proportions in the early 1980s, a number of books were culled from the collection and dispatched in one dispersal for $750,000. "Essentially what happened is that they went in over a weekend and chose what they believed to be duplicates, and sold them off," Fraker said. "That caused a bit of a hullabaloo, but it planted the seed for what came later." In 1991, the society's misfortunes led to the foreclosure sale of its elegant Horticultural Hall across Massachusetts Avenue from Symphony Hall in Boston to the Christian Science Church for the bargain basement price of $1.6 million, and as financial problems continued to mount, attitudes began to polarize around two points of view. The traditionalist faction called for "keeping faith with the founders," as one dissident told me, while the other—a majority of the trustees, as it turned out—saw the literary holdings as a quick and easy way to subsidize its renovation of a thirty-six-acre preserve it had acquired in suburban Wellesley known as Elm Bank, underwrite the annual flower show, and pursue the prospect of establishing a $70 million "Garden Under Glass" project on municipal land near South Station in Boston being made available by the massive underground highway project known as the Big Dig. Although he is said to have exerted some effort toward keeping the library intact early in his tenure, the latter view was ultimately embraced by John C. Peterson, president and chief executive officer of the Horticultural Society since 1992, and it was his support that carried the day.

Because the society enjoys the status of a nonprofit organization, it was required by Massachusetts law to file a business plan with the state attorney general's office detailing its intention to sell off some of its assets, explaining in the process why it needed the money, and estimating how much it expected to realize in the dispersal. According to documents submitted in the 2002 filing, the society claimed to have taken on too many ambitious projects and was "suffering," as a consequence, from "a chronic operating shortfall and lack of available cash." Peterson justified the sale by asserting that the rarest books in the collection were seldom consulted, and that the cost to care for them had become excessive. He asserted that the proceeds—projected in the filing to be in the area of $5 million—would be used to pay debts, restore the endowment, and underwrite the 2003 New England Spring Flower Show. On July 30, 2002, the state's Supreme Judicial Court gave the Mass Hort permission to proceed with the dispersal.

Seven months before that decision was handed down, Paul Rogers, a professional gardener, stepped down as chairman of the board of trustees to protest the impending book sale. "If I am to retain a sense of morality that I can live with, I must disassociate myself from the society—completely," he wrote in his letter of resignation. "Even to have chaired a meeting that included this subject was uncomfortable to me." He was followed out the door by half a dozen other trustees, including the entire finance committee, and the treasurer, Frederick Good III, owner of a plant supply business in suburban Boston, who promptly organized the Committee for a Better MHS (www.bettermhs.org), a dissident group committed to ousting Peterson from his position. When Good began supplying information alleging managerial ineptitude at the organization to the attorney general and the *Boston Globe*, the society sued him in Superior Court, claiming that he had breached his fiduciary duty by spreading "false information." On August 2, 2002, Superior Court Justice Jeffrey A. Locke dismissed the suit summarily, writing that he saw no evidence that Good's conduct "represented anything more than a good faith attempt to address what he perceived as financial mismanagement of a nonprofit organization."

That distraction notwithstanding—and armed with the court's bless-
ings to proceed—Mass Hort went full steam ahead with its plans, adopt-
ing a two-pronged strategy that would place the major portion of the
research materials, 2,219 books and some two thousand horticultural journal titles, with the Chicago Botanic Garden in exchange for an undis-
closed amount of money, but about $3 million, according to documents
on file at the Massachusetts attorney general's office. Reported on the
front page of the *Chicago Tribune,* the acquisition in October 2002 was
greeted with jubilation in the Windy City. "There are complete runs of
journals going over decades, some going back to the seventeenth century
and eighteenth century," Edward J. Valauskas, librarian of the Chicago
Botanic Garden, said. "It's the history of horticulture as an academic discipline. They are remarkable records of the earliest scientific descriptions
of plants and their distribution, many of which are extinct." Peter Fortsas,
a local bookseller who appraised the material for the Chicago group, was
incredulous at the value of what was coming in one fell swoop to an
organization that had been established just thirty years earlier, and was
intent on building the premier horticultural library in the Midwest. "It
would take me fifty years and millions of dollars to put together that collection of books, if it could be done at all."

Had all of the Mass Hort books gone to Chicago, then few critics could
have realistically challenged the transaction, since the collection would
have remained together as a unit, and would have simply been transferred
from one research institution to another, one that was much better
equipped—and quite clearly, much better financed—to maintain it. But it
was the second phase of the dispersal—the selling off at public auction of
the choicest, most glamorous, most exquisitely illustrated books in the
Massachusetts collection—that occasioned condemnation of the sale.
"This is destruction through incompetence," Frederick Good said of the
impending sale. "Those books are going to get chopped up, and as far as I

am concerned, they are lost forever. This is the final deflowering of the Mass Hort."

In a terse statement inserted in the Christie's sale catalog, John Peterson justified the dispersal by claiming the society would be served best by enriching "our endowment and reserve funds" to support the Elm Bank Horticultural Center, and on projects "dedicated to encouraging and improving the science and practice of horticulture and developing the public's enjoyment, appreciation, and understanding of plants and the environment." He also made clear that some books were being kept by the society, most prominently a "legacy collection" of seven hundred rarities, not necessarily because they were especially welcome, it would later be disclosed, but because they were given to the Mass Hort by donors who had the foresight to attach strings to their bequests.

On December 18, 2002, 131 items, described modestly in the sale catalog as "important botanical books from the Massachusetts Horticultural Society," went on the block at Christie's in New York, bringing in $2.45 million. Just nineteen lots were "bought in," meaning that 86 percent of the books met their reserve, averaging $21,895 for each item sold, bringing the grand total derived from the deaccession to just under $5.5 million. The strongest performer in the afternoon sale was the exceedingly scarce first-edition copy of James Bateman's *The Orchidaceae of Mexico and Guatemala*, described in the catalog as "perhaps the most renowned and sought-after of all orchid books," sold to an anonymous buyer for $196,000, or $46,000 above the high estimate. The book—a gift to the society in 1961, and issued in 1843 in an edition of just 125 copies—is said to be "probably the finest, and certainly the largest, botanical book ever produced with lithographic plates," and includes illustrations of some orchids that are now extinct.

While that book was bought by a collector, Pierre-Joseph Redouté's *Les Liliacées* was sold to an unnamed American dealer for $152,500, raising the question of whether or not the six volumes in that lot would be broken up for their exquisite illustrations. Indeed, seven of the ten highest-priced books hammered down in the sale were bought by unnamed dealers, not collectors, prompting similar concerns on what would happen to them. In a statement released through the Christie's press office, Peterson chose to look on the positive side of the ledger, finding "most gratifying" the fact that "a large number of the books were acquired by private collectors, preventing them from being broken up for their plates." Edward Valauskas told me the next day that the Chicago Botanic Garden bought modestly at the sale, acquiring Carolus Linnaeus's *Flora Lapponica* (1737), Johan Joseph Peyritsch's *Aroideae Maximilianae* (1879), and *The Orchid Album* (1882–1897) of Robert Warner, Benjamin Samuel Williams, and Thomas Moore, spending $44,693 for the three lots. As to whether or not any of the books his organization was unable to acquire—"but would dearly love to have been able to afford"—might be stripped of their illustrations, Valauskas said he was "keeping his fingers crossed" that they would remain intact. "But the truth is that I have very little confidence in what some dealers are willing to do with illustrated books. If Dante were alive today, I'd urge him to set aside a special circle in hell for these people." Contacted after the sale by the *Boston Globe*, John Peterson said he considered the matter closed. "I think the reality is that you can't make everybody happy," he said. "I don't have any regrets because, quite honestly, those books hadn't been used in decades."

Robert Fraker had another view, one he told me he expressed to the Mass Hort trustees in 1999 when he was urging them to hold on to their library. "There was this general attitude among some of the board that this was a mishmash of things given by former members, things that were never used, but my feeling then and my feeling now is that this was a very deliberate, very purposeful gathering of books. I told them, please, don't blame the books; it's not their fault that they aren't being used. But it was like they were bent on punishing the library. So finally I told them that if they chose to go through with the sale, do it with the knowledge that this was one of the great horticultural collections to be found anywhere, and that whatever you get for the books today—I don't care *how* much you make—it will seem like a pittance in ten years."

Visitors to a dazzling exhibition early in 1999 at the Pierpont Morgan Library in New York were treated to a comprehensive selection of books assembled with exceptional taste and tenor over the previous thirty years by John Paul Getty Jr. (1932–2003) of England, son of the late American oil billionaire Jean Paul Getty, and knighted by Queen Elizabeth II in 1998 in recognition of his many benefactions to British cultural causes. Given a display case by itself in the lobby outside the main gallery was the copy of Geoffrey Chaucer's *Canterbury Tales* edited and ushered through the press in 1477 by England's first printer, William Caxton, and purchased the previous July at Christie's in London for $7.5 million, the highest price ever paid to that point at auction for a printed book. "You could wait a lifetime and never get a chance to buy that Caxton," Robert J. D. Harding of Maggs Bros. Ltd. of Berkeley Square in London said with evident satisfaction while giving me an informal tour of the exhibition. The Maggs firm was Sir Paul's agents for all of his book purchases, and Bryan Maggs, one of the principals, had the additional distinction of being librarian for the collection he helped to shape, which is called the Wormsley Library for the restored house and estate in the English countryside west of London on the Buckinghamshire-Oxfordshire border where it is maintained. "You have to grasp great opportunities when they are presented," Harding said, and to buttress the point he walked me over to a display case containing three of his personal favorites, not because they are necessarily the dearest items in the Wormsley Library collection of some eight thousand books—although they are quite extraordinary—but because they confirm his contention that great material is still out there, somewhere, available to intrepid collectors, sometimes from the most improbable of sources.

"This section here represents discards from American institutional libraries," he said with an ironic smile. The items lying open under protective glass before us included a twelfth-century folio manuscript on vellum known as the Zacharias Chrysopolitanus, acquired in the 1987–1989 sale at Christie's of the Edward Laurence Doheny Memorial Library in Camarillo, California; it was Number 4 in the Morgan Library exhibition catalog. The item designated Number 2 was a quarto manuscript of 264 leaves from 1164 on vellum known as the Ottobeuren Gradual, with text in a Germanic Romanesque minuscule, including three full-page and two half-page miniatures, along with fourteen historical initials and many elaborated initials, formerly the property of the John Carter Brown Library in Providence, Rhode Island, and acquired by Getty in 1981 at a Sotheby's sale. And listed as Number 1 in the catalog—pride of place—was a piece of text on vellum from the mid-seventh century containing parts of four chapters from a history of the early Christian church by the historian Eusebius, possibly the oldest portion of a book produced in England still in existence. The manuscript survives because it was used in the sixteenth century as a wrapper in the bindings of two medical texts now the property of the Folger Shakespeare Library in Washington, D.C., where it was discovered in 1984 when restoration work was being done on the volumes; Sir Paul acquired that item in 1989.

William M. Voelkle, curator of medieval and Renaissance manuscripts at the Pierpont Morgan Library and one of the organizers of the Wormsley Library exhibition, pointed out that transactions of this nature are not unusual when the materials in question fall outside an institution's collecting interests. "Most of the great items in the world are now in private collections or in the public domain, so the only way you are going to get major pieces like these is if a library has a major shift in focus, and decides to sell," he said. The John Carter Brown Library concentrates on Americana, he pointed out, so it was not surprising when officials decided to sell what Voelkle described as a "German luxury manuscript" they had received as a gift; similarly, the seventh-century sheet discovered at the Folger fell well outside the area of Elizabethan and Jacobean literature that is the specialty there. Maggs bought the Zacharias Chrysopolitanus for Sir Paul in the landmark sale of the Doheny Library, which had been consigned in its entirety to Christie's by the Archdiocese of Los Angeles, and sold for $37.4 million between 1987 and 1989, the most ever realized at auction for the contents of one library. "Nobody discards these books because they think they're worthless," Voelkle said. "They sell them because they realize they are quite valuable, and that they can use them to further their own interests." In fact, it was a good-natured discussion along those very lines that set in motion the decision to allow some Wormsley treasures to be shown in New York in the first place. "I had met Sir Paul through a mutual friend a couple of years ago, and when I met him, he asked me how the Morgan was doing," Charles E. Pierce Jr., director of the Pierpont Morgan Library, told me. "I said we were doing just fine, and he said he was sorry to hear that because he was rather hoping he could buy a few of our things. He was really very sweet and funny about it, so I said, 'Well, that's not the situation, but would you ever consider allowing the library to host an exhibition of some of your favorite books relating to the art of books?' One thing led to another, and eventually it came to pass."

About the same time that Getty was agreeing to send a selection of his books to New York City, a university library in Great Britain that was not doing very well financially decided, without informing anyone else in the tight-knit library community of the United Kingdom, to sell fourteen hundred rare mathematical books, including a number of early editions from the personal library of Sir Isaac Newton, for £1 million. The collection had been built up over fifty years by an eccentric civil servant in the Scottish Education Department named Charles Turner and given to Keele

University in 1968. David Ingram, a retired professor whose friendship with the benefactor led to the gift, told an interviewer that Turner lived frugally in order to buy books, and that he decided to give his collection to a recently established university instead of one with a rich tradition, since it "had not had the opportunity or good fortune to acquire such an important special collection." Ingram said he knew nothing of the transaction while it was being negotiated with a consortium of London booksellers, identified in the *Guardian* as Robert Downie, Daniel McDowell, and Simon Finch.

"This sale is a national disgrace," Professor David Singmaster, a historian of mathematics at South Bank University, said when told of what had happened. "I estimate the collection was worth several million. The Newton material alone might have brought a million at auction." The whole affair was "beneath contempt," Dr. Judith Field, president of the British Society for the History of Mathematics, fumed. Dr. John Fauvel, senior lecturer in the history of mathematics at the Open University and a former president of the society himself, said the sale "marks the desecration of Turner's wishes. He collected it to leave it to the nation and young scholars. For it to be turned into a private collection is ghastly." David McKitterick, the librarian for Trinity College at Cambridge University, the institution where Sir Isaac Newton was a fellow and where most of his books are kept, said he was told nothing about the sale before it was concluded. "Keele never consulted me. Some libraries would have worked extremely hard to pay. Pounds one million would not have been impossible." Officials at the Royal Society and the Bodleian Library at Oxford University confirmed that they had not been contacted either. Professor Ingram, the former head of physics at Keele University, was singularly upset, since it was his friendship with Charles Turner that had facilitated the donation in the first place. Turner had lived in the top floor of a "minimum house" in Wimbledon that was lined with shelf upon shelf of mathematical books, he recalled. "There wasn't any expensive furniture. There was a slightly musty kind of feeling rather like a house in Victorian times. He lived on his own and this was his main interest in life. He was a quiet kind of chap, very polite, a charming gentleman." Professor Singmaster saw a moral in the whole affair: "It just shows that you should never leave anything to a university."

Writing six months later in the *Book Collector* about what was now being called "The Keele Affair" in library circles, David McKitterick pointed out that Newton's own annotated copy of Boyle's *Medicina Hydrostatica* of 1690 and part of a manuscript draft of a lecture delivered in the 1670s were among the materials sold. "The incunabula include a remarkable composite volume of half a dozen works published at Leipzig and Venice in the 1490s, still in its original wooden boards." Acknowledging that Keele had recently fallen on hard times financially, McKitterick condemned the university nonetheless for selling off some of its most precious holdings without attempting to place them in another research library. "To disperse a collection is to demolish a potentially fruitful source of inspiration, scholarship and learning," he wrote, and concluded that Keele had "broken its trust: a moral one both to its benefactor and to the country."

That the money was reported to be going toward the purchase of new computers and on-line access services was especially galling, McKitterick felt. The Keele library, he offered, "is notable for its high-profile commitment to information technology rather than to books. Indeed, the current postgraduate prospectus joins libraries and information services together under the heading of 'Information,' and altogether omits to mention the word 'book' at this point. It is not entirely irrelevant to such a world to point out the obvious: that while books have some lasting value, virtually everything depending on computers has to be replaced or reformatted at least once every five years." In the end, he reasoned, such an exchange "is lopsided" in that "once sold, exceptional books cannot be replaced. Collections of a kind such as Turner's cannot be re-created. The loser in the end is the university, whatever the temporary comfort given to university administration by a fat cheque."

That other options are available to administrators in situations like this was demonstrated quite convincingly by the Catholic University of Nijmegen in the Netherlands in 2001 when curators there were looking for ways to thin twelve hundred titles from its admirable holding of books published in the Low Countries before 1800. "These were all duplicates in their collection, and they came to us as a one hundred percent gift," William A. Gosling, librarian at the University of Michigan in Ann Arbor, told me in May 2002 during a walking tour of "Netherlandic Treasures," an exhibition of rare books that had just opened in the special collections unit. We were admiring half a dozen items in one display case, by no means the most spectacular pieces in the exhibition—there were some truly fabulous pieces from the university's own collection of books and manuscripts from the Netherlands and Belgium under glass nearby—but what was special about these was the circumstance of their accession.

"When we were contacted about the books, the clear understanding was that they would never be sold by us to anyone else, and that if there ever came a time when we decided we had no use for them, they would go to another repository where they would be available to scholars," Gosling said. "But of course that will never happen, since the reason they came here, as you can readily see around you, is because we have such an important holding of our own in this area. These books are especially welcome here for another reason: We already had a rich gathering of the high spots, which includes many thousands of maps, atlases, and pamphlets, a number of important manuscripts, but we were weak in the second-tier material, exactly the kinds of things you need to enrich a major collection, and exactly the kinds of things we acquired by way of this gift." The University of Michigan, Gosling pointed out, began building a strong research collection of material from the Low Countries early in the twentieth century under the direction of William Warner Bishop, the university librarian from 1915 to 1941, who personally supervised a massive acquisition program in Europe. Within the university, a Netherlands visiting professorship has been sponsored every year since 1950, and more than twenty Dutch authors have been invited to be writers-in-residence over the same period. The twelve hundred duplicates from Nijmegen, according to Peggy Daub, director of special collections at the University of Michigan, "forms an unusual addition to Netherlandic studies since they document the minority Catholic viewpoint in the Low Countries" prior to 1800, when all of them were published. Most are quite scarce, in good condition, in their original bindings, and therefore quite desirable on the antiquarian market, had raising money been the strategy chosen by their former custodians. "It was really a generous gift," Gosling said, "and a perfect fit for us."

At the Library of Congress in Washington, D.C., every book that arrives—and some twenty thousand items a day, on average, pour into the cavernous Madison Building on Capitol Hill and various satellite facilities—does not necessarily become part of the national collections. "We have guidelines that strictly define what we can keep," Diane N. Kresh, director of preservation and acting director for public service collections, told me. "We have a selection office, and the people there examine everything that comes in, be it by copyright or by purchase or gift or exchange, to make sure it is within our scope. There is, as you know, a mandatory deposit requirement for all books published in the United States, but whether or not we keep them depends on whether or not they fall within our collections policy guidelines. These have been carefully developed and are a matter of public record."

At that point, Kresh slid a blue loose-leaf notebook containing a set of Library of Congress policy statements across the top of her desk, "yours to keep," she noted, and suggested I pay particular attention to what are called the "canons of selection" for the national collections. "As you know—and as you will readily see in that notebook—we have a thorough plan here that is second to none, but there is still no way that we can collect everything. Once we do choose to place something in our permanent collections, however, we will keep it forever. It is true that we don't keep dust jackets, and I think that is a mistake, because there is a whole history of social life and customs that you can get from dust jackets, and newspapers for the most part have been replaced by microfilm, which we regard as a viable copy of the original. We will not keep multiple copies of superseded textbooks either. But acquisitions, and how we take care of things, are at the heart of what we are all about."

Sometimes the deaccessioning of unwanted materials raises questions that have nothing to do with dwindling storage space or shrinking budgets, and everything to do with the loss of important information, however distasteful or out of fashion it may be to prevailing sensibilities. This, at least, was the epiphany that came to one Massachusetts educator who attempted to locate a copy of a controversial book that was once held in numerous research libraries, but had since been discarded to the point that no "last copy" was available for consultation in any American institution. Titled *Die Freigabe der Vernichtung lebensunwerten Lebens* (Permitting the Destruction of an Unworthy Life), the highly polemical monograph had been written in the early years of the twentieth century by two German academics, Dr. Alfred Binding, a prominent defense attorney and widely published emeritus professor of law at Leipzig University, and Dr. Karl Hoche, a professor of psychiatry at the University of Freiburg and the prolific author of numerous medical essays. Published in 1920 by Felix Meiner Verlag of Leipzig, the treatise appeared at a volatile juncture in European history when Germany was reassessing its humiliating defeat in World War I and groping for ways to reclaim its international stature. By presenting a chilling argument in favor of state-supported programs of euthanasia, Binding and Hoche gave credence to an argument then gaining support in their homeland that one way for a people to assure collective strength was to eliminate the weaker elements of its population. Robert Jay Lifton, professor of psychiatry and psychology at John Jay College in New York and the author in 1986 of *The Nazi Doctors,* called the collaboration of the two prominent nationalists "the crucial theoretical work" that German politicians needed to justify the "medical killing" of 200,000 chronically sick, physically disabled, and mentally ill adults and children. More ominously, it helped shape a "psychology of genocide" that led ultimately to the unspeakable atrocities of the Holocaust. "Binding and Hoche turned out to be the prophets of direct medicalized killing," Lifton declared unequivocally.

In its time, the soft-cover pamphlet was a "minor best-seller" in Europe, Dr. Patrick G. Derr, chairman of the philosophy department at Clark University in Worcester, Massachusetts, told me, and copies were acquired by numerous medical schools, law schools, and research libraries. Derr said his interest in examining the monograph had been spurred in the fall of 1988 during an international conference he had organized at Clark on the general topic of "euthanasia and the future of medicine." Three hundred physicians, attorneys, academics, and clergy from North America and Europe attended, with papers read by many prominent speakers, C. Everett Koop, Ralph McInerny, Fred Rosner, Mark Siegler, Arthur Dyck, Milton Heifetz, and Moshe Tendler among them.

"I was struck by the repeated reference in their remarks to this monograph," Derr said. "There was no question in anyone's mind that it was an important document, and when it became clear to me that nobody who mentioned it had actually seen it firsthand, I thought it would be worthwhile to make an English version available to the scholarly community." Walter E. Wright, an associate professor of philosophy at Clark who is fluent in German, agreed to do a translation, and *Issues in Law & Medicine,* a journal published by the National Legal Center for the Medically Dependent and Disabled, agreed to publish it. But when the two scholars tried to locate an intact copy of the original German text, no copies could be found in any research library. Derr and his colleague finally located a "miracle copy" that had been deposited years earlier in the archives of the Leipzig publisher that issued it, and produced their translation in 1992. In a preface, they detailed at length their "strangely difficult" experience in trying to make the work available to a new generation of scholars. A photocopy of the German edition is now held by Clark University's Robert H. Goddard Library, and is available there for anyone who wants to study the text in its original version; no copies are available for reference in any other library that reports its holdings to the OCLC WorldCat database. Derr, meanwhile, has since located a first edition signed by Hoche through the antiquarian market for his personal library, proving once again how it is the collector who oftentimes serves as a final line of defense against the loss of important material.

"What we discovered is that a good number of American libraries had once owned this book, and there are ample records to document that," Derr said. "Only Harvard Medical School claimed to still have a copy, but after repeated attempts, they finally admitted that they couldn't locate it for us. We were told simply that it could not be found, and that was that." As to why the influential work might have been tossed out by so many institutions, Derr said he could offer only an educated guess. "Americans, for the most part, have recoiled in horror from a eugenics program that our own scholars helped to create," he surmised. "Scientific eugenics is an American-English invention, and the fact of the matter is that it is extremely embarrassing to us. Nazi universities gave honorary degrees to a number of American race scholars. You can check that out. It is a matter of record. I'm pretty ignorant of the politics that go on in research libraries, but cultures do tend to erase the disagreeable aspects of their own history, and there has been a fairly strong backlash against race theory in the United States. One of my abiding professional interests is the evolution of medical ethics, and this is an extremely important document in that history." Derr said there is an entire list of books of "scientific racism," some of them written in the early years of the twentieth century by prominent scholars, that can no longer be found in American libraries either, and he cited Allan Chase's book *The Legacy of Malthus: The Social Costs of the New Scientific Racism* (New York: Alfred A. Knopf, 1977) as an important reference to consult on the subject.

Kerr told me he deplores the discarding of any book that is essential to the pursuit of serious scholarship, however abhorrent the premise may be that it propounds. "That's one of the questions that fascinated me at the conference we had. There were so many people here who had mentioned this book, but none of them, it seemed perfectly clear, had actually ever read it, and undoubtedly that was because none of them were able to lay their hands on a copy. Well, mentions aren't good enough for scholarship. The larger point to all this, I think, is that somebody has to keep the books that document the foundations of hate."

The summary expulsion of the Binding-Hoche monograph is an example of a book of considerable social consequence being allowed to slip through the cracks of custodial oversight, and only through the persistence of two stubborn professors was the loss discovered before it was too late. In the vast majority of cases, discarded books pass into oblivion without any ceremony at all, their titles largely forgotten, and whatever benefit they might have offered future inquiry vaporizes along with them. But every once in a while there are indications of where specific items, however obscure or unpopular they may have been when they were cast adrift, have created a discernible void merely by their absence. "Prodigal Text," a brief article published in the Cornell University alumni magazine for January-February 2000, reported the efforts of a student in the university's agriculture school, located in Geneva, New York, to locate an old reference book to supplement his research. Here is the item in its entirety:

> When plant pathology grad student Nathaniel Mitkowski couldn't find an out-of-print nematology text in the Geneva Ag Station library, he searched on the Internet. A Nevada-based website yielded a copy of the 1961 primer on microscopic worms for $20. Mitkowski bought it, and when it arrived he noticed a stamp on the inside cover: New York State Agricultural Experiment Station Plant Pathology Library, Geneva—DISCARDED. The book, it turns out, had been jettisoned a few years earlier to make room in the library. After a 6,000-mile round trip, it sits on Mitkowski's shelf, ten feet from where it was before.

Paradoxically, it is precisely this kind of book—a title that very few people know very much about, or care very much about for that matter—that is of mounting concern to preservationists, since collections of unquestioned rarity such as those sold by the Hill Library, the Keele Library, and the Massachusetts Horticultural Society are not likely to fall victim to neglect or indifference even if they are deaccessioned. Those books simply go someplace else where they will find a more welcoming home. Academic titles that are in constant circulation or support ongoing research programs are not likely to be discarded either. It is the huge reservoir of material in the middle—books no longer in demand, books that are decidedly dated, books that do not appeal to prevailing tastes, "brittle" books that are not high-priority items for repair—that are most immediately at risk. In an effort to protect some—but by no means all—books in this nebulous limbo zone, a number of research libraries, Columbia University in particular, have established a category called "medium rare," and have transferred books at risk from their general circulation stacks to restricted areas. These titles do not receive the same archival attention accorded to special collections by any means, but access to them is monitored, they cannot be removed from the library, and photocopying is permitted only on a case-by-case basis after a determination has been made that page-by-page exposure to the rigors of a machine will not inflict excessive damage.

A deaccession symposium held at Brown University in 1981 addressed the general issue head-on, noting, in the words of keynote speaker David H. Stam, at that time the Andrew W. Mellon Director of the Research Libraries of the New York Public Library, that the subject was "a hot topic at the moment," and it remains hot two decades later. Part of the problem librarians face, Stam offered then, was "a widespread cultural belief in the sacredness of the book, the printed word, and even the written word," and they continue to deal with that "problem" today. "We're told it was there in the beginning, and that includes moving a book from one library to another. Every librarian has been burned by that issue, having discarded or transferred something that someone else thinks valuable." Stam offered this further caution on the politics of discarding:

> The library should also ascertain to the best of its ability the uniqueness, rarity or scarcity of materials being considered for disposal and assess the possible effects of dispersal on the access of the scholar or a more general public to the material. If an accession, by definition, makes something accessible, we should remember that a deaccession may make that item inaccessible. This is a particular problem with archival collections where a decision to discard is often irrevocable and the material is lost forever, though usually no proceeds are involved.

Another set of discard issues not discussed by Stam at the Brown symposium was a federally funded program of "preservation by surrogate" begun in the 1970s at many research libraries throughout the United States, including the New York Public Library, that involved disbinding aging books, almanacs, and pamphlets at the spine so they could be microfilmed, and then discarded. The Ardsley, New York, collector of Americana, Michael Zinman, went to unprecedented lengths in 1997 to inform the book world of a huge cache of material, including some "last copies" he had acquired that were formerly the property of the New York Public Library. Zinman—a collector who coined the term *critical mess* to describe his approach to gathering material in bulk with little regard to physical condition—had bought thousands of almanacs, old periodicals, and booklets known as series tracts at the flat-rate price of a dollar a pound from a bookseller, who had acquired them from the library for the price of scrap paper.

As a holiday greeting to several hundred influential people in and around the book world, including every member of the board of trustees of the New York Public Library, Zinman sent out a poster reproducing the bookplates of some of the items he had obtained. Printed above the illustrations was a quotation purportedly used by an American military commander during the Vietnam War: "In order to save the village we had to destroy it." One of the people on Zinman's mailing list was the *New Yorker* feature writer Mark Singer, who promptly wrote a "Talk of the Town" piece for the magazine, causing no small measure of dismay to NYPL officials when it appeared in print on January 10, 1998.

"There are a lot of good things they do at the New York Public Library," Zinman told me, "but what has one got to do with the other? What I was condemning was a fundamental policy of the library, and my question is this: Is it something that is endemic to the library world at large? Who knows? I certainly don't, and it's beside the point in this instance as far as I'm concerned. These things are worth thousands of dollars, but money is not the issue. This is an institution that should never, within reason, throw anything out. There are alternatives to discarding, the easiest being packing material up and putting it in cold storage. If somebody absolutely needs to see the original, charge a fee that will cover the cost of getting it out to examine, and for treating it while it's out."

In the library's defense, the long-term microfilming project represented conventional wisdom regarding preservation strategies in vogue when the program began in the 1970s. Robert Darnton, a professor of history at Princeton University, a noted author of scholarly nonfiction, and a trustee of the New York Public Library (see chapter 9), told me that the embarrassment brought on by the *New Yorker* article prompted the board to demand a new policy that would outline in specific detail procedures to be followed involving discards. "One thing we were adamant about," Darnton said, "is that there be no more guillotining. There has to be another way to do this. And original materials must be preserved." The library administration responded by drafting a twenty-one-page set of guidelines governing the "deaccession and disposition of library materials," which was adopted on February 17, 1999.

In the new statement, the library acknowledged that "prior to 1998" the library "considered microfilmed surrogates of brittle materials to be duplicates of the original artifacts," and that if the original "was not considered rare, unique, or possessing special features," curators were free to dispose of the artifact and keep the copy, which was done in thousands of instances. That practice was terminated forthwith, although the library did reserve the right to make exceptions on an individual basis in the future. It was also decided that original materials that have been "reformatted"—either scanned digitally or copied on microfilm—will be kept by the library, "or transferred to other research institutions or libraries as deemed appropriate."

A year after the new policy was adopted, Paul LeClerc, president of the New York Public Library, told me that as welcome as the changes may be, they were made possible only because the financial health of the library had improved to such a point where the privately funded institution could even consider implementing them. Just as significant, he added, was the construction of a new off-site storage facility in New Jersey owned jointly by the library with Princeton and Columbia Universities, which provided storage space that was not available in the past. "This is a substantially complicated issue," he emphasized. "You have to take a look at the financial condition of this library in the 1970s. It was not what it is today; our economic and financial capacity now is vastly superior, night and day, from what it was twenty-five years ago. There were physical capacity issues to consider then too, concerns about whether or not the library had sufficient resources then to keep everything that it owned forever, and there were preservation concerns as well. Preservation then was synonymous with microfilming, and that attitude is now changing. So what this administration did when it looked at those old practices was to do what we consider to be the best thing for right now, given our own changing attitudes toward maintaining our collections. This is not by any means our dilemma alone, of course; this is an issue for all research libraries."

Of more immediate concern is the desperate status of archival newspaper collections, which have been routinely discarded by research libraries everywhere in favor of black-and-white microfilm copies. In the fall of 1999 the novelist and essayist Nicholson Baker, fresh from drawing international attention to the wholesale destruction of antiquated card catalogs and the indiscriminate dumping of books at the San Francisco Public Library, launched a last-minute effort to rescue seven thousand bulky volumes containing hundreds of old newspapers, each bearing the stamp "Discarded by the British Library" on the cover. The enormous archive was sold in a silent auction conducted by the British Library on September 30, 1999, and included an uninterrupted cycle of Joseph Pulitzer's heavily illustrated *New York World*, 1866 to 1930, neatly bound in eight hundred hardcover volumes. Along with long runs of other newspapers, many of them ethnic publications published in rural America in the late nineteenth and early twentieth centuries, Baker acquired every copy of the *Chicago Tribune* printed between 1888 and 1958, all of the *New York Times* from 1915 to 1958, and perhaps the most exciting resource of all, the *New York Herald Tribune,* from its founding in 1886 straight through to its lamentable demise in 1975. Imparting a sense of urgency to the undertaking for Baker was the knowledge that full runs of these original materials are no longer held by research libraries in the country of their origin, and that the British Library dispersal represented a final opportunity for anyone to acquire extensive sets in their original formats. Most North American repositories, including the Library of Congress, at one time the largest repository for newspapers in the country, have systematically replaced their cumbersome collections with compact black-and-white microfilm images, finding that small spools of film are much easier to store than bulky sheets of aging newsprint, even though the quality is decidedly inferior, and casual browsing is an enormously difficult, if not impossible, exercise to undertake. A notable exception to this trend is the American Antiquarian Society in Massachusetts, which collects everything that was printed in what is now the United States of America—the AAS has a cut-off date of 1876—and the Boston Public Library, which steadfastly refuses to discard any of its newspaper collections. "A million people a day once read Pulitzer's *World,*" Baker wrote in the *New Yorker;* "now an original set is a good deal rarer than a Shakespeare First Folio or the Gutenberg Bible."

To free up space for its own national newspaper collections—and the foreign publications targeted for discard took up two miles of shelving in the Colindale warehouse north of London—the British Library had followed the lead of its sibling institutions and adopted microfilm as the exclusive source for the materials. As part of an ongoing "overseas disposal project," the library had already gotten rid of its European, Russian, and South American collections, including newspapers from Nazi Germany, occupied France, and prerevolutionary Russia. Baker recalled how he had pleaded with English officials to spare the collections, or at the very least donate them to the American Newspaper Repository, a nonprofit foundation he had established "in a mad rush" to "acquire, preserve, and make available to the public, original newspapers of historic and scholarly interest that would otherwise be destroyed or dispersed into private ownership." Several prominent book people on both sides of the Atlantic—most notably G. Thomas Tanselle, the American bibliographer and vice president of the John Simon Guggenheim Memorial Foundation, and Nicolas Barker, the estimable editor of the *Book Collector* and the former head of conservation for the British Library—openly supported Baker's effort. Baker wrote an impassioned letter to John Ashworth, the British Library chairman of the board, to caution him that selling off the American newspapers under conditions of secrecy—the *Daily Telegraph* of London would later report that "not a word appeared in the press to mark" the sale—had the potential of creating an "international scandal."

Baker submitted winning bids for most of the runs he had targeted—the invoice from London read "Deselection (Newspapers) £19,282.00"—with the notable exception of the *Chicago Tribune*. When Baker later learned that the *Tribune* is not held in any depth by any major repository in the United States, he contacted the high bidder, a Pennsylvania entrepreneur who does a spirited business in the sale of "souvenir" pages stripped from old newspapers, with hopes of negotiating a deal. Bolstered by a grant from the MacArthur Foundation, Baker paid $63,000 for another "ten tons of major metropolitan history," or about $50 a volume. Subsequent support from the Knight Foundation enabled him to locate the American Newspaper Repository (www.oldpapers.org) in a nineteenth-century industrial building in Rollinsford, New Hampshire.

Hard on the heels of Baker's *New Yorker* essay came his book *Double Fold*, published in 2001. With an expanded version of the newspaper controversy at its core, Baker went further afield to allege professional misconduct on the part of some librarians, suggesting that they signed on too easily on reformatting what they were led to believe are brittle books, claiming, in essence, that the problem was overstated, and had led to the discarding of close to a million books throughout the United States that still had a lot of life left in them. Baker, as I discussed in a chapter of *Patience & Fortitude* dealing with the recent misfortunes of the San Francisco Public Library, is no stranger to library controversy—indeed, he does not dispute assessments that describe him as a "library activist"— but the response to *Double Fold* was unusually pointed, garnering international attention from the world media, winning for its author a National Book Critics Circle award for nonfiction. On May 16, 2001, it also occasioned a memorable confrontation with Richard J. Cox, professor of library and information service at the University of Pittsburgh, at a forum in Boston sponsored by Simmons College before a packed auditorium of librarians, archivists, journalists, and students.

Candidly describing himself as "obsessed" with Baker's sudden celebrity in what most general observers would regard as the otherwise arcane community of bibliographical and archival professionals, Cox engaged *Double Fold* point for point, getting back as good as he gave in return. A year after the debate, Cox published an expanded version of his rebuttal, *Vandals in the Stacks: A Response to Nicholson Baker*, making clear that his title came from a review of *Double Fold*, and not from *Double Fold* itself. At the center of Cox's argument was the contention that Baker is an amateur sailor adrift in a stormy sea best navigated by professional mariners. "This chapter plays with the fact that Baker is a novelist and it is difficult to see how the story Baker tells is more than a good story, not very different from some of his other fiction," he offered as an opening salvo. "The public can find better sources than *Double Fold* or any of Nicholson Baker's other writings to gain an appreciation of the nature and function of libraries," he suggested elsewhere, and so on throughout his book, which Cox acknowledged would probably appeal principally to the "modern information professions" than it would a general readership. That qualification aside, *Vandals in the Stacks* is instructive for those interested in the other side of the argument propounded by Baker and his supporters, if only to appreciate how contentious the issue is, and how complex it remains. For Cox, the most challenging theme raised by Baker in his book, and the one he feels is the most naïve, is the suggestion that "*everything* should be saved, an argument that has found resonance with the media and public."

As the furor raised by *Double Fold* receded, Baker's commitment to preservation of the original artifacts remained constant, and as the second anniversary of the publication of the book approached in 2003, he remained hopeful that an agreement would be reached with a major research library to take permanent custody of the newspapers he had saved from desecration. When we exchanged e-mail early in the year, he told me that discussions were ongoing with the Firestone Library at Princeton University, although other institutions had expressed strong interest in the holdings as well. "Specifically, it would be a deposit agreement that would become a gift after a transition period," he made clear. "One thing is for certain—this eventually will be a gift, not a sale. Selling is what got us into this mess in the first place."

7.

Ingenious Cipher

※ ※

The physical book is never more than an ingenious and often beautiful cipher by which the intellectual book is communicated from one mind to another, and the intellectual book is always a structure in the imagination which may hang for a time above a folio page in ten-point type with a half-calf binding only to be found thereafter on a different page above a different type and even in another language.

—ARCHIBALD MACLEISH, "OF THE LIBRARIAN'S PROFESSION,"
IN THE *ATLANTIC MONTHLY* (1940)

※ ※

T
he idea that a book is an artifact that has relevance beyond its content is a concept that involves many points of view, any number of which bear directly on whether or not these objects have lives in and of themselves, or that their purpose is to function merely as carriers of information. A word of recent coinage that has entered the general debate—*paratexts*—was introduced in the 1980s by the French literary theorist Gérard Genette to identify and describe the various "liminal devices and conventions, both within and outside the book, that form part of the complex mediation between book, author, publisher, and reader," and include such familiar "framing elements" as titles, dedications, forewords, prefaces, epigraphs, epilogues, endnotes, afterwords, illustrations, dust jackets, indexes, appendices, paper, type design, and bindings. The paratext, Genette contended, provides some commentary on the text and influences how the

text is received. Whenever the suggestion is broached that a text exists independently of its "delivery system" or, by contrast, that the medium is merely the vehicle by which words are passed on and received, it is elements like these that are taken into account.

Precisely *how* a text is presented becomes particularly crucial in the poetry of Emily Dickinson (1830–1886), the reclusive "belle of Amherst" who wrote nearly eighteen hundred poems that were never published in her lifetime. Instead, she organized most of them into her own idea of a book, copying each poem onto sheets of letter paper and fastening all of them together with string. "In her isolation and poetic silence, these manuscript books, known as fascicles, may have served privately as publication, a personal enactment of the public act that, for reasons unexplained, she denied herself," Ralph W. Franklin wrote in the introduction to a facsimile edition of the handwritten verses. Seeing the poems not only as they were written, but as they were bound and gathered, is of considerable importance, "for the manuscripts of this poet resist translation into the conventions of print. Formal features like her unusual punctuation and capitalization, line and stanza divisions, and display of alternate readings are a source of continuing critical concern." Because Dickinson's poetic vision exists in one holographic copy, the only way anyone other than a serious scholar with impeccable credentials will ever get to read her work as she intended it to be read is in facsimile—a copy of the original that attempts to reproduce as faithfully as possible not only the idiosyncrasies of language, but the physical presentation itself. How the poems were edited and prepared for traditional publication, moreover, how her language is presented, and whether or not the poems appear in the precise sequence that Dickinson arranged them, are all paratextual factors that will influence how her work is "received" and "processed" by readers.

The inspired coupling of words and images has never been demonstrated more dramatically than by the work of William Blake (1757–1827), the English genius who combined the considerable skills of an accomplished artist, a penetrating poet, and an innovative engraver to produce books that were unique from one copy to the next. The son of a London tradesman, Blake began writing poetry as a child; at fourteen, he was apprenticed to the engraver for the Society of Antiquaries. Largely self-educated—he taught himself Greek, Latin, Hebrew, and Italian so that he could read classical works in their original languages—Blake had a driving passion to create art that synthesized the various intellectual disciplines he had mastered.

A firm believer in mystical presences, Blake maintained that a new method of engraving was revealed to him in a dream by his beloved brother Robert, who had died at the age of nineteen. The result was the creation of an art form known as relief printing, which allowed him to publish his illustrated lyrics without using the traditional letterpress process. Before Blake's refinement of this technique, the standard method of printing words with pictures on the same page required the assembly of etched plates of illustrations with lines of movable metal type in a tray. Blake began his procedure by sketching out working designs for both elements on sheets of copperplate with chalk. Then, using a camel-hair brush and a quill pen, he painted the images and words he wanted on each sheet with a mixture of salad oil and candle grease, a concoction he had determined would resist a coating of nitric acid that bit into the surrounding metal. Three or four hours after application of the acid, the words and images would emerge in *relief* as one integrated design on a single plate, which Blake then used to pull prints on paper. He produced illuminated copies of *Songs of Innocence* through the last years of his life in this manner, and no two were ever alike. His hand-coloring varied distinctively from print to print, and the poems never appeared in the same order, producing what amounted to unique literary artifacts. Blake's poetry has been printed in dozens of editions since his death, but reading the text in plain type apart from his visual art is a truncated experience—aesthetically, emotionally, and intellectually.

In diverting contrast to Blake are the curious productions of Nicolas-Edme Restif (1734–1806), known as Restif de la Bretonne, who wrote numerous realistic and erotic novels in which he extracted morals and proposed sweeping social reforms. Like Blake, Restif was born to humble parents and trained to pursue a craft in the graphic arts. After serving his apprenticeship as a printer in Auxerre, he moved to Paris in 1755 and got a job in the royal printing press. Around 1765 he began writing the first of what one critic has described as a "bewildering multitude of books" on many subjects, about two hundred volumes all told. Restif was no stranger to poverty and intrigue, and he drew heavily on his own experiences for his writings, which depict the ancien régime on the eve of the French Revolution. Among his more noteworthy efforts are *Le Pied de Fanchette* (1769), a novel, and *La Pornographe* (also 1769), in which he offered a plan for the regulating of prostitution. He wrote many short stories, and toward the end of his life began *Monsieur Nicolas,* an autobiography in sixteen volumes that spared nothing—remembrances, opinions, commentary on politics and morality, petty hatreds, and endless recitations on the romantic interludes that occupied much of his life. "Restif de la Bretonne has genius, but no taste," the president of the National Academy sniffed in 1795, when declining to approve his nomination for membership.

Restif's works are of interest to antiquarians and bibliographers, since he set the type and printed the sheets for much of his own work, employing a typographic method that was decidedly his. Frequently at odds with the censors, Restif would print a few copies of his books in compliance with their corrections, and then rearrange the type and print the material as he had wanted it to appear in the first place; he apparently was never caught in this deception. In his memoirs, Restif made clear that his greatest satisfaction as a writer came while working with type in the pressroom. Speaking of himself in the third person, Restif described what for him was the most productive technique: "He worked on all of these titles in the printing press. He was at the same time author and compositor: he composed entire passages without a manuscript, and these instances where he set the work directly in the cases without a written copy were always the best—the best written, the best thought out." Although critics are mixed on the quality of Restif's prose, his first editions—the books he himself coaxed through the printing press with his own hands in the heat of composition—routinely command five-figure prices in the antiquarian book market.

One of the most imaginative English novels of the eighteenth century, *The Life and Opinions of Tristram Shandy, Gentleman,* by Laurence Sterne (1713–1768), is an example of a book in which an author has taken extraordinary steps to "interact" with readers in ways that went well beyond enticing them to comprehend words printed on paper. Written in nine volumes between 1759 and 1767, *Tristram Shandy* ranks among the most eccentric, extraordinarily complex, and endlessly convoluted works ever to appear in English literature, and continues to charm those who attempt to engage it in the manner conceived by Sterne. Part of its continuing fun comes with the realization that this was an experimental work, one that by every account was intended by its author, an Irish-born English clergyman obsessed with achieving great success as a man of letters, to be experienced as a physical object, and he accomplished this by breaking away from the conventions of what then were held to constitute a novel.

As the title suggests, the hugely discursive work purports to narrate the life story of one Tristram Shandy, beginning with his conception, but because there is so much to relate about his eccentric family, he is not born until the fourth volume. A work that delights in parody and satire, *Tristram Shandy* has moments of bawdy humor that remain hilarious more than two hundred years after they were written, but layered just beneath the frivolity are stark images of disconnection and human isolation, leading Shandy to wonder how much he can ever know about himself. As quite possibly the first author to write a novel about the writing of novels,

Sterne frequently speaks directly to the reader, creating a dialogue in which he expounds on his views of the book as a material object.

Very much a part of Sterne's scheme is the mindful combination of verbal elements with visual contrivances, and a case can be made that the only way to appreciate *Tristram Shandy* in the manner that he intended is to handle an edition of the book that faithfully reproduces the physical characteristics he insisted it embody. Just about every page contains an intricate system of hyphens, asterisks, and occasional crosses, with flamboyant use in particular made of the dash; varying in length, these marks are often treated as though they are words in their own right. Just as important as the experimental use of typography is Sterne's playful manipulation of the pages. In one instance the figure of a crucifix appears when a character crosses himself; a black page "mourns" the death of another, squiggly lines indicate the not-so-linear progress of the narrative, blank pages suggest text that has been torn out, and a very different kind of page gives the reader an opportunity to draw an original depiction of a woman's supposed beauty. Other oddities of the first edition included the insertion of hand-marbled pages where each side was uniquely different, the use of parallel texts in Latin and English, chapters that consist of a single sentence, misplaced chapters, and sections that are missing altogether. In volume 4, for example, the pagination jumps from page 146 to 156—and there is *no* chapter 24 at all—with the result that all the subsequent pages to the right are assigned even numbers, not odd, quite a departure in traditional book-making form, since every page on the left side of an opening should always be even. It is through repeated peculiarities such as these that the reader's attention is drawn to the *appearance* of the page, drawing notice to the unconventional form, which has a decided impact on the way the text itself is received.

To make sure that his grand scheme of the novel was fully realized, Sterne personally ushered each volume through the press. Letters he wrote to his publisher document in exacting detail the care with which he chose the format, paper, type, and layout of the work. To protect himself against piracy, he autographed every first- and second-edition copy of volume 5 on the title page, and the first-edition copies of volumes 7 and 9, signing his name, it has been estimated, no fewer than 12,750 times. As a crowning touch, he persuaded the great satiric artist of the period, William Hogarth (1697–1764), to design a pair of distinctive plates as frontispieces for two of the volumes. Given these material peculiarities— what Genette, once again, would call *paratextual* elements—it is clear that the book was meant by Sterne to be taken in and savored as much as it was intended to be read as an innovative work of fiction.

In 1996, Pantheon Books published a new English translation of *Dead Souls,* a satiric epic of life in the Russian provinces during the middle of the nineteenth century first published in 1842 and considered the master-piece of Nikolai Gogol (1809–1852), a dramatist, storyteller, and novelist who was trained originally as a painter. One of the translators of the new version, Richard Pevear, began his introduction by recalling a curiosity of the book's early history. "Gogol designed the title page for the first edi-tion of *Dead Souls* himself. It is an elaborate piece of not-quite-symmetrical baroque scrollwork, surrounded by airy curlicues in which various objects and figures appear." Pevear's precise description of this single page pays close attention to Gogol's various drawings, and to the size and style of lettering he chose for the words *Chichikov's Adventures* at the top, printed in the smallest possible characters, and then, in very small cursive, the word *or,* followed by *Dead Souls* in large, bold script at the center of the page.

"I want to say something about the words Gogol distinguished so carefully by the size of their lettering and their placement on the page," Pevear noted, and for the next five pages he outlined how the book ran afoul of the czar's imperial censor in Moscow—a devout member of the

Russian Orthodox Church, it happened—for daring to suggest that "immortal souls" could possibly be "dead," even after the author insisted that he was talking not about spiritual matters but of deceased serfs who were still listed on the tax rolls. "Even worse," the chief censor replied. "That means it is against serfdom." Because Gogol was regarded as the leading literary light in Russia at the time, his work was finally approved for publication, but only after he had agreed to modify the title by adding *Chichikov's Adventures* to it. "That is how those two words in the plainest and smallest letters appeared at the top of Gogol's design for the title page, though the title was and has always remained *Dead Souls* and nothing else." Knowing that telling circumstance—and actually seeing it before embarking on a reading of the text itself, along with the author's sketches—is an essential part of appreciating Gogel's concept of his own novel, yet for some unexplained reason, the publisher of the new English-language edition chose not to include a reproduction of this telling element in the new translation.

A similar circumstance applies to the novel *Vanity Fair*, which made its debut appearance in a series of monthly installments between January 1847 and July 1848, followed by release of a book that was decorated with forty full-page plates of illustrations, plus an engraved title page and 150 woodcuts, all drawn by the author, William Makepeace Thackeray (1811–1863). Taking into account the subtitle of the magazine series, *Pen and Pencil Sketches of English Society*, and the physical appearance of the book itself, there can be little doubt that Thackeray considered his art an indispensable part of the total work. "That first appearance undoubtedly is the book that Thackeray wanted to be read, yet very few editions published since his death have been illustrated with these pictures," noted Terry Belanger, university professor and director of the Rare Book School at the University of Virginia in Charlottesville, and a keen observer of just how books are made. "The reader is being deprived of something that the author of a great nineteenth-century novel felt was important to include."

Another "teaching tool" that Belanger uses in his courses is a collection of four hundred copies of a romantic novel in verse published in Britain and the United States between 1860 and 1927 in an abundance of formats, designs, and sizes, some of them illustrated, some not. Written by Owen Meredith, the pseudonym of the poet and statesman Edward Robert Bulwer, the first earl of Lytton (1831–1891), *Lucile* enjoyed a tremendous run of popularity in the years leading up to World War I, but is virtually unknown today. I asked Belanger why it was necessary for a research institute with finite storage space to have so many copies of one obscure book when they all "say" essentially the same thing. "First of all, why not?" he answered, pointing out that the purpose of the center he directs is to study the book as an artifact—a "container" of information—not the "intellectual construct" that comprises the content. "This is a laboratory for the book arts, it is not a library," he made clear. "With *Lucile*, we want to show students what it really means to be a best-seller. We don't read books down here anyway; they do that upstairs in the library. What we do is look at the containers."

Belanger expressed similar pride over the 107 copies Rare Book School has of H. W. Janson's *History of Art*, a textbook first published in 1962 and known to millions of college students worldwide over the past four decades. "Not only have there been six editions of this book published in the United States, but there are more than forty printings within these editions, and since most of the *printings* exist in two states, the total number of variants is substantial even before you start counting the many foreign-language versions that used American edition sheets containing the illustrations, overprinted locally with texts and picture captions in German, French, Italian, Swedish, Finnish, Japanese, and several other languages." Taken together, the Jansons demonstrate how design, typography, and illustration of one book have evolved over four decades. "The text and the choice of illustrations have changed as a result of the revisions, but there is a core of several hundred illustrations which have remained unchanged from the first printing through the one currently in print." Students using various editions of the *History of Art* can look up the *Mona Lisa*, for example, and see how Leonardo da Vinci's masterpiece appears reproduced in black-and-white gravure, black-and-white duotone lithography, color relief, color lithography on coated stock, or color lithography on uncoated stock. "She looks very different in these various configurations," Belanger said, "and the whole sequence is a study in miniature of the changes in printing history over the past forty years. Over time, any frequently reprinted art book would show the same sort of variation in printing processes as Janson." Belanger chose this classic survey because it was widely available for purchase in its various editions and printings, an excellent "textbook of the history of printing in the second half of the twentieth century."

Beyond differences in packaging and presentation, variant editions of important books often raise a number of substantive issues as well. Any librarian who discards early "containers" of the novels of Honoré de Balzac (1799–1850) on the assumption that later editions of the great oeuvre first gathered in 1842 under the collective title *La Comédie humaine* makes the others redundant, for example, would be missing out on important prefaces that appeared only in those copies. Similarly, when Henry James (1843–1916) was working on what became known as the New York Edition of his collected works between 1905 and 1909, he tinkered furiously with some material that had been published years earlier, making modified versions of what was regarded as "completed" work, and he wrote eighteen new prefaces that are exceptional works of literary commentary in their own right. "With a courage and zeal few writers had shown, he rewrote his early works to bring them up to the level of his maturity," the Pulitzer Prize– and National Book Award–winning biographer of Henry James, Leon Edel, observed. "And he was ruthless in his omissions. As his publisher announced, the New York edition contained 'all of the author's fiction that he desires perpetuated.' "

In a trenchant essay on the "future of primary records," G. Thomas Tanselle recounted an instance in which the famous Harvard University literary critic F. O. Matthiessen wrote an essay in which he discussed at some length the phrase "soiled fish of the sea" as it appeared in Herman Melville's novel *White-Jacket.* The phrase Melville actually used when he wrote the novel—and the phrase that appeared in the original English and American editions of 1850—was "coiled fish of the sea." Matthiessen had read an edition published in 1922, and based his commentary on a typographical error committed long after Melville had died. The incident, in Tanselle's view, supports his contention that "every textual artifact, however it may be classed in terms of 'originals' or 'reproductions,' is potentially worthy of future study as a primary record. Even a private xerographic copy can be a primary record if a person who used it becomes a subject of historical inquiry—or, of course, if one's topic is the history of reproductions."

In *Curiosities of Literature,* a marvelously readable collection of literary and historical anecdotes published in six volumes between 1791 and 1834, the remarkably well-read London pedant Isaac Disraeli (1766–1848) showed little patience for what he called "the incorrectness of our English classics, as reprinted by our booksellers," and cited several examples to elucidate the point. "We have an edition of the Bible, known by the name of *The Vinegar Bible;* from the erratum in the title to the 20th Chapter of St. Luke, in which 'Parable of the *Vineyard,* is printed 'Parable of the *Vinegar.'* It was printed in 1717, at the Clarendon Press." In another edition of the Bible, a publisher made the frightful mistake of "omitting the negation" by printing one of the Ten Commandments as "Thou shalt commit adultery," resulting in "one of the heaviest penalties on the Company of Stationers that was ever recorded in the annals of literary history." Disraeli—father of Benjamin Disraeli, Queen Victoria's great prime minister and a formidable intellect in his own right—expressed vehement intolerance for cases in which "some stupid printer often changes a whole text intentionally" to correct what is unwittingly perceived to be errors in earlier editions:

> The fine description by [Mark] Akenside of the Pantheon, "SEVERELY great," not being understood by the blockhead, was printed *serenely great*. [Jonathan] Swift's own edition of "The City Shower," has "old ACHES throb." *Aches* is two syllables, but modern printers, who had lost the right pronunciation, have *aches* as one syllable; and then, to complete the metre, have foisted in "aches *will* throb." Thus what the poet and the linguist wish to preserve is altered, and finally lost.

In 1980 the novelist Tim O'Brien won a National Book Award for *Going After Cacciato,* arguably the first "great" literary work of fiction to emerge from the Vietnam War, and still read and discussed in college classrooms across America. A dozen years after it first appeared in print, O'Brien spent six months rewriting key sections that he inserted into a new paperback edition that was released by Houghton Mifflin without any formal announcement of what had been done. "I had a guy call me up, a professor who teaches the book in a course, and he said, 'This isn't the same novel here, I have one copy in hardcover and the kids have another in paperback,'" O'Brien told me in a 1994 interview, and he expressed no misgivings whatsoever about revising a work that represents a formative period of his creative life. "I was talking a while back with the poet David Justice, who had just reissued his poems in a new edition, and he said to me, 'I just don't hold with those people who say you shouldn't play with these things, because you're trying to leave a gift to the world that ultimately is beautiful.' I totally agree with that. As far as I am concerned, this paperback edition of *Cacciato* is the one that's going to last. The last one you do is the one that matters. I fixed some dumb little things in there like punctuation mistakes, but there are big things there too. There are cartoonish parts of *Cacciato* I didn't like at all, that I went overboard with on the first time around, and it's a hell of a lot better book now." When we spoke, O'Brien said he also planned to perform the same kind of reconstructive surgery on a paperback edition of his 1990 Vietnam novel, *The Things They Carried*.

As extreme an approach as this might sound, it is by no means unique. When the publisher Horace Liveright rejected *Flags in the Dust* in 1927, the novelist William Faulkner reworked the manuscript into *Sartoris*, which was issued in 1929 by Harcourt Brace and Company; the Nobel laureate's original manuscript was brought out without changes in 1973, eleven years after his death. Similarly, Nelson Algren reworked his 1935 novel *Somebody in Boots* into *A Walk on the Wild Side*, which appeared twenty-one years later to much greater acclaim. In October 2000 the University of South Carolina Press published *O Lost: A Story of the Buried Life*, the original version of Thomas Wolfe's classic work of 1929, *Look Homeward, Angel*, with 22 percent of the original manuscript that had been excised by the legendary Scribner's editor Maxwell E. Perkins now back in again. A year later, Harcourt Brace released a "restored" version of *All the King's Men*, Robert Penn Warren's resonant political novel loosely based on the shenanigans of Huey "Kingfish" Long of Louisiana, "reissued," according to a statement on the dust jacket, "as it was originally written."

The fundamental change to the novel—which won a Pulitzer Prize in 1947 and has never been out of print—was the inclusion of about one hundred pages of text that had been removed by Warren's original editors, including an opening chapter that had been left out altogether, and the use throughout the text of the name Willie Talos for the leading character in place of Willie Stark, since Talos was the name Warren used in his manuscript, now at the Beinecke Library of Yale University. Acknowledging that *All the King's Men* has been a "significant part of the Ameri-

can literary landscape for more than half a century," the textual editor of
the new edition, Noel Polk, explained in an afterword that "as good as it is
in its 1946 published version, the novel Warren wrote is even better." So
does this edition, then, "replace" the thousands of copies maintained in
libraries throughout the world? Obviously it does not, as a check of the
OCLC database readily indicates, although more than five hundred
libraries did add the new version to their collections within the first year
of its release, clear evidence that one does not supplant the other, and that
both versions are necessary, especially since Robert Penn Warren never
once demanded an amended edition after he became recognized as a
canonical writer—and he lived for another forty-three years—which
means that he just may have been happy leaving well enough alone.

Perhaps the best-known example of fictional retooling in recent times
involved the novelist Stephen King, who in 1990 arranged for a reissue of
his 1978 novel *The Stand* in which 150,000 words he claimed "company
accountants" at Doubleday had required him to cut from the original manuscript to minimize production costs were restored. By that time King was
much better known, of course, prompting his publisher to order a printing
of 400,000 copies; at 1,160 pages, the updated version of the horror novelist's work was 257 pages longer than the true first edition. Far less fanfare
was involved in December 1913, when Marcel Proust learned that an attentive reader with a passion for accuracy had annotated a copy of *Swann's
Way* with close to a thousand corrections. Proust promptly arranged to
acquire the volume so that he could get the appropriate changes into a new
edition that was then in the works. "What a delight it is for me to leaf
through the copy," he wrote the man, "and how grateful I feel!"

There are other cases where authors who find themselves embarrassed
by their early work take steps that are far less invasive than trying to quietly insert revised versions into the marketplace. E. L. Doctorow simply
does not allow any new editions of his second novel, *Big as Life*, to be
published at all, preferring instead to let the relatively small first printing

of several thousand copies crumble into dust and disappear from libraries, "preferably from the face of the earth," he told me in one of four interviews we have had over the years. Of Doctorow's ten books published between 1960 and 2000—and his oeuvre includes *The Book of Daniel* (1971), *Ragtime* (1975), *Loon Lake* (1980), *World's Fair* (1985), *Billy Bathgate* (1989), and *City of God* (2000)—this is the only one that remains out of print. "It's a very rare book now," he agreed when I told him that I had bought a copy in 1989 in superb condition from the California bookseller Ralph Sipper for $200, an unqualified bargain by today's standards. "I believe that I had some decent things in it," Doctorow said of his single attempt at science fiction, "but it was by far the worst thing I've ever done, and I will never let it get back in print." A search of several on-line book-locator services disclosed the availability of several copies, two of them bearing ex libris markings, meaning that at least two institutions—and undoubtedly there are many more—have discarded copies of an early book by a major American author that they will never be able to add to their collections again, unless they are willing to pay $300 or more to rare-book dealers for copies that were all printed on acidic paper in 1966 and are now showing marked signs of deterioration. In the summer of 2002, some 201 institutions worldwide still included the book among their holdings, so it is a far way from approaching "last copy" status.

A few weeks after I met with Tim O'Brien in Cambridge, Massachusetts, I interviewed the widely admired short-story writer and memoirist Tobias Wolff in Syracuse, New York, for a *Publishers Weekly* profile I was writing about him. When the matter of early work came up, Wolff flatly refused to name the title of his first published book—it was a novel issued in England by Allen & Unwin in 1975 and called *Ugly Rumors*, I later learned, and offered early in 2000 by one antiquarian bookseller at $850 for a "superior copy of this rare first book"—because it "mortifies" him just to think about it.

"Most people's juvenalia doesn't get published, but mine did," Wolff explained. "Blessedly, it died, but it had the virtue, at least, of making me feel that somebody else in the world thought I was a writer." I asked Wolff what he thought about fiction writers and poets who tinker with works produced during earlier periods of their lives. "I respect Tim's motives," he said when I told him about O'Brien's decision to rework *Going After Cacciato* and *The Things They Carried*, "but I think it's a mistake, and I'll tell you why. The famous example of a compulsive rewriter is William Wordsworth, who in his old age went back to the works of his youth, his late middle age through his old age, actually. Well, it turns out the earlier versions were superior. The thing you've got to remember as a writer is that you are not the person you were when you wrote that book. And you have to respect that person. I think you're second-guessing yourself. It makes no more sense for me to go back now and rewrite something I wrote ten years ago than it would to rewrite the work of a friend, because I have no more moral authority over that work now than I would over a friend's work."

Wolff's point about the poems William Wordsworth (1770–1850) revised later in life—and, as most critics most definitely do agree, decidedly for the worse—is a famous case of an author second-guessing finished work, but it is by no means the most celebrated. The French art critic and poet Charles Baudelaire (1821–1867) produced substantially different versions of his magnum opus, *Les Fleurs du Mal* (The Flowers of Evil), seeing it through the press twice in his lifetime, each version "a recognizable (if variable) entity, proposed by the poet as a cumulative whole," according to the translator Richard Howard. The first edition, issued in 1857 in a printing of 1,320 copies, was ordered seized by the public prosecutor, who brought suit against the author and publisher on charges of having committed "offenses to public morality." Baudelaire was fined, and six poems were ordered removed. A substantially revised and reorganized second edition of 1,500 copies, including thirty-five new poems, appeared in 1861; a "definitive edition" was issued posthumously in 1868.

The poet Walt Whitman (1819–1892) devoted his adult life to the constant enlargement and refinement of *Leaves of Grass,* beginning in 1855 with a first edition of 795 copies that was printed with his own funds, qualifying it as possibly the most accomplished example of a self-published "vanity" book in the history of American publishing. In 1891, a year before he died, Whitman completed what has since been designated the "deathbed" edition of *Leaves of Grass,* called that because of an authorial statement printed on the copyright page asserting that as "there are now several editions" of the book comprising "different texts and dates" in print—the final edition was the ninth—"I wish to say that I prefer and recommend this present one, complete, for future printing." Two months before he died, Whitman issued a promotional statement announcing that *Leaves of Grass,* "which he has been working on at great intervals and partially issued for the past thirty-five or forty years, is now completed, and he would like this new 1892 edition to absolutely supersede all previous ones."

There is no way of knowing for certain, but chances are that many librarians took Whitman at his word, and substituted the most recent text—the last one—for the others that had come earlier. Whether or not the quality of composition is superior in the first edition, which included a preface explaining Whitman's poetic theories that appeared in no subsequent versions, along with twelve untitled poems, or the ninth, with more than four hundred titled entries, or any of the seven other editions that appeared in between—and they all vary—is a matter of personal taste. But when the Library of America, the nonprofit publishing venture committed to placing in print authoritative editions of the cornerstones of American literature, brought out an edition of Whitman in 1982, the editor of the volume, the Pulitzer Prize–winning Whitman biographer Justin Kaplan, included complete texts of the first and the ninth editions, even though there were, in his words, "some repetitions and overlappings." Kaplan justified the unusual move by pointing out that even though Whitman spent the final thirty-seven years of his life "expanding, articulating, and rearranging his books of poems," the 1855 *Leaves of Grass* "retains a formal, substantive, and genetic character that sets it apart from subsequent editions, some more than four times its page bulk."

What has to be the most embarrassing instance of a library discarding an earlier text for a later edition took place at the Bodleian Library of Oxford University sometime in the seventeenth century when it was determined that a recently arrived Third Folio of the dramatic works of William Shakespeare, published in 1664, made the First Folio acquired in 1623 on legal deposit redundant, and thus irrelevant to the needs of the collection. It was not until 1821, when the library of the great Shakespearean editor Edmund Malone was bequeathed to Oxford, that another First Folio made its way into the Bodleian collections. Eighty-four years after that, the miraculous took place; a dilapidated First Folio being offered for sale by a local bookseller was determined to be the original Bodleian copy. Because seventeenth-century books sent to Oxford on legal deposit arrived in loose sheets, the library routinely arranged for its own distinctive bindings to be mounted on them. Documents on file in the university archives disclosed that the job on the First Folio had been performed by a local binder named William Wildgoose; some inspired detective work showed further that Wildgoose had used identical binding materials on other volumes processed in the same consignment, making a positive identification of the Shakespeare folio possible. A public subscription launched in 1905 to buy the copy for the university resulted in a jubilant return to its original shelf location. A sidelight to this episode—one that strengthens the contention that every book has a story to tell apart from its literary content—is that by examining the pages of this well-worn copy for evidence of use, scholars have determined that the plays seventeenth-century Oxford students thumbed through the most were *Romeo and Juliet* and *Julius Caesar*.

Of immediate concern to textual scholars in this regard is the common library practice of weeding out titles that exist in multiple copies without paying attention to any differences that might exist between editions, what are known among bibliographers and literary scholars as "variants." The First and Third Folios of Shakespeare, in fact, are an excellent example of this. The Third Folio added *Pericles* and six spurious plays to the Shakespeare canon, making the two books different from each other not only in content, but also in the edited versions of plays they had in common, which reflect "a progressive modernizing and regularizing of the text, affecting not only the punctuation and spelling but language and syntax as well," according to the Shakespearean scholar G. Blakemore Evans.

There is even significant variation within the pages of different copies of the First Folio itself, a circumstance that might seem especially odd given that printed books tend to be identical in the same editions. But it was not an unusual practice in the early days of printing for corrections to be made during the course of a long run, "on the fly," so to speak, making for an accumulation of variants along the way. The 1623 collection of Shakespeare's dramatic works is believed to have taken two years to see through the press, and numerous corrections were made in the course of production. During the 1950s a clever bibliographer with a background in naval intelligence invented a special optical device that enabled him to identify each and every variation in the First Folio, page by page. The machine, called the Hinman Collator after Charlton Hinman, the inventor, compared the eighty First Folios that are the centerpiece holdings of the Folger Shakespeare Library in Washington, D.C., with the idea of compiling one "ideal" copy. Still in use at a number of research libraries to this day, including one in the special collections reading room of Alderman Library at the University of Virginia, Hinman's contraption grew out of a process employed during World War II to compare reconnaissance photographs taken before a target was attacked, and just afterward, to assess the degree of bomb damage that had been inflicted. The collator uses electrical lights and mirrors to converge two texts into one, discerning slight variations between the copies by superimposing the image of a page from one copy over the same page of another.

Hinman found 370 points of variance in the tragedies alone, most of them presumably the result of bad proofreading caught during the press run, but some of a substantive nature. Using the best pages from all the copies in the Folger collection, Hinman was able to compile a composite photographic volume known as *The Norton Facsimile of the First Folio of Shakespeare,* published in 1968 by W. W. Norton and Company, and reissued in 1997. "The primary aim of the present facsimile is to furnish a reliable photographic reproduction of what the printers of the original edition would themselves have considered an ideal copy of the First Folio of Shakespeare," Hinman explained in his introduction, "one in which every page is not only clear and readable throughout but represents the latest or most fully corrected state of the text. It is sought, that is, to give concrete representation to what has hitherto been only a theoretical entity, an abstraction: *the* First Folio text." Arguing in favor of such a project was the fact that "no single original" copy of the plays was "either wholly uncorrected or fully corrected throughout" by the first printers, meaning that "none can be said to represent *the* First Folio text: what would be found in a copy showing every page in its latest state."

In a 1978 interview with me, the great Elizabethan scholar Samuel Schoenbaum expressed his conviction that every generation demands at least one new edition of Shakespeare, just as every generation probably should have a fresh translation of Dante and another of Homer. "These are writers who speak for the ages," Schoenbaum said, "but scholarship changes, interpretations change. And every edition is important. It is a continuum." I was reminded of these words on June 20, 2002, when the *New York Times* reported how a Vassar College professor of English literature had just recanted an assertion made seven years earlier—and reported triumphantly at that time on the newspaper's front page—that Shakespeare was the author of an obscure 578-line poem called "A Funeral Elegy," a claim so persuasively documented, it received enthusiastic endorsement from many prominent critics. To arrive at that bold conclusion, the professor, Donald Foster, had used a lexical database of eighty thousand lines known as the Shaxicon to analyze the language of the poem, written in 1612 and signed simply, w. s. His argument was so convincing that three publishers—Houghton Mifflin, Longman, and W. W. Norton—included the elegy in new editions of Shakespeare's works, while the estimable critic Harold Bloom cited it in his 1998 book *Shakespeare: The Invention of the Human*, noting "an affinity" with *Henry VIII*. Foster himself detailed the rationale in his own book, *Author Unknown: On the Trail of Anonymous*, a work of literary detection released in 2000 that was burnished further by details of how he had determined that the Washington journalist Joe Klein was the author of the best-selling political satire *Primary Colors*, which had been published anonymously in 1996.

When faced with compelling evidence gathered by the French scholar Gilles D. Monsarrat that another English dramatist, John Ford, was the more likely author of the elegy—which everyone who read it agreed was a dreadful piece of work in the first instance—Foster gamely admitted that he had been in error. "I know good evidence when I see it," he said in a formal statement. "No one who cannot rejoice in the discovery of his own mistakes deserves to be called a scholar." All well and good, of course, but what happens now to the credibility—and the utility—of all the books that anointed the now-specious elegy as part of the great bard's canon? The obvious answer is that each and every edition has an important place in a scholarly collection.

In a similar vein, the Harry Ransom Humanities Research Center (HRHRC) at the University of Texas in Austin owns twenty-seven of the exceedingly scarce first editions of James Joyce's *Ulysses*, published in 1922 in a run of one thousand copies by Sylvia Beach, owner of Shakespeare & Co., a Left Bank bookstore popular among the "lost generation" of literary expatriates who took up residence in Paris in the years following World War I. A casual critic might regard such a circumstance as an insupportable exercise in excess, but the book, written as it was by an expatriate Irishman in the English language and published by an American bookseller whose Dijon typesetters were fluent only in French, presents innumerable textual problems for contemporary scholars, including an errata sheet listing more than five hundred emendations that continue to cause spasms of anxiety among editors. In addition to its unrivaled collection of printed first editions of *Ulysses*, the University of Texas owns a substantial archive of proof sheets, corrected galleys, and correspondence of Joyce, giving scholars the ability to study the work through every stage of the creative process, up to and including the profoundly different ways it was represented in successive stages of publication.

"Most of our first-edition copies have some kind of provenance, so there is an associative value to keep in mind here as well," Richard W. Oram, librarian of the HRHRC, told me. "Eight contain inscriptions from Joyce to various people. One belonged to Compton MacKenzie, the Scottish novelist and journalist, and another is inscribed to Alfred A. Knopf and his wife Blanche. The copy I like to take out and show to people is the one that belonged to T. E. Lawrence, because after all these years, it still smells strongly of his pipe tobacco. That's something I don't think you will ever get from a digitized copy. There also is the matter of presumed textual variation within the edition to consider here, which after close to eighty years is something that still remains to be examined by scholars, for the very reason that it is such a mammoth undertaking." Although the first edition was numbered 1 to 1,000, Texas has a press copy of *Ulysses* that is totally out of the numerical sequence, "which suggests to us that it was one of the earliest copies of the novel that came off the press." Three different kinds of paper were used in the course of producing the first edition, each of which is represented among the Texas holdings.

The problems associated with printing the 1922 Paris edition are legendary. The first appearance of the masterpiece was replete with printer's errors, something that bothered Joyce enormously, and which he mentioned in letters to his friends and associates. His publisher, Sylvia Beach, included an insert apologizing for "typographical errors unavoidable in the exceptional circumstances." One textual scholar has written that most efforts to "establish a correct text of *Ulysses* appear to have added as many mistakes as they have eliminated," including the six editions of the novel that were issued during the lifetime of the author (1882–1941), who made numerous changes from printing to printing. The first American edition, issued by Random House in 1934, was based on an unauthorized pirated edition, prompting Random House to issue a corrected Modern Library version in 1961.

Quite apart from these textual difficulties has been the long-standing competition among contemporary scholars to establish a "definitive" edition of the novel as Joyce is believed to have intended it to be published. One version prepared by the German scholar Hans Walter Gabler and released in 1984 contained five thousand modifications, and was touted by Random House, its trade publisher, as the "definitive critical edition," but subsequent attacks on its reliability prompted the publisher to restore the text of its 1961 edition to general circulation. The "Joyce Wars," as they have been dubbed, show no sign of cease-fire soon, and several publishers have committed themselves to releasing their own renderings of Joyce's masterpiece once copyright issues are resolved. Normally the book would have passed into the public domain in 1997, seventy-five years after the publication of the first edition in Paris, but Random House has vehemently argued that the beginning date for the lucrative market in North America should be 1934, the year the Supreme Court cleared the novel for publication in the United States.

In his preface to the 1984 *Ulysses: A Critical and Synoptic Edition*, Professor Gabler had promised that his computer-assisted version would "replace the text made public in the book's first printing and every subsequent printing since 1922." The fact that Gabler's own publisher later modified a blurb on the cover proclaiming the edition as "the corrected text" to simply calling it "the Gabler edition" suggests that the quest for perfection remains elusive and ongoing. The larger point to be emphasized here is that a scholarly collection of Joyce is outstanding only if copies of every edition of *Ulysses* are available for side-by-side comparison. "There are libraries that have this notion that if you destroy one copy, you can substitute a duplicate for it," Professor Darnton at Princeton University told me. "But in strict bibliographical terms there is no such thing as a duplicate. And if you are beginning to destroy older books as a matter of policy, then this veers off into vandalism. I think that a lot of librarians faced with the severe problems of preservation who once thought that they could microfilm everything, and who now think they can digitize everything and then discard the original, are making decisions based on what I believe is a misunderstanding about the importance of the book. So I would argue, microfilm, yes, digitize, certainly. But please, do not throw away the original."

Among research librarians, this plea for preservation has had an impact on recent policy, one that has brought about a renewed sense of purpose among many book custodians. In 1999, the Council on Library and Information Resources (CLIR), a nonprofit foundation based in Washington, D.C., formed a seventeen-member task force to study what factors argue for retaining works in their original form, and to advise on the kinds of strategies that might be used to preserve them. Named to chair the Task Force on the Artifact in the Library of the Future was Stephen G. Nichols, the James H. Beall Professor of French and Humanities and chair of the Romance languages department at Johns Hopkins University, and also director of the School of Criticism and Theory at Cornell University. An admitted conservative when it comes to keeping original materials, Nichols told me shortly after his appointment was announced that the group was formed in response to "a serious argument that has been brewing among preservationists as to what constitutes preservation. That is the issue, really, and it goes all the way back to Plato, who was greatly concerned about the context of articulated thought, because he basically felt that if you did not know what the occasion was when a thought was uttered, you would not be able to understand it. When you photograph a book, you have a microfilm, but the microfilm does not preserve the historical materiality of that manuscript. It doesn't have the binding, the other things that you would look at. So what is the definition of an artifact? You start with the materiality of the object. Anything that destroys the materiality of the object is going to destroy the historical specificity of the object."

The task force, which issued a preliminary report in 2001, set in motion the groundwork for a protocol that would preserve not only physical objects but visual materials such as film and prints, and newer materials that exist only in digital formats. "The good news is that our task force is very much a task force geared toward tying to figure out ways to preserve as much as we can," Nichols said. In the area of printed books, the group concentrated primarily on material that has appeared in the last two centuries. "Where we come in is what happens after 1800, since anything printed before that date, by general scholarly convention, has been established to be important, and worthy of preservation for the fact in and of itself."

In cases where seldom-used materials are no longer kept in central repositories, or where they are not even welcome in off-site storage facilities, one option has been to send books on the margins to an independent depository located near the campus of the University of Chicago known as the Center for Research Libraries (CRL). Established in 1949 by ten midwestern universities, the center's mission has evolved to the point where it is now regarded as a sanctuary of last resort for titles that might otherwise be headed for the shredders. Today, this "library for libraries" receives material from several hundred institutions throughout North America, all of it "rarely used" and largely unwanted.

Kevin Guthrie, president of JSTOR (for "journal storage"), the non-profit foundation that is making digital versions of scholarly journals available on-line to researchers worldwide, urged me to see the library when I visited Chicago. CRL came up while I was questioning Guthrie about what JSTOR does with the original serials it obtains once electronic copies are made. "If you are asking whether or not we are going to keep them forever, the answer is no," he said candidly, but he quickly added how that policy applies only to journals that are not "last copies." In cases where JSTOR is dealing with scarce copies of obscure journals, Guthrie said an arrangement had been made with CRL to take custody of them. "What we consider part of our mission is that we take affirmative steps to ensure that the last copy does not get lost. We ensure that it is safely placed in a depository library someplace. That way we know there is a physical last copy."

8.

Into Thin Air

Our revels now are ended. These are actors,
As I foretold you, were all spirits, and
Are melted into air, into thin air;
And, like the baseless fabric of this vision,
The cloud-capp'd towers, the gorgeous palaces,
The solemn temples, the great globe itself,
Yea, all which it inherit, shall dissolve
And, like this insubstantial pageant faded,
Leave not a rack behind. We are such stuff
As dreams are made on, and our little life
Is rounded with a sleep.
—THE TEMPEST, ACT IV, SCENE 1

The realization that books printed on highly acidic paper were disintegrating at an alarmingly rapid rate did not arrive with a sudden flash of perception in the waning years of the twentieth century. Indeed, librarians have known for decades that millions of the books entrusted to their care were breaking apart and crumbling, but since there was very little any of them could do about the situation, very little was done. Curiously, it was not the oldest books in the stacks that were at immediate risk, since most of them were printed on rag paper and doing just fine, but the more recent volumes, those produced since the middle of the nineteenth century with sheets fabricated from a highly acidic wood pulp concoction, that were causing the most anxiety. The transition to lesser-grade stock began around the time of the American Civil War, when increasing demand hastened the development of a cheaper process. To improve strength and to prevent ink from being too readily absorbed by the pulp paper, chemicals such as aluminum sulphate, known as alum, were added to the mix, with the result that documents exposed to humidity produced sulfuric acid, and the molecular structure of the cellulose was weakened. Further deterioration of the fibers was caused by bleaches that were used to brighten the sheets. A warning published in *Scientific American* in 1895 took note of the implications:

> Paper is now made of such inferior materials that it will soon rot, and very few of the books now published have much chance of a long life. The paper maker thus unwittingly assumes the function of the great literary censor of the age. However, his criticism is mainly destructive, and it is too severe. Without the power of selective appreciation, he condemns to destruction good and bad alike.

When William Blades was gathering information for *The Enemies of Books* in the 1860s and 1870s, he noticed that the pesky bookworms he was examining were adapting to the "scarcity of edible books" in ways that did not bode well for the far more valuable volumes manufactured years earlier with traditional ingredients:

> One result of the extensive adulteration of modern paper is that the worm will not touch it. His instinct forbids him to eat the china clay, the bleaches, the plaster of Paris, the sulphate of barytes, the scores of adulterants now used to mix with the fibre, and, so far, the wise pages of the old literature are, in the race against Time with the modern rubbish, heavily handicapped.

Acidic paper was considered serious enough an archival issue in Great Britain in the 1920s to authorize a formal investigation by a professional body known as the Library Association. Its findings, published in 1930 in a document called *The Durability of Paper: Report of Special Committee*, stated the situation in stark terms: "During the last thirty years, many scientists in different countries have pointed out that, owing to the employment of papers manufactured by certain processes, a large part of the printed and written productions of the present age will possibly have perished before they can be utilised by the learned world of the future." The committee proposed the use of certain "grades" of paper for official documents, recommending that "first quality rag or other pure cellulose" products be used for documents where "absolute" permanence was called for, and "properly prepared all-chemical-wood stock" for those requiring "relative" permanence. "Relative" permanence was defined broadly to mean an unspecified period of time "as would give to a reasonably distant posterity the opportunity to use the productions of our age." Deciding which items merit preservation through the centuries, of course, and which ones need go no further than "a reasonably distant posterity," involves a value judgment, and raises the same kind of questions that archivists everywhere argue today over which electronic records should be maintained indefinitely, and which ones can be purged from their databases.

"The difficulty here is that of predicting, at the time papers are written, which will be preserved and should therefore be on permanent paper, and which may be consigned to the cheapest possible material," the Library Association agreed in its report, but stressed that the "all-important" consideration was to make sure "that those who use paper for purposes which involve a serious contribution to knowledge—the publication of books of permanent value or the writing of archives—should realize that grade papers at competitive prices are now actually on the market, and proceed to take practical advantage of that fact."

In the United States, the federal government began mandating the use of permanent paper for its official documents in 1990. Most commercial and noncommercial publishers, spurred on by an aggressive campaign supported by various writers and library groups, are now using alkaline paper, so the greater problem today is not newly published books but "brittle book" technologies peculiar to the past 150 years, which have already brought about the disintegration of many millions of volumes. A 1985 report estimated that 75 million books in North American research libraries were at immediate risk, with the numbers increasing at a rate of 0.6 percent a year. The study, commissioned by the Association of American Universities and the American Council of Learned Societies, calculated further that 12 million endangered volumes were unique copies, meaning that when any one of these books crumbles into dust, no backup copy is available in another research library, and in all probability the book is lost forever to formal scholarship. Those materials in particular became the focus of various initiatives that have included the use of microfilm to make preservation copies, a process that usually involved the guillotining of spines and the discarding of originals.

A walk through the stacks of any large library gives off an aroma that for many bibliophiles is akin to sipping nectar with the gods on Mount Olympus. "It is an intoxicating fragrance, I quite agree," Kenneth E. Carpenter said one morning while escorting me through Widener Library on one of his periodic excursions to select books destined for semiretirement in the off-site storage facility known as the Harvard Depository. "But what you smell is decaying paper." The challenge, according to Roger E. Stoddard, curator of rare books at Harvard, "is how many of these things can you process in an hour. I'd be interested to know the answer to that. Whatever the formula is, it's no good unless it does them by the carload."

Just how daunting the task can be was made clear during a series of tests conducted for the Library of Congress in the 1980s by the National Aeronautics and Space Administration and Northrop, Inc., at the Goddard Space Center laboratory in Landover, Maryland. A deacidification process developed and patented by the library involved placing brittle books in a sealed chamber filled with diethyl zinc, a gas known by the acronym DEZ that was formulated to neutralize the acids. "DEZ is a very good process, very effective, but there are two major disadvantages, and they both involve safety," Kenneth E. Harris, the preservation projects director for the Library of Congress, told me during an interview in his Washington office. "The chemical is pyroforic, which means that you have to exercise explicit safety precautions in handling and converting the chemical. It can blow up in the presence of oxygen and water." In fact, on at least two occasions the chemical did exactly that. During one test a technician apparently pulled the wrong switch, allowing the DEZ to mix with water and causing a moderate explosion. Nobody was injured, but an army demolition team was needed to put out the fire.

Another process developed by Akzo Nobel Inc. of the Netherlands controlled the explosive properties of DEZ but left the books with what one company spokesman described as a "light odor problem." Sonja Jordan, at that time the director of preservation for the University of Notre Dame in South Bend, Indiana, described the offensive scent as "sort of a pesticide smell" that made people "sick." In 1994, after six years of further tests, Akzo wrote off its $2 million investment and abandoned the project altogether. "The challenge is to develop a process that will take care of the acid and restore strength to the paper. That's the trick. The technology is there to treat the books. But what you end up with are pages that have the rigidity of tissue paper."

An extremely promising solution to the problem—one that involved a dramatic departure from conventional methods—was introduced in the early 1990s by a small company located in Cranberry Township, Pennsylvania, a suburb of Pittsburgh. Though scorned at first as something of a wishful solution to a seemingly bottomless morass, the patented process, known as Bookkeeper, has gained sufficient favor in recent years that a number of institutions have made it their option of choice, most notably the Library of Congress, which gave the upstart company a trial run in 1994 out of pure desperation. The chief drawback to Bookkeeper is that it does not treat books by the carload, with the result that the forty employees of Preservation Technologies, L.P., work around the clock in three shifts in a fifteen-thousand-square-foot plant loading a cluster of stainless steel cylinders, one batch after another, twenty-four hours a day. The volumes, eight to twelve at a time depending on their size, are mounted on a narrow rack around a central shaft so that their pages fan out during a half-hour cycle of gentle agitation. When switched into operation, the containers are filled with perfluoroalkane, a heavy, clear liquid used in the manufacture of transistors, and begin to shake like washing machines. The effective agent in the process is magnesium oxide.

"It's kind of like an antacid in your stomach," James E. Burd, president of the company, told me in the first of several interviews we would have over a span of five years. "Bookkeeper works on the concept that if you can get submicron particles—a micron is a millionth of a meter—into the fibers of the paper, they will work as a neutralizer. I am greatly oversimplifying it here, but it amounts to a rather elegant and simple idea that has the side benefit of doing no collateral damage to the books. Since all that you do is add a neutralizing agent, no ink is dissolved. We use no solvents, we have no odors and no toxicity. The beauty of the process is that you can't tell that we did it. The only drawback so far as I can see is a bureaucratic inertia on the part of many institutions to try something that they have never dared attempt before."

This "rather elegant and simple idea" was conceived by Richard E. Spatz, an attorney who spent a number of years directing the Forests Products Group of Koppers Company (now Koppers Industries Inc.), a Pennsylvania chemical corporation that preserves telephone poles, railroad ties, and deck lumber by pressure-treating them. The idea to apply proven industrial science to mass deacidification for books came to Spatz in a moment of pure inspiration while he was reading an article in the *New*

York Times about the pressing need for just such a process in the nation's libraries. "Telephone poles are made out of wood, books are made out of wood," he recalled thinking at the time, and promptly assembled a team of scientists who developed a process that Koppers quickly patented, but chose not to pursue as a commercial venture.

When Spatz retired in 1986 at the age of sixty-two, he acquired the rights to the formula for himself and set up his own company in space leased at a suburban industrial park. To market the idea, he began calling on universities with large libraries, getting a few orders here and there, but nothing sufficient to create a groundswell of enthusiasm for his service. The big break came in 1994 when the largest library in the world gave him an opportunity to prove his mettle. "We had no place else to go, nothing left to try," Diane N. Kresh, the director of preservation at the Library of Congress, recalled. The library has been sending him shipments in ever increasing numbers ever since, and now Spatz has books coming in from repositories all over North America—Yale, Notre Dame, Pennsylvania State University, Northwestern, National Library of Quebec, New York Public Library, University of Maryland, University of California, Georgetown University, Johns Hopkins University, and Florida State University among them—and a European operation has been licensed in the Netherlands. "In lieu of anything else being pursued in the United States today," Kresh said, "this is pretty much the only viable show in town."

In the first six years of Bookkeeper's trial run, 300,000 books were processed for the Library of Congress. Beginning in 2000, a thirty-year program to deacidify about 8 million brittle books in the library's inventory got under way, starting with 100,000 volumes the first year. By 2004 Preservation Technologies will be processing 300,000 volumes a year, and will maintain that pace through 2030. "We believe that by that time we will have treated pretty much all the books we now have that need to be treated," Winston Tabb, the associate librarian for library services at the Library of Congress from 1992 to 2002, and now dean of university libraries at Johns

Hopkins University in Baltimore, Maryland, told me. "The cost for the first five years is fifteen dollars a book, which makes it the least expensive preservation process that was available to us." Deacidification extends the estimated life span of books by as many as two hundred years, depending on the severity of deterioration at the time of treatment. The company's contract with the Library of Congress included the installation of an on-site system at the Madison Building in Washington, D.C., to deacidify single sheets of manuscript material and records. James Burd said he projects treating up to 7.5 million documents through 2004.

On the bright October morning in 1997 that I arrived to visit the newly opened Die Deutsche Bibliothek in Frankfurt—a gleaming national facility designed for the twenty-first century—the main computer had crashed, leaving staff members and researchers intent on finding items listed in the electronic catalog idle for much of the day, and waiting helplessly until a backup system could be brought on-line. "You have an exquisite sense of timing," Klaus-Dieter Lehmann, at that time the director general of the German National Library and now president of the Prussian Cultural Heritage Foundation in Berlin, said in greeting, quickly adding that this was the first time such an inconvenience had occurred since the new building opened five months earlier. He offered the failure as a good example of why his country is committed to conserving original copies of its national collections. "We collect everything about Germany and the German people, and we collect everything that has been printed in the German language, which cuts through all of our history and across all political lines," he said. This arrangement enables three state facilities to operate under one administrative umbrella known collectively as Die Deutsche Bibliothek, with general headquarters maintained in Frankfurt, a book city in league historically with Venice, Leiden, and Paris. Indeed, my meeting with Lehmann and members of his staff came a week before a quarter of a million people inundated the city for a venerable rite of publishing known as the Frankfurt Book Fair, a huge trade show held every October that traces its lineage back to the fifteenth century and remains, by far, the largest such event anywhere in the world. The national library also operates Deutsches Musikarchiv, a music collection in Berlin, and Die Deutsche Bücherei in Leipzig, a facility that served as the German national library through World War II and was used as the official repository for the German Democratic Republic during the years of Communist rule. Absorbed into the federal system following reunification of East and West in 1990, it became the operational headquarters for a concerted government effort aimed at preservation, conservation, and mass deacidification of the national collections. "We keep everything in its original form, so deciding which materials are worthy of preservation is a very simple matter for us," Lehmann said. "We have chosen to preserve them all. If it is in the German language, we are committed to keeping it forever."

Leipzig, a three-and-a-half-hour train ride from Frankfurt, is home to an international book fair of its own, one that has become increasingly popular since reunification allowed more people to come in from the West. I traveled to this beautiful city from Frankfurt to get a look at the complex of innovative preservation processes introduced there in 1994, efforts that are being watched closely by conservators all over the world. In one procedure that I was permitted to observe, a machine the size of four pickup trucks—it looks something like the huge rotary presses used to produce newspapers—divides the decaying sheets of disbound brittle books into halves, and treats them. In the next step, the apparatus, known as a page-splitter, inserts a transparent center layer known as a core sheet between the separated pages to provide strength, then attaches them back together using a clear gelatin as an adhesive. Another repair technique called leaf casting uses a thin mixture of a cellulose pulp known as a slurry to patch the kind of decaying publications that other libraries routinely discard—yellowing city directories, street atlases, superannuated telephone books, and the like. Books of more recent vintage—many of them printed in the 1960s and 1970s—go to a unit that deacidifies 170 kilos per cycle; about 200,000 books are now being treated annually in this manner, with plans afoot to double the volume. Lehmann told me that 13 million books in the national inventory are in need of treatment, and that twenty years will be required to get it done. The German process, developed by Battelle Ingenieurtechnik GmbH of Frankfurt, uses magnesium titanium ethoxide as the active agent. A few months after my visit to Leipzig, the operation was privatized and turned over to an independent limited company known as Zentrum für Bucherhaltung (Center for Book Preservation), which has begun offering its services to institutions outside Germany, including many in the United States.

Elsewhere, other initiatives have been moving forward, some employing the Bookkeeper approach, some experimenting with the German strategy, others following their own courses. What librarians and curators around the world find particularly encouraging are the strides that have been made toward correcting the brittle book problem at its source, with most new hardcover editions published in North America and Europe now being printed on more durable alkaline paper. In the United States, a good deal of the credit for that enlightened attitude belongs to Barbara Goldsmith, a historian, philanthropist, and trustee of the New York Public Library, whose campaign got under way about the same time that the Library of Congress was conducting its volatile experiments in Maryland. Her plan—exerting pressure on publishers by enlisting major authors to join her cause—was striking for its simplicity, yet resoundingly successful in achieving results.

On March 7, 1988, Goldsmith's lobbying efforts were honored at a gala event in the Celeste Bartos Forum of the New York Public Library. During the formal program, John P. Baker, director of the library's preservation division, held up a copy of Euclid's *Geometry*, printed in

Venice in 1482, and invited the gathering to admire the creamy white pages that had retained their brightness and flexibility over the previous five hundred years. He then held up a copy of a biography of the composer Giovanni Pierluigi da Palestrina, printed in Milan in 1925; there were gasps as one of the pages crumbled between his fingers. Because a preservation copy of the book had already been made on microfilm, the information was not lost, but the artifact itself was beyond repair. Baker was not seeking converts to the cause by the demonstration, since the people he was addressing that night—a group of authors that included Tom Wolfe, Kurt Vonnegut Jr., Robert A. Caro, Maurice Sendak, Frances Fitzgerald, and Susan Isaacs—had already signed a declaration insisting that all future first-edition hardcover copies of their books be printed on acid-free paper. Some forty publishing houses had also affixed their names to the manifesto, and by the end of the decade, more than three thousand authors had endorsed the demand, a measure of "unending satisfaction" for Goldsmith, the daughter of Joseph I. Lubin, a former chairman of Pepsi-Cola Company. Her 1988 gift of $1 million revitalized a preservation laboratory in the basement of the New York Public Library. "It took a lot of arm-twisting to get people on board, and the publishers were the toughest ones of all to convince," Goldsmith told me. "I am in this for the long haul, and I intend to stay involved. Book preservation has become my passion."

In 1853, Charles Coffin Jewett, the librarian of the recently established Smithsonian Institution in Washington, D.C., announced a proposal for a long-term record of America's literary heritage that some of his colleagues felt was a clever joke. Addressing a gathering of librarians and bibliographers meeting in New York City, Jewett suggested that a bibliographical listing of all books produced in the United States be inscribed on clay tablets and baked in ovens to assure permanence. Such a project, he believed, would serve as a measured start toward documenting a "great national library" that could withstand the withering forces of nature. As far as anyone could tell, this was the first time that an American or European book professional of any standing had proposed using processes employed thousands of years earlier by the Sumerians and Babylonians to secure longevity of their writings, but given Jewett's stature—he was chairman of the New York gathering "and its leading spirit," according to the library historian Samuel Swett Green—his words "were listened to by all the members with admiration and profound respect."

As the responsibility for building a comprehensive print collection shifted away from the Smithsonian Institution to the Library of Congress, Jewett's plan fell by the wayside, though not for lack of effort. His concept was endorsed by a unanimous vote at the 1853 meeting, "and an amendment was made to the resolution of approval in order to claim it as an American invention." Some thirty-three years later, an aging contemporary of Jewett's, William Frederick Poole, entertained the inaugural convention of the American Library Association with some firsthand reflections of what he described as his late colleague's unusual "scheme" for preservation: "The material he used was a clay from Indiana. Congress made an appropriation for executing the plan! I recollect that librarians of the country generally favored it, and that I did not. I remember that I spoke of it at the time as 'Prof. Jewett's *mud* catalogue.' My views concerning it were based on some practical knowledge of legitimate typography, and from specimens of the work which Prof. Jewett exhibited."

The ultimate failure of Jewett's plan, Poole believed, was brought on by "mechanical defects" in the process, "the shrinking and warping of the blocks in baking" in particular, "and the intractable nature of the material when baked, which made the exact adjustment of the blocks on the press impossible." Other attempts at permanent preservation of the bibliographic record would be made in succeeding years, a number of them toying with the idea of depositing selective accounts of the human experience in receptacles known as time capsules, a throwback to the Babylonian model of burying archival material in bunkers to await discovery in future generations, archives archaeologists call "foundation documents," not for the nature of their content, but for the actual location in the buildings where they are found, more often than not in what is determined to be the cornerstone of the structure. While this hole-in-the-ground approach runs counter to the open-access concept of a library, it does serve the ancilliary purpose, at least, of keeping a partial record, however inaccessible it might be for the short run. But even then there are no guarantees of permanence, as an organization based at Oglethorpe University in Atlanta, Georgia, known as the International Time Capsule Society, has demonstrated. Of ten thousand time capsules known to have been buried in North America during the twentieth century, only a thousand or so will ever be found; most have already been lost, many of them victims of their sponsor's failure to document their precise whereabouts, or to leave any record that they even existed.

One of the most ambitious examples attempted to date resides in a reinforced chamber twenty feet long by ten feet wide by ten feet high—a converted indoor swimming pool—built on the campus of Oglethorpe University. Known as the Crypt of Civilization, the vault was completed in 1940 and filled with hundreds of everyday trinkets that purported to offer a "running story" of American customs prevailing at the time the steel door was welded shut. The chamber is supposed to remain closed until 8113, a calculation based on the number of years that had passed from a point in the distant past when the Egyptians are said by some scholars to have introduced the first calendar. Dr. Thornwell Jacobs, the Oglethorpe president who masterminded the undertaking, had added an equal number of years to 1936—the year he began preparing the subterranean installation—and came up with 8113. Though undeniably outlandish, the venture has some relevance to the written record in that many of the materials selected for deposit were books and newspapers, and a good deal of effort and imagination went into ensuring that these amulets from the twentieth century would withstand the passage of six thousand years.

Among the curiosities deposited in the Atlanta chamber were several stainless steel canisters containing 640,000 pages from eight hundred "classics in the arts and sciences" that had been reproduced on microfilm, and hermetically sealed in nitrogen gas to prevent oxidation. Even with those precautions, the U.S. Bureau of Standards projected a life span of six centuries, although that admonition did not deter the Hollywood producer David O. Selznick from donating an original copy of the film script of *Gone With the Wind*. Because the likelihood of anyone speaking English in the ninth millennium is remote, Dr. Jacobs left a device he called the "Language Integrator" inside, along with a small windmill to generate electrical power, and a pronunciation guide.

As the twentieth century drew to a close, the interment of time capsules became an increasingly common, some might even say tedious, exercise, with one of the more ambitious projects carried out by the *New York Times*, which devoted a special issue of its Sunday magazine to the effort as the culmination of a six-part series covering the approaching millennium. "Figuring out what we might say to our descendants a thousand years from now is one thing; actually writing it down and putting it in a strongbox is something else altogether," Jack Hitt wrote in an entertaining overview of this peculiarly American indulgence, and of plans for the newspaper's own high-profile project, christened Times Capsule, to be opened in the year 3000. With $60,000 committed to building a two-ton enclosure designed by the Spanish architect Santiago Calatrava to stay the course over ten centuries, the magazine's editors assembled a team of experts schooled in archaeology, geology, materials preservation, and, in their words, "the esoteric field of deep-time messaging" to decide on what should go inside. A point of agreement for everyone on the panel was the folly of storing anything written in digital form, especially if it were to be recorded on magnetic tapes or CD-ROMs, which are notoriously perishable. "One of the problems," a member of the task force said, "is that when digital material corrupts, it corrupts absolutely. We've been used to analog materials, which deteriorate rather gracefully."

Interestingly enough, the strategies the *Times* experts came up with involved new applications of what were at root decidedly traditional techniques. For openers, they recommended printing some materials on acid-free paper with ink and storing them in a "proper container." It was reasoned that even though the documents would fade over a thousand years, they had a higher probability of remaining legible "long after all the newer technologies had turned to dust."

As a high-tech backup, they commissioned Norsam Technologies of Portland, Oregon, to imprint a series of microscopic images onto a wafer-thin nonferrous metal known as an HD-Rosetta data disk. Developed at Los Alamos National Laboratory in New Mexico to protect classified government information in the event of a nuclear attack, the high-density storage process uses an ion beam to etch up to 100,000 pages on a nickel medallion about the size of an Oreo cookie, and can store gray-scale or color images. Since the information is not digital, it does not require a computer or software program to make sense out of zeroes and ones, and is readable with an electron microscope; to read data with a conventional optical microscope—a device familiar to every high school chemistry student—Norsam officials recommend a reduction of twenty thousand pages per disk. Either way, the key to storing historical documents "permanently and safely" for up to a thousand years, they maintained, is to make sure they are set down in analog form. In tests conducted by company engineers, the nickel disks survived exposure to temperatures of 570 degrees Fahrenheit and extended immersion in seawater, and were impervious to abrasion, electromagnetic pulses, and atmospheric changes.

Burying books in the ground may sound extreme, but it is not without its supporters, and it has already become operational in one national library in Europe. I first heard about the Depository Library at Mo i Rana in Norway from Winston Tabb, formerly of the Library of Congress and now dean of libraries at Johns Hopkins University, who told me that this throwback approach to protecting cultural treasures was something he would like to see considered for serious use in one fashion or another in the United States. In the instance of the Norwegian initiative, a desolate site just below the Arctic Circle was selected for the book depository. "It's what you might call the 'deep-freeze' approach to long-term preservation," Tabb said of the brace of tunnels that was hollowed out of a rugged mountainside by the Norwegians. "They are using these caves for their national patrimony collection. One copy of every new book they receive on legal deposit stays where it is available to researchers, and another goes north to this environmentally controlled facility that is totally secure from the outside world. My understanding is that this copy is not to be moved unless absolutely necessary."

Located a thousand kilometers north of Oslo, the depository was authorized in 1989 as a matter of political expedience for a community of twenty-five thousand people. "Mo i Rana is a city that needed work," Jonny Edvardsen, the assistant director of the facility, told me in a telephone interview I arranged after talking with Tabb. "There was a big steel plant here owned by the state that had closed down, and the Norwegian government had to find some work for those people who were left without jobs. One of the government institutions being enlarged at the time was the national library, and what we have here today grew out of that. The policy we have now is that one copy of every new book printed in Norway goes inside the mountain. We put newspapers on microfilm in there too, as well as recordings from state broadcasting." All told, about fifteen thousand new books are received each year on legal deposit. Blasted out of solid rock on four levels, the storage vaults were completed in 1992 and have a capacity of forty-two thousand shelf meters, with plenty of room available for expansion. Temperatures inside are kept at

8 degrees centigrade, humidity at 35 percent, and air is circulated once an hour.

"We don't know how long books will survive in there, but we are sure they will survive a lot longer there than if we put them someplace else," Edvardsen said. "We believe some of the materials could last a thousand years." In addition to the mountain vault, a more readily accessed section of the repository is used for material that exists in multiple copies. "We save the original newspapers as well as the microfilm, since we hold the artifact to be just as important as the content. We also are building a huge digital repository inside the mountain. Up until now we have not had occasion to go into the mountain collection, but if something has to come out, we will make a copy on the spot. The mission here is preservation, and the copy we put inside the mountain we call the safety copy, and it stays there forever in pristine condition."

A visit to Archives II, an imposing seven-story building just outside the District of Columbia in College Park, Maryland, that serves as the principal repository for America's official documents, begins with the awareness that within the stone walls of this 2-million-square-foot structure of steel and glass resides something in the area of 4 billion pieces of paper. There are 9.5 million photographs as well, half a million films and videos, and 2.6 million maps and charts, numbers that keep growing at the rate of 1.5 million cubic feet of records a year. Of these, about one third will be permanently stored, and then there is the world of electronic records to consider, the most vulnerable and uncertain historical artifacts of them all. For people comfortable in libraries, an archive is an interesting concept to consider, a repository established and maintained with a similar mandate to preserve, but with differences in function and philosophy.

"The basic difference between the two is that we deal with records, not information that is necessarily meant to be published," Kenneth Thibodeau, since 1988 the director of electronic records for the National Archives, told me in a wide-ranging interview one morning that took in a number of issues that went well beyond the preservation of digital data. "Records are simply instruments and by-products of doing your job. They are not produced for a general audience, they are produced for people with whom you are interacting in the course of general business. Basically, to understand a record, you have to understand the context in which it was created. We do not organize things the way a library does. Archives are organized by where they come from, by their provenance, by the person or the office generating it, and not by subject. If you have related materials, they are not necessarily going to be kept together in an archive." To help people determine context, it is necessary for archivists to "perfect the arrangement," Thibodeau said. "If records come in that are obviously disordered, we will try to figure out what the original arrangement was, if that's possible. The point is that with records, if you take any one of them out of its original context, it will be greatly impoverished. The golden rule is that you don't mess with the way the creator organized the records, because that is how they were using the information."

Paper records in the National Archives are stored in boxes that contain up to one third of a cubic foot of material. "You can assume that the average box in this building is not pulled off the shelf once in ten years," Thibodeau said. "The most highly active stuff is military casualty information and genealogical material. In our building here there is a room with ninety-eight microfilm readers, and there are days when you wait in line to use one of them. We get something in excess of three hundred thousand people going in there each year, and a comparable number at our various units around the country. Most of these people are interested in records, not what the government was doing at any particular time. The National Archives has oversight responsibility for the whole government, and our job is to preserve the materials we think have historical value. In general, archivists all over the world in the last ten years have focused on what we call 'evidential value.' That is the stuff that will tell you how the government worked, what the decisions were, what followed those decisions."

From an archival point of view, the great paradox of our age is that for all the wonders of modern technology, there is the real possibility that enormous chunks of our common legacy are at immediate risk of disappearing forever, in many instances without a trace. Because so much cultural heritage is at stake, the search for a durable preservation medium has never been more compelling a concern than now, with uneasiness centering as much on digital technology as it does on the decay of brittle books. At a time when the life span of electronically generated data is measured in terms of months and decades, not generations or centuries, the ongoing challenge is to make sure that important material is transferred from one computer format to another, from one software system to another, from one operational unit to another, from one piece of hardware to another, a dilemma not unlike one confronted in the early Middle Ages, when classical texts deemed unworthy of copying from their papyrus originals faced the high likelihood of extinction. As Jeff Rothenberg, a noted computer scientist who writes and lectures worldwide on the situation, has put it, the greatest challenge confronting archivists of the twenty-first century is the overriding need to "ensure the longevity of digital documents." Rothenberg has become the champion of a strategy called emulation, a way of keeping up with software and hardware changes by building machines that will, in a sense, allow for what amounts to the cloning of antiquated systems and hardware to access archived material in the future. An alternative approach to the one championed by Rothenberg—one that would not stress saving the original software, as he favors, but one that merely provides the means for future machines to extract data from long-abandoned programs—has been proposed by Raymond Lorie, a researcher at the Almaden Research Center in San Jose, California, a unit of IBM. Lorie's idea, called a "universal virtual computer," would extract the data stored in a particular file and transfer it to a system designed to be so logical and accessible that computer developers of the future would be able to write instructions to download the information easily on their new machines. For that strategy to work, the system would have to be adopted as an international standard. The central elements of Lorie's universal computer have been tested by the Dutch national library and deemed promising. For his part, Rothenberg believes the strategy is not ambitious enough. "It will give you the contents—or rather, what someone thought were the meaningful core contents—in some future form," he told Anne Eisenberg of the *New York Times*. "But it won't preserve the original."

Anyone whose first computer used 5.25-inch floppy disks, anyone who wrote correspondence, reports, or journalism on WordStar or kept business records on VisiCalc, anyone whose attempt to access a website is greeted by an "Error 404" response—an indication that the site has been abandoned and is inaccessible—has a sense of the crisis being faced on a far more massive scale by librarians, archivists, and curators all over the world. "While books printed 300 years ago work the same way as those bound today, data recorded just 20 years ago can be indecipherable on today's equipment," David M. Ewalt wrote in an article for *Information Week*. "What use is a perfectly preserved Word file, if a thousand years from now, nobody has a copy of Microsoft Office or a Windows machine to run it on?" The dilemma was brought into sharper focus by Peter Lyman and Howard Besser, two participants in a 1998 conference sponsored by the Getty Conservation Institute in Los Angeles. "In fact, our digital cultural heritage is disappearing, almost as fast as it is recorded," they wrote in the introduction to the final report. "Atoms, as in ink on paper, tend to persist. Digital records tend to become inaccessible, rendered unreadable by media deterioration, or obsolete by the pace of innovation in information technology."

Like the brittle book crisis, the enormity and complexity of preserving electronic records has been understood for some time, and alarms have been sounded for at least a decade, though none with the degree of hysteria that gripped much of the world in the frenetic months leading up to the arrival of the year 2000 during what was called the Y2K crisis. On a governmental level, the implications of the problem were outlined in a congressional report prepared by the Committee on Government Operations in 1990 called *Taking a Byte Out of History: The Archival Preservation of Federal Computer Records,* and regarded today as the first official warning of the serious problem that was at hand. "Federal records document the history and intent of public policy and form the basis of our national history," the authors of the report began, though they quickly pointed out that a record "remains useful only as long as the medium on which its information is stored can be read and understood."

Like all good government reports, this one had a few horror stories to pass on, most notably the status of information gathered for the 1960 census. Because the type and format of computer tapes used in the national survey became obsolete within a few years, there were "only two machines in the world that can read the original data." One of the devices, by 1990 already regarded as a relic, was in the Smithsonian Institution; the other was in Japan. "If a computer record cannot be read," the committee declared, "then for all practical purposes, the record no longer exists. Like Stonehenge, it is possible that a computer tape can be seen but not understood." Another concern was the increasing use of electronic mail, for which no preservation guidelines were in place. "The Iran-Contra Affair illustrates the importance of an electronic mail system as a repository of information crucial not only for historians but for current policy, oversight, and investigatory purposes. The incident also illustrates the lack of attention that has been paid to the preservation of some computerized records."

No immediate solutions were proposed in the report, but a first warning was issued, and other cautionary tales would follow. One of the more widely reported instances involved disclosures that 20 percent of the information collected on Jet Propulsion Laboratory computers during the 1976 *Viking* mission to Mars had been stored on magnetic tape that deteriorated so severely it was presumed lost. Another revealed that some prisoner-of-war and missing-in-action records and casualty counts from the Vietnam War gathered by the Department of Defense were no longer readable. At the National Climate Data Center in Asheville, North Carolina, it was announced that weather information gathered by satellites from the mid-1970s to 1996 had been stored on a tape system called the U-matic that is no longer manufactured. "We're down to only a couple of machines that can read them," John Jensen, chief of the division, said in the fall of 1999.

Prevailing wisdom today involves a concept known as "migration" that allows for the transfer of important materials as technology advances, a process that virtually guarantees the loss of data in transition. "The point right now is that basically there is no archival medium for permanent storage," Kenneth Thibodeau at the National Archives told me. "Magnetic tape is a horrendous medium—it doesn't last, it self-destructs, it is extremely fragile, it is sensitive to mold, humidity, and to changes in temperature—but I kind of regard it as the devil I know. And the problem is that because of the market drive toward miniaturization, it gets less and less stable. But even if there was an archival medium for this data, we wouldn't use it, because as long as the technology continues to change, it becomes obsolete anyway. Since we started taking stuff in digital form here at the National Archives in 1971, we have been using one form of magnetic tape or another, and since then we've had a policy that when any tape gets to be ten years old, we are going to copy it. And that's worked out pretty well. Some organizations even use a five-year refreshment."

Everyone involved in the discussion has agreed that the ultimate challenge lies in deciding what information will be saved, and what allowed to disappear. "The problem with the Internet is that it gives you everything, reliable material and crazy material," the semiotician and novelist

Umberto Eco told Celestine Bohlen in the fall of 2002. "So the problem becomes, how do you discriminate? The function of memory is not only to preserve, but also to throw away. If you remembered everything from your entire life, you would be sick."

For materials that are not "refreshed" or "migrated," there will be certain losses, regardless of their significance. In recent months the debate has turned to whether maintaining preservation copies of every electronic document is a good idea, regardless of how achievable it may be. The upshot to all this abundance, Deanna B. Marcum, the president of the Council on Library and Information Resources, wrote in an op-ed piece for the *New York Times*, "is that the easier it is to create and store information, the harder that information is to manage, and the greater is the threat that we will not be able to find something when we need it. There is simply too much to sort through."

While there are no easy answers, the solution clearly is not "to save every tidbit of data generated," Marcum argued, and one reason research libraries in the United States are so useful to scholars is because "they were shaped by men and women who used their critical judgment to select items that would be of value. They did not just hit the 'save' button." People do not routinely preserve every restaurant receipt, dry-cleaning ticket, junk mail flyer, and chewing gum wrapper, and then "deed them to their descendants with the injunction that they be kept forever. That would be irresponsible, self-centered and lazy."

A palpable sense of the volume of data now being generated worldwide each year was offered in the fall of 2000 by Peter Lyman and Hal Varian of the School of Information and Management Systems (SIMS) at the University of California at Berkeley, in a study called "How Much Information?" Culling their data from industry and academic research reports, Lyman and Varian used a unit of measurement called the terabyte to compare the size of information being stored in several forms of physical media: paper, film, optical (CDs and DVDs), and magnetic. In this scheme, one terabyte is equivalent to a million megabytes, which is roughly equivalent to the textual content of a million books. Their research disclosed that 93 percent of the information now being produced is stored in digital form, with hard drives in stand-alone personal computers accounting for 55 percent of the total. At the time the report was issued in October 2000, material directly available on the World Wide Web consisted of some 2.5 billion documents, and was growing at the rate of 7.3 million pages a day. One clear indication of just how rapidly the figures are expanding is evident by the fact that the Lyman-Varian report was issued not in a paper edition but posted electronically as a "living document" that can be constantly updated and modified.

One of the study's most sobering conclusions was clear evidence of what they called the "dominance of digital" content in today's world, and the "paucity of print." Lyman and Varian reckoned that if all printed material published in the world each year were to be expressed in ASCII (American Standard Code for Information Interchange), the character sets used in most computers, it could be stored in fewer than five terabytes. "This doesn't mean that print is dead," they stressed. "What it means is that it has become a very efficient and concentrated form for the communication of information."

It is instructive to emphasize that the title of the Berkeley study concludes with a question mark—"How Much Information?"—and while nobody knows the precise volume of data that will be produced in the years to come, Lyman and Varian offered some idea of the logistics that would be involved to store it: "The world's total yearly production of print, film, optical, and magnetic content would require roughly 1.5 billion gigabytes of storage. This is the equivalent of 250 megabytes per person for each man, woman, and child on earth." In the fall of 2000 the cost of magnetic storage was said to be "less than $10" per gigabyte, and "dropping rapidly" toward the $1 level by the year 2005. "Soon it will be technologically possible for an average person to access virtually all recorded information. The natural question then arises: how much information is there to store? If we wanted to store 'everything,' how much storage would it take?"

At least one ambitious project has been undertaken that addresses that very question. In the fall of 2002, the Massachusetts Institute of Technology launched a program it christened DSpace, an electronic repository in which faculty, students, and researchers will be able to save the fruits of their efforts and make it available to others on the Internet, not only now, but in the years to come in a "federation of systems" that make available the "collective intellectual resources of the world's leading institutions," according to the "vision" statement posted on its website (dspace.org). Working in collaboration with Hewlett-Packard Co., which underwrote the two-year project with a $1.8 million grant, MIT engineers said they hope to create a "superarchive" that will preserve "trillions of bytes" of digital information, including everything from records of classroom lectures and experiments to brain scans and surveys of the ocean floor. Materials submitted to the repository are organized within a "community," be it a school, department, laboratory, or research center, and every document will be assigned a unique and permanent URL. Each community sets its own standards and determines who will be authorized access to the documents, though material posted with unrestricted access may be viewed by anyone.

"If you look at the landscape of digital repositories, there seem to be two types," observed MacKenzie Smith, associate director for technology for the MIT Libraries and the institute's project manager for DSpace. "One concerns library holdings that happen to be in digital format. The other is a preprint archive that is tailored to scholarly papers in a discipline and is a vehicle for getting them out quickly. They are not concerned with long-term preservation." DSpace, however, is committed to preserving not only published papers, but also their supporting documentation.

A goal of DSpace is to store uncataloged information that is likely to be lost unless a suitable repository is created. Every year MIT researchers create at least ten thousand papers, data files, images, collections of field notes, and audio and video clips. The studies frequently appear in professional journals, but the rest of the research material remains stored in personal computers, websites, and departmental servers, accessible to only a few scholars.

When DSpace was launched, MIT had already archived about a thousand files totaling more than 2 terabytes of data. By contrast, the content of every book in the Library of Congress, excluding pictures, is estimated to total 20 terabytes. In time, MIT expects to be saving petabytes, or thousands of terabytes, of data. "I think the problem that libraries are going to have is what they don't put into it," Hal Abelson, an MIT computer science and electrical engineering professor who works on the project, said, given the limitless potential for storage.

In another ambitious initiative, a nonprofit company based in San Francisco known as the Internet Archive is using a network of sophisticated "crawling" devices to download copies of every Web page that has been publicly posted on the Internet since 1996. Conceived by Brewster Kahle, cofounder of Alexa Internet, a Web navigation company now owned by Amazon.com, the Internet Archive has been gathering Web pages and storing them in tape drives the size of two soda machines, each capable of preserving 10 terabytes of data, again, about one half of the contents of the Library of Congress. While an efficient means of cataloging and accessing the raw material remains to be devised, Kahle's long-term goal is to "preserve our digital heritage." To do that, he told a reporter for the *San Francisco Chronicle*, it is necessary "to capture all the dreck you could ever want." Driving Kahle's project is the realization that the average life span of a page on the World Wide Web is seventy-five days, a circumstance that explains the frustration so many "surfers" feel when their attempts to log on to a targeted site is met with an "Error 404" message, a gentle way of saying that the page no longer exists, or has moved to a different address without a known link. "Using the saved files in the future may require conversion to new file formats," Kahle wrote in an article for *Scientific American*, a tacit acknowledgment that what he has set in place is little more than a first step.

Forty miles north of Dallas, meanwhile, in the basement offices of the A. M. Willis Library of the University of North Texas at Denton, a repository created in 1997 to archive the digital records of defunct federal agencies and commissions receives anywhere from twenty thousand to thirty thousand queries a month for material once available on the World Wide Web. Formally known as the CyberCemetery, the endeavor is operated with the assistance of the Government Printing Office, which had been directed by Congress to find a suitable way of saving the data gathered on the discontinued websites. The material appears exactly as it did on the day that such agencies as the Office of Technology Assessment, the National Bankruptcy Review Commission, the Census Monitoring Board, and the National Partnership for Reinventing Government—fifteen all told in the fall of 2002—closed shop. "Federal bureaucracies are born in Washington," Christopher Lee wrote in an article for the *Washington Post*, "but they go to Texas to die."

A few weeks before I was scheduled to give a talk in Chicago in the summer of 2000 at the annual meeting of the American Library Association on the subject of the library as *museum*—are books and manuscripts on their way to becoming artifacts of the past to exist only as outmoded curiosities, in other words—I attended a conference at the John F. Kennedy Library in Boston called Digital Reality II. All the big names in the field were there, including Tim Berners-Lee, the MIT scientist credited with single-handedly creating the Internet-based hypermedia initiative for global information known as the World Wide Web, and Jeff Rothenberg, who put forth his "emulation" proposal in an illustrated lecture, and who readily acknowledged that the concept remains on the drawing board all the same. What was apparent to everyone in attendance was just how much of a cottage industry electronic preservation has become, and how little tangible progress has been made toward preserving the digital record. The lesson to be learned, as I suggested in my Chicago remarks, was that the book had plenty of life left before it could be sealed under glass and put on display as a dimly recalled anachronism. In closing, I quoted the words of the essayist William H. Gass, who in an homage to the printed book written a year earlier for *Harper's Magazine* declared that "words on a screen" have visual qualities that "darkly limn their shape, but they have no materiality, they are only shadows, and when the light shifts they'll be gone."

Make Haste Slowly

Yet this little body of thought that lies before me in the shape of a book has existed thousands of years; nor since the invention of the press, can any thing short of an universal convulsion of nature, abolish it. To a shape like this, so small, yet so comprehensive, so slight, yet so lasting, so insignificant, yet so venerable, turns the mighty activity of Homer, and so turning, is enabled to live and warm us forever.

—LEIGH HUNT (1784–1859), "MY BOOKS"

I have claimed that I was the first person in the world that ever had a telephone in his house for practical purposes; I will now claim—until dispossessed—that I was the first person in the world to apply the type-machine to literature. That book must have been The Adventures of Tom Sawyer. *I wrote the first half of it in '72, the rest of it in '74. My machinist type-copied a book for me in '74, so I concluded it was that one. That early machine was full of caprices, full of defects—devilish ones. It has as many immoralities as the machine of today has virtues.*

—MARK TWAIN (1835–1910),

UNPUBLISHED AUTOBIOGRAPHY, 1904

In the opening sentence of a respected survey on the history and technique of bookbinding, a famed New York craftswoman who was trained in Europe in the early 1900s by such giants as Thomas James Cobden-Sanderson and the firm of Francis Sangorski and George Sutcliffe placed the evolution of *books* in fine perspective. "The book form has gone through very few changes in physical appearance since its inception," Edith Diehl wrote, "and it is interesting to note that each change of form has been the natural and even the compelling result of a change in the character of the tools and materials used for recording the text." At the very time that Diehl was writing those words, a monumental shift in the character of tools and materials for recording words was already in its embryonic stage of development, and had in fact been foreseen a full year before her two-volume study was published with uncanny perception by Dr. Vannevar Bush, the director of the Office of Scientific Research and Development for the United States during World War II, and responsible for marshaling the technology that produced such weapons systems as radar, the proximity fuse, amphibious weapons, and the atomic bomb. With the end of global warfare in sight, Dr. Bush had written a contemplative essay for *The Atlantic Monthly* titled "As We May Think," which addressed itself to novel ways of dealing with the mass of technical information being developed by the world's scientists. As coordinator of the secret government project that led to the nuclear bombings of Hiroshima and Nagasaki, Bush enthused over how "exhilarating" it had been for thousands of individuals to have worked so closely as one unit in pursuit of a common cause. "Now, for many, this appears to be approaching an end," he wrote just a few weeks before the warplane *Enola Gay* lifted off from Midway Island for the Japanese mainland, carrying in its bomb bay a certain resolution of the hostilities, leading him to ask: "What are the scientists to do next?"

The purpose of the article was not to speculate so much on what technological frontiers were about to be explored, but to propose a "new relationship" that would enable scientists to combine "the sum of our knowledge" in the pursuit of meaningful research. To achieve these goals, Bush believed it was necessary to develop "mechanical aids with which to effect a transformation in scientific records." When read today, his language is outdated, but what he was contemplating was nothing less than the management, filing, storage, and retrieval of vast amounts of information with remarkable devices then winsomely being referred to by incredulous outsiders as "electronic brains." Having just supervised six thousand scientists in the development of horrific "destructive gadgets," none of which he was free to describe at the time, Bush knew as well as anyone the limitless potential of the human intellect. "There is a growing mountain of research," he hinted, but there was an exasperating problem in dealing with it. Methods of access had become hopelessly antiquated, rendering the material useless to other scientists.

"The summation of human experience is being expanded at a prodigious rate, and the means we use for threading through the consequent maze to the momentarily important item is the same as was used in the days of square-rigged ships," he complained. "The investigator is staggered by the findings and conclusions of thousands of other workers—conclusions which he cannot find time to grasp, much less to remember, as they appear." Further on in his essay, Bush suggested that the problem torments researchers everywhere, not just those working in the sciences. "There may be millions of fine thoughts, and the account of the experience on which they are based, all encased within the stone walls of acceptable architectural form; but if the scholar can get at only one a week by diligent search, his syntheses are not likely to keep up with the current scene." Never did Bush use the word *computer*—it had not yet become a fixture in the language to identify the miraculous machines we live with so intimately today—but the research and reading tools he described as imminently forthcoming, and their functions, are eerily familiar all the same.

He wrote of "new and powerful instrumentalities" coming into use, of "photocells capable of seeing things in a physical sense," of advanced photography "which can record what is seen or even what is not," of "thermionic tubes" capable of controlling potent forces under the guidance of less power "than a mosquito uses to vibrate his wings," of cathode ray tubes "rendering visible an occurrence so brief that by comparison a microsecond is a long time," of relay combinations that will carry out involved sequences of movements "more reliably than any human operator and thousands of times as fast," any one or all of which could be used, he believed, to build "mechanical aids with which to effect a transformation in scientific records."

Bush proposed a word, *memex,* for a machine that he suggested would use mechanical components and microfilm to store and process data, but the coinage never quite made it into the language. The computer jargon of today, *software, hypertext, memory, search engines, byte, link, word processing, artificial intelligence, Internet,* and perhaps the most consequential of all in the modern world of information storage and transmission, *database,* is nowhere to be found in his essay either, but many of the functions we take for granted now were beginning to appear on the horizon in 1945, as he so enthusiastically speculated. "One might, for example, speak to a microphone, in the manner described in connection with the speech controlled typewriter," he mused, predicting voice recognition systems of half a century later. Bush may not have foreseen the arrival of transistors and microchips, the miniaturization of processors, the obsolescence of vacuum tubes, the potential of optical fibers, or the myriad possibilities of digital scanning, but he clearly understood that the only way to sort through vast quantities of information was with technology. When discussing the potential of the memex, Bush was anticipating the furious trend toward making things smaller and faster and lighter. "The cards may be in miniature, so that they occupy little space. They must move quickly. They need not be transferred far, but merely into position so that the photocell and recorder can operate them." The applications were vast, and in his view inevitable. "It might even be of use in libraries," he opined at one point, "but that is another story."

Bush had many opportunities to consider his speculations over the remaining twenty-nine years of his life, and in 1967 he revisited the subject in a collection of essays he wrote as a kind of meditation on his life's work titled *Science Is Not Enough*. In a chapter called "Memex Revisited," he asked the basic question: "Now, is this all a dream? It certainly was, two decades ago. It is still a dream, but one that is now attainable. To create an actual memex will be expensive, and will demand initiative, ingenuity, patience, and engineering skill of the highest order. But it can be done." The matter of whether or not it would be done is what vexed him the most, and accomplishing it, he felt, was a matter of national will. "The great digital machines of today have their exciting proliferation because they could vitally aid business, because they could increase profits. The libraries still operate by horse-and-buggy methods, for there is no profit in libraries. Government spends billions on space since it has glamour and hence public appeal. There is no glamour about libraries, and the public do not understand that the welfare of their children depends far more upon effective libraries than it does on the collecting of a bucket of talcum powder from the moon. So it will not be done soon. But eventually it will."

For all the successful methods that humans have devised to transmit their thoughts and images through the centuries, many thousands of schemes that were not so successful have fallen by the wayside and been abandoned, forgotten to all but a sentimental few. A fascinating exhibition mounted by the Getty Museum in Los Angeles in 2000–2001 called *Devices of Wonder* took respectful notice of the many ways people of imagination have used various "eye machines" through the centuries, featuring such dazzling optical instruments as the camera obscura and the anamorphic cone that produced paintings that were comprehensible only from specific vantage points. On view elsewhere in the Getty gallery were captivating displays of multiplying mirrors, magic lanterns, perspective theaters, zograscopes that make two-dimensional pictures appear lifelike, and a crank-operated moving-picture mechanism known as the choreutoscope that prefigured the cinema. "Given the age-old promise of assisted exaltation, it is not surprising that the human-machine interface stretches back to the sorcerer's mirror, Alexandrian automata, the 'input-box' of the *Wunderschrank*, the lenses of a telescope or microscope, the scrolling mechanism of the panorama, and the individualized menus of the diorama," Barbara Maria Stafford noted in a learned introduction to the exhibition catalog: "The desktop processor's collection of overlapping windows and iconic taskbars is an extension of this ancient world of mediating and transporting apparatus that takes us directly to another reality by clicking on a relevant link."

For people who study this phenomenon, several websites have been established, the most sophisticated known as the Dead Media Project, created in the mid-1990s by Bruce Sterling and Richard Kadrey, two well-known science-fiction writers whose passion for fabulous contrivances come into play in the shaping of their fanciful stories. Though not writing surfaces in the strictest sense, these forsaken artifacts offer dramatic, sometimes amusing evidence of the lengths to which people have gone to enhance their ability to communicate, not only across great distances but across time. Soliciting nominations from visitors to their website—and spiritedly encouraging anyone so disposed to use the material they have gathered as the raw material for a much-needed "field guide for the communications paleontologist"—the Dead Media Project has archived a treasure trove of documentation for systems and objects that have lapsed into disuse over the centuries. "We need a book about the failures of media, the collapses of media, the supercessions of media, the stangulations of media, a book detailing all the freakish and hideous media mistakes that we should know enough now not to repeat, a book about media that have died on the barbed wire of technological advance, media that didn't make it, martyred media, dead media," Sterling explained in a mission statement he titled "The Dead Media Manifesto."

Among the scores of curiosities that have been itemized on the website are such objects and concepts as a counting device composed of dyed cotton cords with knots tied in them known as the Incan quipu. Others equally as arcane have such enigmatic names as the Tlascaltec nepohualtzitzin, the Okinawan warazan, the Bolivian chimpu, American Indian wampum, and Zulu beadwork. To these are added more familiar and now abandoned practices as smoke signals, carrier pigeons, and town criers, along with doodads known as the telescriber, refrigerator-mounted talking notepads, a medieval form of authenticating copies of documents on vellum by using a cutting device known as the cyrograph, a visual jukebox from the 1960s called the scopitone. And then there were the telegraph balloons used by the Union army during the Civil War and 16-inch aluminum transcription disks used to document live radio broadcasts in the years before magnetic tape, altogether a fascinating menagerie.

On a more focused level are the fervent collectors of early computing devices that are no longer in use, contraptions like the Commodore ZX, the Eagle II, the AT&T 7300, the NEC PC8201a, the Inmos Transputer, the UNIX PC, the Sun-3 that are now regarded as dinosaurs. At the Computer History Museum in Mountain View, California—the very heart of Silicon Valley—some thirty-five hundred objects spanning thirty-five years of computer development are maintained, and regular exhibitions are mounted. Another California organization sponsors an annual Vintage Computer Festival that is well attended by collectors from all over the world, and more often than not the rarest of examples are no more than twenty-five or thirty years old. The founder of the organization, a computer engineer named Sellam Ismail, has amassed a personal collection of fifteen hundred computers, thirty-five hundred computer-related books (from as early as 1875), twenty thousand magazines, thousands of software programs, manuals, games, and game hardware, and has made a successful business out of providing services and equipment to individuals and companies who suddenly find themselves in need of obsolete technology they can find no place else.

For the Mel Fisher Maritime Museum in Key West, Florida, for instance, Ismail retrieved 130,000 digitized photographs of gold doubloons, bars of bullion, and silver ingots recovered from the seventeenth-century Spanish galleon *Nuestra Señora de Atocha* that had been archived on VHS tapes, a short-lived mode of encoding binary data in the 1980s that fell out of favor quickly and was abandoned altogether. Modern computer systems were unable to accept the tapes, let alone read them, giving Ismail an opportunity to strut his stuff and effect a full rescue. He told a reporter for the *Guardian* in London that he began stockpiling old machines by the hundreds in several rented warehouses when he started to travel around to flea markets and discovered he was not alone in his zeal. "I guess that's when I officially became a collector, because there was really no rational reason for me to have these stupid old computers. I thought I would be the only one dumb enough to collect stuff like this."

Among other private collectors, certainly one of the most passionate is Nathan P. Myhrvold, at one time the chief technology officer for Microsoft Corporation, whose vast holdings of gee-whiz knickknacks include seven supercomputers, enormous machines of great power and sophistication that cost as much as $20 million when new, but now are virtually worthless. An amateur paleontologist who has funded important field research, Myhrvold also owns an actual dinosaur or two; the fossilized remains of several prehistoric creatures enjoy prominent positions in the massive warehouse he uses as a private gallery for his collection outside Seattle, Washington. Myhrvold told one interviewer that he went through a phase of acquisition in which he was "actively scouting for machines that were about to be junked." Part of the motivation, he added, is rooted in a basic premise: "The technology industry doesn't respect its past. No one thinks of saving old stuff."

As these examples suggest, the idea of using machines to facilitate the production and acquisition of knowledge is by no means a recent conceit, and is well rooted in history. One scheme that was *not* included in the Getty exhibition since it was never actually produced but continues to excite the imagination appears in a wonderful sixteenth-century engraving of an intricately designed apparatus identified by its creator as a "reading wheel." Conceived by the Italian inventor Agostino Ramelli, the apparatus was intended to enable a reader to sit before a large cylinder outfitted with a series of revolving shelves operated by the feet and to consult a number of books at the same time, a precursor to the hyperlinks Web surfers find so indispensable today. A caption accompanying the drawing, published in Italian and French, offered this description:

> This is a beautiful and ingenious machine, very useful and convenient for anyone who takes pleasure in study, especially those who are indisposed and tormented by gout. For with this machine a man can see and turn through a large number of books without moving from one spot. Moreover, it has another fine convenience in that it occupies very little space in the place where it is set, as anyone of intelligence can clearly see from the drawing. This wheel is made in the manner shown, that is, it is constructed so that when the books are laid on their lecterns they never fall or move from the place where they are laid even when the wheel is turned and revolved all the way around. Indeed, they will always remain in the same position and will be displayed to the reader in the same way as they were laid on their small lecterns, without any need to tie or hold them with anything. This wheel may be made as large or small as desired, provided the master craftsman who constructs it observes the proportions of each part of its components.

Illustrations of the reading wheel are reproduced frequently, recently in Alberto Manguel's wonderfully accessible *History of Reading* and in *The Scholar in His Study*, Dora Thornton's richly illustrated examination of working spaces favored by Renaissance thinkers. Although it was never built during Ramelli's lifetime, a modern adaptation of the reading wheel was constructed in 1986 by the architect Daniel Libeskind for an exhibition in Venice. "The machine seeks to represent the triumph of spirit over matter, of candlelight over electrical light or darkness," Libeskind wrote of the project. "It's made solely from wood as are the books." Describing the finished product, Libeskind noted that when the wheels and the gears move, "it's truly beautiful—the fascination of a multiplying circle. The experience one has is that the books on the top shelf, which are rotating, appear to be falling on top of you." But instead of cascading on top of the operator during the rotation, the volumes remain "in an ideal position to a hypothetical reader—a reader who isn't there. That's the reading experience: one cog of the entire machine."

Another machine that was never constructed in real life—but whose premise has been a source of great amusement in the two and three quarter centuries since it was first described by Jonathan Swift in *Gulliver's Travels*—is the Literary Engine demonstrated by a professor of "speculative knowledge" in the wacky Academy of Lagado, a device created by the satirist to poke fun at the Royal Society. Lemuel Gulliver, the deadpan narrator, gives a firsthand description of the "engine," designed, he has been told, to enable even "the most ignorant person" to write serious books on any scholarly subject, "without the least assistance from genius or study." Positioned around a large square box in the middle of a room are thirty-six students, all poised to begin cranking individual iron shafts at a professor's command. Attached by wire to every rod are "bits of wood" covered with numerous pieces of paper, each bearing a different word. As the scrambled lexicon is churned, sifted, and shuffled about, the tiny papers randomly form "three or four words together that might make a sentence," and are dictated in quiet monotones to four other students whose assignment it is to function as scribes. The shuffling is repeated several times, and at every turn the words shift from place to place:

> Six hours a-day the young Students were employed in this Labour, and the Professor showed me several volumes in large folio already collected, of broken sentences, which he intended to piece together, and out of those rich materials to give the world a complete body of all arts and sciences; which however might be still improved, and much expedited, if the Public would raise a fund for making and employing five hundred such Frames in Lagado, and oblige the managers to contribute in common their several Collections.
>
> He assured me, that this invention had employed all his thoughts from his youth, that he had emptied the whole vocabulary into his frame, and made the strictest computation of the general proportion there is in books between the numbers of particles, nouns, and verbs, and other parts of speech.
>
> I made my humblest acknowledgement to this illustrious person for his great communicativeness, and promised if ever I had the good fortune to return to my native country, that I would do him justice, as the sole inventor of this wonderful machine; the form and contrivance of which I desired leave to delineate upon paper, as in the figure here annexed.

The "figure here annexed"—a drawing of the machine—is the only illustration included in the 1726 first edition of *Gulliver's Travels* that was not a map; since there are no credit lines for any of the plates, there is some speculation that Swift himself may have drawn the amusing picture. Recent scholarship has suggested that he borrowed the idea for his Literary Engine from a Japanese model, and as preposterous as the premise may be, a few chroniclers of computer history have cited it as being the first mention in print of a mechanical word processor.

The contention that a book is measurably more than a gathering of paper stitched between two covers is not an argument that emerged full-blown in the computer age as a withering defense of print. In fact it is a creed that has been articulated passionately over the years by numerous observers, none more eloquently than the graceful essayist Charles Lamb (1775–1834), an insatiable consumer of literature who confessed in one of his Elia pieces that he dedicated "no inconsiderable portion" of his time to consuming other people's thoughts: "When I am not walking, I am reading; I cannot sit and think. Books think for me." His tastes were decidedly eclectic—"I have no repugnances," he made clear—but there were a few basic qualifications to put on the record just the same. "I can read anything which I call *a book*. There are things in that shape which I cannot allow for such." Lamb thereupon itemized his own "catalogue of *books which are not books—biblia a biblia,*" specifying such imposters as "Court Calendars, Directories, Pocket-Books, Draught Boards, bound and lettered on the back, Scientific Treatises, Almanacs, Statutes at large," precisely the kinds of materials, in fact—lexicons, research reports, telephone numbers, and the like—that are ideally suited to the database of today. "With these exceptions," Lamb wrote, "I can read almost anything. I bless my stars for a taste so catholic, so unexcluding."

Robert Darnton, a professor of history at Princeton University and the author of numerous scholarly books that have earned the dual distinction of being internationally respected and widely read, is one of the world's leading practitioners of a discipline pioneered in France in the 1960s known as *l'histoire du livre*, the social aspect of the "history of the book," and in his writing an unwavering champion of print. "The notion that you are going to read everything from another sort of machine, a computer, is to misunderstand the nature of reading and the nature of books, the nature of book culture," he told me in an interview. Darnton said that in the attempt to replace the codex with on-line books—"however benighted" the intention may be—the "actual tactile sensation" of reading is inevitably lost. "When you read a book, you have contact with the page, and of course with the paper itself. One of the losses in computerized reading is this sense of contact, of turning pages back and forth, of thumbing books and letting your eyes wander, that luxurious feeling of going across the landscape. It could be argued that you're doing that with a computer, but you're not, scrolling up and scrolling down is not the same sensation. The little dots on the screen, the pixels, are not the same as the codex." Darnton said there are studies to support this view, but he used an example from recent American history to illustrate the point. In the late fall of 1998, the U.S. House of Representatives released on the Internet the full text of Kenneth W. Starr's "referral" to Congress recommending the impeachment of William Jefferson Clinton as president of the United States. Every word of the text was available on-line, and it could be downloaded immediately, free of charge. Some 6 million hits were recorded on various government websites offering the Starr report during the first twenty-four hours of its availability. Within a matter of weeks, however, a printed edition of the report was riding on top of all best-seller lists as well, clear evidence that serious readers still preferred to have a hard copy of texts they plan to spend some time with.

"At first we thought we could create an electronic space, throw everything into it, and leave the readers to sort it out," Darnton wrote in "The New Age of the Book," an essay published in the *New York Review of Books*. "Then we learned that no one would read a book on a computer screen or wrestle through heaps of printouts." A second casualty, perhaps not quite as romantic as the tactile experience but more consequential, is the impact a total reliance on electronics has on scholarship itself. "I think that whoever is preaching a library-less library in the university doesn't understand the way books work," Darnton told me with a hint of exasperation. "So many things in a book are conveyed by its physical quality. The actual meaning of a text depends to some extent on the way it is embedded on the pages, the way it's been thought out and put together as a package, the running heads, the indexes, the footnotes, the front matter. You get yourself organized as a reader, it seems to me, by the way you approach a book. You open it, you take it in through all of your senses, and then you begin to use it."

When we first spoke in 1999, Darnton was serving as president of the American Historical Society, and a project he had chosen to champion during his one-year term came as something of surprise, given his views on the primacy of printed books. "I have decided to take on one major initiative during my tenure, and that is to work on the electronic publication of dissertations, and the best way to establish a precedent, I thought, would be to do one of these electronic books myself." What he had in mind, he continued, was to publish the third volume of a trilogy he had been working on for several decades, and to do it entirely in electronic format. Darnton said he agreed with Librarian of Congress James H. Billington, who went on record in an interview with me stressing his belief that electronic publishing is an ideal way for doctoral candidates to get their theses published.

"There are already dissertations on the Web, but the idea I am pursuing is to try and set policy standards, peer group refereeing, editing; in other words, to transform a raw dissertation that is not yet a book, something that is still a scholarly exercise, into a genuine book, the way monographs are done now, and publish it electronically. And the reason for that is that the scholarly monograph is in great danger. It is almost impossible to publish scholarly monographs now, and there is a real crisis in periodicals, and library budgets are gravely restricted. This does not preclude publication in codex form; they can come out as paperbacks, whatever. But at the same time, they will be published electronically." Darnton feels the "electronic book" is ideally suited to dissertations and specialized studies, where the linking capabilities will be particularly helpful. "People don't want to read a whole book on a computer screen, so computers aren't very good for serious reading on a large scale. But they are good for other things, searching, putting facts and figures together, making connections. What I hope will happen is that we will produce monographs of a very high quality."

In his "New Age of the Book" essay, Darnton shared some of the horror stories endemic to publishing scholarly monographs in the traditional manner:

> Every editor has a collection of stories about superb monographs that did not sell. Sanford Thatcher at the Penn State University Press tells of a book on nineteenth-century Brazil that won two prizes and sold fewer than 500 copies and of another on Islam in Central Asia that received ecstatic reviews and four awards but sold only 215 copies in cloth (it sold a mere 691 in paperback). Roy Rosenzweig of George Mason University says that one of the best books in a series he edits sold 282 copies. My own favorite horror story concerns a superb monograph on the French Revolution. It won three major prizes and sold 183 copies in cloth, 549 in paper.

Darnton told me he considers the comparison of photography and the fine arts, and how the arrival of film in the 1800s actually allowed traditional artists to explore new modes of artistic expression, a useful one to make. "I like that parallel," he said. "I think it's illuminating. It's quite wrong to imagine a fight to the death between the printed book and the electronic book. It seems to me they are complementary, and that the electronic book is going to open up new possibilities, even new ways of reading, a kind of vertical reading made possible by various clicks, not the more linear form of horizontal reading."

Among the "clicks" Darnton had in mind were options that would reveal a series of "layers arranged like a pyramid," with the one on top comprising "a concise account" of the subject. "The next layer could contain expanded versions of different aspects of the argument, not arranged sequentially as in a narrative, but rather as self-contained units that feed into the topmost story. The third layer could be composed of documentation, possibly of different kinds, each set off by interpretative essays. A fourth layer might be theoretical or historiographical, with selections from previous scholarship and discussions of them. A fifth layer could be pedagogic, consisting of suggestions for classroom discussion and a model syllabus. And a sixth layer could contain readers' reports, exchanges between the author and the editor, and letters from readers, who could provide a growing corpus of commentary as the book made its way through different groups of readers."

Shortly after Darnton and I spoke, the Andrew W. Mellon Foundation awarded the American Council of Learned Societies a $3 million grant to help underwrite the History E-Book Project. In addition to support for Darnton's experiment, the money would be used to convert five hundred previously published books of "major importance to historical studies"— titles from what is known as the "backlist" that are frequently cited and are not widely available—to electronic format. In the spring of 2003, plans were being finalized to make Darnton's keenly awaited project, *A Literary Tour de France: An Electronic Book about Books in the Age of Enlightenment*, available, for a fee, at www.historyebook.org.

Because it is being "born digital," the Darnton project will begin its life on the World Wide Web in phased installments, allowing readers to see it while it is, in effect, a "work in progress" and still developing. For other works of nonfiction that have had their first renditions in print, the on-line book allows authors and editors a facile way of adding new material to what would once have been regarded as completed work. In 1995 the classicist James O'Donnell posted an electronic version of *Cas-*

siodorus, a biography he had issued many years earlier in hardcover. "This book was published in 1979, had a successful life in print until selling out in 1993," he explained in a prefatory note on his website. "At that point, I reclaimed the rights to the book from my valued collaborators at University of California Press and began preparing this hypertext version 'postprint.' " Initially, he included just the original text, with the footnotes inserted as hypertext links marked by highlighted numbers in double brackets, and appended a bibliographical supplement that actually is larger than the original. "Over time, I hope to link this to other resources, to add new material, and to make the WWW page the site of a virtual second (and ongoing) edition of this work." O'Donnell stressed that he will take steps to ensure that readers can "facilitate distinction of original material from the added links," a procedure that has been described as "version control," and is considered essential to maintaining the integrity of earlier work. Such a procedure becomes especially applicable in huge reference works such as the *Oxford English Dictionary,* the *Oxford Dictionary of National Biography,* and the *Encyclopedia Britannica* that are constantly admitting new material, and where linking capabilities to related materials in vast databases are an undeniably useful option.

How the new technologies may affect what up to now have been monumental publishing ventures produced over extended periods of time remains to be seen as well, although it is clear that pressure is mounting in some quarters to publish electronically books that in the past have been the exclusive province of print. The examples of the Bollingen Series of books, first published by Pantheon Books and later by Princeton University Press, and the Belknap Press imprint of Harvard University Press are models of "grand projects" in publishing, publishing in the "purest" sense that may never be seen again. When it was established by Paul Mellon and Mary Mellon in 1941, the Bollingen Series had no precedent in the United States, and given the parameters of such an endeavor, it may never have any successors. The Mellons not only decided the areas of interest that they would pursue, they chose many of the writers and scholars who produced them, and committed more than $20 million to the foundation they established to support its activities; they commissioned Vladimir Nabokov, to cite just one example, to translate Aleksandr Pushkin's *Eugene Onegin*. The Bollingen project had been conceived as a way to publish in English the entire corpus of the Swiss psychologist and psychiatrist Carl Gustav Jung, but was expanded to encompass anthropology, mythology, folklore, archaeology, the arts of all ages, prehistorical and historical records, religion, symbology, and the literature of the imagination. Bollingen, in fact, was the name of the retreat in Switzerland where Jung lived "in modest harmony with nature."

Though the series was chartered as a nonprofit enterprise, many of its titles have been extremely popular, offering dramatic proof that there still is a market for impeccably produced books of high literary merit. *The Collected Works of C. G. Jung* have more than a million copies in print, and Joseph Campbell's *The Hero with a Thousand Faces* has sold more than 750,000 copies; the Richard Wilhelm–Cary F. Baynes translation of *The I Ching; or Book of Changes* has more than 900,000 copies in print. Bollingen Series books were numbered 1 to 100 in Roman numerals, although some entries represented multivolume sets. William McGuire, who edited the books for more than thirty years, described the exercise as "an adventure in collecting the past," and it remains a unique episode in American publishing.

In 1949 Waldron Phoenix Belknap Jr., a wealthy member of Harvard College Class of 1920, left a major bequest to his alma mater with an unusual mandate. According to Thomas J. Wilson, a former publisher of the Harvard University Press, Belknap was "a man of wealth, a bachelor, and a connoisseur" of books, which were the center of his existence. He had unqualified respect for the Houghton Library of Rare Books and Manuscripts at the university, and initially planned on leaving the bulk of his considerable estate to strengthen its collections. But after spending some time in the Bodleian Library at Oxford University during World War II, he conceived of a plan whereby his money "would more usefully be spent in publishing or reprinting great books than in buying rare ones." Belknap made the Houghton Library his beneficiary, but he directed that his bequest be used primarily for the publication of commissioned material. Once the imprint bearing Belknap's name was established within Harvard University Press, the result was immediate. "I saw the change from fear of publishing books at a loss to confidence that we could safely publish any book worthwhile as scholarship," Wilson recalled.

Belknap titles do not always generate very much attention outside scholarly circles, although the publication in 1985 of Volume 1 of the *Dictionary of American Regional English,* a monumental work that at that time was twenty years in preparation, did attract widespread coverage. Some writers compared Frederic Cassidy's exhaustive enterprise with the effort put in by the lexicographers who spent seventy-one years seeing the thirteen-volume *Oxford English Dictionary* through to completion. Volumes 2 and 3 of the *Dictionary of American Regional English* were published in 1994 and 1997, bringing the project up to the letter O. Picking up at P and continuing through Sk, Volume 4 arrived in January 2003, by that time under the general editorship of Joan Houston Hall, a senior scientist at the University of Wisconsin who assumed direction of the project in 2000 following the death of Cassidy at the age of ninety-two, who died after more than four decades committed to the effort. The fifth and concluding installment is expected to arrive in 2005 in time for a fortieth-anniversary celebration. The *Oxford English Dictionary,* meanwhile, launched an on-line version in 2000, signaling what could well be the eventual demise of the printed version.

Projects like the *Oxford English Dictionary* and the *Dictionary of American Regional English* are typically commissioned by university presses with the understanding that they may lose money, but like the Bollingen and Belknap projects at Princeton and Harvard, they go forward on the strength of their intrinsic merits. In 1951, Harvard University Press began publishing three generations of Adams Family Papers —John Adams, John Quincy Adams, Charles Francis Adams—a project that is expected to include more than one hundred volumes when it concludes several decades from now; the editing is being done at the Massachusetts Historical Society, which owns the huge archive. Since 1960, Yale University Press has been publishing the papers of Benjamin Franklin at the rate of a volume a year, with a total of forty-six volumes projected through the year 2006, while editors of an even larger project at Princeton University Press devoted to the papers of Thomas Jefferson suggest that another fifty years will be required to complete that eighty-five-volume job; the first installment was published in 1950. In 1993, Princeton published the sixty-ninth and final volume in its Woodrow Wilson Project; not only was that series completed within a comparatively tidy thirty-five years, it enjoyed the remarkable distinction of having one general editor, Arthur S. Link, at the helm through the entire process. "Working without benefit of modern word processing technology," the biographer Terry Teachout marveled in a lengthy essay on the accomplishment, Link "personally chose every document, wrote most of the longer footnotes and saw each volume through the press; he also carried a full teaching load at Princeton, published two dozen books of his own, underwent seven back operations and helped raise four children."

On the West Coast, the University of California Press won numerous awards following publication in 1980 of *The Plan of St. Gall,* an extensive architectural, historical, and anthropological reconstruction of the Benedictine monastery outside Zurich that was based on a ninth-century drawing on vellum found in the church library in 1704. The three-volume set, weighing twenty-two pounds and containing 1,073 illustrations and foldout charts, was thirteen years in preparation and a marvel of fine bookmaking that made it an instant collector's item. Issued in a single printing of two thousand sets priced at $350 apiece, the run quickly sold out. Reviews were extraordinary, and orders for copies came pouring in, but a second edition was never considered because of impossibly high production costs. Today, sets show up periodically on the antiquarian market priced as high as $2,000, depending on condition.

Another University of California venture of even greater scope and ambition—a fifty-year project to edit and publish the complete corpus of Samuel Langhorne Clemens, the canonical American writer known by millions of readers as Mark Twain—also made its debut in 1967, but in this instance there was never any guarantee that the goals as originally conceived would be realized. Through the first thirty-five years of the Mark Twain Project, twenty-eight volumes have appeared in print, with dozens more projected for completion by the year 2021, including a comprehensive, chronological setting forth of about twelve thousand letters. Though editorial work has continued without interruption, the shape forthcoming editions might take remains unclear, dependent in large measure on the National Endowment for the Humanities—which has provided funding throughout the project—and whether or not university officials will insist on doing the rest of the series electronically, a possibility that the director of the program told me in the summer of 2000, and again two years later, he worries about constantly.

"I am getting enormous pressure to move entirely over to the Internet," Robert H. Hirst, general editor of the project and curator of the Mark Twain Papers at the Bancroft Library, told me as the deadline approached for him to submit an application for continued government support in the summer of 2000.

We are getting these signals from within the university, and from funding sources at the NEH. What I am being told is that these books are too scholarly and too old-fashioned as they exist now in print, and that perhaps the best way to do them from here on out is electronically. There has already been one attempt to pull the plug on us. At one point I received word from the vice chancellor's office here that we should start developing a plan for winding the whole project down altogether, and to think about setting up a termination schedule that would allow us to complete works-in-progress. So far, thankfully, that has not been forced upon us, but it is a daily battle to stay alive. Speaking for myself individually, and in my position as chairman of the Committee on Scholarly Editions for the Modern Language Association, I believe this very definitely is something that should go up on-line, but I also believe that the subject is of sufficient weight and relevance to American culture that a scholarly edition should appear in print as well. This is Mark Twain we are talking about here, after all. You do this once, and it will be there forever.

The University of California began the Mark Twain Project in the mid-1960s as a condition of accepting permanent custody of the Clemens papers from the author's estate, comprising a million pages of material all told. Included in this enormous archive were the manuscripts of four hundred literary works, fifty of which have never been available in any form. Hirst has been involved with the project from the beginning, starting as an editor while still in graduate school at Berkeley, and taking over as director in 1980. He is the only member of the team who is paid directly by the University of California; the five editors on his staff rely on government funding and matching grants for their salaries. Since 1967, NEH has committed a total of $5.7 million to the Mark Twain series.

Charles B. Faulhaber, director of the Bancroft Library, acknowledged that the University of California is "looking very seriously at the possibility" of introducing an electronic Mark Twain edition that would "basically divorce the content of a particular text from the medium in which it is displayed," and allow readers to print out or download the specific materials they might want at any given time. Just when that kind of a program might be implemented, Faulhaber could not say, but he does believe profound change is in the offing nonetheless, and that it will arrive sooner rather than later. "What this means for the Mark Twain Project is that we will be able to keep an evolving edition on a website that is always up to date with whatever changes or additions come along in the scholarship." He would not rule out supporting the production of more printed books in the series, particularly reading texts of the literary works, but changes, he said, are definitely forthcoming.

Right now academic monographs sell, on average, about three hundred copies, so what we see is that the prices keep going way up, and the readership goes way down. This is why the electronic model is so attractive. It makes it possible for us to do all sorts of things you couldn't do otherwise. I am thinking specifically here in regard to the letters, where you might put up machine-readable transcriptions of all the known letters of Mark Twain, you make that material immediately available in an electronic edition, and then, over time, you deepen the edition, so it is not a matter of taking a small chronological chunk at a time, and being stuck with it forever in a printed text. The electronic edition means you can add material that might come along later, you can supplement it with worthwhile commentary as it is produced, and you would establish procedures to document when the revisions and additions are made. I think this is exciting progress, and I believe that it is going to revolutionize scholarship. There is an enormous amount of editorial and scholarly conservatism that needs to be overcome. People are suspicious. We know what we have now. And we don't know just yet what will replace it. But looking twenty years ahead, I don't think there is any doubt that projects like this will be totally electronic. What I don't know right now is how we're going to get there.

James Herbert, director of the Division of Research Programs at the National Endowment for the Humanities in Washington, told me that the agency's guidelines do not favor one publishing medium over another, but he did not deny that electronic projects have gained favor within the NEH over print. "I would say there is a drift toward combining comprehensive electronic publishing with selective publication," he told me in 2000. "What lies behind all of this is money. Our budget for 1996 was cut by 40 percent overall, and at that time we were supporting about one hundred long-term editing projects. Everything was going fine up to that point, but the funding was severely reduced, and we have had to take a hard look at how to go on from here."

The fact that the Mark Twain Project has been ongoing for more than thirty years does not necessarily give it top priority, Herbert said.

All of these editing projects—and I am talking in general, not specifically about Mark Twain—represent the most basic kind of scholarly research. It's easy to be glib about this, but the question is not how long is it going to take to do something, the question is what is the scope of the endeavor, and how detailed it has to be in references and annotations and things of that nature to make it viable. Another false reference often used in this context is the number of volumes published, and will the project be successful only in that one medium. Relevance in some cases can be measured by considering such fundamental issues as how many institutions now offer doctorates in English or history in the United States, for instance, and determining how many of them will be offering doctorates in those disciplines fifty years from now, because we are concerned about the long-term scholarly applications of the projects that we fund.

Outside of the humanities, funding for various scholarly editions also comes from the National Historical Publications and Records Commission, a federal agency affiliated with the National Archives.

When I spoke with Hirst again in the summer of 2002, he had a number of developments to report, most notably that the NEH had, in fact, followed through on its unwillingness to underwrite any more printed books. "They made it clear that they are willing to fund electronic versions, period," he said. "This means that if the print edition is going to continue, it has to be funded by the university and by private donors." With that alternative now the only option, Hirst said he was relieved to report an initial grant of "several hundred thousand dollars" from the Barkley Fund, a philanthropic foundation based in California. But the most important development of all, in Hirst's view, was a "renewed resolve" from the University of California to see the project through. "I am much more optimistic now than I was before, to tell you the truth, because it is clear that the university is not going to let this very important project die. They have committed themselves to raising funds for it. I agree with my colleague Charles that things are going to change over the long haul. But I think they will change not by eliminating books altogether, but by combining features that exploit the best qualities of both."

The redefinition of priorities at the University of California and the National Endowment of the Humanities notwithstanding, ambitious undertakings continue apace elsewhere, and print remains very much a part of the long-range planning. At Yale University Press, two programs were launched in the 1990s at a time when the Internet's implications for conventional publishing were readily apparent, yet the scholarly works being produced in the two ventures are appearing between hard covers all the same. For the Culture and Civilization of China (CCC) Project, "several hundred scholars" are working together in a joint undertaking with the People's Republic of China, according to John G. Ryden, director of the press, with seventy-five volumes expected to appear in print by the year 2020; thirteen titles alone were released between 1991 and 2002. "It is a wonderful, exciting, rewarding, and sometimes difficult undertaking," he said about the massive effort that is striving to produce works that will illumine three thousand years of Chinese art, architecture, painting, sculpture, calligraphy, carvings, and folk art on one front, and classical Chinese literature on another, including the preparation of new translations and a final section of references on Chinese civilization.

In addition to the printed books, there also will be electronic versions "that will be ten to twenty times larger, something that is relatively easy to accomplish with databases," Ryden said. "But we never once considered that there wouldn't and couldn't and shouldn't be a book side to this as well. Here we can use this new technology as a way of enhancing and supplementing the book." The first title released in the series, *Three Thousand Years of Chinese Painting*, an oversize, beautifully illustrated survey issued in 1997, won the Association of American Publishers' top prize for scholarly publishing. "We have already sold ten thousand copies, and we are in our third printing," Ryland said in the summer of 2000.

Launched in 1995, an even more unconventional long-term Yale endeavor called the Annals of Communism Project is publishing English and Russian editions of various archival papers found in the once top-secret Kremlin files of the KGB, the military, the Presidium, the Central Committee, and the foreign ministry that were made available to Western scholars after the fall of the Soviet Union. Fourteen titles in the series, called the Annals of Communism, were released between 1995 and 2002, with another twenty-five to fifty volumes projected. "The rationale for doing these as printed books is pretty straightforward, and I speak here as a publisher who keeps an eye on the bottom line," Ryden said. "There is a demand for them."

Writing in *The Atlantic Monthly* in 1905, the American publisher Henry Holt expressed grave misgivings on the future of "serious literature," and he blamed the disquieting trend he saw on a changing marketplace that valued profits over merit and sales over substance. Holt felt that the development was driven by the sudden availability of cheaply produced books and new technologies that allowed for mass production. In his essay "The Commercialization of Literature," Holt decried the growing influence of literary agents in negotiating contracts, and a new dynamic that required the expenditure of thousands of dollars on advertising to keep up in a world that had become, almost overnight, fiercely competitive.

"I cannot but think that lately many American publishers were as crazy about advertising as the Dutch were about tulips, or the French about the Mississippi Bubble," he complained. "A book is a thing by itself: there is nothing like it, as one shoe is like another, or as one kind of whiskey is like another. Intelligent book buyers want *that* book; no other will fill its place; no amount of advertising of another will substitute it." Yet here books were anyway, he groused, being grouped in the same company with "patent medicines, drinks, tobaccos, food stuffs, clothes, real estate investments, and other things demanded by everybody with money to pay for them."

With fewer and fewer books able to "pay for themselves" as before—or "earn out" their advances on royalties, to use today's jargon—Holt was not optimistic about what he felt lay ahead. "The literature of our mother tongue has been commercialized to an extent not dreamed of in any time of which I have knowledge," and the "trade of publishing has come to a pass such that great changes must take place before it can deserve the name of 'profession,' and before the suggestion in connection with it of anything like 'glory,' can cease to sadden more than it inspires." What Holt was saying, in essence, was that the book as he knew and published it was a creature of the past. But as events turned out, Holt continued to publish such authors as Robert Frost, A. E. Housman, and Frederick Jackson Turner, and the future was not nearly as gloomy as he had anticipated. The author of a scholarly study on the blossoming of printing arts in post–World War I America has suggested, in fact, that the increased production of high-quality limited-edition books in the 1920s and 1930s came about as a direct reaction to a society that suddenly found itself teeming with cheap magazines, sleazy tabloid newspapers, crowded movie theaters, and vapid radio broadcasts. The motto embraced in 1923 by Porter Garnett, founder in Pittsburgh, Pennsylvania, of the Laboratory Press at the Carnegie Institute of Technology, and one of the innovators of "fine printing" in America, expressed the guiding philosophy of the movement succinctly: *Nil vulgare, nil pertriti, nil inepti*—nothing commonplace, nothing hackneyed, nothing tasteless.

IO.

Music of the Spheres

*I could sketch a fairly orderly model of impersonal forces, factors, and trends that
theoretically should have a predictable influence on the course of communications
media over the next twenty or thirty years. I suspect, however, that some
schoolboy, now fourteen years old, whose name I do not know, is going to conceive
of an idea in 1981 that will have more influence on what communications are like
in 2000 than anything I or my colleagues could logically project today.*

—HEDLEY DONOVAN, EDITOR IN CHIEF, *TIME* MAGAZINE,

SPEAKING TO THE AMERICAN ACADEMY OF ARTS AND SCIENCES (1966)

*Advances in technology are inevitable—we have already got the atomic bomb, the
supersonic airbus, men on the moon and, I believe, a television set which prints out
what it shows. But what matters most is that men and women should remain
human beings; for as long as we are that, we will continue to make and read
books. It does not matter how they are written or printed. It also does not matter
how many other media of communication there are: they all have their uses. The
function of writing is, however, necessary, and so is the function of reading
which, it must be remembered, is a creative and active, not a passive occupation.*

—RUARI MCLEAN, IN THE AFTERWORD TO

THE BOOK THROUGH FIVE THOUSAND YEARS (1972)

W hen people gather today to talk seriously about "books of
the future," the discussion inevitably is driven by what
some see as the ubiquitous triumph of modern technology

and the certain obsolescence of print. The book as we know it, in other words, if not dead, is certainly moribund. Curiously enough, this kind of debate is not especially new, and has been argued in one form or another for decades, often with great passion and conviction on both sides of the issue. There are parallels, in fact, between the "paradigm shift" so ardently proclaimed now and the positions that emerged five and a half centuries ago when scriptoria throughout Europe were being displaced by printing shops. Johannes Gutenberg's introduction of movable metal type had three immediate effects on Western civilization, Elizabeth L. Eisenstein has demonstrated in *The Printing Press as an Agent of Change,* a landmark work on the subject: standardization of content, widespread dissemination of intellectual dialogue, and, most important of all, fixity of the product. But a few observers hardened in the old traditions felt that printing would have an adverse impact on refined civilization, and some of them put up spirited arguments against its growing dominance.

The most prominent dissenter of them all was Johannes Trithemius (1462–1516), the abbot of the Benedictine monastery of Sponheim in the diocese of Mainz in northwest Germany from 1483 to 1505 and a dedicated humanist who served briefly as a counselor to Emperor Maximilian I; if his detractors present credible testimony, he was also a closet magician and necromancer who dabbled in the black arts. In addition to carrying out his holy obligations, Trithemius found time to become an enormously influential author who expounded on a multitude of lay subjects, including one commentary on communicating with spirits that remained unpublished for a hundred years and was banned by the Roman Catholic Church when it finally was released. A trilogy he worked on toward the end of his life called *Steganographia*—the title means "hidden writing" in Greek, though the work itself was written in Latin—is regarded as the first known treatise on cryptography. John Dee (1527–1608), the eminent English astrologer, bibliophile, and mathematician whose readings of the heavens were called upon by Queen Elizabeth I to select a propitious coronation day, was elated to have acquired a bootleg copy of the notorious manuscript. Dee confided to a colleague how others had offered as much as 1,000 Dutch crowns to make their own copies, only to be rebuffed in their efforts. The third volume of *Steganographia*, written under the guise of occult astrology, contained a secret code that remained largely unbroken until the 1990s.

A bas-relief sculpture on Trithemius's tombstone depicts the lifelike countenance of a middle-aged man with a pudgy face, a pronounced cleft in the chin, alert eyes, and a self-assured expression that suggests deep intelligence and amused disdain for the mundanities of a temporal world. Clutched tightly to the figure's breast is the shape of an open book adorned with a jeweled binding, an apt tribute to a man who used every means at his disposal to nourish the library he supervised at Sponheim. "I readily admit my boundless and unceasing love of studies and books," he wrote in an autobiographical sketch toward the end of his life. "Neither could ever satisfy my desire to know everything which can be known in the world. It is my greatest pleasure to own and to know all books I ever saw or which I knew to have appeared in print, however trivial and unimportant they have been. To my regret I could never satisfy my desire." Sworn to poverty by his holy orders, Trithemius complained about the shortage of money available to sustain "the satisfaction of my passion for books," but he still found energetic ways to increase the abbey's holdings from the thirty or so titles that were there when he arrived at the age of twenty-two, to "about two thousand volumes, both handwritten and printed, on every subject and science which is held of utility among Christians," by the time he left. He offered this further boast as to the measure of his collecting acumen: "I have never seen in all of Germany, nor have I heard to exist anywhere, such a rare and marvelous library."

To keep current with what was newly available, Trithemius attended the famous book fair held annually in nearby Frankfurt, and he ordered titles directly from dealers in Italy. In his memoir, he gloried in visiting "very many cloisters" in "scattered provinces" during his twenty-two-year tenure as abbot of Sponheim, and to having "thoroughly examined many libraries." Whenever he found instances of duplication along the way, he offered either a swap of materials from his own collections or a sum of money in exchange. "Trithemius was not above exploiting monastic ignorance to achieve his desired results," the American scholar Noel L. Brann observed of the abbot's aggressive acquisition methods. *Liber de Scriptoribus Ecclesiasticis,* a scholarly work published in 1494 and considered to be Trithemius's most important book, listed about seven thousand theological writings by 963 authors, and prompted the noted bibliographer Theodore Besterman to anoint him the "father of bibliography."

Because Trithemius commanded such widespread respect among his contemporaries, his views on the new technology that had taken Europe by storm over the previous half century were not likely to be dismissed out of hand. In 1492 he vigorously stated his case in a small work of sixteen concise chapters titled *De Laude Scriptorum* (In Praise of Scribes). Trithemius's principal concern was with the study of scripture and the need to train new generations of copyists, but it is what he had to say in Chapter 7 that makes him an amusing topic of conversation at "future of the book" conferences held routinely today, especially among those who see futility in stemming the mounting tides of innovation. The full title of the chapter, in Latin, is "*Quod propter impressuram a scribendis voluminibus non sit desistendum*" ("That monks should not stop copying because of the invention of printing"). A contemporary equivalent might be, "Don't give up the day job just yet."

Astute readers will note that many of the same arguments raised today over the pros and cons of modern communications technologies were put forth more than five centuries ago in this paean to scribal craft, the only difference being one of degree. The abbot raised issues that critics today would categorize variously as "preservation," "migration," "professional accountability," "aesthetics," "economy," even the "retrospective conversion" of old formats to new. "All of you know the difference between a manuscript and a printed book," Trithemius submitted in a tone that would not be out of place in an introductory-level college course devoted to the history of communications. "The word written on parchment will last a thousand years. The printed word is on paper. How long will it last? The most you can expect a book of paper to survive is two hundred years. Yet, there are many who think they can entrust their works to paper. Only time will tell."

There also was the matter of quality control to consider: "Printed books will never be the equivalent of handwritten codices, especially since printed books are often deficient in spelling and appearance. The simple reason is that copying by hand involves more diligence and industry." For those among his colleagues who might argue that every important text had already been transformed into print, making the mission of the copyist irrelevant, Trithemius insisted that worthwhile material was everywhere, lying neglected and waiting to be discovered:

> Yes, many books are available now in print, but no matter how many books will be printed, there will always be some left unprinted and worth copying. No one will ever be able to locate and buy all printed books. Even if all works ever written would appear in print, the devoted scribe should not relax his zeal. On the contrary, he will guarantee permanence to useful printed books by copying them. Otherwise they would not last long. His labor will render mediocre books better, worthless ones more valuable, and perishable ones more lasting. The inspired scribe will always find something worth his trouble. He does not depend on the printer; he is free and as a scribe can enjoy his freedom. He is by no means defeated by the printer; he must not cease copying just because the art of printing has been invented. He should pursue his path without looking back; he should be certain that in the eyes of God his reward will be no less, without regard to anyone else.

Trithemius concluded with a clarion call to the community of scribes everywhere, many of them, like himself, spiritual descendants of Saint Benedict, the maker of the monastic rule that gave energy and purpose to their handiwork: "He who gives up copying because of the invention of printing is no genuine friend of holy Scripture. He sees only what is and contributes nothing to the edification of future generations."

What some critics find particularly telling about all this is that Trithemius chose to issue his polemic for general distribution through the very medium he was taking to task, and that for all its heat and bombast, *De Laude Scriptorum* does not survive today in the hand of its author. In a further twist of circumstance, one of the earliest printed editions was produced in Mainz, the city where Gutenberg introduced Europe's first press forty years earlier. "Trithemius knew very well that a printed book was bound to reach a much larger audience than a manuscript," Klaus Arnold noted in an excellent introduction to a 1974 translation of the work. "If his instructions in the art of copying were to be effective, he had to ensure the greatest possible circulation for them."

It has been estimated that as many as 8 million books were printed in Europe between 1450, about the time when Gutenberg began to print, and 1500, a half century later—and Trithemius, it turns out, was an eager contributor to the ever-accelerating numbers. The Mainz firm he retained was operated by Peter von Friedberg, a printer who did so much job work for the abbot that his operation "could almost be called the Sponheim abbey press." Of twenty-five titles produced by Friedberg in the 1490s, thirteen list Trithemius as author, with six others written by his close associates.

In describing a curious interlude at the cusp of the Reformation he called "monastic humanism," Noel Brann noted how Trithemius openly lamented a steady weakening of Benedictine will in the monastery he had worked so hard to strengthen, which could very well explain the conservative posture he adopted. James J. O'Donnell, a former professor of classical studies at the University of Pennsylvania where his collateral duties included direction of information systems and computing, has taken special pains to note that seventeen years after Trithemius wrote his encomium to the scribal life, he was offering up effusive praise for the new technology, calling it "that wondrous and previously unheard-of art of printing books." Named provost of Georgetown University in 2002, O'Donnell, who has championed the use of electronic tools in his classics courses—insisting in some instances that students submit nothing on paper, only by e-mail—wondered if Trithemius should be regarded as "our patron saint of indecision." O'Donnell thinks not, suggesting instead that the abbot's "true topic is the undermining of the ethos of the monastery and its scriptorium" by the move to print. "The fact that he focused on preserving, not adapting, the monastic community was his failure."

Still, there is a moral here, one that goes well beyond technological change and the constrictions of monastic life. Similar examples abound, and they extend back to the golden age of Athens when Socrates was advising his students to seek truth through human inquiry, not from the reading of books. In the dialogue known as *Phaedrus*, Plato recalled an anecdote that his mentor liked to tell about Thamus, an Egyptian king who legend holds one day entertained the god Theuth, also known as Thoth, a deity credited with inventing the magical art of writing among other fascinating diversions, the rolling of dice and the board game we call checkers among them. Instead of marveling over the gift, which Theuth/Thoth had proclaimed would "improve both the wisdom and the memory of the Egyptians," Thamus, as Socrates told the tale, saw a threat to the very nature of philosophical discourse. Here is what the Egyptian king supposedly told the clever god:

> Theuth, my paragon of inventors, the discoverer of an art is not the best judge of the good or harm which will accrue to those who practice it. So it is in this; you, who are the father of writing, have out of fondness for your off-spring attributed to it quite the oppo-

site of its real function. Those who acquire it will cease to exercise their memory and become forgetful; they will rely on writing to bring things to their remembrance by external signs instead of by their own internal resources. What you have discovered is a recipe for recollection, not for memory. And as for wisdom, your pupils will have the reputation for it without the reality. They will receive a quantity of information without proper instruction, and in consequence be thought very knowledgeable when they are for the most part quite ignorant. And because they are filled with conceit of wisdom instead of real wisdom they will be a burden to society.

This disdain for the written word suggests the kind of argument raised in the nineteenth century by some American educators who were opposed to putting erasers on pencils, the misgiving being that the ease with which youngsters could correct their mistakes would encourage them to develop sloppy work habits and make more errors, or the more recent opposition to allowing students the use of portable calculators when taking mathematics examinations. When Plato recorded the words of Socrates about 360 B.C., writing had been around for several thousand years, and had already extended its reach to all levels of educated society. Literacy, in fact, was no longer limited to an elite corps of scribes and priests, and what the two philosophers apparently feared most of all was what today would be called the "virtualization" of knowledge in signs and symbols, and the continued erosion of the "art of memory," a technique of impressing places and images in the mind usually classified as "mnemotechnics." It is noteworthy that the Greek goddess of memory, Mnemosyne, was also the mother of the Muses, the true creative spirits. Socrates, for his part, maintained that oratory was the art of enchanting the soul, and everything else was a distraction.

When the daguerreotype ushered in the era of photography in 1839, people were captivated by snapshots that were absolutely faithful representations of reality, images of events that were "captured in time." But not everyone was thrilled with that development either, particularly the portrait artists whose tools were oils, brushes, and canvas, not optical lenses mounted on wooden boxes, and certainly not the chemicals used to tease pictures out of glass plates. When the French artist Paul Delaroche was shown one of the first examples of the innovation, he was disconsolate. "From today," he exclaimed, "painting is dead." For the British proto-impressionist J. M. W. Turner, it was "the end of art." The French poet and art critic Charles Baudelaire belittled the new "photographic industry" as "the refuge of every would-be painter," and condemned the process as having "contributed much to the impoverishment of the French artistic genius." Photography had a "true duty," he believed, and that was to function as "the servant of the sciences and arts—but the very humble servant." In 1906 Pablo Picasso despaired at the implications of the medium, which by then had been around for sixty-seven years. "I have discovered photography," he said. "Now I can kill myself. I have nothing else to learn." But Picasso lived *another* sixty-seven years, all the while exploring innovative modes of creative expression that served to liberate his vision, achieving recognition as among the most renowned artists of the twentieth century. And he is by no means alone, of course; in the years that have elapsed since the invention of photography, the world has celebrated the achievements of painters such as Winslow Homer, Claude Monet, Henri Matisse, Vincent van Gogh, Childe Hassam, Mary Cassatt, Willem de Kooning, and Jackson Pollock, and introduced phrases like impressionism, postimpressionism, modernism, abstract expressionism, and postmodernism to identify the various movements they pioneered. Collectors and museums, meanwhile, have paid unprecedented sums to acquire their masterworks, proof positive that artistic brilliance is timeless, whatever the medium.

With the introduction of color film in the 1930s, the abandonment of black-and-white imagery was feared to be imminent, though nobody convinced such giants as Eliot Porter, Walker Evans, Edward Weston, Eve Arnold, Margaret Bourke-White, Henri Cartier-Bresson, or the incomparable Ansel Adams, whose 1947 visualization of a dramatic landscape in New Mexico, *Moon Rise over Hernandez*, just may be the most perfectly composed photograph ever made. With the arrival of the digital camera in the closing years of the twentieth century, the long-term prospects of film itself came under intense scrutiny, an awareness not lost on the manufacturers of conventional cameras who assiduously positioned themselves to secure a share of the burgeoning market. "Electronic images are quite wonderful and remarkable," Herbert C. Burkholz wrote in the journal of the Photographic Society of America at a time when the new medium was beginning to make a modest impact, but "they are not photographs," he insisted. They may be pictures or images, he allowed, but "a photograph, and the photographic process, refer to a chemical process and none other." True enough, perhaps, but whatever edge the picture captured on film continues to maintain, it is in the superior sharpness of its image, although resolution factors for digital cameras, measured in what are known as "megapixels," continue to improve, and it is only a matter of time before they are of comparable quality. Matters involving storage of the pictures—ownership of a computer is a requirement for those who favor digital imagery—and the need for greater power sources are other factors to consider as well. The champion of the instant photograph, meanwhile, the Polaroid Corporation, sought protection from its creditors in the fall of 2001, having lost to the new technologies the single most attractive feature of its product—the novelty it offered of being able to enjoy immediate visual gratification. On the day the company filed Chapter 11 papers in U.S. Bankruptcy Court in Boston, its stock was trading on the New York Stock Exchange at 28 cents a share, down from a ten-year high of $60.31 recorded in July 1997.

As the nineteenth century drew to a close, fin-de-siècle conferences were mounted on both sides of the Atlantic to celebrate the era that lay ahead and to augur an age of "fraternity, progress, prosperity, and peace" among the peoples of the world. Well-attended meetings in Paris, Vienna, and Philadelphia set the tone for an ambitious Congress of Arts and Sciences that was convened in Saint Louis, Missouri, in September 1904 to mark the centenary of the Louisiana Purchase. The full spectrum of human knowledge was divided into seven categories, with each field broken down into numerous subdivisions, and specialists were brought in from around the world to speak. To provide a permanent record, the entire proceedings were published in eight volumes the following year by Houghton Mifflin Co. of Boston.

Among the authorities to attend were the German sociologist Max Weber, the Princeton scholar and future president of the United States Woodrow Wilson, the Nobel Prize–winning social activist Jane Addams, and the French mathematician Jules-Henri Poincaré. Invited to address the Historical Science section on developing trends in research methods was Dr. Guido Biagi (1855–1925), director of the Biblioteca Medicea Laurenziana in Florence and curator of a major exhibition at the Paris Exposition of 1900 that documented the evolution of the book in Italy. A respected Renaissance scholar, Biagi was the author of numerous important monographs on the literary patrimony of his native country, and as chief custodian of one of the world's great collections of illuminated manuscripts, he drew on his dual professional background to discuss what he saw as the future of scholarly inquiry and the changing role of libraries. Looking ahead to a century that was still decades away from defining itself, Biagi was convinced that a panoply of exciting new inventions was about to alter forever the way primary research would be conducted, and a good deal of that progress, he predicted, meant the eventual demise of print. What might surprise many book custodians of today is that this eminent librarian welcomed the shifting balance with great enthusiasm, not uneasy trepidation.

Offering a bit of historical perspective, Biagi reminded the gathering that "the copyist or the scribe is replaced by the compositor, the miniaturist by the engraver, the draftsman by the lithographer, the painter by the color-printer, the engraver by the photographer and zincographer." Typewriters and wireless telegraphy were already in general use, Biagi observed, and human voices were being recorded on graphite disks by a contraption known as the graphophone. Soon, he believed, libraries everywhere would be storing hundreds of sound *disks*—and he used that word—on their shelves, "just as the libraries of Assyria preserved the clay tablets inscribed with cuneiform characters." These "disks," he asserted, "now so much derided, will form a very large part of the future library."

With the development of long-range dirigibles expected to shorten transoceanic travel time dramatically, and with the eventual linking of all continents by communications cables, Biagi believed that the concept of a universal library was about to take on a whole new dimension. "The electric post or the air-ships will have then shortened distances, the telephone will make it possible to hear at Melbourne a graphophone disk asked for a few minutes earlier from the British Museum," he enthused. "There will be few readers, but an infinite number of hearers, who will listen from their own homes to the spoken paper, to the spoken book." And the transformation would be just as profound on college campuses, he predicted. "University students will listen to their lectures while they lie in bed, and, as now with us, will not know their professors even by sight. Writing will be a lost art. Professors of paleography and keepers of manuscripts will, perhaps, have to learn to accustom their eye to the ancient alphabets. Autographs will be as rare as palimpsests are now. Books will no longer be read; they will be listened to; and then only will be fulfilled [the nineteenth-century Oxford educator and critic] Mark Pattison's famous saying: 'The librarian who reads is lost.' "

Undoubtedly there were people in the audience who rolled their eyes at Biagi's forecast, and even today's reader might smile at the quaintness of his language. He conceded as much at the outset, claiming the right to speculate on the future by virtue of his heritage. "The first founders of public libraries having been Italian, it will perhaps be neither strange nor unfitting that an Italian, the custodian of one of the most ancient and valued book-collections in the world, should speak to you of their past. He may, however, appear presumptuous in that he will speak to you also of their future, thus posing as an exponent of those anticipations which are now fashionable."

Granted, Biagi was off course a few degrees in his long-term reckoning of what miracles the new gadgetry would allow, but he knew major change was in the offing, and he was in no way lost at sea without a compass. The graphophone in particular, developed in the 1880s by Chichester A. Bell and Charles Sumner Tainter in competition with Thomas Alva Edison's phonograph, logged a period of modest popularity but never put up the kind of challenge to books that Biagi had anticipated. At one point it was used in drugstores as a primitive jukebox, not exactly what its backers had in mind. A competing invention known as the Gramophone, developed by the German émigré Emile Berliner, enjoyed a lively run as well, but the focus was always on music, not the "spoken paper" or "spoken book." Dirigibles flourished for several decades, but with the Hindenburg catastrophe of 1937, the era of the floating airship came to a decisive end, and another technology entirely—the fixed-wing aircraft—achieved dominance of the skies.

Biagi was not the only librarian who saw the phonograph and the telephone as posing a serious threat to the printed book. Justin Winsor, a founder of the American Library Association and a pioneer of the public library movement in the United States, recalled having been present among a small circle of friends when Alexander Graham Bell "made a rude instrument in the rooms of the American Academy" in Boston "give out" a refrain of "Home, Sweet Home" that actually was being "played on a distant piano." Greatly impressed by the performance, Winsor became "one of the first to put the telephone to practical use in the Boston

Public Library," and he speculated enthusiastically on what other miracles of aural communication might be forthcoming. "We don't know yet what will become of the phonograph. Edison's first instrument was sent to Boston, to be shown to some gentlemen, before its character had been made known. I never expect again to see quite such awe on human faces as when Gray's 'Elegy' was repeated by an insensate box to a company of unsuspecting listeners. I look to see its marvelous capacities yet utilized in the service of the librarian."

In 1962, John Rader Platt (1918–1995), a University of Chicago physicist whose books included such titles as *The Excitement of Science* and *Systematics of the Electronic Spectra of Conjugated Molecules,* wrote an informed essay for the scholarly journal *Horizon* in which he speculated on the imminent arrival of a "universal library" made possible by scientific breakthroughs, though today's reader would be perplexed to learn that the computer did not figure at all in the scenario he felt was just around the corner, nor was there any apparent movement toward the "spoken book" championed by Guido Biagi half a century earlier. "Physicists these days are discussing a question that is going to be of interest to every literate person," Platt began. "How small a book can we make—and still read?"

Platt projected the development of microscopic processes that would allow for what he called creation of a "pinhead library" in which countless numbers of books could be stored in a minimum of space, and not just by libraries and institutions, but by individuals eager to have access to "everything." Already, he enthused, it was possible to create "ultramicrobooks" with photographic reductions that were five hundred to a thousand times smaller in height and width, "so that each letter and each drawing and photograph is reduced in area by as much as one million times." And that was just the "optical limit" of miniaturization, he quickly added. Yet another "degree of reduction" then at hand—one that would involve storing words and pages near the limit of magnification of the electron microscope—"can go as far beyond this as the hydrogen bomb goes beyond the atomic bomb." For his purposes, though, Platt was excited enough about a setup that would allow him to read by use of a basic scientific instrument immediately available to anyone with the inclination to have one. "With an optical-microscope system permitting a reduction in area of about one million times, our 20 million volumes could be photocopied into 20 average volumes, about half the size of a standard encyclopedia. Each sheet in our hypothetical 20 volumes might contain, say, 2,000 books of 500 pages each; and each volume 500 sheets, or one million books; with a total of 10,000 sheets in all the 20 volumes, about the number in an encyclopedia today."

With the prospect of having "all the world's literature and learning" at his fingertips, Platt had little room for romantic notions regarding the enjoyment of handling a real book, anticipating similar arguments pitting the advocates of content against the champions of artifacts that would emerge four decades down the road. "We must remember that what is precious is not the physical 'artifact' of a system of writing but the 'metafacts,' the human communications they contain," Platt wrote. "When our books change into new forms, children brought up to love the things of the mind will come to treat these forms with the same feelings of respect and familiarity and pleasure that we have had for the old ones." To ease things along, he suggested that creation of "a complete Library of Congress within reach of every student and teacher and scientist might be comparable to the value of our great highway systems, and the initial development might be deserving of similar government support."

There was the small matter of the machinery that would be needed, of course, an "interface" in today's language, the development and logistics of which did not seem to cause Platt too much concern. Especially amusing in this essay are the droll caricatures of people pictured browsing items at the bookstalls on the river Seine in Paris or reading their morning newspapers through microscopes, the direction Platt seemed to be suggesting the world was going at the time. In 1960s dollars, he projected a price of "maybe a thousand dollars or two" to buy a full run of micro-printed books, two or three hundred more for a projection microscope, another thousand or two to cover royalties and copyright fees, "the total cost per Universal Library might then be in the three to six thousand range," he felt. "This could cost far less and be worth more, and would certainly have more buyers, than those desk-top computers that have been talked about for years. The sum is not much more than many students and professional people pay for books and journals over, say, a twenty-year period, and is much less than the cost of a reading room or study in a new home, so that such a library system might be built into many houses and apartments, much as hi-fi systems are built in today."

As the events of the twentieth century continued to unfold, however, and as the twenty-first approached, other technological innovations challenged the dominance of print, but they came in the form of microchips, supercomputers, digital scanners, communications satellites, and optical fibers, not blimps, crank telephones, and primitive recording machines, not even the "talking movies" that made their debut in 1929 or the television sets that began to captivate the world in the 1950s, and not the microscopic projectors envisioned by John Rader Platt. Libraries everywhere continued to be libraries in the traditional sense, and it was the apparent certainty of this circumstance—maintaining the status quo—that at least one pedant and occasional man of letters, Archibald Philip Primrose (1847–1929), the fifth earl of Rosebery and the prime minister of Great Britain from 1894 to 1895, found curiously distressing in the years leading up to World War I. In addition to his public service, Lord Rosebery was also the author of books on William Pitt, Sir Robert Peel, and Napoleon Bonaparte, and an academic administrator who served as lord rector at Aberdeen, Edinburgh, and Glasgow Universities in his native Scotland. Speaking at dedication ceremonies of the Mitchell Library in Glasgow in 1911, the onetime champion of British imperialism caused something of a stir among his listeners by challenging, apparently in dead seriousness,

the rationale behind keeping vast piles of unread books in central repositories for years on end, a good deal of them in his view worthless undertakings in the first place and deserving at best a decent Christian burial.

"I feel it a depressing thought to enter one of these huge storehouses
of knowledge, and to feel how hopeless it is in any degree or in any way
to overtake the opportunities that they afford," he said before proceeding
to his central point: "In the main, most of the books are dead. Their bar-
ren backs, as it were, appeal for someone to come and take them down and
rescue them from the passive collection of dust and neglect into which
most of them have deservedly fallen." If by chance his views were not
clear enough, he fashioned a number of provocative phrases to describe
the notion of a public library, calling the institution generally a "great
mass of disappointment," a rampart "of wrecked hopes," and most sting-
ing of all, "this cemetery of books, because, after all, most of them are
dead." Given Lord Rosebery's view on the unending dilemma that some
bibliophiles drolly describe as "so many books, so little time," it is mildly
amusing to note that the peer's one-year residence at Number 10 Down-
ing Street was made possible by the retirement of Sir William Ewart
Gladstone (1809–1898), the dominant public servant of Queen Victoria's
long reign and a towering intellect who from the age of sixteen on kept a
voluminous diary in which the titles of twenty thousand books were
scrupulously recorded and discussed. For all the rigors of a demanding
workload—and he spent sixty-three years as a member of Parliament,
including four separate terms as prime minister—Gladstone read an average of 250 books a year for every year of his adult life. Author of fourteen
books of his own, Gladstone also included in his literary credits a diverting little essay on how to design and arrange a home library. "If you go
into a room filled with books," he wrote, "even without taking them
down from their shelves, they seem to speak to you, to welcome you."

Among the most heatedly discussed views in communications circles during the 1960s were the sweeping pronouncements of Marshall

McLuhan, the Canadian oracle whose dire predictions of "a paper-less society" in *The Gutenberg Galaxy*—which the *Times Literary Supplement* debunked as an "anti-book"—and *Understanding Media* provided a watershed moment in the debate. "It is like the dinosaur just before he disappeared," McLuhan predicted. "It is having its last big splurge." Significantly, McLuhan chose paper as the way to circulate his obituary for the printed word, not the television screens that had so captured his fancy. "Most reassuring of all to advocates of the book, however, is the reflection that *Understanding Media* itself is the work of a thoroughly book-trained man, who has ransacked a library to write it," Gordon N. Ray, an unapologetic "book-addict" and from 1963 to 1985 president of the John Simon Guggenheim Memorial Foundation, wrote in a review of McLuhan's forecasts. This was a wise hedge on McLuhan's part, it turns out; not only are books still alive, but radio and movies are doing just fine as well, while television—which was supposed to force the publishing and film industries out of business—now finds itself in the curious position of losing market share to the Internet.

A series of lectures, presented at the University of Newcastle upon Tyne in the United Kingdom in 1966, had as its working title "The Computer and the Library," and the proceedings were considered important enough to publish on both sides of the Atlantic. "The first use of computers to mechanize a library procedure was but a half-dozen years ago, so that throughout the second-half of the 1960s, libraries will still be in the earliest stages of their most major innovation of the past century," Frederick G. Kilgour said in his welcoming remarks. So that everyone would be on the same page, as it were, he defined a computer as a "central processing unit where the main operations of any processing task take place," and described its elements as containing "a relatively small store of high speed memory, a set of command instructions that will count, sort and otherwise manipulate the records that are in the high speed memory, and a means for storing the programme, which consists of the instructions necessary to accomplish the task at hand."

The thrust of the conference was to streamline record handling and bibliographic housekeeping chores in the world's libraries. Concepts discussed in the presentations such as "speed" and "storage capacity" are hopelessly antediluvian by today's standards, which may explain why my copy of *The Computer and the Library* contains the ex libris stamp of Cornell University and the discard date of October 22, 1984. By far the most entertaining observation to be found within its hard covers appears on the very first page of text, where a gentleman identified as W. T. Williams is quoted as saying that the most important advantage humans have over machines is that "man is the only computer yet designed which can be produced entirely by unskilled labor."

Technology is just one part of a much larger discussion, of course, and the role of the people who manage libraries is quite another, as a younger contemporary of Guido Biagi and Lord Rosebery, the influential Spanish philosopher and political scientist José Ortega y Gasset (1883–1955), suggested in a speech delivered before an international conference of bibliographers and librarians gathered in Paris in 1934 to consider the evolving nature of their professions. "There are already too many books," the Spaniard declared, a startling comment from someone whose curriculum vitae included an interlude as a publisher of political tracts in Madrid. Like Lord Rosebery twenty-three years earlier, Ortega y Gasset saw a predicament that was only getting more intolerable as time went on. "If each new generation continues to accumulate printed paper in the same proportion as the last few generations, the problem posed by the excess of books will become truly terrifying," he warned, adding that the "culture which has liberated man from the primitive forest now thrusts him anew into the midst of a forest of books no less inextricable and stifling." Not only were books being produced in a "torrential abundance"; their content, he felt, was highly suspect. "Many of them are useless and stupid; their existence and their conservation is a dead weight upon humanity which is already bent low under other loads."

Unlike Lord Rosebery, who offered little in the way of a solution, Ortega y Gasset proposed an aggressive strategy of dealing with the deluge at the point of origin, and the people he believed were most suited to determine which writings merited publication were the very people listening to his speech. In putting forth this audacious premise, he wondered aloud if it might be "too Utopian to imagine" a time in the "not too distant future" in which librarians were "held responsible by society for the regulation of the production of books, in order to avoid the publication of superfluous ones and, on the other hand, to guard against the lack of those demanded by the complex of vital problems in every age." Mindful that he was speaking just a year after Nazi zealots had made bonfires out of "offensive" books in the public squares of the Third Reich just one border away to the east, Ortega y Gasset never used the word *censorship* in his remarks. But for those in attendance who might offer the "foolish objection" that such an enterprise "would be an attack on liberty," he declared that liberty "has not come upon the face of the earth to wring the neck of common sense. It is precisely because some have wished to employ it in such an enterprise, because they have pretended to make of it the chief instrument of madness, that liberty is having a bad time at present." Thus it is the "librarian of the future," he reasoned, who must lead readers through the *selva selvaggia*—the dense forests—of books without end, and the mission "ought to be, not as it is today the simple administration of the things called books, but the adjustment, the setting to rights, of that vital function which is the book." As to how the "librarian of the future" would be able to accomplish this, he offered these thoughts:

> He will be the doctor and the hygienist of reading. On this point
> also we find ourselves in a situation quite the reverse of that in

1800. Today people read too much. The condition of receiving without much effort, or even without any effort, the innumerable ideas contained in books and periodicals has accustomed the common man to do no thinking on his own account; and he does not think over what he has read, the only method of making it truly his own. In addition, there is that gravest and most radically negative character of the book, and we must dedicate our utmost effort of attention to it. A large part of today's terrible public problem proceeds from the fact that ordinary minds are full of ideas received in inertia, ideas half understood and deprived of their virtues. Ordinary minds are thus stuffed with pseudo-ideas. In this aspect of his profession, I imagine the librarian of the future is a filter interposed between man and the torrent of books.

The published text of Ortega y Gasset's address does not indicate how the International Congress of Bibliographers and Librarians responded, but his remarks were translated into several languages, printed in many scholarly journals, and given wide distribution. Whatever the librarians of the 1930s might have thought of the proposal, they kept it among themselves, and however radical the sentiment may seem, it did not come without precedent. Indeed, at a time in the mid-nineteenth century when there were no "library schools" anywhere—Melvil Dewey's pioneering program at Columbia University did not accept its first students until 1887—there was a growing belief among some observers that professionals trained to "mediate" between readers and authors were needed, people who could function, to anticipate Ortega y Gasset's therapeutic metaphor, as the "doctor and the hygienist of reading." Ralph Waldo Emerson addressed himself directly to the issue in an 1870 essay called "Books." He began by noting how easy it is "to accuse books" of failing in their mission to inspire and inform, since so many "bad ones are easily found." The best books, he felt, are those which "take rank in our life with parents and lovers and passionate experiences," and the challenge was how to go about finding them among the morass of the second-rate. Emerson's solution called for the training of a kind of intellectual guru—a "gatekeeper," in today's parlance—to mediate between readers and resources, and he took special aim at colleges, which he allowed "provide us with libraries" in great abundance, but "furnish no professor of books" to guide students to the treasures that they hold:

> In a library we are surrounded by many hundreds of dear friends, but they are imprisoned by an enchanter in these paper and leathern boxes; and though they know us, and have been waiting two, ten, or twenty centuries for us,—some of them,—and are eager to give us a sign and unbosom themselves, it is the law of their limbo that they must not speak until spoken to; and as the enchanter has dressed them, like battalions of infantry, in coat and jacket of one cut, by the thousand and ten thousand, your chance of hitting on the right one is to be computed by the arithmetical rule of Permutation and Combination,—not a choice of three caskets, but out of half a million caskets, all alike.

By the end of the twentieth century, the concept of librarianship was still being defined and debated, with a number of universities modifying their programs to train "information specialists" drilled in the skills and techniques of computer operations, while others were dropping their library science programs altogether. Among the more noteworthy casualties were the two most prestigious academic programs of them all, the Library School at the University of Chicago, the first to offer a doctorate in the field, and the Columbia University School of Library Service, a graduate program founded by Melvil Dewey, the originator of the Dewey decimal system, and at the time of its closing in 1992 the oldest active library school in the world. Reasons cited for these abandonments vary, but the consensus reason given by those touched most by the terminations is the most cynical of all.

"It came down to money, and not enough of it," was the succinct appraisal offered by Terry Belanger, who taught library science at Columbia, and is now university professor and honorary curator of special collections at the University of Virginia in Charlottesville. When Belanger left New York, he took with him a massive collection of artifacts called the Book Arts Press, a "bibliographical laboratory" he formed at Columbia in 1972 that is concerned with the history of books, printing, descriptive bibliography, the antiquarian book trade, and rare-book and special collections librarianship. Its resources include a working collection of printing and etching presses, two hundred cases of type, assorted pieces of bookbinding equipment, and fifteen thousand books and five thousand prints dating from the fifteenth century to the present. "It became apparent that the cash cows in universities today are law schools, medical schools, and business schools," Belanger said. "Librarianship is not a profession that figures to bring in enormous gifts a few years down the road either." Beyond the issue of money was the unacknowledged subtext, an apparent conviction among key administrators in these universities that books in the traditional, artifactual sense were becoming marginalized in the information age, and were low-percentage bets to make in a long-distance race fraught with many unforeseen obstacles.

How many books may be contained in the world's libraries is anyone's guess, but when the directors of fifty of the most prominent repositories on the planet gathered in New York City in April 1996 to consider their changing role in the digital age, something in the neighborhood of 500 million volumes were represented in their collections. Called "Global Library Strategies for the Twenty-first Century," the conference was organized by Paul LeClerc, the president of the New York Public Library, with an eye toward balancing priorities between factions that call for greater reliance on electronic media and those who resist the shift away from print. In a reassuring keynote address, Paul M. Horn, senior vice president for research at the International Business Machines Corporation, suggested that librarians are the people who will "become an even more important asset as patrons attempt to wade their way through—and make sense of—new media and systems." For all his support of libraries, though—and he unequivocally declared himself "bullish" on their future—Horn's most widely reported comment, one that was excerpted in a recently published anthology of quotations, was this: "Technology can help libraries increase their collections exponentially, without experiencing a corresponding expansion in square footage. At IBM, for example, we are working on a new kind of optical microscope. It has the potential of imaging a single atom in visible light, which would be unprecedented. It turns out that this same technology may eventually enable dense storage devices that can pack the entire collection of the Library of Congress—that's 16 million books—on a diskette the size of a penny."

The Massachusetts Institute of Technology calls the gray building off Memorial Drive in Cambridge where it develops information strategies for the future the Media Laboratory, an apt name for a place that one instructor there has called "a high-tech womb for the incubation of new communication devices." A visit to this unadorned complex is an introduction to the fantasies of the third millennium, complete with all the solemnity and purpose such a voyage into uncharted territory can involve. Opened in 1985 as part of the university's School of Architecture, the Media Lab is unique at MIT in that all of its work is funded "almost exclusively" by corporations, according to Nicholas Negroponte, the founding director. Fifty percent of the $25 million annual budget comes from American companies like IBM, 3Com Corporation, Xerox Corporation, and the New York Times Company. Twenty-five percent of the others are European patrons such as Siemens Nixdorf Information Systems, Deutsche Telekom, and

British Airways; the remainder, including Canon, Hong Kong Telecom, Kodansha Ltd. Publishers, and Mitsubishi, have headquarters in the Far East. Each of these corporate sponsors has a vested interest in the various trinkets that emerge from this building hard by the banks of the Charles River, and each commits an average of $200,000 a year in support of the programs pursued.

Negroponte offered some idea of what electronic wonders he believes lie in store for us all in *Being Digital,* an exuberant introduction to the electronic tools of the future, a good many of them now being developed at the Media Lab. The advent of "books without pages" was inevitable, and as far as he was concerned, not soon enough. "Being dyslexic, I don't like to read." Negroponte envisioned a scenario in the not-too-distant future where reading about an exotic place "can include the sensory experience of going there," and engaging a book "can be a conversation" with the author. Like it or not, the age of "hypermedia"—a cousin of "hypertext"—has arrived, he proclaimed. "Think of hypermedia as a collection of elastic messages that can stretch and shrink in accordance with the reader's actions," and of a world where ideas "can be opened and analyzed at multiple levels of detail." The change from "atoms to bits is irrecoverable and unstoppable," Negroponte concluded, making the "digital planet" of tomorrow "look and feel like the head of a pin." And the art of bookmaking, he declared in an essay for a computer magazine shortly after *Being Digital* was published, "will probably be as relevant in 2020 as blacksmithing is today."

There was one nagging point Negroponte had to address, of course, and that was the little matter of why he had chosen to offer his weighty prognostications between the hard covers of an "old-fashioned book" composed of "atoms," and not through the magical "bits" of digital wizardry that were readily available to him. The crux of his answer came down to the clear admission that "the current interface is primitive—clumsy at best, and hardly something with which you might wish to curl up in bed." Put another way, Negroponte knew that if he wanted the right medium to spread his message of imminent doom, he had to put his money on a proven winner, even if it meant following a pattern that has become tedious in its predictability.

Two years after *Being Digital* had enjoyed a spirited run on all of the major best-seller lists, I made my first visit to the MIT Media Lab, drawn there not so much by Negroponte's ebullience as by reports that had cropped up in various journals of research being done by one of his young instructors on a reading machine that would have the look and feel of an honest-to-goodness book, a device with pages to flip through that an old bibliophile like myself just might wish to "curl up" with while crossing the timeline into a virtual wonderland. MIT's e-book, I quickly learned, is a serious project, and the identity of the companies that were supporting it—Advance Publications, Motorola, Phillips Electronics, the Hearst Corporation, and Lucent Technologies are among those who have signed on as "strategic partners"—made clear that it was being funded to go the distance.

"What distinguishes our project is that we are attempting to preserve the tactile experience of turning the pages," Joseph M. Jacobson, an associate professor at MIT and director of the research project, told me. It turns out that the in-house code name for the physicist's adventure is "the last book," a not-so-subtle prediction that every conventional codex is in jeopardy of being rendered disposable by an electronic device that can make thousands of books available on demand by temporarily "printing" them on surfaces that have the look and feel of real paper.

There was no prototype available when we first spoke in 1996, merely plans, drawings, and various concepts, and none had yet been built when we spoke again four years later. But he was delighted to inform me when we touched base in the spring of 2003 that a working model with two functioning pages would be unveiled before the year was out, in time, he hoped, to show at the Frankfurt Book Fair. "You'll be able to load a few dozen novels in it, and it will be able to display text in a variety of types and illustrations," he said. Although the device is being built in Japan by Top-pan Printing Company, Ltd., "this is all our technology," Jacobson empha-sized, and by "ours" he meant E Ink Corporation, a private company based in Cambridge that was formed in 1997, with more than $100 million raised from "strategic investors." In May 2002, E Ink demonstrated the world's thinnest TFT, or thin film transistor, display. "It is three hundred microns thick—that's about three and a half pieces of paper in thickness. Our goal is to make something on the order of eighty microns, which will bring it down to the thickness of a regular piece of paper. So, slow but sure, we're getting there." Indeed, Jacobson has insisted all along that "getting there" presents no major problems, as he made clear in our second interview: "These are technologies that are not particularly difficult to manufacture, and they will get cheaper and cheaper as time goes on. The goal is to make them as inexpensive as possible so they will be irresistible to consumers. It's the same strategy that is applied in the marketing of safety razors and mobile telephones, where what you are really selling is razor blades and air time. Here, it's the content that matters. To get to that stage, you have to make the e-book a part of people's lives."

Unlike other reading machines that have flooded the market to decid-edly mixed reviews, Jacobson's e-book will have the look, heft, and feel of an authentic codex. Unlike the others, which display their text on a single solid surface, Jacobson intends that his device will have a series of paper-like "substrates" bound inside actual covers, creating what in essence are gatherings of resilient computer screens that have the appearance of con-ventional pages. With the continued compression of processing technol-ogy and the exponential increase in storage capacity, Jacobson foresees a day when millions of books could be stored in a single volume. To use it, a reader would select a title by simply spinning a little dial embedded in the spine. Any published work that has been downloaded into the system will be called up and displayed on the "pages." Such a book will work on a supply of low power that is readily rechargeable. It will recognize and store "marginal annotations," it will faithfully replicate the appearance of various typefaces, it will adjust the size of words to suit a reader's tastes, and it also will reproduce illustrations. Jacobson's plan is to engineer a book with about four hundred of these flexible pages, bound in cloth as a conventional book, in leather if the owner really wants to splurge. The mechanics of determining exactly which books can be downloaded remains to be worked out. Titles already in the public domain pose no problem at all; newly released works and those still protected by copyright are more problematic, and a system of accessing material over the Internet once royalties have been paid would have to be developed.

An article Jacobson wrote for *IBM Systems Journal* titled "The Last Book" outlined a detailed explanation of how his device would function. Reduced to its basic elements, the plan calls for installing circuits in the spine that would activate electrodes in each page, causing millions of tiny spheres, half of them positively charged white capsules, the other half negatively charged black capsules, each about the diameter of a human hair, to orient themselves up or down, forming words. Jacobson explained in the essay why he thought successive pages were better than the single display unit most commonly associated with computer terminals. Over thousands of years, he offered, human beings have evolved a "highly sophisticated spatial map" in their brains that enables them to find, "with high specificity," information "that was seen only briefly" on the right or left side of a printed page. The reason for this, he opined, is that a person's "haptic connection with the brain's spatial map comprises a highly natural and effective interface when such information is embodied on actual multiple physical pages." Put another way, people are more comfortable reading words on pages than they are reading words on screens. Or even simpler than that—they like reading books more than they like reading on computer terminals. The arrival of competing e-books on the market has convinced Jacobson that he is on the right track with electronic ink, and that the "tactile" strategy makes tremendous sense. "I continue to have enormous respect for the traditional book, and I believe that paper is a medium for the future," he said, adding that with "traditional" books there is "no startup, no log-on, no button click," and the "presentation is immediate."

What Jacobson could have added is that there are no batteries involved with the conventional codex either, which every owner of a laptop computer, mobile telephone, or video recorder knows remain as short-lived as ever and are not likely to become more efficient in the immediate future. Unlike processors, which keep getting faster, smaller, and more powerful, the batteries needed to operate the kind of portable units an electronic book demands continue to frustrate the best efforts of scientists everywhere. A battery—which has not changed dramatically in the two hundred years since its invention by Alessandro Volta—is basically an electrical generator that uses a chemical reaction instead of a mechanical dynamo to create current. It is the product of chemistry, not physics, and the search for lightweight, long-lasting batteries is said to be the Holy Grail of the portable computer industry. "Batteries remain the worst obstacle to progress in designing the next generation of portable computer or electric car," the noted science writer James Gleick wrote in 1997. "They have not obeyed Moore's Law—the observation that chips of a given size and price double in capacity every year and a half. If they had, our automobiles would be running quietly and fumelessly for months on AA's."

Hoping to provide some relief for laptop computer users who have learned through experience to bring spare battery packs on long airplane flights, an engineer for Compaq Computer Corp. in Houston, Texas, patented a keyboard embedded with magnets and coils that spark a current each time a letter is struck. The basic concept being advanced was to feed all the kinetic electricity produced from typing into a power generator, which in turn would charge a capacitor in the battery. The more a person types, the more electricity would be fed to the charger, sort of like a fan belt in an automobile, but with nothing approaching the same veloc-ity. How this invention could be applied to an e-book remains uncertain, since other than turning the pages, reading requires no repeating hand movements.

Another problem that has proved almost as perplexing, and one that is absolutely relevant to the willingness of people to accept electronic books, is the continuing presence of the "flickering pixel" and the clear certainty of one irrefutable fact, which was underscored early in 2000 by Ian Austen in the *New York Times:* "Uncounted billions of printed words have migrated to the computer, but few people would rather read on screen instead of reading on paper." One of the reasons people prefer print is that it is easier on the eyes. At the University of California at Berkeley, Dr. James E. Sheedy, a clinical professor of optometry, has established a Computer Eye Clinic to treat people with a screen-related eye strain called computer vision syndrome, or CVS. Symptoms include headaches, dry or irritated eyes, neckache or backache, sensitivity to light, and double vision.

"What we're dealing with on our computer screens doesn't approach the quality of paper," Dr. Sheedy emphasized to me in a telephone inter-view. Although screen presentation is improving constantly, Sheedy said he has seen nothing that would persuade him to anticipate the demise of the printed book any time soon. "The immediate difference between the two presentations is that displays are flickering images, printed books are not," he said. "You also have reflections on computer screens that reduce contrast, and you have images that are formed with fewer dots per inch than on the printed page. Another factor more important than all the oth-ers is that computer displays are fixed in space and users have to adapt their postures to read them."

Engineers at Microsoft Corporation have introduced a software they call ClearType, a technology they hope will make on-screen type appear three times sharper than conventional displays. "It will look like professionally published work," one company spokesman cheerfully promised, but the true nature of the situation was put into some degree of perspective by an executive with Adobe, another company with a stake in the electronic book industry. "Are we a culture in which the concept of reading on-screen is just a little too foreign?" Harold Grey asked. "Is it easier to read on paper, or is it just something we're more comfortable with? It will be interesting to see what happens to the kids growing up with screens." In the meantime, those who wanted to make an appointment with Dr. Sheedy at the Computer Eye Clinic were told by staff at the dawn of the twenty-first century that bookings were being made weeks in advance, and that immediate tips on how to relieve the strain and the anxiety could be found on their website.

In fiction, the first genuine head-to-head challenge to the printed novel came early in 2000 with the release of *Riding the Bullet,* a sixty-six-page novella by Stephen King, the Maine author of books about horror and the supernatural whose blockbuster sales make him a phenomenon in publishing, uniquely positioned to carve out his own destiny in the marketplace. Available for purchase only in an encrypted electronic format, half a million "copies" were downloaded within a week of its release, "causing a cyberspace traffic jam of epic proportions," according to Jonathan Yardley of the *Washington Post,* who was quick to point out that most of the "sales" were actually given away free by Amazon and Barnes & Noble as splashy promotions for their on-line services. Regardless of whether the downloads were complimentary inducements or bought and paid for outright, the fact remained that people who use Stephen King as an index to project long-range publishing patterns do so at their own risk. It is no secret in the industry—and in the antiquarian book world as well, where prices for first editions of his earliest works are off the scale—that King's readership cleaves to its own dynamic and thrives by its own rules. King recognized as much himself in a statement issued a day after *Riding the Bullet* was scooped up by his fans worldwide. "While I think that the Internet and various computer applications for stories have great promise, I don't think anything will replace the printed word and the bound book." In an interview with *Time* magazine, he suggested that electronic publishing is best suited to writers "who have been disenfranchised by the shrinking list of publishers" willing to take their work, and are unable to "do their stuff" between hard covers

Just four months later, however, King was offering readers an opportunity to buy directly over the Internet a tongue-in-cheek epistolary novel about a writer who sends a carnivorous vine to a New York paperback publishing house that had rejected his work. *The Plant* was offered in monthly installments at $1 a download, payable directly to him on the honor system. But there was a catch—if fewer than 75 percent of the people who downloaded chapters failed to pay their dollar, the offer would end. "If you pay, the story rolls," King wrote; "if you don't the story folds." The consensus opinion among writers, literary agents, and publishers was that only a celebrity with the clout of a Stephen King could even consider such a ploy, especially with an unpublished manuscript such as this one that had been gathering dust in a desk drawer for fifteen years, and a few questioned the wisdom of putting out work that had eschewed the traditional processes of editing, marketing, and oversight, creating, in effect, a self-published vanity book of historic proportions. "No reader is asking for e-books," one publishing executive said, putting the development in some perspective. "This is not the Sony Walkman."

Still, this *was* Stephen King, and his followers began downloading copies of the first chapter in droves, some 140,000 the first month, enough of them paying their dollar to keep the experiment going. By the time the fifth chapter was reached, however, only 40,000 readers were still hanging in there, and fewer still were paying. "Suspense Doesn't Sell at E-Speed," a headline in the *New York Times* trumpeted; "King's Plant Wilts as Readers Fail to Pay," the *Daily Telegraph* reported in London; "Deadbeats Prompt King to Yank Internet Book," the *Washington Post* offered. As an exit strategy, King announced that he was "putting on ice" the final four chapters. "Am I displeased with how things have turned out?" he asked in an essay written for *Time* magazine. "Nope. I've had terrific fun working on *The Plant,* and so far it's grossed about $600,000." Besides, he concluded, there was still another life for the novel, as plans were being finalized to bring the entire work out in print to be sold exclusively over the Internet. "And for that, my friend, you'll need your credit card."

Quite apart from King's adventure with *The Plant* were the results of a study released in August 2000, just a month after his electronic serial was launched amid great hoopla, indicating that while millions of Americans may be willing to *read* books on a variety of electronic platforms, only 12 percent are likely to *pay* for the privilege. What made the report newsworthy was the nature of the people whose opinions were sampled, and the organization that had conducted the poll. The study was commissioned by Seybold Research, an organization that sponsors seminars in electronic publishing in the United States, and the three thousand people they questioned were attendees at one of the company's own shows; the results were announced on "E-Book Day" at Seybold San Francisco 2000. Fully two thirds of the respondents said they were "not at all likely" to purchase either an e-book or a device dedicated to digital reading in the next twelve months, and for all the interest most expressed in digital reading, only 28 percent of those surveyed said they would consider using an electronic book for recreational reading any time soon.

Emboldened, meanwhile, by its success with *Riding the Bullet,* King's hardcover publisher, Simon & Schuster, proceeded with plans it had announced in the spring of 2000 to offer consumers a variety of reading "options," including e-books, for the forthcoming releases of Mary Higgins Clark, who signed a $64 million contract to write five suspense novels with the expectation they would be released in a variety of formats. A company official said that the electronic alternative would aim to replace sales in the mass-market paperback field, which had come upon difficult times, and not the hardcover editions. "The baby boomers, the 'paperback in your back pocket' people of the 1960s and 1970s, are now older and more affluent and are buying hardcovers and are walking around with reading glasses in their back pockets," Jack Romanos, president and chief operating officer of Simon & Schuster, said of the strategy. "And that is coupled with the fact that we are losing ground to the electronic media, which young people are turning to for their leisure time."

A ringing rebuttal to that analysis came within weeks by way of *Harry Potter and the Goblet of Fire*, the fourth installment in a series of books written by the British author J. K. Rowling that have caused a frenzy among young readers worldwide, recording sales of such magnitude that the *New York Times* was forced to add a new category to its best-seller list, works for children. Rowling's American publisher, Scholastic Press, issued a first printing of 3.8 million copies that was quickly exhausted, and put an order in for 3 million more. Amazon Books—which promised day-of-issue deliveries by Federal Express—claimed to have sold just under 350 tons of the book during the initial rush. Although sales were unprecedented, of particular gravity was the fact that millions of youngsters worldwide were ignoring their on-line chat rooms and video games to read a 734-page book totally devoid of "interactive" diversions. All they were guaranteed—and that clearly was quite sufficient—was a satisfying reading experience about the continuing adventures of an orphan with a lightning bolt scar on his forehead who attends a boarding school for young wizards. A headline in the *Boston Globe* described the July 8, 2000, launch date for the novel as "The Day the Kids Sat Still."

At a conference in 1994 at the then newly established Center for Semiotic and Cognitive Studies at the University of San Marino in California under the general rubric of "The Future of the Book," the noted novelist and semiotician Umberto Eco went on record as declaring that books as we know them "will remain indispensable not only for literature, but for any circumstance in which one needs to read carefully, not only to receive information but also to reflect about it." Computers, he declared, "are diffusing a new form of literacy but are incapable of satisfying all the intellectual needs they are stimulating." Geoffrey Nunberg, a professor of linguistics at Stanford University and a principal scientist at Palo Alto Research Center in California, was chairman of the conference, and editor of a book published two years later by the University of California Press that collected the remarks. Since then, Nunberg has been quoted by some journalists as saying that the book as we know it is a terminal species, an assessment he qualified considerably when he spoke with me. "What I actually have said is that most bound books will disappear, but only the uninteresting ones," he said. "Most bound books—and by bound I mean volumes printed on paper—are parts catalogs, telephone directories, and things of the like. That is what I am talking about, books that have no real cultural content, whose occurrence in this form is a mere contingency, whose replacement by digitized media should be of concern to nobody." Nunberg said he agrees with Librarian of Congress James Billington that the digital revolution will permit the printed book to achieve its true potential as a creative medium. The growing use of print-on-demand technology, he added, will mean essentially that no book will ever go out of print. "Pretty soon—and I mean in the immediate future—you should be able to walk into most any bookstore and order any title on the backlist, and just download it and print it up right then and there, and for twenty or thirty dollars you will be able to have a professionally produced hard copy of whatever it is that you want. That development suggests to me the continuing popularity of the conventional book."

Indeed, the annual rites of the publishing industry known in Europe as the Frankfurt Book Fair and in the United States as BookExpo America, each a massive event that draws thousands of booksellers, publishers, literary agents, and authors from all over the world into one massive exhibition hall for several days of shop talk and previews of forthcoming releases and products, have in recent years featured as star attractions demonstrations of print-on-demand technology, known by the acronym POD. Though not electronic books in the conventional sense, since a traditional printed copy is what is being produced, the innovation is very much a product of the new technology. Texts, be they old books scanned and stored in databases or entirely new works that are "born digital," are transmitted electronically to retailers equipped with the machinery, and within a matter of minutes copied in sturdy paperback editions. Still, by the end of 2000, most major American publishers were making plans to establish imprints, or divisions, that were entirely electronic. "We want to see electronic publishing blow the covers off of books," Laurence Kirshbaum, chairman of the books division of AOL Time Warner, said at a Midtown Manhattan news conference in which a number of prominent publishing people expressed their commitment to penetrating the uncharted territory they were certain lay hard on the horizon.

Ann Godoff, former president and publisher of the Random House Trade Group and creator of that company's digital imprint, called AtRandom, acknowledged that she had never read a book of any sort from start to finish off a computer screen, but recognized the wisdom in preparing for the future all the same. She was particularly enthusiastic about how the technology would allow a publisher to sell books with limited appeal at a profit by eliminating the need to clog up warehouse space with large inventories. The new division moved quickly to acquire the kinds of books considered best suited to the medium, primarily self-help books and reference works, although a few commercial novels by first-time authors were signed up too. "This is the brave new world we want to see," Godoff said. "No printing, no paper and binding, no need for a sales conference or printed catalogue—we don't know the size of the market, but it could be potentially very profitable for us."

Before the year was out, however, the AtRandom name and logo had been scuttled by Random House amid widespread industry reports of consumer indifference to electronic books. "Forecasts of an E-Book Era

Were, It Seems, Premature," a headline in the *New York Times* proclaimed in the summer of 2001. "The main advantage of electronic books appears to be that they gather dust," David D. Kirkpatrick wrote. "Almost no one is buying. Publishers and online bookstores say only the very few best-selling electronic editions have sold more than a thousand copies, and most sell fewer. Only a handful have generated enough revenue to cover the few hundred dollars it costs to convert their texts to digital formats." Asked to comment on his unbridled enthusiasm of a year earlier, Laurence Kirshbaum said that perhaps "we were too-early adapters. We were the early birds who went out to catch the early worms and there weren't very many." Patricia Schroeder, president of the Association of American Publishers, which had commissioned a study that had predicted electronic books would account for 10 percent of all book sales by 2005, acknowledged later that the forecast appeared overly ambitious. "I think everybody has hit the pause button on e-books for the moment," she said. That sentiment was expressed a bit more pointedly in an article published in the *Washington Post* on July 6, 2002, under the headline, "E-Books Not Exactly Flying Off the Shelves." In the lengthy article, the newspaper's publishing correspondent, Linton Weeks, noted the profound change in attitude at the industry's most important convention:

> At BookExpo America in 2000, the annual gathering of book-sellers and publishers, more than 60 e-vendors strutted around McCormick Place in Chicago like so many vultures over a fallen doe. Around that time publishing houses were launching e-book divisions. E-book companies were popping up like nutrias along the information superhighway. Writers were in an angst-ridden dither about digital rights.
>
> But a couple of months ago, BookExpo America 2002 in New York was virtually devoid of e-book chatter. The two-year-old International eBook Award Foundation folded this year due to lack

of funding—and interest. About the only time you hear the topic mentioned in publishing circles these days is when this question comes up: Where have all the e-books gone?

The first entry for *computer* in the *Oxford English Dictionary* identified a person, a human being, who computes—a "calculator" or a "reckoner"—not a device made by people to do the computing for them. Listed among the earliest citations for the word were Sir Thomas Browne in 1646, Jonathan Swift in 1704, and Horace Walpole in 1744. A 1986 supplement to the OED offered a variety of primary references that were more to the point of current usage, one going back to 1897 in which a certain apparatus was described as "of the nature of a circular slide rule." The earliest citation to make sense in a contemporary context—although the word itself was misspelled—appeared in 1944 in a *Sunday Times* of London article about an electronic device called the Mark XIV. It was characterized as "a rectangular box called the computor, which might be called the brains of the machine."

Those two words—*brains* and *machine*—have come full circle in ways that the writer of that article, and perhaps even the inventors of the Mark XIV and its numerical forebears, would have considered inconceivable half a century ago, and the gap is closing all the time. "Computers are still one billion times simpler than the human brain," Ray Kurzweil, an author, inventor, engineer, and admitted "futurist," told me early in 1999, but the good news, as far as he was concerned, is that parity will arrive sometime within the next two decades. "By the year 2019, the computer is going to match the human brain in capacity," he said. "By 2030 it will be equal to a thousand human brains. That is the hardware; I agree that just having the hardware does not automatically give you human intelligence, but that's where the reverse engineering of the human brain comes in."

I met with Kurzweil in the Boston suburb where he operates a number of high-tech companies to discuss his unequivocal belief that the world is changing so rapidly that questions about books, paper, and traditional methods of preserving culture will be rendered irrelevant by the end of the present decade, never mind the end of the twenty-first century. Our conversation was occasioned by the publication of his third book, *The Age of Spiritual Machines: When Computers Exceed Human Intelligence*. Once named inventor of the year by the Massachusetts Institute of Technology, his alma mater, Kurzweil pioneered pattern recognition systems now used in voice dictation programs and worked on developing various artificial-intelligence technologies. He also designed the world's first print-to-speech reading machine for the blind. His 1990 book, *The Age of Intelligent Machines*, predicted the emergence of the World Wide Web, the imminent defeat of a human chess champion by a computer, and the widespread use of synthesizers to create commercial music.

"The human brain does a hundred trillion things at a time," he said. "Right now it is one million times faster than our fastest computer. And that difference of one million is the difference between the rich, subtle behavior of humans and the relatively primitive behavior of the computer. But I also can see, within the next three decades, the emergence of nonbiological entities, called machines, that will be more like people, and will gain a level of intelligence equal to the flexibility and depth and breadth of human intelligence." And once this begins to happen, machines will design their own next generation, "but not in a way to suggest that this is an invasion of aliens," he quickly added. "They are already a part of our civilization. They are already extending our bodies and our minds. We are very intimate with our computers." On the delicate matter of intimacy, Kurzweil predicted that by 2019, people will be choosing the "personality of their computer assistants," and be able to establish "any type of experience" they want, regardless of physical proximity.

"People have a certain conception of the computer as something confined strictly to calculation. People figure, okay, this machine is very good at calculating, but it could never think in an intuitive way, that there is something qualitatively different from what humans do." Kurzweil foresees a time in the near future when machines will not only make music and creative art, but they will play jazz with humans in jam sessions—and enjoy it. All of which brought us to the future of the printed book, which Kurzweil unequivocally predicted in *The Age of Spiritual Machines*— itself a printed book—to be in its final agonizing death throes. The debate over whether books as we know them will survive is meaningless, in Kurzweil's view, if not downright ludicrous and a depressing waste of time. "I did not predict the end of paper in my last book," he said, but he now believes that in the year 2099, most information will be published using "standard assimilated knowledge" that can be "instantly understood" through the implantation of microchips in the human brain. Conventional books are not a part of that scenario at all. "One hundred years from now, we will be able to bypass this kind of language," he said, dismissing with a weary wave the continuing debate over whether or not books and bytes will coexist in the years to come. "People really will go away from paper, and they will do so over the next decade."

Indeed, more will happen in the next twenty years "than happened in the last hundred," he said. "When you consider the exponential growth of technology, the enormous power that these very powerful computers will have, the extent to which they are going to be deeply embedded in our society—you put that all together—and it has a pretty formidable effect." And the technology will be there, he insisted, to change forever the way we live. "We can build computers the same way the human brain is built, and the brain is a physical entity. We already understand how substantial clusters of neurons work, and we know that the brain is made up of a hundred billion neurons. That is not something beyond comprehension. We can manage that level of complexity." Because "biological intelligence" is "relatively at a standstill"—and by that Kurzweil means that human intelligence is "really not developing at all"—the time is coming when he believes "there is not going to be a clear distinction between man and machine." He also believes that the technology is at hand—perhaps as early as two or three decades—to "scan our minds" and "upload copies of ourselves" into machines, making the possibility of human immortality a viable concept.

Because of Kurzweil's impressive credentials, and because he has had some success in making predictions, his long look into the future cannot be dismissed out of hand, although one prominent critic characterized his predictions as "preposterous science." Writing in the *New York Review of Books*, John R. Searle, professor of philosophy at the University of California at Berkeley, suggested that Kurzweil's entire argument is one that "rests on the assumption that the main thing humans do in their lives is compute." Writing in *Science* magazine, another philosopher, Diane Proudfoot of the University of Canterbury in New Zealand, described Kurzweil as one of a species of contemporary writer "who anthropomorphizes machines," and termed his book "an excellent example of the blurring of fact and fiction so common in discussions of artificial intelligence." This field, she maintained, is "littered with the wrecks of fantastical predictions of machine capabilities and, in consequence, with grant applications rejected by eventually disenchanted funding bodies."

Kurzweil is sanguine about the criticism he has received, and steadfastly believes that time is on his side. Because he is a human being subject, like all other human beings, to the inexorable certainties of mortality, he has a third book to his credit—a self-help paperback on nutrition and health. Kurzweil keeps himself fit and well groomed, and toward the end of our conversation I asked him whether he uses an electric shaver or a conventional razor blade on his face each morning. "What has that got to do with anything we've been talking about?" he replied with an edge of testiness, but then quickly saw my point. Electric shavers have been around for more than fifty years, yet for all their supposed superiority, they have not come close to supplanting the traditional method of soap and hot water, as messy and outdated an exertion as that might be. "Okay, I use a Gillette Mach III, but not because it's an anachronism, but because the technology makes it superior to everything else that is available," Kurzweil allowed. What he did not say is that he prefers the wet manual method over the dry electronic because some things are just better in and of themselves. But as another MIT alumnus with a flair for prediction, Dr. Vannevar Bush, wrote in 1945, albeit in a decidedly different context, that is another story.

Two years after my interview with Kurzweil, I had an opportunity to meet John E. Warnock, a man of considerable vision who with Charles M. Geschke in 1982 founded Adobe Systems, Inc., with the idea of imparting a sense of authenticity to digitized documents, making it possible to create pages on computers that appear in every way as if they were the "real thing." The result of their collaboration was the introduction of what is known as the portable document format, or PDF, the standard method of distributing digital documents worldwide, and with the introduction in 1993 of Adobe's Acrobat software, millions of people are now able to transmit electronic versions of reports, newspapers, and books complete with artwork, photographs, and typefaces. Even more pervasive is the impact the company's other products—PostScript, Photoshop, and InDesign are some of the other names—have had on the revolution in desktop publishing. "We had no idea what we were starting," Warnock told me in a wide-ranging interview in 2001, but five years after the onetime Xerox PARC (Palo Alto Research Center) engineers had launched Adobe, they took the company public, a turn of events that allowed the former mathematics professor with a doctorate in electrical engineering the means to indulge a newfound interest in acquiring books of exceptional rarity. During a trip to London with his family in 1987, Warnock's son Christopher showed him a copy of Euclid's *Elementa Geometria*, printed in Venice in 1482, while they were strolling through the booths of an antiquarian book fair. "My undergraduate and master's degrees are in mathematics, and I really like geometry," Warnock said. "I looked at this book, I felt it, and I said, 'We have to have this—*I* have to have this.' So what happens next is that you bring this book home, you put it on the shelf, and then you say, 'Well, it clearly needs friends,' and as you know, that's a very slippery slope. But that's when I started."

Before long, Warnock had assembled a choice collection of rare books, high spots of Western culture and accomplishment for the most part, but high spots of such irrefutable significance that he knew he had the kind of material that very few people would ever have the opportunity to enjoy firsthand, books like Isaac Newton's *Philosophiae Naturalis Principia Mathematica* (1667), Nicolaus Copernicus's *De Revolutionibus Orbium Coelestium* (1543), Charles Darwin's *On the Origin of the Species* (1859), Andreas Vesalius's *De Humani Corporis Fabrica* (1543), Galileo Galilei's *Sidereus Nuncius* (1610), Hans Holbein's *Icones Historiarum Veteris Testamenti* (1547), Robert Hooke's *Micrographia* (1665), Gerardus Mercator's *Atlas sive Cosmographicae Meditationes de Fabrica Mundi et Fabricati Figura* (1595), a copy of the exquisitely illustrated Kelmscott Press edition of *The Works of Geoffrey Chaucer* (1896), a first printing of the Bill of Rights (1791), believed to be the only copy in private hands.

Although he was actively involved in creating a publishing revolution with Adobe, Warnock said he had little idea of just how intoxicating the experience of handling such timeless objects could be. "I hadn't realized that all the early books were in such wonderful shape and hadn't deteriorated because they all had rag-based papers, and I hadn't really appreciated the diversity of typography that they had used. So here I am, holding an artifact of history, and it was an absolutely palpable sensation for me, one that engaged all the senses. The thing that really struck me is that before I became a collector, I didn't even know these books existed. I mean, I knew they *existed*, but as artifacts available to somebody like myself, that was new to me. And the other thing is, let's face it, the general public has no access. I mean, if you go to the British Library, you have to say, 'I am a researcher, I have a specific need,' then you have to demonstrate your need to see this and establish your bona fides. I said, 'Well, this is a shame,' because while the libraries obviously have the charter to protect these things and keep them from being damaged, you would think that they might also want to make them more available to the public."

The idea that he could apply the technology he had given to the world in such triumphant fashion to share his books with others—Adobe's revenues in 2001 were $1.26 billion, down somewhat from the previous year but robust and healthy in an otherwise sluggish economy just the same—came to Warnock after he had been asked by several groups to talk about his newfound passion. Deciding that showing examples of what he was collecting was far more effective than simply talking about them, Warnock selected a few titles from his shelves and brought them along to the lectures. At one of the events, he followed an appearance by the young Chinese dissident who gained international recognition in 1989 by facing down an army tank in Tiananmen Square. "He talked about his father, who is an academic, who had been in prison in China, and how important intellectual freedom is," Warnock said. "Then it was my turn—and it happened that one of the items I had brought along with me was my copy of the Bill of Rights—and I said, simply, 'Well, here's the Bill of Rights.' There wasn't a dry eye in the place, and I realized then and there just how effectively artifacts can transport you back in history. The text alone doesn't do that. You feel you're seeing something the same way that Darwin saw it, or the way Newton saw it."

In 1997, Warnock established Octavo Corp., a company that would create precise digital reproductions of rare books and make them available on CD-ROM, and the books the company began with came from the John Warnock Library. "I'm the only collector of these things so far as I know who has come up with a way to share them with other people," he said, and he explained what had encouraged him to get the project going.

"We brought out technology in 1983 that in two decades completely changed printing—I mean, really, completely, changed printing. Not a little bit, but across the boards. Newspapers, magazines, textbooks, all advertising publishing, PDF became the standard, and a very ubiquitous standard. And so almost everything that you see visually that is printed uses our technology, whether they're packaging labels on grocery store shelves or the packages for Frito-Lay, or the printing of a Coke can, they all use our technology." Warnock said that as a writer of computer software, there was an awareness—he did not quibble when I suggested the word *perception*—that he was driving at a process that could somehow replicate the original, if only as an image.

"With Adobe, we figured out how to bring all of the graphic elements, all the type elements, all the image elements together on a common open platform. All the systems prior to that were special-purpose kinds of things, and we sort of flattened the playing field and made it open. It just changed publishing. So in the process of sort of inventing Acrobat as part of Adobe, I said the technology is getting to the point where it is feasible to capture these books and make them available on a much broader basis. And that became part of what we are doing now with Octavo." In addition to offering high-resolution photographic images of every page in each book, Octavo has developed software features that offer "live text" applications that give translations by inviting the reader to click onto various passages on the pages. Readers also can zoom in and out, enlarge letters or phrases, search for specific words, access commentary, and examine illustrations in minute detail. This is not the "real thing," to be sure, but it is as close as most people without academic standing will ever get to handling such rarities, and even institutions eager to restrict unnecessary use of its most precious holdings have recognized its potential. By 2003, forty books had been made available by Octavo, and partnerships had been established with more than a dozen libraries, most notably with the Library of Congress to prepare a digitized edition of the nation's copy of the Gutenberg Bible, one of only three perfect copies printed on vellum in the world, and with the Folger Shakespeare Library to make a disc using an exquisite copy of the First Folio of 1623 from its matchless collection.

I first met Warnock in April 2001 in Washington, D.C., at a forum of collectors, booksellers, and librarians sponsored by the Center for the Book at the Library of Congress in which he made clear his unwillingness to place his books in any institution that does not take steps to make them available to a wider audience. One of his more memorable statements was the observation that with something on the order of twenty thousand objects coming into the building each day, the nation's largest library "is like Niagara Falls coming in and a garden hose going out." When we sat down to talk in San Francisco two months later, Warnock had come up to the Bay Area from his home in Palo Alto to meet with rare-books-and-manuscripts librarians who were attending the annual meeting of the American Library Association, and had invited them all to an elegant reception at the Fairmont Hotel with hopes of introducing them to what his pet project has to offer. He explained his motivation:

What I hope I can impress upon these people is my firm belief that all the technological advances in printing and publishing have always at the end given the librarian an artifact, namely a book. The librarian has never particularly cared how the book is produced, what intellectual processes go into its making, what you get is the book, and your job is to protect this book and make it available to people. My feeling is that this view of the library will be replaced over time with the fact that there is going to be a companion electronic set of documents and information surfaces, and they have it in their bibliography files right now, but in the *content* itself, it's going to be very important how the thing was produced and how it spews out information and interrelates that information to other content. So, in the end, you do have to stop thinking about the book as an artifact, and start thinking about the lighter problem of information management and storage and technology, and not worrying about whether they give you another artifact like a CD, but worry about this wide body of knowledge that will go forward.

As to whether electronic texts will totally supplant print, Warnock— who observed his sixty-third birthday in 2003—said he does not dismiss the possibility out of hand, but feels it will not come in his lifetime. "I think it will happen when kids learn how to read off of the screen, and by that I mean when their primal learning process about information doesn't come from a book, but comes from a screen, and they actually learn to read off a screen, then that will sort of wire all their cells to prefer that mode. But that will be a long time." In the meantime, he firmly believes that the use of paper must be reduced drastically, if only to save natural resources. "Printing does not disappear," he made clear, "but I do believe that paper as a transportation medium does go away. This is not something that is terribly fuel-efficient, it is bad for the environment—think of all the trees it kills unnecessarily—and the fact of the matter is that there are much more efficient ways to communicate information. But to *read* information—paper is not going away anytime soon, which is one reason why I see a great future for print-on-demand services."

For all his acceptance of the change that is in the offing, Warnock said he remains committed to the spirit of creativity, which partly explains why he chose to continue as chief technology officer at Adobe after stepping down as chief executive officer in 2001. "I'm an amateur painter. I think of myself as a very visual person, and all of Adobe's products are really trying to focus how you sort of bring the left side of the brain together with the right side and allow artists to use tools that they couldn't in the past. To accomplish something like that I think you need somebody who straddles the fence and who sees both sides and who knows what the value systems on both sides are." As a tool, Warnock said the printed book "will probably outlast most of the other media around today. I have a 1468 copy of *Summa Theologica* that was printed in Basel—it was William Morris's copy—and it has these incredible boards and the original chain, it was attached to the library bench, and the book was never pressed, so the pages undulate with these impressions of the type. It has this texture that is just breathtaking. And it is five hundred years old. It is just an amazing experience." That response prompted me to ask Warnock what he thought about Ray Kurzweil's prediction that the age of print was in its twilight years, doomed by the end of the decade. "I know Ray," he said, and laughed good-naturedly. "Ray's been wrong before."

In the waning months of the twentieth century, the eminent Yale historian Jonathan D. Spence addressed an international conference at the Library of Congress not unlike the one gathered in Saint Louis ninety-five years earlier in which Dr. Guido Biagi of the Laurentian Library predicted the imminent arrival of the "spoken book." Spence's remarks centered on how the "mechanics of scholarship" might change in the future, given that so many historical records will exist only in electronic formats. "Never have so many discordant voices been clamoring at once, pursuing such utterly different agendas, using such different methods to assess their data and to get their points across, and with so little unanimity on what they are trying to do," Spence observed in an apparent call for calm. "We can see that the world of technology is constantly introducing new challenges and new techniques that will affect the future of historical work in ways we can only guess at." Regardless of the technological changes that come along, Spence stressed his belief that historians will continue "to apply their intellects to the workings of the past," and continue "to scrutinize whatever records they can find with integrity, intelligence, and imaginative strength."

When Ernest Cushing Richardson (1860–1939) accepted an invitation to discuss the "beginnings of libraries" at the New York Public Library in 1912, the study of library science was still in its infancy. A theological scholar and bibliographer with several dozen important works to his credit, Richardson was serving as librarian of Princeton University at the time and fully qualified to speak authoritatively on a number of pertinent subjects, but he chose to open his remarks at the most fundamental of levels. "What is a book?" he asked rhetorically. "To this it may be answered that a book is any record of thought in words. Here again neither size, form, nor material matters; even a one word record may be a book and that book a library. This leads again however to still another question: What is a word?" Following a carefully considered line of thought, Richardson concluded forcefully that the "very simplest library consists therefore of a single recorded sign kept for use," and that the root of "library wisdom is to seek out diligently the nature of these rudimentary libraries." Among these "rudimentary" libraries, he suggested, was a subset of some "alleged libraries," a few he described as "antediluvian" repositories consulted by a multitude of deities and various biblical patriarchs, Adam and Noah among them:

Almost all the great god families, Indian, Egyptian, Babylonian, Persian, Greek, and Scandinavian, had their own book-collections, so it is said. According to several religions there were book-collections before the creation of man; the Talmud has it that there was one before the creation of the world, the Vedas say that collections existed before even the Creator created himself, and the Koran maintains that such a collection co-existed from eternity with the uncreated God. It is obviously idle to try to trace libraries back farther than this.

"Alleged" libraries aside, the earliest repositories of which we have irrefutable knowledge were maintained in Babylonia five thousand years ago, yet even then, Richardson reminded his audience, the possibility of systematic accumulation was an infinite concept. "To the ancient Babylonians the stars of heaven were themselves books in which could be read the secrets of heaven and earth and the destiny of mankind. The whole firmament was thus a library of celestial tablets—tablets of destiny or tablets of wisdom from the 'house of wisdom,' which was before creation, or carried upon the breast of the world ruler."

Three quarters of a century after Richardson offered these soaring thoughts in the newly opened New York Public Library, a writer who came of age in Reading Room 315 of that same building offered some measured speculations of a different sort. Philip Hamburger—a contributor of gracefully written profiles to the *New Yorker* since 1939—admitted a sinking queasiness when he saw that eight thousand oak drawers full of three-by-five classification cards were being replaced by an electronic catalog system in the 1980s, and confessed to being depressed when he considered all the other rippling changes that seemed to be in store. Visiting the library one day shortly after the conversion had become a reality, Hamburger stopped by a computer terminal in the massive room "that I and millions of others had been using since we could remember first going into the library," and entered on a keyboard the name of a writer whose works he knew had been listed in the antiquated system, one that he was sure should be included in the new database as well. The name he was trying to locate was his own. Suddenly, a string of green letters blinked back at him on the black screen. "Type HELP," he was advised. Hamburger took a deep breath and puttered along about his way, leaving the inquiry for another day:

> I realized that I was in the grip of technology, and needed patience, perseverance, and an open mind. I felt blue about this until I walked into one of the enormous reading rooms behind the

catalogue room. There sat hundreds of people, quietly reading. There was a slight murmur in the room, almost a whisper, and it sounded like low music of the spheres. As long as there is this reading room, these people, this murmur, I thought, we are safe. Perhaps.

Perhaps, indeed, but as the abbot Trithemius suggested five hundred years earlier on a matter of comparable historic consequence: *Hoc posteritas iudicabit*—"only time will tell."

Proper Passage:
A Coda

One of my central goals throughout these explorations has been to characterize the life cycle of books and to examine the quirky experiences of the people who have safeguarded them across the decades. Just as pertinent have been issues relating to the choices individuals inevitably face regarding the future of their precious possessions, with a fundamental concern often involving questions of whether treasures should be set free and allowed to nourish the next wave of collectors, or if they should go into institutions and be removed from circulation forever. As we saw in the chapter called "Shelf Life," this latter option does not always guarantee that books will remain in the same safe place indefinitely, giving rise to yet another consideration, the various ways some benefactions occasionally come to be deaccessioned and sent off to uncertain fates.

One of my favorite examples of what can happen when benevolence and bibliomania come together involved the creation of a magnificent research library outside Los Angeles in the early years of the twentieth century by the California railroad magnate Henry E. Huntington (1850–1927). When asked once to explain why he suddenly decided at the age of sixty to become one of the most important book collectors of all time, Huntington—who had been thinking a lot then about the fragility of life and his place in history—had a simple answer: "Men may come and men may go, but books go on forever. The ownership of a fine library is the surest and swiftest way to immortality." True to his word, Huntington used his vast personal wealth to achieve exactly that, and all it took was fifteen years to get it done. Significantly, one of the collections Huntington drew on to supply his fabulous repository on the grounds of an old orange grove in the San Gabriel Valley—he became known, in fact, as a "collector of collections"—had been assembled by Robert Hoe III (1839–1909) of New York City, arguably the greatest American book collector ever, and one who had chosen a different course of action entirely for the disposition of his remarkable treasures. Hoe's rationale for authorizing a high-profile auction in Manhattan that would attract the most prominent book people of the day: "If the great collections of the past had not been sold, where would I have found *my* books?"

The point of these two stories is as valid now as when I told them in *A Gentle Madness,* and it bears emphasizing again here, that regardless of the destinations responsible collectors choose for their books, steps are usually taken to ensure proper passage, and as I conclude these ruminations, it seems appropriate that I share a final example of this essential dynamic, one that fittingly involves what the late librarian Lawrence Clark Powell called the "trinity" of book collector, bookseller, and librarian to assure success, one that touches on many of the issues addressed in *A Gentle Madness, Patience & Fortitude,* and *A Splendor of Letters.*

The death in 1999 at the age of ninety-one of Paul Mellon was observed respectfully around the world, with just as many superlatives issuing forth from Great Britain in tribute to the great American philanthropist as from the United States. "His generosity was matched only by his modesty and avoidance of publicity," the *Guardian* of London proclaimed in its obituary, pointing out that Mellon's numerous gifts to English institutions and universities qualified him as "the greatest collector and benefactor of British art" in the twentieth century, a level of generosity that earned him an honorary knighthood from Queen Elizabeth II in 1974. By all accounts a modest man who preferred having his name left off the scores of bequests he had made to dozens of universities, museums, theaters, and libraries during his lifetime, the very scope of Mellon's philanthropy ensured that it would by no means remain a secret, and indeed a lengthy appendix to *Reflections in a Silver Spoon,* his 1992 autobiography, outlined in thorough detail the extent of his gifts. Dispersing more than $600 million during his lifetime and many additional millions afterward, Mellon believed deeply in the power of art and literature to shape individual lives, and the pattern he established was to expedite the gifts while he was alive.

During the twenty-two years he was president of the board of the National Gallery of Art in Washington, D.C., 1963 to 1985, for instance, Mellon underwrote the $95 million construction of the east wing of the building designed by I. M. Pei, and along with his sister, Ailsa Mellon Bruce, gave numerous French and American masterpieces to adorn the galleries. Beloved paintings by the English artists George Stubbs, J. M. W. Turner, Joshua Reynolds, and others, were already installed in the Yale Center for British Art, which he had established in 1977, and for good measure had stocked with an extraordinary collection of early maps and atlases, including the earliest surviving chart showing the route of Sir Francis Drake's circumnavigation of the globe from 1577 to 1580. Mellon had also committed to the center an unparalleled collection of seventy-five hundred sporting books, a passion he had begun to indulge as an undergraduate at Clare College, Cambridge University, during the 1930s.

Mellon had made no secret of the fact that he had a taste for rare books, but the general perception of his collecting had always been that the fine arts took precedence over everything else he pursued. He had taken passing note of a bibliophilic interest toward the end of his autobiography with a brief mention of how in 1959 he had bought "the surviving intact portion of the library of John Locke," and then decided, eighteen years later, "that since I had little leisure to read or study the books, I should let the Bodleian Library" at Oxford University "have them immediately," and not wait until his estate went to probate, which as events turned out would have involved another twenty-two years before this essential research tool would have been made available to scholars. Mellon had nothing else to say in his memoir about the remaining contents of his library, however, and since he had stopped buying rare books in the 1970s, few people were aware of what he owned. Shortly after his death, it developed that there were still a few surprises, and it turned out that they involved what may have been his most treasured possessions of all, a rich gathering of Americana that he had acquired between 1950 and 1973 and kept in a second-floor library of his elegant country home in Upperville, Virginia, known as the Brick House. "Because it ceased to be an active collection, and was not in an area with which he was commonly identified, Mellon's Americana collection was not noticed even by those familiar with his many collecting interests," William S. Reese, the noted New Haven, Connecticut, bookseller, wrote in an essay for the *Yale University Library Gazette*. "In fact, it was one of the greatest collections ever formed in that field."

In his will, Mellon directed that the books, pamphlets, maps, manuscripts, broadsides, print portfolios, and ephemera from this collection, 1,827 objects all told, be shared equally among the principal rare-book libraries of Yale University, his alma mater, and two major research institutions in his adopted state, the University of Virginia and the Virginia Historical Society, with the task of deciding precisely who would get what left for his estate to determine. Among the ground rules his executors established was a commitment to honor a wish often expressed by Mellon to ensure that material relating to Virginia—documents such as King James I's *Order Banishing Rogues to New Found Lands* (1603), the earliest printed proclamation relating to Virginia, for instance, or various handwritten letters of great historical importance by Thomas Jefferson and George Washington—remain in the state. At the same time, there was a determined effort to avoid duplication of materials already held by the various libraries and to build on the strength of existing collections. Furnished with detailed lists of the holdings, the curators were asked to choose the items they wanted most by assigning values of one to five for every object, with five being the most desirable, and to indicate their top ten choices. With these "wish lists" in hand, Reese and Beverly Carter, Mellon's longtime librarian and one of his executors, were able to designate equal numbers of "fives," "fours," "threes," "twos," and "ones" among the repositories. "The system worked remarkably well, so that the vast majority of the items could be assigned to the institution that most wanted them," Reese reported later in a talk given to the Virginia Historical Society. "In only a few instances were Solomaic decisions required." When all was said and done, some 900 items had gone to Yale, and an equal number had gone to the two libraries in Virginia. Although it is impossible to summarize here the materials they received, the richness and depth of the gifts suggested by exhibitions the three institutions promptly mounted to showcase some of the choicest items and in the catalogs they issued to accompany them indicates a true splendor of letters all the same. "We stand in awe and gratitude," wrote Barbara A. Shailor, director of the Beinecke Rare Book and Manuscript Library at Yale, expressing a sentiment shared by her colleagues. "I can think of no other instance in the history of institutional collecting in this country where so great a collection was divided in such a fashion to the complete satisfaction of all the parties involved," Reese said. "The result fulfilled Mr. Mellon's desire to make his collection part of the cultural resources available to researchers under the auspices of two great universities and a great historical society." What one of the wealthiest people in the world understood as much as anyone, it bears emphasizing, is that he really *owned* nothing of great artistic or historical value, that he had a responsibility as caretaker to preserve and pass on, which is the essence of stewardship.

As I write the concluding words to this book, the gutted shell of the National Library of Iraq still smolders in Baghdad, the victim on April 14, 2003, of wholesale looting and wanton destruction that took place in the aftermath of the American seizure of the city. Among irreplaceable treasures reported lost in the ensuing chaos were historical documents from the Ottoman era and books in manuscript that survived the Mongol conquest of 1258, many of them medieval poems, odes, and lyrical descriptions of the desert. Just as devastating were the barbarities inflicted a few days earlier on the National Museum of Iraq; among the thousands of Mesopotamian artworks and antiquities reported to have been plundered there were cuneiform tablets from the Sumerian, Akkadian, Assyrian, and Babylonian eras, including eight hundred clay tablets known as the Sippar Library that had been unearthed outside Baghdad in the 1980s. Dating from the sixth century B.C., the collection included hymns, prayers, glossaries, astronomical observations, and scientific texts, along with a previously unknown fragment of the *Epic of Gilgamesh* and a copy of the prologue to the great legal code compiled in the eighteenth century B.C. by King Hammurabi.

"Trust in the survival of the word, as well as the urge to destroy it, is as old as the first clay tablets," the author Alberto Manguel wrote of the incalculable losses in the *New York Times*. "To hold and transmit memory, to teach through the experience of others, to share the knowledge of the world and of ourselves are some of the powers (and dangers) of books, and the reasons why we both treasure and fear them." Manguel concluded his lamentation by quoting from the copy of Hammurabi's Code that was carved on a massive cone of polished black basalt thousands of years ago, and is preserved today at the Louvre Museum in Paris: "If one is sufficiently wise to be capable of maintaining order in the land, may he heed the words I have written on this stele."

Notes

This work draws substantially from the author's personal interviews, which are listed in the Bibliography. Biographical information for the principal subjects is contained in the body of the text and can be located by referring to the Index. Sources cited in the Notes by the author's last name or by a short form of the title are to be found in the Bibliography.

Preface

xiv   "pleasurist . . . noble poem": Macaulay, xv–xvii. For a brilliant photographic consideration of this book, see *Roloff Beny Interprets in Photographs Pleasure of Ruins by Rose Macaulay*, ed. Constance Babington Smith (New York: Henry Holt, 1977). Also, for a recent exercise in "ruin questing" of more modest scale, see Christopher Woodward, *In Ruins* (New York: Pantheon, 2001).

xv   "Scrawled . . . world": Amery and Curran, 50.

xvi   "We were the first": Quoted in Scott Macleod, "Lost Cities," *Time Europe*, June 17, 2002. See also William Mullen, "2,000 Years Under the Sea," *Chicago Tribune*, Sept. 22, 2002; Stephanie Pain, "Sunken Cities of the Nile," *New Scientist*, Oct. 19, 2001; Jean Yoyotte, "The Naos of Herakleion," posted at http://www.underwaterdiscovery.org/english/projects/canopicregion/history/history_02.asp.

xvi   "found the bottle": Anne Warren, "Post Office Would Have Been Faster," *Cape Cod Times*, July 20, 2001.

Chapter 1: Marbles and Names

2   "A fine thing": Sickinger, 1; for an alternative translation, see Chris Carey, *Aeschines* (Austin: University of Texas Press, 2000), 190.

2   *On the Crown:* Loeb Classical Library, *Demosthenes,* trans. C. A. and J. H. Vince (Cambridge, Mass.: Harvard University Press, 1926), vol. 2.

3   "not with ink": A. H. Clough, ed. *Plutarch's Lives* (Boston: Little, Brown, 1885), "Solon," Vol. 1, 184. Plutarch may have been speaking metaphorically about Draco, but such, apparently, is not the case with Saddam Hussein of Iraq, as John F. Burns wrote in the *New York Times* on Dec. 15, 2002: "Inside a special sanctum, treated by the mosque's custodian with the reverence due a holy of holies, there are 650 pages of the Koran—written, it is said, in Mr. Hussein's blood. As the official legend has it, 'Mr. President' donated 28 liters of his blood—about 50 pints—over two years, and a famous calligrapher, Abas al-Baghdadi, mixed it with ink and preservatives to produce the handsome writing now laid out page by page in glass-walled display cases."

3   "No book is to be taken": *Oxford Companion to Classical Civilization,* ed. Simon Hornblower and Antony Spawforth (Oxford, England: Oxford University Press, 1998), 414–415; for an alternate translation, see Staikos, 123: "No books may be removed from the premises. Opening hours six a.m. to twelve noon."

4   "No one can know": *Ausonius,* trans. Hugh G. Evelyn White (New York: William Heinemann, 1919), 159; another version in Schnapp, 39.

4   "inventors . . . day": Josephus, *Antiquities of the Jews,* book 1, chap. 2.

6   Charters of Freedom: see Warren E. Leary, "New Homes for the 'Charters of Freedom,'" *New York Times,* Sept. 12, 2000; Alfred Meyer, "Daily Rise and Fall of the Nation's Revered Documents," *Smithsonian* 17:6 (Oct. 1986): 134. For additional information on the handling of the Constitution over time, see David C. Mearns and Vernon W. Clapp, *The Constitution of the United States together with an account of its travels since September 17, 1787* (Washington, D.C.: Library of Congress, 1948). For more on the challenges facing conservators, see Lynn Amlie, "The Charters of Freedom: Support Paper for the Re-encasement Project," *Hand Papermaking* 16 (1) (summer 2001): 14–19.

7   When originals no longer exist: Umberto Eco, *Foucault's Pendulum* (New York: Harcourt Brace Jovanovich, 1989), 131.

8   "My overriding": *New York Times*, Jan. 25, 1987.

8   Faksimile Verlag Luzern: http://www.faksimile.ch/index2.html.

9   "It is a marvelous thing": Marjorie Anders, "Metropolitan Museum Gets First Pages of Book of Kells," Associated Press dispatch, June 2, 1987; Douglas McGill, "Ireland's Book of Kells Is Facsimiled," *New York Times*, June 2, 1987.

9   "The driving . . . Real McCoy": Schwartz, 11.

10   "Is it the ideas": Michael Scott, "Imitation Leonardo," *Vancouver Sun*, Oct. 3, 1998.

11   "Mr. Spiegelman": Benjamin Weiser, "Sentence by Judge Reflects Historic Documents' Value," *New York Times*, Apr. 25, 1998.

11   "Such an act has graver implications": Quoted in Benjamin Weiser, "What Is the True Measure of a Lost Book?" *New York Times*, Mar. 21, 1998.

12   "Multiply that huge number": Ibid.

12   "A document worth $10": Lewis A. Kaplan, "The Cultural Value of Books: United States of America v. Daniel Spiegelman, Defendant," in *Gazette of the Grolier Club, New Series,* ed. Donald Oresman, intro. Jean W. Ashton, No. 50, 1999, 9–25. Also: *United States of America v. Daniel Spiegelman*, U.S. District Court for the Southern District of New York, 4 F Supp. 2nd 275; 1998, 97 Criminal 309 (LAK).

14   Stephen C. Blumberg: See Basbanes, *Gentle Madness*, chap. 13, and preface to the 1999 Owl edition for an update on his activities.

14   Spiegelman's 1984 forgery conviction: John Sullivan, *New York Times*, June 17, 1995.

15   "In callously stealing": Kaplan, op. cit.

15   arrested again: "Convicted Thief Charged with Selling Stolen Papers," Associated Press, Oct. 5, 1999.

17   Hill Monastic Manuscript Library: See www.hmml.org/Default.htm.

18   UMI: Power, 93.

19   "Each copy": Ibid., 17.

19   "British agents . . . Schweinfurt": Ibid., 135.

20   "genuine . . . around": Ibid., 154–160.

22   "Librarian as Gambler": Russell Chandler and Patt Morrison, "Controversy Shatters a Librarian's Quiet," *Los Angeles Times*, Sept. 24, 1991.

22   "This victory": Vermes, 9. For Moffett as "liberator," see Shanks, 56–58, and Wise et al., 6–8. For more on the cartel, see Baigent and Leigh.

23   For more on Silvestre de Sacy as bibliomane: See Basbanes, *Gentle Madness*, 10.

23   Copying the Rosetta Stone: Pope, 62–84; W.V. Davies, in Hooker, 119–128; *Sunday Telegraph*, June 30, 1999; Fagan, *Eyewitness to Discovery*, 79, 88; for printing techniques, Parkinson, 20.

24   "In most of the places": Quoted in Adkins and Adkins, 124–125.

25   Académie des Inscriptions et Belles Lettres: Hooker, 126; Pope, 208; Parkinson, 32–34.

25   Champollion's trip to England: Parkinson, 38.

25   "I will continue": Quoted in Adkins and Adkins, 212–213.

25   "I will not try . . . degree": Ibid., 254.

26   "Museums are full . . . a dialogue": Parkinson, 13.

Chapter 2: Editio Princeps

27   Papyrus monopoly: Strabo VIII, 60–61. For more on Pergamum and Alexandria, see Basbanes, *Gentle Madness*, chap. 2, and *Patience & Fortitude*, chap. 1.

27   "our civilization": Pliny, *Natural History*, vol. 4, book XIII; quoted in Hunter, 19–23.

28   "palm-leaves . . . documents": Pliny, op. cit., 141.

28   best quality . . . Virgil: Ibid., 149. The ancient Greeks applied similar standards of quality to the choice of materials they used for important inscriptions. R. E. Wycherley wrote in *The Stones of Athens* (Princeton, N.J.: Princeton University Press, 1978) how the Athenians "became more and more addicted to having all their activities inscribed on stone for public scrutiny, and the stelai accumulated in hundreds and eventually thousands." The finest marbles of them all—from nearby Pentelikon—were reserved for the most important architectural, artistic, and writing projects. "Alongside the statues, and in far greater numbers, stood the inscribed stelai, the best of which were true works of sculptural art, made of fine marble, well-proportioned and carefully designed, with the text meticulously set out in elegant lettering" (77). In a postscript detailing the specific nature of the stones they used, Wycherley quoted no less an authority than Xenophon: "Attica has a plentiful supply of stone, from which are made the fairest temples and altars, and the most beautiful statues for the gods" (267).

28   "that is original": Boyle, 7.

29   Caesar's dispatches on animal skins: Irwin, 116.

29   "You who want my little books": *Martial* (1.2.7–8); D. R. Shackleton Bailey, Loeb Classical Library, *Martial Epigrams*, vol. 1, p. 43; see Bailey's introduction for an excellent essay on the evolution of the epigram as a literary form.

29   Invention of paper: See Carter, chap. I; Hunter, 60, and for a superb chronology, 464–582. For more on the spread of paper through Europe, see Jonathan M. Bloom.

30   *Liber Augustalis:* Hermann Conrad, Thea Von Der Lieck-Buyken, and Wolfgang Wagner, eds., *Die Konstitutionen Friedrich II. Von Hohenstaufen für Sein Königreich Sizilien* (Würzburg: Böhlau Verlag Köln Wien, 1973), 122–125.

30   Loss of Tacitus's books: Ronald Haithwaite Martin, in *Oxford Classical Dictionary* (Oxford: Oxford University Press, 1996), 1469.

31   "Whenever I had taken": John C. Rolfe, trans., *The Attic Nights of Aulus Gellius* (Cambridge, Mass.: Loeb Classical Library, 1920), vol. 1, xxvii.

32   "written account . . . company": N. G. Wilson, 25.

33   "It is": Ibid., 18. For more on Cardinal Bessarion, see Basbanes, *Patience & Fortitude*, 104–107.

33   "born in Egypt": N. G. Wilson, 158.

34   "odious and impious": Ibid., 167.

34   "In style": Ibid., 54.

34   "Read a novel": Ibid., 104.

34   "patriarch . . . point of view": Quoted in ibid., 2.

34   "Was he . . . surviving copy": Ibid., 6.

35   The execution of Michael Servetus for the writing of the *Christianismi Restitution* and the survival of just three copies of the book have been the subject of numerous studies, most recently Lawrence Goldstone and Nancy Goldstone, *Out of the Flames* (New York: Broadway Books, 2002).

36   "*cacoethes scribendi . . .* well": Ditchfield, viii–ix.

36   Aristotle on book worms: This translation from the Rev. J. S. H. O'Connor in *Facts About Bookworms* (see bibliography), a delightful nineteenth-century monograph dedicated "to all lovers of books," with the added wish that "their thoughts may live triumphant over the ravages of the work of worm or of time." Other versions of the quotation are to be found in various translations of Aristotle, *History of Animals*, book IV, part 7.

37   "There was . . . books": Reynolds and Wilson, 32.

38   "not because . . . obsolete text": Ibid., 76.

38   palimpsests: In the early 1800s, Thomas Hartwell Horne (see bibliography) used the phrase *Codex Rescriptus* (Latin for "written over") to describe "a parchment, from which the original writing has been partially or totally erased, and on which a new work has been written in its stead" (vol. 1, 112). He reported further that the "custom became so common, in Germany, in the fourteenth and fifteenth centuries, that at length it was perceived how dangerous it might prove, to employ erased parchments for public instruments, and efficacious measures were adopted to prevent this disorder. Accordingly, the patents, by which the emperors of Germany elevated individuals to the rank of a count, with power to create imperial notaries, usually contained the following clause:—'on condition, that they should not make use of old and erased parchment, but that it should be *virgin* (i.e. made of abortive skins) and quite new' " (Ibid., 117–118).

38   "buried under": Reynolds and Wilson, 68.

38   A thorough history of the Archimedes palimpsest is included in papers filed for *Greek Orthodox Patriarchate of Jerusalem v. Christie's Inc.*, U.S. District Court, Southern District of New York, Personal Property (QDS:02761536), summarized in *New York Law Journal* (Sept. 3, 1999): 25.

39   "invisible": *The Book Collector,* spring 1999, 116; see also William J. Cannon, "Archimedes Unbound," *American Scientist* 87:4 (July 1, 1999): 36.

39   *De republica* of Cicero: Kenyon, 71.

40   "unique tri-lingual quintuple palimpsest": A. S. Atiya, in Hellmut Lehmann-Haupt, ed., *Homage to a Bookman: Essays on Manuscripts, Books and Printing Written for Hans P. Kraus on His 60th Birthday* (Berlin: Gebr. Mann Verlag, 1967), 75–85.

40   "One cannot . . . trace": Reynolds and Wilson, 90.

40   For more on John Heminge and Henry Condell, see Charles Connell, *They Gave Us Shakespeare* (Northumberland, England: Oriel Press, 1982).

41   no known manuscripts: Reiman, 8–9.

42   tattoos: See Jane Caplan, ed., *Written on the Body* (Princeton, N.J.: Princeton University Press, 2000).

42   dendroglyphs: See transcript of report filed on National Public Radio Morning Edition, July 6, 2000, by Tristan Clum; Mark Shaffer, "Trees Are Living History: Basques Made Their Marks 100 Years Ago," *The Arizona Republic,* Aug. 1, 1999; Chris Fiscus, "Flagstaff's Telltale Trees: Aspen Bark Reveals Sheepherders' History and Humor," *The Phoenix Gazette,* Oct. 23, 1994.

42   Petroglyph National Monument: See Linda DuVal, "The Writing on the Wall," *Baltimore Sun,* July 25, 1999; also http://www.nps.gov/petr/.

43   *PT-109*: In July 2002, a *National Geographic* expedition led by explorer Robert Ballard found the sunken remains of John F. Kennedy's *PT-109.*

43   maps on silk: See Debbie Hall, "Wall Tiles and Free Parking: Escape and Evasion Maps of World War II"; http://www.mapforum.com/04/escape.htm.

44   Wallpaper newspapers: See Clarence S. Brigham, "Wall-Paper Newspapers of the Civil War," in *A Tribute to Wilberforce Eames: Bibliographical Essays*

(New York: Burt Franklin, 1968 facsimile reprint of 1924 edition), 203–209; see also "Famous Fakes 4: Vicksburg *Daily Citizen* Facsimiles," in *Archival Chronicle* 21.1 (March 2002), posted at http://www.bgsu.edu/colleges/library/cac/ac0203.html. For image of the paper, see http://www.loc.gov/exhibits/treasures/images/vc46a.4p1.jpg.

45   ostraca: See http://www.usc.edu/dept/LAS/wsrp/educational_site/ancient_texts/ostraca.shtm/pennnews/releases/2002/Q1/hamlet.html.

47   "very convenient method": Petroski, 179.

47   Engine Company 22: See Glenn Collins, "With Chalk on Slate, History Is Preserved," *New York Times*, May 17, 2002.

48   Diamond Sutra: Carter, chap. VII; Hunter, 61.

49   "beyond the point": Stein, *Sand-Buried Ruins*, xix, 405.

49   "It was not sand . . . and other rubbish": Ibid., 367. For a consideration of "what our garbage tells us about ourselves," with specific attention given to the Fish Kills landfill on Staten Island, N.Y. (where the debris from the World Trade Center was taken and sorted in 2001–2002), see William Rathje and Cullen Murphy, *Rubbish! The Archaeology of Garbage* (New York: HarperCollins, 1992).

49   "the first specimens": Ibid., 371.

49   "On the south . . . perfectly preserved": Stein, *Ruins of Desert Cathay*, vol. 1, 393–394.

50   Papyri: For full texts of recovered materials at Oxyrhynchus, see Loeb Classical Library, A. S. Hunt and C. C. Edgar, *Select Papyri*, 4 vols. (Cambridge, Mass.: Harvard University Press, 1932). For a recent bilingual edition of the works of Sappho, featuring a photograph of an Oxyrhynchus papyri on the dust jacket and superb endnotes on the individual poems, see Anne Carson, trans., *If Not, Winter: Fragments of Sappho* (New York: Alfred A. Knopf, 2002). Also, for a profile of Dirk Obbink, curator of the papyrus collection at Ashmolean Museum, see Tom Dunkel, "Puzzle Master," in *Smithsonian* 33:6 (Sept. 2002): 36–38.

52   "Storage" "treasury," . . . "burial": Jeff Sharlet, "Jewish-Studies Project Aims to Catalogue Documentary Bonanza of Jewish Archive," *Chronicle of Higher Education*, Nov. 12, 1999.

52 "When the spirit": Quoted in Bentwich, 136.

52 "very ancient": Ibid., 138.

52 "I am just back . . . reveals itself to us": Deborah B. Karp, in *Women's League Outlook*, June 30, 1997.

53 Albert D. Friedberg grant: *Christianity Today* 43:14 (Dec. 6, 1999): 23.

54 "anonymous dealer": John Darnton, "Fragile Scrolls Cast New Light on Early Buddhism," *New York Times*, July 7, 1996.

54 "These birch . . . fragile": Salomon, xiii.

54 "reliable information . . . value": Ibid., 20.

55 "There was a gradual . . . then to China": *New York Times*, July 7, 1996.

55 "Unfortunately . . . preparation": Salomon, 107. For a textual evaluation of the birch bark scrolls, see Richard Salomon, *A Gāndhārī Version of the Rhinoceros Sūtra* (Seattle: University of Washington Press, 2001), vol. 1. The historic region known as Gandhara where the scrolls were located came to the attention of the world in March 2001 when Taliban fanatics deliberately destroyed two colossal statues of Buddha that had been carved into the cliff face at Bamiyan two thousand years ago. For a photographic appreciation and a poignant essay of the statuary unique to the area, see Bérénice Geoffroy-Schneiter, *Gandhara: The Memory of Afghanistan* (New York: Assouline, 2001).

56 "They were two": R. C. Longworth, *Chicago Tribune*, Dec. 21, 1988.

56 For more on Vindolanda discoveries, see Bowman.

57 Centre for the Study of Ancient Documents: http://www.csad.ac.uk.

57 "It is mainly . . . these precious records": Stein, *Sand-Buried Ruins*, 367.

Chapter 3: The Ozymandias Factor

59 human beings: Schnapp, 11–12.

60 "We have to engage": Ibid., 18.

61 "But the *Voyager* record": Sagan et al., 42.

62   "He made good laws": *The Complete Works of Lord Macaulay* (London: Longmans, 1898), vol. 11, "On the Royal Society of Literature," 219–227.

62   Great Rock of Behistun: See Fagan, *Return*, 70–82.

63   "On reaching . . . Rosetta Stone": Quoted in Fagan, *Eyewitness*, 100–104.

65   "The inscription": Blair, 3.

65   For more on Halbherr and Gortyn Code, see Godart, 21–34.

66   Museum of Classical Archaeology: See http://www.classics.cam.ac.uk/museum/guideearlyclass.html.

68   Nineveh: See Austen H. Layard, *Discoveries in the Ruins of Nineveh and Babylon* (London: John Murray, 1853); Gordon Waterfield, *Layard of Nineveh* (London: John Murray, 1963); Fagan, *Eyewitness*, 90–99, and *Return*, 90–137.

69   "furnish us . . . transcribed": Ibid., 129; see also Russell, 28–29.

70   "relating the command": Ryan and Pitman, 46–47.

70   "It's the most important piece": Fawn Vrazo, "In Storage Area of British Museum, Researcher Makes a Key Discovery," *Philadelphia Inquirer*, Nov. 30, 1998. For geological evidence of the great deluge that may have inspired the Gilgamesh epic, see Rosie Mestel, "Noah's Flood," *New Scientist*, Oct. 4, 1997, 24. For evolution of *Gilgamesh* as a literary work, see Tigay.

71   "the centre": Matthiae, 225.

71   Royal Archives of Ebla: See Alfonso Archi, in Weiss, 140–148.

72   "These documents": Archi, in Weiss, 140.

72   "A new world": Pettinato, 3

73   Claudius as Etruscan scholar: See Haynes, 185.

73   *haruspices*. Tacitus, *Annals*, 11.15; Haynes, 386

74   "Etruria is the originator": Quoted in Keller, 79.

74   "For an unknown language": Velther Valerius, *The History of Etruria*, at http://www.mysteriousetruscans.com/history4.html.

74   "There is no *point d'appui*": Massimo Palottino, *The Meaning of Archaeology* (New York: Harry N. Abrams, 1968), 161; see also Bonfante and Bonfante, 330, 333.

75   "It is no Rosetta Stone": Bonfante and Bonfante, 346.

75   "The number of surviving mirrors": Ibid., 347.

76   *abacus:* For a photo of the Etruscan counting board, see ibid., 344.

76   *Liber Linteus*: See Gabor Z. Bodroghy, "The Etruscan Liber Linteus," at http://users.tpg.com.au/etr/etrusk/default.html.

78   Mawangtui discovery: Henricks, *Lao-Tẓu Te-Tao Ching*, passim.

78   "documents of which": Ibid., xii–xiv.

78   Guodian discovery: Henricks, *Lao Tẓu's Tao Te Ching*, passim.

79   "They became so brilliant": Andrea Shen, "Ancient Script Rewrites History," *Harvard University Gaẓette*, Feb. 22, 2001, text posted at http://www.news.harvard.edu/gazette/2001/02.22/07-ancientscript.html.

79   "Chinese equivalent": http://www.dartmouth.edu/~news/releases/1998/apr98/chinese.html.

80   Copper Scroll: See Wise et al., 188–199; Vermes, 583.

81   Nag Hammadi Library: See Rudolph.

81   *Gospel According to Thomas:* Pagels, xv.

81   "The focus that brought . . . movement": James Robinson, 1–3.

82   Michael Ventris and Linear B: Andrew Robinson, passim. See also Ceram, 102–110; John Chadwick, in Hooker, 167; Singh, 130–142.

83   "The disc is of high quality": Godart, 61.

84   "first typewritten document": Chadwick, in Hooker, 114, 190.

84   "Why was it found": Godart, 16.

84   "English . . . foreign language": Foster, xv.

85   "with a pen of iron": Quoted in Baike, 30.

86   "not only . . . the king": Mercer, vol. 1, xi.

86   Derivation of *paper* and *volume*: Alma Davenport, 6?

87   "sacred carved letters": Parkinson, 138

87   Derveni Papyrus colloquium: Laks and Most.

88   "I don't think": Quoted in John Noble Wilford, "Mummy's Bequest: Poems From a Master," *New York Times*, Nov. 26, 2002. See also Lara Suziedelis Bogle, "Rare Greek Scroll Found With Egyptian Mummy," *National Geographic News*, Oct. 28, 2002.

90   For more on Philodemus Project, see: www.humnet.ucla/edu/humnet/ classics/philodemus/philhome.htm.

90   "Works of Latin . . . revelations": Quoted in Shirley Hazzard, "Quest for a Fabled Ancient Library," *New York Times Magazine*, May 10. 1987. See also Deiss, passim.

91   "They are written . . . through the ages": Gigante, 3

91   "We are dealing": Alan Riding, "A Battle of Words and Stones; Near Vesuvius, the Hunt for a Library Faces Modern Politics," *New York Times*, July 15, 1997.

92   "grave danger": "Great Cultural Treasure at Risk," *Times* (London), Mar. 13, 2002.

Chapter 4: Ex Libris Punicis

93   "All history": George Orwell, *1984* (New York: Harcourt, Brace, 1949), 41.

94   "Who controls the past": Ibid., 251.

94   Holocaust diaries: For excerpts from fifty-five journals written throughout Europe during World War II and discovered since the publication of *Anne Frank: The Diary of a Young Girl* in 1952, see Alexandra Zapruder, *Salvaged Pages: Young Writers' Diaries of the Holocaust* (New Haven, Conn.: Yale University Press, 2002).

94   "Dear finder, search everywhere": Patterson, 274.

95   "After the house search": Victor Klemperer, *I Will Bear Witness: A Diary of the Nazi Years 1942–1945* (New York: Random House, 1999), 61.

96   "I laid . . . it might be": Ringelblum, xxi.

96   "There are illegal": Ibid., 132.

97   "Only a handful of our friends": Ibid., xx.

97   "The historiography of the Holocaust": Leon Wieseltier, *New Republic*, May 3, 1993, 16. Ringelblum's works have been translated and published in eight languages; an advocate of armed resistance, he was the model for the hero of John Hersey's *The Wall* (New York: Alfred A. Knopf, 1950), the first novel written by an American about the Holocaust. A similar archival project was undertaken in the Kovno Ghetto of Lithuania from 1941 to 1944. One of the participants, George Kadish, took hundreds of clandestine photographs, many of them through a buttonhole, using film he stole from a hospital X-ray laboratory where he worked. Many of his photos were displayed at a 1997 exhibition at the U.S. Holocaust Memorial Museum. See Hank Burchard, "Kovno's Terrible Time Capsule," *Washington Post*, Nov. 28, 1997.

98   "The Jewish Quarter": Stroop, title page.

99   "an obsession with documentation": Andrzej Wirth, introduction to Stroop.

99   Nazi plans to pulp books: *New York Times*, May 11, 1933.

100   Jewish Studies Without Jews: Fishman, 4.

100   "Museum of an Extinct Race": See Altshuler, passim. See also "The Jewish Museum in Prague Renewed," in *Jewish Heritage Report* 1:2 (summer 1997), electronic version posted at: http://www.isjm.org/jhr/no2/museums2.html; Carolyn Barta, "A Daunting History," *Dallas Morning News*, Sept. 12, 1999.

100   "Paradoxically, the Nazis": Altshuler, 8.

100   "During the final . . . Czech Jews": Ibid., 36–38.

101   "covered with caviar" and "covered with sour cream": Marianna Tax Choldin in *Censorship in the Slavic World*, catalog of an exhibition at the New York Public Library, 1984.

101   "You not only had": David Remnick, "Russian Resurrected; Unmuzzling Soviet Writers—and Their Literature," *Washington Post,* Aug. 26, 1990.

102   "I see their eyes": Solzhenitsyn, 25.

102   "the eradication": Hedrick, 246.

104   "After the Conquest": Savage, 45.

104   "the rapid displacement": Baugh, 117.

104   By 1248: Savage, 45.

105   "God forbid": Baugh, 164.

105   In 1362: Ibid., 181–182.

105   John Gower is discussed incisively by Michael Schmidt in *Lives of the Poets* (New York: Alfred A. Knopf, 1999), 30–48; for the seventeenth-century antiquarian Sir Robert Cotton's collecting activities, see Basbanes, *Gentle Madness,* 89–96.

106   Solidarity with the English: Baugh, 179.

106   "The first finder": Thomas Hoccleve (1368–1450), in the poem *The Regiment of Princes* (c. 1411), line 4978.

106   Charles Blockson: Basbanes, *Gentle Madness,* 398–404.

107   "Perhaps they asked her": Gates and McKay, xxxi.

107   "We whose Names": Ibid., xxxi–xxxii.

108   For more on the life and pottery inscriptions of Dave the Potter, see Koverman.

111   For publication history of the *Aeneid,* see Kenneth Quinn, *Virgil's Aeneid,* 23–64.

112   Quotations from *The Aeneid* are from the Loeb Classical Library edition of *Virgil* (vol. I), translated by H. R. Fairclough, revised by G. P. Goold (Cambridge, Mass.: Harvard University Press, 1999): "the capital of all nations," 203; "smitten with a grievous love-pang," 423; "with equal sovereignty," 429; "Let no love or treaty," 465.

113   Quotations from *Appian's Roman History* are from the Loeb Classical Library edition (vol. I, "The Punic Wars"), translated by Horace White

(Cambridge, Mass.: Harvard University Press, 1982): "has been severely criticized," xi; "Gentlemen . . . wonderful success and power," 491; Byrsa, 403; Cato, 515; "They became a match," 405; Carthaginian harbor, 567.

113   "all too ready": Grant, *Readings,* 523.

115   UNESCO archaeologists: Lancel, 427.

115   Qart Hadasht: Starr, 479.

115   "from Phoenicia": Michael Brett, "Carthage: The God in Stone," *History Today* 47:2 (Feb. 1997): 44.

115   "these Phoenicians:" Frank Moore Cross, in Senner, 78–79.

116   For an overview of research on Phoenician and Punic languages, including illustrations of alphabetic characters and surviving inscriptions on coins, see J. Brian Peckham, *Development of the Late Phoenician Scripts* (Cambridge, Mass.: Harvard University Press, 1968).

116   *sopherim:* Lancel, 357; Peckham, chap. 5.

116   "Neopunic" religious inscription: Lancel, 437; Di Vita and Di Vita-Evrad, 33; Peckham, passim.

116   "Many . . . the state": Aristotle, *Politics,* rev. Oxford trans. (Princeton, N.J.: Princeton University Press, 1984), vol. 2, 2019–2021.

117   African princes: Lancel, 358.

117   Quotations from the *Natural History* of Pliny are from the Harvard Classical Library edition, trans. H. Rackham (Cambridge, Mass.: Harvard University Press, 1945); see Lancel, 274, 358.

117   *bibliothecae* of Pliny (book XVIII, 22–23), discussed in Lancel, 358.

117   "could very well have imitated": Lancel, 358.

118   "What men inhabited . . . *ex libris Punicis*": Loeb Classical Library edition of *Sallust,* trans. J. C. Rolfe (Cambridge, Mass.: Harvard University Press, 1921; revised 1931), 171.

118   "I have undertaken": Quoted by Henri Troyat in *Flaubert* (New York: Viking, 1992), 159.

119   Carthaginian inscriptions: See Pedley.

119   "*Why this emptiness*": Quoted in Di Vita and Di Vita-Evrad, 4.

119   "It is remarkable": Disraeli, vol. 1, 67.

120   "burning of the books": Gallankamp, 11–14.

120   "We found a great number . . . caused them great grief ": Pagden, 124; for reproductions of the four surviving Maya codices, see Coe and Kerr, 169–182; Landa's Maya "signs" and "alphabet" reproduced in Coe, 102–105.

120   "a stupid zeal": Quoted in Coe and Kerr, 89.

121   "It lay . . . impenetrable mystery": Quoted in Fash, 9.

121   Maya writing system: Coe and Kerr, 63; Floyd G. Lounsbury, in Senner, 214. For the earlier development of Zapotec writing, see John M. D. Pohl, *Exploring Mesoamerica* (Oxford, England: Oxford University Press, 1999), 50.

121   "The books": Thomas A. Lee Whiting, "The Maya Codices," in Peter Schmidt, ed., *Maya* (New York: Rizzoli, 1998), 206–215.

123   "It is a fact . . . writing": Coe, 99–100.

123   "I will set . . . *ad infinitum*": Pagden, 43, 124; Coe and Kerr, 36, 169–170, 229.

123   Yuri Knorosov: Coe, 145–166. (Michael Coe dedicated *Breaking the Maya Code* to the memory of the Russian epigrapher.)

124   "critical mass": Norman Hammond, "Ancient Civilizations Lost and Found," in *Times* (London), Dec. 5, 1992; see also Coe, 50.

124   Book burnings in Germany: Frederick T. Birchall, "Nazi Book-Burning Fails to Stir Berlin," *New York Times*, May 11, 1933.

125   "You can burn": Quoted in Stern, 3.

126   "They got my name wrong": Quoted in "Book Burning Recollections," an editorial, *Washington Post*, May 31, 1977.

127   From Mehring: "I was driven," 18; "I was not," 176; "A man can become," 18; "Never had I possessed," 256.

128   "one of the seminal figures": See David Rosand, "Reason's Secrets," *The New Republic*, Aug. 23, 1999, 33; Joseph Leo Koerner, "Paleface and Redskin," *The New Republic*, March 24, 1997, 30.

129   "He believed his library": Chernow, 286.

129   "From floor to ceiling": Gombrich, 332.

129   Declared off-limits to scholars: Ibid., 404.

130   Move to London: Chernow, 265. For more on the Warburg Institute see http://www.sas.ac.uk/Warburg.htm.

131   "The Anglo-Saxon culture": Ibid., 408. The Warburg Institute was not the only instance of a library migration during World War II. The transplantation of books from the Vilna Ghetto in Lithuania to New York City and the relocation to Manhattan of the YIVO Institute for Jewish Research were carried out by a very resourceful group of people known as the "paper brigade" who used a variety of smuggling schemes during the war to get books out of occupied Europe, and by various acquisitions afterward. For a full account of the growth and institutionalization of the collections in New York, see Dawidowicz, 262–264; Fishman, passim.

Chapter 5: From the Ashes

133   For detail on destruction of National and University Library of Bosnia and Herzegovina, and a summary account of its holdings, see András Riedl-mayer, "Libraries Are Not for Burning: International Librarianship and the Recovery of the Destroyed Heritage of Bosnia and Herzegovina," *INSPEL* 30:1 (1996): 82–91.

134   "What is more important": Archibald MacLeish, "The Premise of Meaning," a speech given at the dedication of Scott Library, York University, Toronto; published in *American Scholar* 41:3 (summer 1972): 357–362.

134   Muslims, Serbians, and Croatians: Len A. Costa, "The Libraries: Another Kind of War Victim," *New York Times,* June 13, 1998.

136   "The Serbs did not": Mark Danner, "Bosnia: The Turning Point," *New York Review of Books,* Feb. 5, 1998. For more on the destruction of the library: Ellen Barry, "How the Vijecnica Was Lost," *Metropolis,* June 1999; Ivan Lovrenovic, "The Hatred of Memory," *New York Times,* May 28, 1994.

136   "culturecide": Robert Fisk, *Independent* (London), June 20, 1994. For more on "ethnic cleansing," see Michael A. Sells, *The Bridge Betrayed: Religion and Genocide in Bosnia* (Berkeley: University of California Press, 1996).

138   Bosnian Manuscript Ingathering Project: www.applicom.com/manu/ ingather.htm.

139   Sabre Foundation: Established in 1969, the organization shipped 3.7 million books abroad during its first thirty years of operation, most of them works in the English language donated by two hundred North American publishers, with a retail value of $105 million. In 1999, Sabre donated nearly half a million books to twenty-two different countries, including eighty-five hundred volumes to Somalia, a nation that for years had lacked a functioning central government. Focusing mostly on "developing and transitional" societies, Sabre's program began in central and eastern Europe, and expanded to countries in the former Soviet Union, Asia, Africa, the Caribbean, and Latin America. Source: "Sabre Foundation, Inc.: Report for 1999." See http://www.sabre.org.

140   WorldCat: Ron Chepesiuk, "From Rubble to Reconstruction: Rebuilding Bosnian Libraries," *American Libraries* 31:2 (Feb. 1, 2000): 22. For more on OCLC project, see: www.oclc.org/oclc/research/publications/review96/ bosnia.htm.

142   "sinister figures . . . burned": Whitlock, vol. 1, 168.

142   "in nine or ten hours": Quoted in John Horne and Alan Kramer, "German Atrocities and Franco-German Opinion, 1914: The Evidence of German Soldiers' Diaries," *Journal of Modern History* 66:1 (March 1994): 39.

143   "At Louvain": Ibid., 387.

143   ninety-three German professors: Horne and Kramer, 1–33.

143   "We shall wipe it out": Quoted in Martin Gilbert, *The First World War: A Complete History* (New York: Henry Holt, 1994), 42–43.

143   "Oxford of Belgium": John Keegan, *The First World War* (New York: Alfred A. Knopf, 1999), 82–83. See Stubbings, chaps. 7 and 8.

144   Article 247 of the Treaty of Versailles: *American Journal of International Law* 13:3 Suppl: Official Documents (July 1919): 277.

144   For split of the University of Louvain, see Stephen Milligan, "Belgium: A Most Unnatural Country," *The Economist,* Jan. 19, 1980.

146   For more on Sarajevo Haggadah, see András Riedlmayer, "*Convivencia* Under Fire: Genocide and Book Burning in Bosnia," in Rose, 266–291.

148   "At about 9:30 P.M.": Kemal Bakaršic, "The Libraries of Sarajevo and the Book that Saved Our Lives," *The New Combat* (autumn 1994): 13–15. Complete text of the essay posted at http://www.openbook.ba/obq/no3/kemo.htm.

151   San Lazzaro Island: See Yardemian, passim.

151   Apostle of Armenia: Evans, in *Glory*, 351.

152   coinage of word *genocide:* Marilyn Henry, "A Genocide Denied," *Jerusalem Post*, May 28, 1999; see Weitz, passim.

153   From *Lord Byron's Letters*, vol. 5: "I am studying," 130; "I had begun," 137; "a very pretty," 140–141; "I can assure you," 156. From vol. 6: "You must not," 29.

155   "distinctive": Evans, 351.

155   Polish collections in Russia: Danuta Górecki, "The Zaluskis' Library of the Republic of Poland," *Journal of Library History* 13:4 (1978): 408–431; Mary Stuart, *Aristocrat-Librarian in Service to the Tsars: Alexsei Nikolaevich Olenin and the Imperial Public Library* (Boulder, Colo.: East European Monographs, 1986), 30–33; Mary Stuart, "The Evolution of Librarianship in Russia: The Librarians of the Imperial Public Library, 1808–1868," *The Library Quarterly* 64:1 (Jan. 1994): 1–29.

155   Catherine the Great: Stanley Meisler, "The Hermitage," *Smithsonian* 25:12 (Mar. 1995): 40. See also Malcolm Bradbury, *To the Hermitage* (London: Picador, 2000), a lively novel based on Diderot's relationship with Catherine; Katya Galitzine, *St. Petersburg: The Hidden Interiors* (New York: Vendome Press, 1999).

156   Polish Library in Paris: Francisca Granier, *Les Tribulations de la Bibliothèque Polonaise de Paris* (Paris: Les Amis de la Démocratie en Pologne, 1956); Irene Galezowska, *Bibliothèque Polonaise de Paris 1839–1939* (Paris: Bibliothèque Polonaise, 1946). See also William G. Atwood, *The Parisian Worlds of Frédéric Chopin* (New Haven, Conn.: Yale University Press, 1999).

156   Systematic program to eradicate Polish culture and loss of books: See Stubbings, chaps. 2 and 3; Barbara Bieńkowska, *Losses of Polish Libraries During World War II*, trans. Krystyna Cekalska (Warsaw: Polish Cultural Heritage, 1994); Marek Sroka, "The University of Cracow Library under Nazi Occupation: 1939–1945," *Libraries & Culture* 34:1 (winter 1999): 1–16. For more

on the partition of Poland, see Norman Davies, *God's Playground: A History of Poland* (New York: Oxford University Press, 1982).

158   "tens of thousands": *New York Times,* July 26, 1989. See also: Beth Van Schaack, "The Crime of Political Genocide: Repairing the Genocide Convention's Blind Spot," *Yale Law Journal* 106:7 (May 1997): 2259–2291; Jeanne Malmgren, "One Woman's Mission to Save Cambodia," *St. Petersburg Times,* Oct. 8, 2000.

158   "We must rid": Quoted in Chandler, 44. See also Van Schaack; op. cit.; Chandler, 43.

159   "Since cultural knowledge": Seth Mydans, "Khmer Dancers Try to Save an Art Form Ravaged by War," *New York Times,* Dec. 30, 1993.

159   Cornell project: See John F. Dean, "The Preservation of Books and Manuscripts in Cambodia," *American Archivist* 53 (spring 1990): 262–297; John F. Dean, "The Preservation and Conservation Needs of the Upper Regions of Southeast Asia," *Libri* 47:3 (Sept. 1997): 123–138; "Cornell Tries to Help Cambodia Preserve Its Past," *New York Times,* July 26, 1989.

162   S-21: Chandler, 41–76; Michael Kimmelman, "Poignant Faces of the Soon-to-be-Dead," *New York Times,* June 20, 1997.

163   Tuol Sleng Museum of Genocide: A 1997 exhibition at the Museum of Modern Art in New York, "The Killing Fields," presented twenty-two of the haunting images.

171   "entire corpus": See Library of Congress catalog entry at http://www.loc.gov/acq/devpol/colloverviews/tibetan.html.

171   "Four Olds": See Karan, passim, and Althea Hennedige, "The Cultural Revolution and Its Legacy in Tibet," *Columbia East Asian Review* 2:1 (spring 1998), for detail on Chou En-lai's decision to preserve just fourteen monasteries, along with additional pertinent essays by Lisa Keary, Matthew Bell, Brian Lafferty, and others; posted on-line at http://www.columbia.edu/cu/ccba/cear/issues/spring98/text-only/hennsidebar2.htm.

172   "everything under the sun": Quoted in Barbara Stewart, "War Resister Becomes Savior of Tibet's Literature," *New York Times,* June 15, 2002. See also Michael Paulson, "One for the Sages: Tibetologist Aims to Turn Archive into a Resource," *Boston Globe,* Apr. 20, 2001, and Lopez, passim.

173   Fragile Palm Leaves Project: See http://www.palitext.demon.co.uk/subpages/project.htm.

174   Repatriation of Icelandic manuscripts: See Greenfield, 10–46.

175   "outstanding example": Oliver Meyer, *The International Lawyer* 25:4 (winter 1991): 1096.

176   Árni Magnússon collection: See Robert Wernick, "Sagas Are Still Alive and Kicking for Icelanders," *Smithsonian* 16:10 (Jan. 1986): 114. See the institute website: http://www.hi.is/HI/Ranns/SAM/main.html.

177   "The prose literature": Smiley, in Thorssen, ix.

Chapter 6: Shelf Life

182   "Are these titles . . . read-by date": Ian Watson, "A Short Shelf Life," *New Scientist,* June 15, 1996.

183   Sturgis Library: See Eugene Exman, *A Short History of the Sturgis Library* (Barnstable, Mass.: The Sturgis Library, 1997), and Helen Lathrop Taber, *A New Home in Mattakeese: A Guide to Reverend John Lothrop's Barnstable* (Yarmouth Port, Mass.: privately printed, 1995), both available through the library.

186   "book-breaking": One of the more flagrant episodes of text desecration in recent years involved Gilbert Bland ("the Al Capone of cartography"), whose activities are explored by Miles Harvey in *The Island of Lost Maps: A True Story of Cartographic Crime* (New York: Random House, 2000).

187   Sale of Audubon to Sheik: See *"Birds of America* Takes Off," *Maine Antiques Digest,* May 2000; on-line version available at: http://www.maineantiquedigest.com/other/cont0500.htm.

188   "artistic vandalism": Geraldine Norman, "How Art Dealer Did a Pounds 13m Swap with Rulers of Iran," *Independent* (London), Oct. 17, 1994.

188   Houghton *Shahnameh*: For details on the making of the book, and for exquisite reproductions of the plates, see *The Houghton Shahnameh*, intro. and descr. Martin Bernard Dickson and Stuart Cary Welch, 2 vols. (Cambridge, Mass.: Fogg Art Museum/Harvard University Press, 1981).

190   For more on Thomas Hoving and Arthur Houghton, see Thomas Hoving, *Making the Mummies Dance: Inside the Metropolitan Museum of Art* (New York: Simon & Schuster, 1993), passim.

190   Arthur Houghton as bibliophile: For background on the sale of his private library at auction in 1979, see Basbanes, *Gentle Madness*, 229–231.

191   "powerful" person: Nicolas Barker, obituary of Arthur Houghton, *Independent* (London), Apr. 12, 1990. See also George James, "Arthur Houghton Jr., 83, Dies; Led Steuben Glass," *New York Times*, Apr. 4, 1990.

191   *Shahnameh* remnants to Iran: For more on David Geffen's role in acquiring the de Kooning painting, see Tom King, *The Operator: David Geffen Builds, Buys, and Sells the New Hollywood* (New York: Random House, 2000).

192   "a great day for commerce": Souren Melikian, "Destroying a Treasure: The Sad Story of a Manuscript," *International Herald Tribune*, Apr. 27, 1996.

193   "The present edition": Michael Levy, "The Very Rich Hours of the Shah," *New York Review of Books*, Oct. 7, 1982.

193   James Jerome Hill Reference Library: *The James Jerome Hill Reference Library*, a brief history published by the library in 1996 in conjunction with its seventy-fifth anniversary. See Robert Franklin, "Hill Family and Foundation Squabble Over Charity's Future," *Star Tribune* (Minneapolis), Jan. 31, 1994. For life of founder: Michael P. Malone, *James J. Hill: Empire Builder of the Northwest* (Norman: University of Oklahoma Press, 1966); Albro Martin, *James J. Hill and the Opening of the Northwest* (St. Paul: Minnesota Historical Society Press, 1991).

198   Seth Eastman: See Patricia Condon Johnston, "Seth Eastman's West," *American History*, Oct. 1996

200   "A basic disregard," "ongoing decimation," "If it's not bolted": Quoted in Richard Chin, "Sale of Hill Art Sets Scene for Intense Conflict, *St. Paul Pioneer Press*, July 2, 1995.

200   "It seems . . . vision for the library": ffolliott and Krech, in Boehme et al., xxi.

201   *New York Times* reporting of the New-York Historical Society deaccession controversy: Douglas C. McGill, "Museum's Downfall: Raiding Endowment to Pay for Growth," July 19, 1988; Douglas C. McGill, "Criticism Moves Historical Society, a Little," July 25, 1988; Ralph Blumenthal, "Try-

ing to Keep the Historical Society a la Mode," Dec. 6, 1994; Michael Kimmelman, "Should Old Masters Be Fund-Raisers?" Jan. 8, 1995. The controversy is detailed thoroughly in Guthrie. For history of the society, see Walter Muir Whitehill, *Independent Historical Societies* (Boston: Boston Athenæum, 1962), 38–64; Glenn Collins, "Lost and Found: Historic Treasures," *New York Times,* July 31, 2000.

202   "If you start": Quoted in Guthrie, 5.

202   word leaked out: See Geoff Edgers, "Seeking a Solution in the Books," *Boston Globe,* Aug. 14, 2002.

203   Mass Hort Library: See Robert Fraker, "The Building of the Massachusetts Horticultural Society Library," *Journal of the New England Garden History Society* 8 (fall 2000): 38–45.

205   "suffering . . . available cash": Edgers, op. cit.

205   "If I am to retain": Quoted in Geoff Edgers, "Horticultural Society in a Fiscal Squeeze," *Boston Globe,* Mar. 21, 2002.

206   "There are complete runs": Quoted in William Mullen, "Botanic Garden Gets Book Bonanza," *Chicago Tribune,* Oct. 29, 2002.

207   "our endowment": Quoted in *Important Botanical Books From the Massachusetts Horticultural Society: Wednesday, 18 December 2002* (New York: Christie's, 2002), 9.

209   Wormsley Library: See Fletcher. For profiles of John Carter Brown, Henry Clay Folger, and Estelle Doheny as collectors, see Basbanes, *Gentle Madness,* 12–13, 161–162; 184–185, 197–199; 29–30, 215–218.

212   "had not . . . special collection": Quoted in Oliver Swanton, "Wave Goodbye to the Silver," *Guardian* (London), Feb. 2, 1999.

212   "This sale": Ibid. See also Oliver Swinton, "Lost Pages of History: A University Library Needs Funds. What to Do? Sell the Books, of Course," *Independent* (London), March 19, 1999.

212   "beneath contempt": Quoted in Roger Highfield, "Fury at Pounds 1m Keele Sale of Maths Collection," *Daily Telegraph* (London), Dec. 22, 1998.

212   "marks the desecration": Ibid.

212   "Keele never": Quoted in Swanton, op. cit.

212   "There wasn't . . . university": Quoted in Highfield, op. cit.

213   "The incunabula . . . a fat cheque": McKitterick, 202–207.

214   Low Countries collections and University of Nijmegen accession: See *Netherlandic Treasures at the University of Michigan Library,* catalog of an exhibition, June 3–Aug. 16, 2002 (Ann Arbor: University of Michigan Library, 2002).

217   "crucial theoretical work": Robert J. Lifton, "German Doctors and the Final Solution," *New York Times Magazine,* Sept. 21, 1986.

217   *Issues in Law & Medicine* essays: Patrick G. Derr, "Hadamar, Hippocrates, and the Future of Medicine: Reflections and the History of German Medicine," 4:4 (Mar. 22, 1989): 487; Karl Binding, "Essay One: Legal Explanation; Permitting the Destruction of an Unworthy Life," 8:2 (Sept. 22, 1992): 231; Alfred Hoche, "Essay Two: Medical Explanation; Permitting the Destruction of an Unworthy Life," 8:2 (Sept. 22, 1992): 255.

220   "When plant pathology . . . before": *Cornell Magazine* 102:4 (Jan.-Feb. 2000).

221   "a hot . . . involved": Stam, 5–10. The deaccession symposium at Brown was occasioned by the decision of the trustees of the John Carter Brown Library to sell at auction a small collection of extremely valuable European manuscripts that had been given to the institution over the years as gifts, but which were clearly not within the "scope" of the library's mandate to "collect everything printed during the colonial period that reflects what happened as a result of the discovery of the New World." In a three-page introduction to the sale catalog, *Western Illuminated Manuscripts* (New York: Sotheby Parke Bernet, 1981), the trustees explained how and why the decision to sell the material was reached. They quoted from the will of one of the principal benefactors, Louisa Dexter Sharpe Metcalf, who stipulated when she made her bequest that the library could sell the manuscripts at any time if they thought the proceeds would benefit the institution. One of the most important items sold at the sale—the Ottobeuren Gradual and Sacramentary, circa 1164—was bought by John Paul Getty Jr., and is today regarded as one of the prize possessions of his Wormsley Library (see chap. 6).

222   Mark Singer: Mark Singer, "Missed Opportunities Dept." (The Talk of the Town), *The New Yorker,* Jan. 12, 1998, 29–30. For profile of Zinman's collecting, see Basbanes, *Gentle Madness,* 301–307; in 2000, Zinman's collection of American Imprints was sold to Library Company of Philadelphia for

$8 million, of which $3 million was a gift. See Stephan Salisbury, "Library Company Gets Rare Early Documents," *Philadelphia Inquirer*, Mar. 5, 2000.

223 "prior to 1998 . . . as deemed appropriate": New York Public Library Policy on Deaccession and Disposition of Library Materials, dated Feb. 17, 1999, copy furnished to the author.

224 Sale of British Library newspaper discards: See Nicholson Baker, *Double Fold* (New York: Random House, 2001); Susannah Herbert, "The Sale of the Century's History," *Daily Telegraph* (London), July 24, 2000. For more on Nicholson Baker as "library activist," see Basbanes, *Patience & Fortitude*, chap. 9.

227 "obsessed": Cox et al., 5.

227 "This chapter": Ibid., 7.

227 "The public can find": Ibid., 13.

228 "*everything* should be saved": Ibid., 2.

Chapter 7: Ingenious Cipher

229 "liminal devices . . . bindings": Genette, 1–16. For paratextual qualities of manuscripts, see Cerquiglini. A fascinating component of the paratextual element is explored in chap. 7 of Brown and Duguid, by Paul Duguid, who writes about a medical historian who sniffs 250-year-old letters for traces of vinegar to chart the course of cholera in an eighteenth-century Colonial American community. The condiment was used as a disinfectant during times of epidemic.

230 "In her isolation . . . critical concern": Ralph W. Franklin, *The Manuscript Books of Emily Dickinson* (Cambridge, Mass.: The Belknap Press of Harvard University Press, 1981), vol. 1, ix

231 For a full consideration of William Blake's creation of unique books, see Viscomi; see also Peter Ackroyd, *Blake: A Biography* (New York: Alfred A. Knopf, 1996), chap. 9. For a thorough appreciation of the elegant results, see *William Blake: The Complete Illuminated Books* (New York: Thames & Hudson, 2000).

232   "bewildering multitude . . . no taste": Palache, 247.

232   "He worked . . . thought out": Porter, 400–401.

233   *Tristram Shandy:* In October 2000, the Special Collections department of the University of Glasgow library featured Laurence Sterne's comic masterpiece as its "book of the month," and posted a detailed discussion of the making of the book at its website, with learned commentary by Julie Coleman, director of the department, and featuring numerous reproductions of the novel from first-edition copies among its holdings. See http://special.lib.gla.ac.uk/exhibns/month/oct2000.html. For more on Sterne's "hands-on" approach to the making of the novel, see Lewis Perry Curtis, ed., *Letters of Laurence Sterne* (Oxford: Oxford University Press, 1935); in one letter to Robert Dodsley in London, his first publisher, he stated his wish to "feel the pulse of the world" with his innovative book, and to accomplish that hopeful goal, he made clear his intention to "correct every proof myself, it shall go perfect into the world, and be printed in so creditable a way as to paper, type, &c, as to do no dishonor to you, who, I know, never chuse to print a book meanly" (80–81).

235   "Gogol . . . nothing else": Nikolai Gogol, *Lost Souls,* ed. Richard Pevear and Larissa Volokhonsky (New York: Pantheon, 1996), vii–viii.

237   *Lucile:* Sidney F. Huttner, director of special collections at the University of Iowa, has also made a project of obtaining every possible edition of Owen Meredith's novel, and in a spirit of cooperation with a colleague, exchanges duplicate copies with Terry Belanger at the University of Virginia. Huttner is the only collector I have ever met who has devoted an entire wall in his home—some seven hundred volumes—to the shelving of a single title. One essential rule he applies is that he not spend more than $25 for any copy of the book, although he did acknowledge having "strayed" on occasion to acquire a particularly coveted example. He has created an informative website documenting the endeavor at: http://staffweb.lib.uiowa.edu/shuttner/huttner.htm.

238   "With a courage . . . perpetuated' ": Leon Edel, *Henry James: A Life* (New York: Harper & Row, 1985), 624.

239   "every textual . . . reproductions": Tanselle, 100. See also "Statement on the Significance of Primary Records," in *Profession 95* (New York: Modern Language Association, 1995), 27–28, in which "physical evidence in manuscripts and printed matter" are regarded as "indispensable." Texts, accord-

ing to the statement, "are inevitably affected by the physical means of their transmission; the physical features of the artifacts conveying texts therefore play an integral role in the attempt to comprehend those texts. For this reason, the concept of a textual source must involve attention to the presentation of text, not simply to the text as a disembodied group of words."

239   "the incorrectness . . . lost": Disraeli, vol. 1, 116.

240   Revising published work: See John Blades, "Leaving Well—or Bad—Enough Alone," *Chicago Tribune*, Jan. 3, 1992.

241   "as good as it is": Robert Penn Warren, *All the King's Men*, ed. Noel Polk (New York: Harcourt, Brace, 2001).

242   *The Stand* reissued: Edwin McDowell, "Putting Back the Words," *New York Times*, Jan. 31, 1990. In 2003, the Modern Library issued a new version of Joyce Carol Oates's 1967 novel, *A Garden of Earthly Delights*, revised and updated, the author explained in an afterword, so that the "singular voices" of the characters could "infuse the text" more effectively than they were able to do thirty-six years earlier, prompting one critic to observe the following: "Revising years later may be the riskiest thing a writer can do. At best it adds a sophisticated gloss to a youthful text; at worst, it interpolates anachronistic detail and violates the integrity of the original. Revision of this sort can even be seen as cannibalism, the devouring of the younger self by the older." (Judith Shulevitz, "The CLOSE Reader; Get Me Rewrite," *New York Times Book Review*, Apr. 6, 2003.)

242   "What a delight": Quoted in William C. Carter, *Marcel Proust: A Life* (New Haven, Conn.: Yale University Press, 2000), 559.

244   "a recognizable (if variable) entity": Richard Howard, in *Les Fleurs du Mal* (Boston: David R. Godine, 1982), xix; Denis Holler, *New History of French Literature* (Cambridge, Mass.: Harvard University Press, 1989), 737.

245   "there are now . . . future printing": *Whitman* (New York: The Library of America, 1982), 148.

245   "which he has": Ibid., 1352–1354.

245   "some repetitions . . . bulk": Ibid.

246   Bodleian First Folio deaccessioned and recovered: William Dunn Macray, *Annals of the Bodleian Library* (Oxford: Oxford University Press, 1890), 52; Rogers, 78.

247   "a progressive modernizing": G. Blakemore Evans, *The Riverside Shakespeare* (Boston: Houghton Mifflin, 1974), 32.

248   "The primary aim . . . First Folio text": Charlton Hinman, *The Norton Facsimile of the First Folio of Shakespeare* (New York: W. W. Norton, 1968, reissued 1997), xxii.

249   "I know good evidence": Quoted in *New York Times,* June 20, 2002.

249   Multiple copies of *Ulysses* at Texas: A similar rationale is put forth by curators of the Alderman Library at the University of Virginia in Charlottesville to explain why it is necessary to keep eleven copies of the first edition of Walt Whitman's *Leaves of Grass* in its collections; only 795 copies were printed by the poet in 1855.

251   "establish . . . eliminated": Charles Rossman, "The Problems of Hypertextualizing *Ulysses,*" *Studies in the Novel* 22:2 (summer 1990): 13. Complete text of the essay posted at http://www.cwrl.utexas.edu/cwrl/v3n1/dgold/5_problems.html.

251   Joyce Wars: See John Kidd, "The Scandal of Ulysses," *New York Review of Books,* June 30, 1988, 32–39; Bruce Arnold, *Scandal of Ulysses* (New York: St. Martin's Press, 1992).

252   Task Force on the Artifact in the Library: For full report, see http://www.clir.org/pubs/reports/pub103/contents.html.

Chapter 8: Into Thin Air

256   "Paper . . . bad alike": "The Life of Our Present Literature," *Scientific American* 72:5 (Feb. 1895): 73.

256   "One result": Blades, 83–84.

257   "During the last . . . that fact": *The Durability of Paper: Report of Special Committee,* 1930. For American government guidelines, see Abby Smith, *The Future of the Past,* 5–7.

258   1985 report: Ibid.

259   explosion: Marjorie Sun, "The Big Problem of Brittle Books," *Science*

240:4852 (Apr. 29, 1988): 598; Richard O'Mara, "Rescue of Books Set Back," *Baltimore Sun,* Feb. 14, 1994.

259   "light odor problem": Quoted in John Fialka, "Library of Congress Thinks Pulp Fiction Isn't Simply Trash; It Hires Mr. Spatz to Save a Decaying Collection Using Dunking Machine," *Wall Street Journal,* July 10, 1997.

264   Barbara Goldsmith honored: Eleanor Blau, "Publishers Swear Off Acidic Paper," *New York Times,* Mar. 8, 1989; see also Eleanor Blau, "Saving Books From the Paper They're Printed On," *New York Times,* Nov. 27, 1994. In January 2000, the New York Public Library named the Preservation and Conservation divisions in Goldsmith's honor.

266   "great national library . . . press impossible": Samuel Swett Green, *The Public Library Movement in the United States, 1853–1893* (Boston: Gregg Press, 1972 facsimile reprint of 1913 edition), 3–4.

267   Time capsules: See Pamela LiCalzi O'Connell, "Time in a Bottle," *New York Times,* Apr. 22, 1999.

267   Crypt of Civilization: http://www.oglethorpe.edu/itcs/crypt.htm.

268   Times Capsule: *New York Times Magazine,* Dec. 5, 1999; "Figuring out," Ibid.; "One of the problems," Ibid.; "long after," Ibid. For contents, see http://www.amnh.org/exhibitions/timescapsule/contents.html.

268   "deep-time messaging": See Benford, passim, and Brand, in particular chap. 12, "Burning Libraries," and chap. 15, "10,000-Year Library," in which a proposal for a repository that takes a "long view of things" is considered, to wit: "Earth's Moon might be an ideal eventual location for the 10,000-Year Library. Over that time frame humanity's main story would be of global convergence followed by a massive diaspora into space. The diaspora's point of origin would be a prime candidate for record keeping, and the Moon offers a stable, durable site, easily accessible from space, with a good view of grandmother Earth" (98). As for collections, the library "should specialize in trends too slow to notice but that gradually dominate everything as they accumulate" (100).

269   Rosetta data disk: http://www.norsam.com/rosetta.html.

269   tests conducted: David Dorman, "Technically Speaking," *American Libraries* (Sept. 1998): 78.

270   Mo i Rana: See Joakim Philipson, senior executive officer, National Library of Norway, Rana Division, "Reviving the Dead: A Common Market for 'Document Recycling' in the Nordic-Baltic Countries?" in Pauline Connolly, ed., *Solving Collection Problems Through Repository Strategies*, Proceedings of an International Conference held in Kuopio, Finland, May 1999.

271   For an overview of storage concerns at the National Archives, see Alexander Stille, "Overload," *New Yorker*, Mar. 8, 1999, 38–44.

272   Preservation strategies: See Jeff Rothenberg, "Ensuring the Longevity of Digital Documents," *Scientific American* 272:1 (Jan. 1995): 24–29; *Avoiding Technological Quicksand: Finding a Viable Technical Foundation for Digital Preservation*, Jan. 1998, posted at http://www/clir.org/pubs/reports/rothenberg/contents.html.

273   "universal virtual computer": Anne Eisenberg, "A Universal Tool to Rescue Old Files From Obsolescence," *New York Times*, Aug. 29, 2002.

274   "While books printed": David M. Ewalt, "Preserving Data Virtually," *Information Week*, Oct. 22, 2001.

274   "In fact . . . technology": Lyman and Besser, in Ben H. Davis, ed., *Time and Bits: Managing Digital Continuity* (Los Angeles: J. Paul Getty Trust, 1998), 11.

275   From House Report 101-979, *Taking a Byte*, 101st Cong., 2nd sess.: "Federal records document," 2; "only two machines . . . but not understood," 3–4; "The Iran-Contra . . . computerized records," 9–10.

276   "We're down to only": Mark Johnson, "Information Age Artifacts in Danger of Disappearing," *Tampa Tribune*, Oct. 11, 1999. Just how far-reaching the problem has become was dramatized in two videos: *Into the Future: On the Preservation of Knowledge in the Electronic Age* (1997), and *Slow Fires: On the Preservation of the Human Record* (1987) by Terry Sanders, produced in association with the Commission on Preservation and Access and the American Council of Learned Societies and aired on PBS; they are available from the American Film Foundation, 1333 Ocean Ave., Santa Monica, Calif. 90406.

276   "The problem with the Internet": Quoted in Celestine Bohlen, "A Lover of Literary Puzzles," *New York Times*, Oct. 19, 2002.

277   "is that the easier . . . self-centered and lazy": Deanna B. Marcum, "We Can't Save Everything," *New York Times*, July 6, 1998.

277   "How Much Information?": Full report posted at http://www.sims.berkeley.edu/how-much-info/summary.html. Don Herskovitz writes in

"Data Storage and the Coming Millennium," *Journal of Electronic Defense* 21:5 (May 1998), that "data managers have moved from the realm of terabyte storage and are now locking horns with petabytes of data." If a typewritten page contains about 2,000 bytes of data, a megabyte represents 500 text pages, a terabyte 500 million pages, and a petabyte 500 billion pages, "a number so vast as to defy comprehension."

278   Gigabytes: The basic unit of data storage, the megabyte, is a million bytes of information (one letter in the alphabet is equivalent to one byte; five megabytes can store the complete works of Shakespeare.) Next on the scale, the gigabyte, is one thousand megabytes, or 1 trillion bytes. (Most new personal computers are equipped with between 10 to 80 gigabytes of disk storage.) A terabyte, by extension, is one thousand gigabytes—ten could hold the entire printed collection of the Library of Congress—and a petabyte is one thousand terabytes of data (two of these could contain the contents of all research libraries in the United States). An exabyte is one thousand terabytes (1,000,000,000,000,000,000 bytes)—five of these would store every word ever spoken in the annals of humanity—a zettabyte is one thousand exabytes, and a yottabyte is one thousand exabytes ("a whole yotta data," according to Roy Williams of the California Institute of Technology, who created the "Data Powers of Ten" system of data measurement). See http://www.calacademy.org/research/library/biodiv/biblio/poften.htm.

279   DSpace: See Florence Olsen, "MIT's Open Window: Putting Course Materials Online, the University Faces High Expectations," *Chronicle of Higher Education*, Dec. 6, 2002; Peter J. Howe, "MIT to Create Digital Library," *Boston Globe*, Nov. 4, 2002; Jeffrey R. Young, " 'Superarchives' Could Hold All Scholarly Output," *Chronicle of Higher Education*, July 5, 2002; Sally Atwood, "A Digital Repository Will Revolutionize the Way Research Is Shared and Preserved," *Forbes*, Dec. 2002–Jan. 2003; see also http://libraries.mit.edu/dspace.

280   "preserve our digital": Quoted in Rajiv Chandrasekaran, "In California, Creating a Web of the Past," *Washington Post*, Sept. 22, 1996.

280   "to capture": Quoted in Carolyn Said, "Archiving the Internet: Brewster Kahle Makes Digital Snapshots of the Web," *San Francisco Chronicle*, May 7, 1998.

281   "Using the saved": Brewster Kahle, "Archiving the Internet," *Scientific American* 276:3 (Mar. 1997), on-line text available at http://www.archive.org.

281   CyberCemetery: Christopher Lee, "Just Like the Day They Died," *Washington Post*, Oct. 21, 2002; see also http://www.npr.gov/ and http://govinfo.library.unt.edu/.

281   Digital Reality II Boston conference: See http://nelinet.net/conf/pres/pres00/digital.htm.

282   "words on a screen . . . they'll be gone": William H. Gass, "In Defense of the Book: On the Enduring Pleasures of Paper, Type, Page, and Ink," *Harper's Magazine* 299 (Nov. 1999): 4–51.

Chapter 9: Make Haste Slowly

284   "The book form": Diehl, vol. 1, 3.

284   "Now . . . is another story": See Bush, "As We May Think," passim.

287   "Memex Revisited": Bush, *Science Is Not Enough*, 81–12.

288   Dead Media Project: http://www.deadmedia.org/.

289   "Manifesto": http://www.deadmedia.org/modest-proposal.html. For a scholarly examination of "binary coding in the Andean knotted-string records" of the Inka Empire (c. A.D. 1450–1532)—of what might just possibly, in other words, have been the first documentable use of record-keeping techniques that have parallels today with computer technologies, which process vast quantities of information by manipulating sequences of zeroes and ones—see Gary Urton, *Signs of the Inka Khipu* (Austin, Texas: Univeristy of Texas Press, 2003).

289   Computer History Museum: http://www.computerhistory.org/.

289   Sellam Ismail: Nick Pandya, "Be There for Geeks Bearing Gizmos," *Guardian* (London), Apr. 6, 2002. See also http://www.vintage.org/.

290   "actively scouting": Finn, 159.

291   "This is . . . components": Ramelli's drawing first appeared in *Le Diverse et Artificiose Machine* (Paris, 1588); a copy was given to the University of Delaware in 1974 as its one millionth book. Ramelli's description was translated by Martha Teach Gnudi in *Various Ingenious Machines of Agostino Ramelli* (New York: Dover Books, 1976).

292   "The machine . . . entire machine": Libeskind, 40–47. In April 2003, after an intense competition, Libeskind was selected to design a September 11, 2001, memorial for the Ground Zero site in New York where the Twin Towers complex once stood.

293   "Six hours . . . here annexed": Jonathan Swift, *Gulliver's Travels* (New York: Penguin Classics Edition, 1985), 229–230.

294   "When I am not . . . so unexcluding": Lamb, 273.

295   "At first . . . printouts": Robert Darnton, "The New Age of the Book," *The New York Review of Books,* Mar. 18, 1999.

297   "Every editor": Ibid.

298   "layers . . . readers": Ibid.; see also Robert Darnton, "A Historian of Books, Lost and Found in Cyberspace," *Chronicle of Higher Education,* Mar. 12, 1999.

298   James O'Donnell's *Cassiodorus* book goes electronic: See http://ccat.sas. upenn.edu/jod/texts/cassbook/toc.html.

299   Bollingen Series: See McGuire, passim.

300   "a man . . . scholarship": Quoted in Wilson, vii–viii.

302   "Working . . . four children": Terry Teachout, "35 Years with Woodrow Wilson: The Journey of a Long-Distance Editor," *New York Times Magazine,* Oct. 31, 1993, 33.

303   Mark Twain Project: See Charles Burress, "Making Their Mark on Twain," *San Francisco Chronicle,* Jan. 30, 1998; John Boudreau, "Uncertain Future for the Works of Mark Twain," *Los Angeles Times,* Apr. 29, 1992. See also http://www.lib.berkeley.edu/BANC/MTP/.

309   "serious literature . . . inspires": Holt, 595.

310   *Nil vulgare:* Benton, 2.

Chapter 10: Music of the Spheres

312   Trithemius: See Brann, passim; Arnold, 1–24; Kahn, 130–137; Eisenstein, 96–97; O'Donnell, 79–83; Balsamo, 26–28.

313   1,000 Dutch crowns: Kahn, 866.

313   Secret code broken: See Gina Kolata, "A Mystery Unraveled, Twice," *New York Times,* Apr. 14, 1998.

313   bas-relief sculpture: See Arnold, plates 4 and 5.

313   "I readily . . . library": Quoted in Arnold, 4–5.

314   "Trithemius was not above": Brann, 14.

314   "father of bibliography": Quoted in Balsamo, 26; Eisenstein, 97.

314   "All of you . . . generations": Arnold, 63–65.

316   "Trithemius knew . . . them": Ibid., 15.

316   8 million books: Eisenstein, 45; in his monograph on bibliography, Balsamo suggests the figure could be as high as 10 million (60).

316   "Sponheim abbey press": Arnold, 15.

316   "monastic humanism": Brann, 11.

317   "that wondrous": Quoted in O'Donnell, 79.

317   "our patron saint . . . his failure": Ibid.

317   "Theuth . . . society": *Phaedrus,* trans. H. N. Fowler, *Plato,* vol. 1, Loeb Classical Library (Cambridge, Mass.: Harvard University Press, 1990). See O'Donnell, 17–28, for a provocative reading of the dialogue.

319   "From today": Delaroche, quoted in William Packer, "Picasso Through a Glass Darkly," *Financial Times* (London), Feb. 9, 1999.

319   "the end of art": Quoted in Christopher Willard, "Paintings From Photographs," *American Artist* 63:680 (Mar. 1, 1999): 12.

319   "photographic . . . servant": Quoted in Alma Davenport, 30.

319   "I have discovered . . . learn": Quoted in Packer, op. cit. For an examination of how artists have used photography to develop their artistic vision, see Dorothy Kosinski, *The Artist and the Camera: Degas to Picasso* (New Haven, Conn.: Dallas Museum of Art / Yale University Press, 1999).

320   "Electronic . . . none other": Herbert C. Burkholz, "There's No Such Thing as Electronic Photography," *PSA Journal* 61:6 (June 1995): 10.

322   "The copyist . . . future library": Rogers, 220.

322   "With the development . . . lost": Ibid., 223.

323   "The first founders . . . now fashionable": Ibid., 216.

323   "made a rude . . . the librarian": Quoted in Robert S. Taylor, *The Making of a Library: The Academic Library in Transition* (New York: John Wiley, 1972), 87–88.

324   "universal library" and "ultramicrobooks": See John Rader Platt, "Where Will the Books Go?" *Horizon* 5:1 (Sept. 1962): 42–47.

327   "I feel . . . dead": Quoted in Norman D. Stevens, "Two Hundred and Twenty Thousand Platitudes," *American Libraries* 29:5 (May 1998): 79.

327   "If you go . . . welcome you": Quoted in Dana Parsons, "Curling Up With a Good Bookstore," *Los Angeles Times,* Jan. 14, 1988. See Roy Jenkins, *Gladstone: A Biography* (New York: Random House, 1997), 7, 176–179; on Gladstone's design for home library, see Fadiman, 139–146.

328   "It is like the dinosaur": *Herald Tribune* (New York), Mar. 21, 1966.

328   "Most reassuring": Gordon N. Ray, *ALA Bulletin*, Sept. 1966, offprint. For a learned discussion of McLuhan, see Eisenstein, 40–41.

328   "The first use . . . at hand": Cox, Dews, Dolby, 7.

329   "There are . . . books": See Ortega y Gasset, passim.

331   "to accuse . . . alike": Ralph Waldo Emerson, "Books," in *Society and Solitude,* 182–184.

333   "Global Library Strategies for the Twenty-first Century": Text of remarks delivered by Paul M. Horn, furnished to the author by the New York Public Library.

334   MIT Media Lab: See http://www.media.mit.edu/.

335   "books . . . a pin": Negroponte, 4. In the fall of 2000, Nicholas Negroponte was succeeded as executive director by Walter Bender, his longtime deputy, signaling a new philosophical direction after fifteen years of existence, according to some observers, focusing more, it was suggested, on "international relations" and increased "fund-raising." See Scott Kirsner, "Technology & Innovation," *Boston Globe,* Oct. 9, 2000; "The Media Lab at a Crossroads," *Technology Review* 103:5 (Sept. 2000): 70–83.

335   "bookmaking . . . today": "The Future of the Book," *Wired,* Feb. 1996.

335   "the current interface": Negroponte, 7.

338   "The Last Book": J. Jacobson, C. Turner, J. Albert, P. Taso, *IBM Systems Journal* 36:5 (Nov. 3, 1997), 457–63. For more on E-ink, see http://www.eink.com/.

339   batteries: Hiawatha Bray, "In Galloping High-Tech World, One Part Can't Keep Current," *Boston Globe,* Oct. 27, 1999; Michael Marriott, "As the Battery Goes, So Goes . . . ," *New York Times,* Nov. 19, 1998.

339   "Batteries . . . AA's": James Gleick, "Fast Forward; Maintenance Not Included," *New York Times Magazine,* July 13, 1997, 18.

339   kinetic keyboard: Jennifer Lee, "A Way to Let Your Fingers Recharge Batteries," *New York Times,* July 29, 1999.

340   "flickering pixel": Ian Austen, *New York Times,* Feb. 3, 2000. See also Karen Springen, "The Dangerous Desk," *Newsweek,* March 26, 2001, 66; Anne Chambers, "Computer Vision Syndrome: Relief Is in Sight," *Occupational Hazards* 69:10 (Oct. 1, 1999), 179; Richard Gawel, "Are You a Victim of Computer Vision Syndrome?" *Electronic Design* 47:19 (Sept. 20, 1999), 32B.

340   "It will look like" and "Are we a culture": Ibid.

341   "cyberspace traffic jam": Jonathan Yardley, "Publishers, the Writing's on the E-Wall," *Washington Post,* Mar. 23.

341   "While I Think": Quoted in Andrea Sachs, "Boo! How He Startled the Book World," *Time,* Mar. 27, 2000, 76.

342   "No reader . . . Walkman": Joseph Menn, "E-Book Publishing: Much Ado About Nothing Much," *Los Angeles Times,* July 24, 2000. See also Stephen J. Dubner, "What Is Stephen King Trying to Prove?" *New York Times Magazine,* Aug. 13, 2000.

342   Headlines: "Suspense Doesn't," Alberto Manguel, *New York Times,* Dec. 5, 2000; "King's Plant Wilts," Jonathan Lambeth, *Daily Telegraph,* Dec. 7, 2000; "Deadbeats Prompt," Linton Weeks, *Washington Post,* Nov. 29, 2000.

343   "Am I displeased . . . turned out?": Stephen King, "How I Got That Story," *Time,* Dec. 18, 2000, 77.

343   Convention study: Paul Hilts, "Seybold Looks at E-Book Market; E-Books Hot Topic of Meeting, Though Survey Finds Few Prepared to Pay for Titles," *Publishers Weekly*, Sept. 18, 2000, 41.

344   "The baby boomers . . . pockets": Quoted in Alex Kuczynski, "Updating a Paperback Heroine," *New York Times*, May 21, 2000.

344   "The Day the Kids Sat Still": Linda Matchan, *Boston Globe*, July 8, 2000.

344   Future of the Book seminar: See Nunberg.

344   "will remain indispensable": Eco, in Nunberg, 300.

346   "This is the brave": Quoted in "Random House to Establish Exclusively Digital Unit," *New York Times*, July 31, 2000.

347   "The main advantage . . . for the moment": Quoted in David Kirkpatrick, "Forecasts of an E-Book Era Were, It Seems, Premature," *New York Times*, Aug. 28, 2001.

347   "At BookExpo": Linton Weeks, "E-Books Not Exactly Flying Off the Shelves," *Washington Post*, July 6, 2002.

351   "preposterous . . . compute": John R. Searle, *New York Review of Books*, Nov. 6, 1999.

351   "who . . . funding bodies": Diane Proudfoot, *Science* 284:5415 (Apr. 30, 1999): 745. In a reply to her review (285:5426 [July 16, 1999]: 339) Kurzweil saw "no harm" in "anthropomorphizing," since he clearly maintained that "today's machines do not have the endearing qualities of humans," and he stood by his assertion that "nonbiological entities" are "going to vastly expand in the breadth, depth, and subtlety of their intelligence and creativity."

352   John E. Warnock: See Andrew Fisher, "View From the Top: John Warnock of Adobe Systems," *Financial Times*, Feb. 7, 2001.

358   Jonathan D. Spence: "History in the Twentieth Century and the Spirit of St. Louis," remarks delivered at "Frontiers of the Mind in the Twenty-First Century," a conference at the Library of Congress, June 15–17, 1999. Complete copy of remarks furnished to the author; excerpts at http://lcweb.loc.gov/bicentennial/symposia_frontiers.html.

359   "What is . . . farther than this": Richardson, *Beginnings*, 27–28. See also Richardson, *Some Old Egyptian Librarians*, for an excellent discussion of

libraries that are "at least half a millennium older than that 'oldest library of which we have details' (i.e. before Assurbanipal)."

360   "I realized": Hamburger, 102.

Proper Passage: A Coda

363   "Men may come": Basbanes, *Gentle Madness*, 194.

364   "If the great": Basbanes, *Gentle Madness*, 173.

365   "surviving intact portion": Paul Mellon with John Baskett, *Reflections in a Silver Spoon* (New York: William Morrow, 1992), 284.

366   "Because it ceased": William S. Reese, "Americana in the Paul Mellon Bequest," *Yale University Library Gazette* 75:3–4 (Apr. 2001), 145. For more on Reese, see Basbanes, *Patience & Fortitude*, 314–325.

367   "The system worked": William S. Reese, "Paul Mellon as Collector of Americana and Virginiana," remarks delivered before the Virginia Historical Society, Sept. 5, 2001, copy of text furnished to the author.

367   Exhibitions and catalogs: See Miles and Reese, passim, and *Treasures Revealed from the Paul Mellon Library of Americana*, passim. See also *Private Passions, Public Legacy*, on-line catalog of exhibition of Paul Mellon bequest to the University of Virginia, at http://www.lib.virginia.edu/speccol/exhibits/mellon/

367   "We stand in awe": Barbara A. Shailor, in Miles and Reese, v.

367   "I can think": Reese, Virginia Historical Society remarks.

368   clay tablets known as the Sippar Library: See Guy Gugliotta, "Looters May Have Destroyed Priceless Cuneiform Archive," *Washington Post*, Apr. 18, 2003, A23.

368   "To hold and transmit": Alberto Manguel, "Our First Words, Written in Clay, in an Accountant's Hand," *New York Times*, Apr. 20, 2003; see also Adam Goodheart, "Missing: A Vase, a Book, a Bird and 10,000 Years of History," *New York Times*, Apr. 20, 2003.

Bibliography

Adkins, Lesley, and Roy Adkins. *The Keys of Egypt: The Obsession to Decipher Egyptian Hieroglyphs.* New York: HarperCollins, 2000.

Aizenberg, Edna. *Books and Bombs in Buenos Aires: Borges, Gerchunoff, and Argentine-Jewish Writing.* Hanover, N.H.: University Press of New England, 2002.

Altshuler, David, ed. *The Precious Legacy: Judaic Treasures from the Czechoslovak State Collections.* New York: Summit Books, 1983.

Amery, Colin, and Brian Curran Jr. *The Lost World of Pompeii.* Los Angeles: Getty Publications, 2002.

Armstrong, Carol. *Scenes in a Library: Reading the Photograph in the Book, 1843–1875.* Cambridge, Mass.: MIT Press, 1998.

Arnold, Klaus, ed. *Johannes Trithemius: In Praise of Scribes* (De Laude Scriptorum). Translated from the Latin by Roland Behrendt. Lawrence, Kan.: Coronado Press, 1974.

Avrin, Leila. *Scribes, Script and Books: The Book Arts from Antiquity to the Renaissance.* Chicago: American Library Association; London: British Library, 1991.

Baigent, Michael, and Richard Leigh. *The Dead Sea Scrolls Deception.* New York: Summit, 1991.

Baike, James. *Egyptian Papyri and Papyrus-Hunting.* New York and Chicago: Fleming H. Revell Co., [1926].

Bakaršic, Kemal. "The Libraries of Sarajevo and the Book That Saved Our Lives." *The New Combat: A Journal of Reason and Resistance* (autumn 1994): 13–15.

Baker, Nicholson. *Double Fold.* New York: Random House, 2001.

Balsamo, Luigi. *Bibliography: History of a Tradition.* Translated from the Italian by William A. Pettas. Berkeley, Calif.: Bernard M. Rosenthal, Inc., 1990.

Barkan, Leonard. *Unearthing the Past: Archaeology and Aesthetics in the Making of Renaissance Culture.* New Haven, Conn.: Yale University Press, 1999.

Basbanes, Nicholas A. *A Gentle Madness: Bibliophiles, Bibliomanes, and the Eternal Passion for Books.* New York: Henry Holt, 1995; Owl paperback, 1999.

———. *Patience & Fortitude: A Roving Chronicle of Book People and Book Places.* New York: HarperCollins, 2001; Perennial paperback, 2003.

Batche, Geoffrey. *Burning With Desire: The Conception of Photography*. Cambridge, Mass.: MIT Press, 1997.

Baugh, Albert C. *A History of the English Language*. New York: Appleton-Century-Crofts, Inc., 1935.

Bell-Fialkoff, Andrew. *Ethnic Cleansing*. New York: St. Martin's Press, 1996.

Benford, Gregory. *Deep Time: How Humanity Communicates Across Millennia*. New York: Avon Books, 1991.

Benton, Megan L. *Beauty and the Book: Fine Editions and Cultural Distinction in America*. New Haven, Conn.: Yale University Press, 2000.

Bentwich, Norman. *Solomon Schechter: A Biography*. Philadelphia: Jewish Publication Society of America, 1938.

Berenbaum, Michael. *The World Must Know: The History of the Holocaust as Told in the United States Holocaust Museum*. New York: Little, Brown, 1993.

Birkerts, Sven. *The Gutenberg Galaxy: The Fate of Reading in an Electronic Age*. Boston: Faber and Faber, 1994.

———, ed. *Tolstoy's Dictaphone: Technology and the Muse*. St. Paul, Minn.: Graywolf Press, 1996.

Blades, William. *The Enemies of Books*. London: Elliot Stock, 1902.

Blair, Sheila S. *Islamic Inscriptions*. New York: New York University Press, 1998.

Bloom, Harold. *Shakespeare: The Invention of the Human*. New York: Riverhead Books, 1998.

———. *The Western Canon: The Books and School of the Ages*. New York: Harcourt, Brace, 1994.

Bloom, Jonathan M. *Paper Before Print: The History and Impact of Paper in the Islamic World*. New Haven, Conn.: Yale University Press, 2001.

Boehme, Sarah E., Christian F. Feest, and Patricia Condon Johnston. *Seth Eastman: A Portfolio of North American Indians*. Afton, Minn.: Afton Historical Society Press, 1995.

Bonfante, Giuliano, and Larissa Bonfante. *The Etruscan Language*. Manchester, England: Manchester University Press, 1983.

Bottéro, Jean. *Mesopotamia: Writing, Reasoning, and the Gods*. Translated from the French by Zainab Bahrani and Marc Van De Mieroop. Chicago: University of Chicago Press, 1992.

Bowman, Alan K. *Life and Letters on the Roman Frontier: Vindolanda and Its People*. New York: Routledge, 1994.

Boyle, Leonard E., O.P. *Medieval Latin Paleography: A Bibliographical Introduction*. Toronto: University of Toronto Press, 1984.

Brand, Stewart. *The Clock of the Long Now: Time and Responsibility.* New York: Basic Books, 1999.

Brann, Noel L. *The Abbot Trithemius (1462–1516): The Renaissance of Monastic Humanism.* Leiden: E. J. Brill, 1981.

Brown, John Seely, and Paul Duguid. *The Social Life of Information.* Boston: Harvard Business School Press, 2000.

Brownrigg, Linda L., ed. *Medieval Book Production: Assessing the Evidence.* (Proceedings of the Second Conference of the Seminar in the History of the Book to 1500, Oxford, July 1988.) Los Altos Hills, Calif.: Anderson-Lovelace, 1990.

Bush, Vannevar. "As We May Think." *The Atlantic Monthly* 176:1 (July 1945): 101–108.

————. *Science Is Not Enough: Reflections for the Present and Future.* New York: William Morrow, 1967.

Byron, George Gordon, Baron. *Letters and Journals.* Edited by Leslie A. Marchand. 12 vols. Cambridge, Mass.: Belknap Press of Harvard University Press, 1973–1982.

Cannon, Christopher. *The Making of Chaucer's English: A Study of Words.* Cambridge, England: Cambridge University Press, 1998.

Caplan, Jane, ed. *Written on the Body: The Tattoo in European and American History.* Princeton, N.J.: Princeton University Press, 2000.

Carpenter, Kenneth E., ed. *Books and Society in History: Papers of the Association of College and Research Libraries Rare Books and Manuscripts Preconference, 24–28 June 1980, Boston, Massachusetts.* New York and London: R. R. Bowker Company, 1983.

Carter, Thomas Francis. *The Invention of Printing in China and Its Spread Westward.* New York: Columbia University Press, 1931 (revised edition).

Castillo, Debra A. *The Translated Word: A Postmodern Tour of Libraries in Literature.* Tallahassee: Florida State University Press, 1984.

Ceram, C. W., ed. *Hands on the Past: Pioneer Archaeologists Tell Their Own Story.* New York: Alfred A. Knopf, 1966.

Cerquiglini, Bernard. *In Praise of the Variant: A Critical History of Philology.* Translated from the French by Betsy Wing. Baltimore, Md.: Johns Hopkins University Press, 1999.

Cerquiglini-Toulet, Jacqueline. *The Color of Melancholy: The Uses of Books in the Fourteenth Century.* Translated from the French by Lydia G. Cochrane. Baltimore, Md.: Johns Hopkins University Press, 1997.

Chandler, David. *Voices From S-21: Terror and History in Pol Pot's Secret Prison.* Berkeley: University of California Press, 1999.

Chartier, Roger. *Forms and Meanings: Texts, Performances, and Audiences, From Codex to Computer.* Philadelphia: University of Pennsylvania Press, 1995.

————. *The Order of Books.* Stanford, Calif.: Stanford University Press, 1992.

Chernow, Ron. *The Warburgs: The 20th-Century Odyssey of a Remarkable Jewish Family.* New York: Random House, 1993.

Coe, Michael D. *Breaking the Maya Code.* New York: Thames and Hudson, 1992.

Coe, Michael D., and Justin Kerr. *The Art of the Maya Scribe.* New York: Harry N. Abrams, 1998.

Cole, John Y. *For Congress and the Nation: A Chronological History of the Library of Congress.* Washington, D.C.: Library of Congress, 1979.

————, ed. *Books in Our Future: Perspectives and Proposals.* Washington, D.C.: Library of Congress, 1987.

————, ed. *The Republic of Letters: Librarian of Congress Daniel J. Boorstin on Books, Reading, and Libraries 1975–1987.* Washington, D.C.: Library of Congress, 1988.

Collections, Content, and the Web. Washington, D.C.: Council on Library and Information Resources, 2000. Full text of CLIR publications are available on the World Wide Web, www.clir.org.

Collins, Herbert Ridgeway. *Threads of History: Americana Recorded on Cloth 1775 to the Present.* Washington, D.C.: Smithsonian Institution Press, 1979.

Colver, Robert. "The Bitter Truth About Acid." *O.P. World* (July 1998): 12–13.

Connell, Charles. *They Gave Us Shakespeare: John Heminge & Henry Condell.* Stocksfield, Great Britain: Oriel Press, 1982.

Coser, Lewis A., Charles Kadushin, and Walter W. Powell. *Books: The Culture and Commerce of Publishing.* New York: Basic Books, 1982.

Cox, N. S. M., J. D. Dews, and J. L. Dolby. *The Computer and the Library.* Hamden, Conn.: Archon Books, 1967.

Crawford, Walt, and Michael Gorman. *Future Libraries: Dreams, Madness, and Reality.* Chicago and London: American Library Association, 1995.

Cummings, Anthony M. et al. *University Libraries and Scholarly Communication: A Study Prepared for the Andrew W. Mellon Foundation.* Washington, D.C.: Association of Research Libraries, 1992.

Curtis, J. E., and J. E. Reade, eds. *Art and Empire: Treasures from Assyria in the British Museum.* New York: Metropolitan Museum of Art, 1995.

Dain, Phyllis, and John Y. Cole. *Libraries and Scholarly Communication in the United States.* Westport, Conn.: Greenwood Press, 1990.

Daniels, Peter T., and William Bright. *The World's Writing Systems.* New York and Oxford, England: Oxford University Press, 1996.

Dankey, James P., and Wayne A. Wigand, eds. *Print Culture in a Diverse America.* Urbana: University of Illinois Press, 1998.

Davenport, Alma. *The History of Photography: An Overview.* Albuquerque: University of New Mexico Press, 1999.

Davenport, Cyril. *The Book: Its History and Development.* New York: D. Van Norstrand, 1908.

Davison, Peter, ed. *The Book Encompassed: Studies in Twentieth-Century Bibliography.* Cambridge, England: Cambridge University Press, 1992.

Dawidowicz, Lucy S. *From That Place and Time: A Memoir 1938–1947.* New York: W. W. Norton, 1989.

De Hamel, Christopher. *A History of Illuminated Manuscripts.* Boston: David R. Godine, 1986.

Deiss, Joseph Jay. *Herculaneum: Italy's Buried Treasure.* Malibu, Calif.: J. Paul Getty Museum, 1989.

Deuel, Leo. *Testaments of Time: The Search for Lost Manuscripts and Records.* New York: Alfred A. Knopf, 1965.

Diehl, Edith. *Bookbinding: Its Background and Technique.* 2 vols. New York: Rinehart & Co., 1946.

Disraeli, Isaac. *Curiosities of Literature.* 9th ed., rev., 6 vols. London: E. Moxon, 1834.

Ditchfield, P. H. *Books Fatal to Their Authors.* London: Elliot Stock, 1895.

Di Vita, Antonio, and Ginette Di Vita-Evrad. *Libya: The Lost Cities of the Roman Empire.* Translated from the German by Liz Clegg and Peter Snowdon. Cologne: Könemann Verlagsgesellschaft MbH, 1999.

Doblhofer, Ernst. *Voices in Stone: The Decipherment of Ancient Scripts and Writings.* New York: Viking, 1961.

Douglas, David C. *William the Conqueror: The Norman Impact on England.* Berkeley: University of California Press, 1964.

Drew, David. *The Lost Chronicles of the Maya Kings.* Berkeley: University of California Press, 1999.

Drucker, Johanna. *The Alphabetic Labyrinth: The Letters in History and Imagination.* London: Thames and Hudson, 1995.

———. *The Visible Word: Experimental Typography and Modern Art, 1909–1923.* Chicago: University of Chicago Press, 1994.

Dyson, Freeman J. *The Sun, The Genome, and the Internet: Tools of Scientific Revolutions.* New York: New York Public Library / Oxford University Press, 1999.

Eisenstein, Elizabeth L. *The Printing Press as an Agent of Change: Communications and Cultural Transformations in Early-Modern Europe.* Volumes I and II. Cambridge, England: Cambridge University Press, 1980 [paperback version of the two-volume 1979 hardcover edition].

Emerson, Ralph Waldo. "Books." In *Society and Solitude* [1870], vol. 12, pp. 181–210. *The Works of Ralph Waldo Emerson.* Boston: Houghton Mifflin, 1883.

Epstein, Jason. *Book Business: Publishing Past Present and Future.* New York: W. W. Norton, 2001.

Ermarth, Michael, ed. *Kurt Wolff: A Portrait in Essays and Letters.* Translated from the German by Deborah Lucas Schneider. Chicago: University of Chicago Press, 1991.

Evans, Helen C., and William D. Wixom. *The Glory of Byzantium: Art and Culture of the Middle Byzantine Era, A.D. 843–1261.* New York: Metropolitan Museum of Art, 1967.

Fadiman, Anne. *Ex Libris: Confessions of a Common Reader.* New York: Farrar, Straus, and Giroux, 1998.

Fagan, Brian M. *Return to Babylon: Travelers, Archaeologists and Monuments in Mesopotamia.* Boston: Little, Brown, 1979.

―――, ed. *Eyewitness to Discovery: First-Person Accounts of More Than Fifty of the World's Greatest Archaeological Discoveries.* New York: Oxford University Press, 1996.

Fash, William L. *Scribes, Warriors and Kings: The City of Copán and the Ancient Maya.* London: Thames and Hudson, 1991.

Febvre, Lucien, and Henri-Jean Martin. *The Coming of the Book: The Impact of Printing 1450–1800.* Translated from the French by David Gerard. London: Verso, 1976.

Finn, Christine A. *Artifacts: An Archaeologist's Year in Silicon Valley.* Cambridge, Mass.: MIT Press, 2001.

Fishman, David E. *Embers Plucked From the Fire: The Rescue of Jewish Cultural Treasures in Vilna.* New York: YIVO Institute for Jewish Research, 1996.

Fletcher, H. George, ed. *The Wormsley Library: A Personal Selection by Sir Paul Getty, KBE.* London and New York: Maggs Bros./The Pierpont Morgan Library, 1999.

Foster, John L., trans. *Ancient Egyptian Literature: An Anthology.* Austin: University of Texas Press, 2001.

Gallenkamp, Charles. *Maya: The Riddle and Rediscovery of a Lost Civilization.* 3rd ed., revised. New York: Viking, 1985.

Gass, William H. "In Defense of the Book: On the Enduring Pleasures of Paper, Type, Page, and Ink." *Harper's Magazine* (Nov. 1999): 45–51.

Gates, Bill [William H. III]. *The Road Ahead.* New York: Viking, 1995.

Gates, Henry Louis Jr., and Nellie Y. McKay, eds. *The Norton Anthology of African American Literature.* New York: W. W. Norton, 1997.

Genette, Gérard. *Paratexts: Thresholds of Interpretation.* Translated from the French by Jane E. Lewin. Cambridge, England: Cambridge University Press, 1997.

Gigante, Marcello. *Philodemus in Italy: The Books From Herculaneum.* Translated from the Italian by Dirk Obbink. Ann Arbor: University of Michigan Press, 1995.

Gingerich, Owen. *The Great Copernicus Chase and Other Adventures in Astronomical History*. Cambridge, Mass.: Sky Publishing Corp., 1992.

Godart, Louis. *The Phaistos Disc: The Enigma of an Aegean Script*. [Greece]: ITANOS Publications, 1995.

Gombrich, E. H. *Aby Warburg: An Intellectual Biography*. Second edition, with a memoir on the history of the library by F. Saxl appended. Chicago: University of Chicago Press, 1986.

Grafton, Anthony, with April Shelford and Nancy Sirasi. *New Worlds, Ancient Texts: The Power of Tradition and the Shock of Discovery*. Cambridge, Mass.: The Belknap Press of Harvard University Press, 1992.

Grant, Michael. *The Visible Past: Recent Archaeological Discoveries of Greek and Roman History*. New York: Charles Scribner's Sons, 1990.

Graubard, Stephen R., ed. "Books, Bricks, and Bytes." *Daedalus, Journal of the American Academy of Arts and Sciences* 125:4 (fall 1996), i–361.

Greenfield, Jeanette. *The Return of Cultural Treasures*. Introduction by Magnus Magnusson. Cambridge, England: Cambridge University Press, 1989.

Guthrie, Kevin M. *The New-York Historical Society: Lessons From One Nonprofit's Long Struggle for Survival*. San Francisco: Jossey-Bass, 1996.

Hamburger, Philip. "Searching for Gregorian." In *Curious World: A New Yorker at Large*. San Francisco: North Point Press, 1987.

Haskell, Francis. *History and Its Images: Art and the Interpretation of the Past*. New Haven, Conn.: Yale University Press, 1993.

Hawkins, Brian L., and Patricia Battin, eds. *The Mirage of Continuity: Reconfiguring Academic Information Resources for the 21st Century*. Washington, D.C.: Council on Library and Information Resources and Association of American Universities, 1998.

Haynes, Sybille. *Etruscan Civilization: A Cultural History*. Los Angeles: J. Paul Getty Museum, 2000.

Hedrick, Charles W. *History and Silence: Purge and Rehabilitation of Memory in Late Antiquity*. Austin: University of Texas Press, 2000.

Henderson, Bill, ed. *Minutes of the Lead Pencil Club: Pulling the Plug on the Electronic Revolution*. Wainscott, N.Y.: Pushcart Press, 1997.

Henricks, Robert G. *Lao Tzu's Tao Te Ching: A Translation of the Startling New Documents Found at Guodian*. New York: Columbia University Press, 2000.

————. *Lao-Tzu: Te-Tao Ching: A New Translation Based on the Recently Discovered Ma-wang-tui Texts*. New York: Ballantine, 1989.

Holt, Henry. "The Commercialization of Literature." *The Atlantic Monthly* 96:5 (Nov. 1905): 577–600.

Hooker, J. T., ed., with essays by C. B. F. Walker, W. V. Davies, John Chadwick, John F. Healey, B. F. Cook, and Larisa Bonfante. *Reading the Past: Ancient Writings from Cuneiform to the Alphabet*. Berkeley: University of California Press/British Museum, 1990.

Horne, John, and Alan Kramer, *German Atrocities 1914*. New Haven, Conn.: Yale University Press, 2001.

Horne, Thomas Hartwell. *An Introduction to the Study of Bibliography: To Which Is Prefixed a Memoir on the Public Libraries of the Antients*. 2 vols. London: T. Cadell and W. Davies, 1814.

Hunter, Dard. *Papermaking: The History and Technique of an Ancient Craft*. New York: Alfred A. Knopf, 1947 [second edition revised and enlarged].

Irwin, Raymond. *The Origins of the English Library*. London: Allen & Unwin, 1958.

Johns, Adrian. *The Nature of the Book: Print and Knowledge in the Making*. Chicago: University of Chicago Press, 1998.

Kahle, Brewster. "Preserving the Internet." *Scientific American* 276:3 (Mar. 1997): 82.

Kahn, David. *The Codebreakers: The Comprehensive History of Secret Communication From Ancient Times to the Internet*. New York: Scribner, 1996 [revised and updated edition].

Karan, Pradyumna P. *The Changing Face of Tibet: The Impact of Chinese Communist Ideology on the Landscape*. Lexington: University Press of Kentucky, 1976.

Keller, Werner. *The Etruscans*. New York: Alfred A. Knopf, 1970.

Kenyon, Frederic G. *Ancient Books and Modern Discoveries*. Chicago: Caxton Club, 1927.

Kernan, Alvin. *Printing Technology, Letters & Samuel Johnson*. Princeton, N.J.: Princeton University Press, 1987.

King, David. *The Commissar Vanishes: The Falsification of Photographs and Art in Stalin's Russia*. New York: Metropolitan Books, 1997.

Koverman, Jill Beute. *I Made This Jar . . . : The Life and Works of the Enslaved African-American Potter, Dave*. Columbia: McKissick Museum/University of South Carolina, 1998.

Kruk, Herman. *The Last Days of the Jerusalem of Lithuania: Chronicles From the Vilna Ghetto and the Camps, 1939–1944*. Edited by Benjamin Harshav. Translated from the Yiddish by Barbara Harshav. New Haven, Conn.: Yale University Press, 2002.

Kurzweil, Ray. *The Age of Spiritual Machines: When Computers Exceed Human Intelligence*. New York: Viking, 1999.

Laks, André, and Glenn W. Most, eds. *Studies on the Derveni Papyrus*. Oxford, England: Oxford University Press, 1997.

Lamb, Charles. "Detatched Thoughts on Books and Readers." In *The Works of Charles Lamb*, edited by Sir Thomas Noon Talfourd, vol. 3. New York: A. C. Armstrong & Son, 1880.

Lambert, Joseph B. *Traces of the Past: Unraveling the Secrets of Archaeology Through Chemistry.* Reading, Mass.: Addison-Wesley, 1997.

Lancel, Serge. *Carthage: A History.* Translated from the French by Antonia Nevill. Oxford, England: Blackwell Publishers, 1995.

Lawson, Alexander. *Anatomy of a Typeface.* Boston: David R. Godine, 1990.

Levy, Reuben, trans. *The Epic of the Kings: Shāh-nāma the National Epic of Persia by Ferdowsi.* London: Routledge & Kegan Paul, 1967.

Libeskind, Daniel. *Countersign.* New York: Rizzoli, 1992.

Linenthal, Edward T. *Preserving Memory: The Struggle to Create America's Holocaust Museum.* New York: Viking Penguin, 1995.

Lopez, Donald S., Jr. *Curators of the Buddha: The Study of Buddhism Under Colonialism.* Chicago: University of Chicago Press, 1995.

Macaulay, Rose. *Pleasure of Ruins.* New York: Walker, 1953.

Macdonald, A. J. *Lanfranc: A Study of His Life, Work and Writing.* London: Oxford University Press, 1926.

McGuire, William. *Bollingen: An Adventure in Collecting the Past.* Princeton, N.J.: Princeton University Press, 1982.

McKitterick, David. "The Keele Affair." *Book Collector* 48:2 (summer 1999): 202–207.

MacLean, Margaret, and Ben H. Davis, eds. *Time & Bits: Managing Digital Continuity.* Los Angeles: J. Paul Getty Trust, 1998.

Magness, Jodi. *The Archaeology of Qumran and the Dead Sea Scrolls.* Grand Rapids, Mich.: William B. Eerdmans, 2002.

Martin, Jean-Henri. *The History and Power of Writing.* Translated from the French by Lydia G. Cochrane. Chicago: University of Chicago Press, 1994.

Matthiae, Paolo. *Ebla: An Empire Rediscovered.* Translated from the Italian by Christopher Holme. Garden City, N.Y.: Doubleday, 1981.

Mehring, Walter. *The Lost Library: The Autobiography of a Culture.* London: Secker & Warburg, 1951.

Mercer, S. A. B., ed. *The Tell El-Amarna Tablets.* 2 vols. Toronto: Macmillan, 1939.

Miles, George A., and William S. Reese. *America Pictured to the Life: Illustrated Works from the Paul Mellon Bequest.* New Haven, Conn.: Beinecke Rare Book and Manuscript Library of Yale University, 2002.

Mirsky, Jeannette. *Sir Aurel Stein: Archaeological Explorer.* Chicago: University of Chicago Press, 1998 (first published in 1977).

Murray, Janet H. *Hamlet on the Holodeck: The Future of Narrative in Cyberspace.* New York: Free Press, 1997.

Naudé, Gabriel. *Instructions Concerning Erecting of a Library.* Translated from the French by John Evelyn, with an introduction by John Cotton Dana. Cambridge, Mass.: Riverside Press, 1903.

Needham, Paul. *Twelve Centuries of Bookbindings: 400–1600.* New York: Pierpont Morgan Library/Oxford University Press, 1979.

Negroponte, Nicholas. *Being Digital.* New York: Alfred A. Knopf, 1995.

Neier, Aryeh. *War Crimes: Brutality, Genocide, Terror, and the Struggle for Justice.* New York: Times Books, 1998.

Nunberg, Geoffrey, ed. *The Future of the Book.* Afterword by Umberto Eco. Berkeley and Los Angeles: University of California Press, 1996.

O'Connor, Rev. J. F. X, S.J. *Facts About Bookworms: Their History in Literature and Work in Libraries.* New York: Francis P. Harper, 1898.

O'Donnell, James J. *Avatars of the Word: From Papyrus to Cyberspace.* Cambridge, Mass.: Harvard University Press, 1998.

On Research Libraries: Statement and Recommendations of the Committee on Research Libraries of the American Council of Learned Societies Submitted to the National Advisory Commission on Libraries. Cambridge, Mass.: MIT Press, 1967.

Ortega y Gasset, José. *The Mission of the Librarian.* Translated from the Spanish by James Lewis and Ray Carpenter. Boston: G. K. Hall, 1961.

Orwell, George. *1984.* New York: Harcourt, Brace, 1949.

Pagden, A. R., ed. and trans. *The Maya: Diego de Landa's Account of the Affairs of Yucatán.* Chicago: J. P. O'Hara, 1975.

Pagels, Elaine. *The Gnostic Gospels.* New York: Random House, 1979.

Palache, John Garber. *Four Novelists of the Old Régime.* New York: Viking, 1926.

Parkinson, Richard, with contributions by W. Diffie, M. Fischer, and R. S. Simpson. *Cracking Codes: The Rosetta Stone and Decipherment.* London: British Museum Press, 1999.

Patterson, David. *Along the Edge of Annihilation: The Collapse and Recovery of Life in the Holocaust Diary.* Seattle: University of Washington Press, 1999.

Peckham, J. Brian, S.J. *The Development of the Late Phoenician Scripts.* Cambridge, Mass.: Harvard University Press, 1968.

Pedley, John Griffiths, ed. *New Light on Ancient Carthage.* Ann Arbor: University of Michigan Press, 1980.

Peek, Robin P., and Gregory B. Newby, eds. *Scholarly Publishing: The Electronic Frontier.* Cambridge, Mass.: MIT Press, 1996.

Petroski, Henry. *The Pencil: A History of Design and Circumstance.* New York: Alfred A. Knopf, 1990.

Pettinato, Giovanni. *The Archives of Ebla: An Empire Inscribed in Clay.* Garden City, N.Y.: Doubleday, 1981.

Pohl, John M. D. *Exploring Mesoamerica: Places in Time.* New York: Oxford University Press, 1999.

Pope, Maurice. *The Story of Decipherment: From Egyptian Hieroglyphs to Maya Script.* Revised ed. New York: Thames and Hudson, 1999.

Porter, Charles A. *Restif's Novels, or an Autobiography in Search of an Author.* New Haven, Conn.: Yale University Press, 1976.

Power, Eugene B. *Edition of One.* Ann Arbor, Mich.: University Microfilms Inc., 1990.

Rees, J. Rogers. *The Pleasures of a Book-Worm.* New York: George J. Coombes, 1886.

Reeves, Nicholas. *Akhenaten: Egypt's False Prophet.* London: Thames and Hudson, 2001.

Reif, Stefan C. *A Jewish Archive From Old Cairo: The History of Cambridge University's Genizah Collection.* Richmond, England: Curzon Press, 2000.

Reiman, Donald H. *The Study of Modern Manuscripts: Public, Confidential, and Private.* Baltimore, Md.: Johns Hopkins University Press, 1993.

Reynolds, L. D., and N. G. Wilson. *Scribes and Scholars: A Guide to the Transmission of Greek and Latin Literature.* 2nd ed. revised and enlarged. Oxford, England: Oxford University Press, 1974.

————, ed. *Texts and Transmission: A Survey of the Latin Classics.* Oxford, England: Oxford University Press, 1983.

Rhodes, Richard, ed. *Visions of Technology: A Century of Vital Debate About Machines, Systems, and the Human World.* New York: Simon & Schuster, 1999.

Richardson, Ernest Cushing. *The Beginnings of Libraries.* Princeton, N.J.: Princeton University Press, 1914.

————. *Some Old Egyptian Librarians.* Berkeley, Calif.: Peacock Press, 1964; originally published by Charles Scribner's Sons, New York, 1911.

Ringelblum, Emmanuel. *Notes From the Warsaw Ghetto.* Edited and translated from the Polish by Jacob Sloan. New York: McGraw-Hill, 1958.

Robinson, Andrew. *The Man Who Deciphered Linear B: The Story of Michael Ventris.* New York: Thames and Hudson, 2002.

————. *The Story of Writing: Alphabets, Hieroglyphs and Pictograms.* London: Thames and Hudson, 1995.

Robinson, James G., gen. ed. *The Nag Hammadi Library in English.* 3rd ed., revised. San Francisco: Harper & Row, 1988.

Rogers, Howard J., ed. *Congress of Arts and Science: Universal Exposition, St. Louis.* Vol. 8. Boston: Houghton Mifflin, 1905.

Rose, Jonathan, ed. *The Holocaust and the Book: Destruction and Preservation.* Amherst, Mass.: University of Massachusetts Press, 2001.

Rosen, Jonathan. *The Talmud and the Internet: A Journey Between Worlds.* New York: Farrar, Straus and Giroux, 2000.

Rothenberg, Jeff. "Ensuring the Longevity of Digital Documents." *Scientific American* 272:1 (Jan. 1995): 42–47.

Rothenberg, Jerome, and Steven Clay, eds. *A Book of the Book: Some Works and Projections About the Book and Writing.* New York: Granary Books, 2000.

Rudolph, Kurt. *Gnosis: The Nature and History of Gnosticism.* Translation edited by Robert McLachlan Wilson. San Francisco: Harper & Row, 1983.

Ryan, William B. F., and Walter C. Pitman III. *Noah's Flood: The New Scientific Discoveries About the Event That Changed History.* New York: Simon & Schuster, 1999.

Sagan, Carl et al. *Murmurs of Earth: The Voyager Interstellar Record.* New York: Random House, 1978.

Saggs, H. W. F. *Babylonians.* Berkeley: University of California Press, 2000.

Salomon, Richard. *Ancient Buddhist Scrolls From Gandhara: The British Library Kharosthi Fragments.* Seattle: University of Washington Press, 1999.

Savage, Ernest A. *Old English Libraries: The Making, Collection, and Use of Books During the Middle Ages.* London: Methuen, 1911.

Sax, Joseph L. *Playing Darts With a Rembrandt: Public and Private Rights in Cultural Treasures.* Ann Arbor: University of Michigan Press, 1999.

Schnapp, Alain. *The Discovery of the Past.* New York: Harry N. Abrams, 1997.

Schiffrin, André. *The Business of Books: How International Conglomerates Took Over Publishing and Changed the Way We Read.* London and New York: Verso, 2000.

Schwartz, Hillel. *The Culture of the Copy: Striking Likenesses, Unreasonable Facsimiles.* New York: Zone Books, 1996.

Sells, Michael A. *The Bridge Betrayed: Religion and Genocide in Bosnia.* Berkeley and Los Angeles: University of California Press, 1996.

Senner, Wayne, ed. *The Origins of Writing.* Lincoln: University of Nebraska Press, 1989.

Shanks, Hershel. *The Mystery and Meaning of the Dead Sea Scrolls.* New York: Random House, 1998.

Sharpe, John, and Kimberly Van Kampen, eds. *The Bible as Book: The Manuscript Tradition.* London and New Castle, Del.: The British Library and Oak Knoll Press, 1998.

Shenk, David. *Data Smog: Surviving the Information Glut.* New York: HarperCollins, 1997.

Shlain, Leonard. *The Alphabet Versus the Goddess: The Conflict Between Word and Image.* New York: Viking, 1998.

Sickinger, James P. *Public Records and Archives in Classical Athens.* Chapel Hill: University of North Carolina Press, 1999.

Singh, Simon. *The Code Book: The Evolution of Secrecy from Mary Queen of Scots to Quantum Cryptography.* New York: Doubleday, 1999.

Smith, Abby. *The Future of the Past: Preservation in American Research Libraries.* Washington, D.C.: Council on Library and Information Resources, 1999.

————. *Why Digitize?* Washington, D.C.: Council on Library and Information Resources, 1999.

Smith, E. Gene. *Among Tibetan Texts: History and Literature of the Himalayan Plateau.* Boston: Wisdom Publications, 2001.

Solzhenitsyn, Aleksandr. *Invisible Allies.* Translated from the Russian by Alexis Klimoff and Michael Nicholson. Washington, D.C.: Counterpoint, 1995.

Sprenger, Maja, and Gilda Bartoloni. *The Etruscans: Their History, Art, and Architecture.* Translated from the German and Italian by Albert Hirmer. New York: Harry N. Abrams, 1983.

Stafford, Barbara Maria, and Frances Terpak. *Devices of Wonder: From the World in a Box to Images on a Screen.* Los Angeles: Getty Research Institute, 2001.

Staikos, Konstantinos Sp. *The Great Libraries: From Antiquity to the Renaissance.* New Castle, Del.: Oak Knoll Press, 2000.

Stam, David H. " 'Prove All Things: Hold Fast That Which is Good': Deaccessioning and Research Libraries." *College and Research Libraries* 43:1 (Jan. 1982): 5–13.

Steig, Margaret E. *Public Libraries in Nazi Germany.* Tuscaloosa: University of Alabama Press, 1992.

Stein, Aurel. *Ruins of Desert Cathay: Personal Narrative of Explorations in Central Asia and Westernmost China.* 2 vols. London: Macmillan, 1912.

————. *Sand-Buried Ruins of Khotan: Personal Narrative of a Journey of Archaeological and Geographical Exploration in Chinese Turkestan.* London: Hurst, 1904.

Stephens, Mitchell. *The Rise of the Image, the Fall of the Word.* New York: Oxford University Press, 1998.

Stern, Guy. *Nazi Book Burning and the American Response.* Text of a lecture delivered to the Friends of the Wayne State University Libraries, Nov. 1, 1989. Detroit: Wayne State University, 1989.

Stroop, Juergen. *The Stroop Report: The Jewish Quarter of Warsaw Is No More!* Translated from the German and annotated by Sybil Milton. Introduction by Andrzej Wirth. New York: Pantheon, 1979.

Stubbings, Hilda Urén. *Blitzkrieg and Books: British and European Libraries as Casualties of World War II.* Bloomington, Ind.: Rubena Press, 1993.

Taking a Byte Out of History: The Archival Preservation of Federal Computer Records. Twenty-fifth Report by the Committee on Government Operations. House

Report 101–978, 101st Cong., 2nd sess. Washington, D.C.: U.S. Government Printing Office, 1990.

Tanselle, G. Thomas. *Literature and Artifacts.* Charlottesville: Bibliographical Society of the University of Virginia, 1998.

Taylor, Isaac. *History of the Transmission of Ancient Books to Modern Times, Together With the Process of Historical Proof.* Revised and enlarged. Liverpool: Edward Howell, 1889 (first edition, 1859).

Tebbel, John. *Between Covers: The Rise and Transformation of American Book Publishing.* New York and Oxford: Oxford University Press, 1987.

Thompson, Edward Maunde. *Introduction to Greek and Latin Palaeography.* Oxford: Oxford University Press, 1912.

Thompson, Thomas L. *The Mythic Past: Biblical Archaeology and the Myth of Israel.* New York: Basic Books, 1999.

Thornton, Dora. *The Scholar in His Study: Ownership and Experience in Renaissance Italy.* New Haven, Conn.: Yale University Press, 1997.

Thorsson, Örnólfur, ed. *The Sagas of Icelanders: A Selection.* Preface by Jane Smiley. Introduction by Robert Kellogg. New York: Viking, 2000.

Tigay, Jeffrey H. *The Evolution of the Gilgamesh Epic.* Philadelphia: University of Pennsylvania Press, 1982.

Treasures Revealed from the Paul Mellon Library of Americana, with an introduction by Robert F. Strohm. Charlottesville, Va.: Howell Press, 2001.

Trever, John C. *The Untold Story of Qumran.* Westwood, N.J.: Fleming H. Revell, 1965.

Van Dyke, J. C. *Books and How to Use Them.* New York: Fords, Howard, and Hulbert, 1883.

Vermes, Geza. *The Complete Dead Sea Scrolls in English.* New York: Allen Lane/Penguin Press, 1997.

Vervliet, Hendrik D. L., ed. *The Book Through Five Thousand Years.* London: Phaidon Press, 1972.

Viscomi, Joseph. *Blake and the Idea of the Book.* Princeton, N.J.: Princeton University Press, 1993.

Walker, Annabel. *Aurel Stein: Pioneer of the Silk Road.* Seattle: University of Washington Press, 1995.

Waterfield, Gordon. *Layard of Nineveh.* London: John Murray, 1963.

Weinreich, Max. *Hitler's Professors: The Part of Scholarship in Germany's Crimes Against the Jewish People.* 2nd ed., with a new introduction by Martin Gilbert. New Haven, Conn.: Yale University Press, 1999.

Weiss, Harvey, ed. *Ebla to Damascus: Art and Archaeology of Ancient Syria.* Catalogue of an exhibition from the Directorate-General of Antiquities and Museums,

Syrian Arab Republic. Washington, D.C.: Smithsonian Institution Traveling Exhibition Service, 1985.

Weitz, Eric D. *A Century of Genocide: Utopias of Race and Nation.* Princeton, N.J.: Princeton University Press, 2003.

Wheatley, H. B. *How to Form a Library.* New York: A. C. Armstrong & Son, 1887.

Whitfield, Peter. *New Found Lands: Maps in the History of Exploration.* New York: Routledge, 1998.

Whitfield, Susan. *Life Along the Silk Road.* Berkeley: University of California Press, 1999.

Whitlock, Brand. *Belgium: A Personal Narrative.* 2 vols. New York: D. Appleton, 1919.

Williams, John, ed. *Imaging the Early Medieval Bible.* University Park: Pennsylvania State University Press, 1999.

Wilson, Edmund. *The Dead Sea Scrolls 1947–1969.* New York: Oxford University Press, 1969.

Wilson, N. G. *Photius: The Bibliotheca.* London: Duckworth, 1994.

Winterich, John T. *Early American Books & Printing.* Boston: Houghton Mifflin, 1935.

Wise, Michael, Martin Abegg Jr., and Edward Cook. *The Dead Sea Scrolls: A New Translation.* With commentary. San Francisco: HarperSanFrancisco, 1996.

Wood, Michael. *In Search of England: Journeys Into the English Past.* Berkeley: University of California Press, 1999.

Wooley, Leonard. *The Art of the Middle East: Including Persia, Mesopotamia and Palestine.* New York: Crown, 1961.

Yardemian, Dajad. *San Lazzaro Island: The Monastic Headquarters of the Mekhitarian Order.* Translated from the Armenian by Vartan Ter-Ghevondian. San Lazzaro Island, Venice, Italy: Mekhitarian Publishing House, 1990.

Yates, Frances A. *The Art of Memory.* Chicago: University of Chicago Press, 1966.

Zachary, G. Pascal. *Endless Frontier: Vannevar Bush, Engineer of the American Century.* New York: Free Press, 1997.

Zapruder, Alexandra. *Salvaged Pages: Young Wrtiers' Diaries of the Holocaust.* New Haven, Conn.: Yale University Press, 2002.

Author's Interviews

KEMAL BAKARŠIC

NICHOLSON BAKER

TERRY BELANGER

THE REV. LEONARD E. BOYLE

JAMES E. BURD

ROBERT DARNTON

JOHN F. DEAN

PATRICK G. DERR

UMBERTO ECO

JONNY EDVARDSEN

CHARLES B. FAULHABER

SHEILA FFOLLIOTT

ROBERT FRAKER

BARBARA GOLDSMITH

FREDERICK GOOD III

WILLIAM A. GOSLING

VARTAN GREGORIAN

KEVIN M. GUTHRIE

ROBERT J. D. HARDING

KENNETH HARRIS

JAMES HERBERT

ROBERT H. HIRST

GILES HOLLINGSWORTH

HELEN HOLLINGSWORTH

THOMAS HOVING

JOSEPH M. JACOBSON

DIANE N. KRESH

RAY KURZWEIL

PAUL LeCLERC

KLAUS-DIETER LEHMANN

CHRISTOPHER LINDQUIST

WILLIAM A. MOFFETT

STEPHEN G. NICHOLS

GEOFFREY NUNBERG

TIM O'BRIEN

JAMES J. O'DONNELL

VÉSTEINN ÓLASON

CHARLES E. PIERCE, JR.

ANDRÁS RIEDLMAYER

ROBERT RULON-MILLER

JOHN G. RYDEN

CHARLES G. ST. VIL

JAMES E. SHEEDY

G. RICHARD SLADE

E. GENE SMITH

JEFFREY B. SPURR

WINSTON TABB

ROBERT S. TAYLOR

KENNETH THIBODEAU

EDWARD J. VALAUSKAS

JAMES A. VISBECK

WILLIAM M. VOELKLE

WILLIAM WALKER

JOHN E. WARNOCK

TOBIAS WOLFF

MICHAEL ZINMAN

Index

Index